THE COMPLETE STEP-BY-STEP CAKES & DESSERTS

Notes on the recipes:

Please note that the measurements provided in this book are presented as 'metric/imperial/US-cups' practical equivalents; certain food and cooking items that are termed differently in the UK and in North America are presented as 'UK term/US term'; and eggs are medium (UK)/large (US) and large (UK)/extra-large (US).

Each recipe has been given a handy Difficulty Rating, from 1 to 5 points; the higher the score, the trickier the recipe – a higher difficulty rating may take into account lengthy preparation time, multiple stages, multiple items of equipment used, precision techniques being necessary to create the required effect, or any combination of these.

Publisher and Creative Director: Nick Wells
Project Editor: Catherine Taylor
Art Director: Mike Spender
Layout Design: Jane Ashley
Digital Design and Production: Chris Herbert
Proofreader: Kathy Steer

Special thanks to Caitlin O'Connel, Laura Bulbeck and Marcus Hardy

12 14 16 15 13

1 3 5 7 9 10 8 6 4 2

This edition first published 2012 by
FLAME TREE PUBLISHING
Crabtree Hall, Crabtree Lane
Fulham, London SW6 6TY
United Kingdom

www.flametreepublishing.com

Flame Tree Publishing is part of Flame Tree Publishing Ltd

All pictures courtesy of Foundry Arts, except the following which are courtesy of Shutterstock.com and © the following contributors:
8l Michael C. Gray; 8r slon1971; 9 Shebeko; 10 Larina Natalia; 11t Paul Cowan; 11b M. Unal Ozmen; 12l Chas; 12r ULKASTUDIO; 13t Andrew S.; 13b Komar Maria; 14bl Obak; 14t Mike Neale; 14br Robyn Mackenzie; 15r Chris leachman; 16 Chas; 17t Danie Nel; 17b Tomas Slavicek; 18 Sychugina; 19b Chas; 20t Ruth Black; 22t Simone van den Berg; 22b Andrea Skjold; 23l Petro Feketa; 23r Denis and Yulia Pogostins; 24t Monkey Business Images; 24br Sandra Cunningham; 26 Foodpictures; 27l StockLite; 27r Nayashkova Olga; 28t Andrea Skjold; 28b Joseph C. Salonis

ISBN 978-0-85775-521-6

A CIP Record for this book is available from the British Library upon request

Printed in China

THE COMPLETE STEP-BY-STEP CAKES & DESSERTS

General Editor: Gina Steer

FLAME TREE PUBLISHING

Contents

Baking Basics 6

This chapter will provide you with all the information you need to start trying your hand at some delicious desserts. It gives you an explanation of essential baking ingredients and basic baking techniques, as well as providing a detailed list of the important equipment you'll need in order to begin your foray into these desserts. Culinary terms are clearly explained and helpful conversions are provided. Tips for working with tricky but delicious ingredients such as chocolate and caramel are given. It also details basic recipes for pastry, batters, icings, fruit and meringues that will prove useful as you try out the many recipes in this book. You will find yourself referring again and again to the important basics provided in this section.

Puddings, Pies & Tarts....................30

This section includes a wide range of classic desserts. There are several traditional puddings, all perfect warm comfort food for a rainy day. The Steamed Chocolate Chip Pudding, the Spotted Dick or the Lemon & Apricot Pudding are sure to be the perfect sticky sweet delight. There are also many different pie and tart recipes included in this section, with various fillings to suit anyone's tastes. Recipes from fruit–filled classics such as Apple Pie and Raspberry Chocolate Ganache & Berry Tartlets to more unusual fillings such as Chocolate Mallow Pie or Fudgy Mocha Pie with Espresso Custard Sauce are provided, and you are certain to find just what you have been looking for.

Everyday Desserts & Cakes 108

Although these desserts are familiar classics suited for any day of the week, it certainly does not mean they are boring! The wide selection of desserts, from cakes, crumbles and trifles to ice creams or buns, in this chapter means that you won't run out of options in a hurry! Why not add a sweet finish to your meal this evening by trying some Easy Victoria Sponge or some Chocolate Chip Ice Cream? Or, if you fancy something more finger food friendly, why not try the Fudgy & Top Hat Chocolate Buns or the Lemon-iced Ginger Squares? The desserts found in this chapter are sure to put a smile on anyone's face!

Special, Exotic & Creamy Concoctions 196

From classics such as Sachertorte and Supreme Chocolate Gateau to new, exciting ideas such as Rose-water Doughballs with Yogurt Sauce and Italian Polenta Cake with Mascarpone Cream, this chapter is filled with dessert ideas for fancier occasions. A Bomba Siciliana or Chocolate Raspberry Mille Feuille will help make your dinner party a hit, while the Hazelnut, Chocolate & Chestnut Meringue Torte or Chocolate Roulade will make you a certain favourite if it is your turn to provide the dessert at a family get-together. The large number of recipes, including classic cakes and gateaux, mousses, ice creams and brûlées, means you certainly wont' have to look far to find a delicious recipe that will impress your family and friends.

Sweet Bites for After Dinner..........266

Fancy a smaller dessert option, or one you can grab on the go? This section is filled with cupcakes, muffins and biscuits, all perfect for a sweet snack after a meal. Easily adaptable for any occasion, the varied dessert options in this section, from sophisticated selections such as Blackcurrant & Lemon Muffins or Black Forest Cupcakes to tasty delights for kids such as Traffic Lights or Fondant Fancies, are sure to provide the simple dessert solution you're looking for. Why not try making Miracle Bars or Raspberry Butterfly Cupcakes? These little dessert bites are bound to delight any sweet tooth.

Index 350

Baking Basics

This chapter will provide you with all the information you need to start trying your hand at some delicious desserts. It gives you an explanation of essential baking ingredients and basic baking techniques, as well as providing a detailed list of the important equipment you'll need in order to begin your foray into these desserts. Culinary terms are clearly explained and helpful conversions are provided. Tips for working with tricky but delicious ingredients such as chocolate and caramel are given. It also details basic recipes for pastry, batters, icings, fruit and meringues that will prove useful as you try out the many recipes in this book. You will find yourself referring again and again to the important basics provided in this section.

Essential Ingredients

Fat

Butter and firm block margarine are the fats most commonly used in baking. Others can also be used, such as white vegetable fat, lard and oil. Low-fat spreads are not recommended as they break down when cooked at a high temperature. Often it is a matter of personal preference which fat you choose when baking, but there are a few guidelines that are important to remember.

Butter and Margarine

Unsalted butter is the fat most commonly used in cake making, especially in rich fruit cakes and the heavier sponge cakes such as Madeira or chocolate torte. Unsalted butter gives a distinctive flavour to the cake. Some people favour margarine, which imparts little or no flavour to the cake. As a rule, firm margarine and butter should not be used straight from the refrigerator but allowed to come to room temperature before using. Also, it should be beaten by itself first before creaming or rubbing in. Soft margarine is best suited to one-stage recipes.

Oil

Oil is sometimes used instead of solid fats. However, if oil is used, care should be taken – it is a good idea to follow a specific recipe as the proportions of oil to flour and eggs are different.

Fat in Pastry Making

Fat is an integral ingredient when making pastry, again there are a few specific guidelines to bear in mind. For shortcrust pastry, the best results are achieved by using equal amounts of lard or white vegetable fat with butter or block margarine. The amount of fat

used is always half the amount of flour. Other pastries use differing amounts of ingredients. Pâte sucrée (a sweet flan pastry) uses all butter with eggs and a little sugar, while flaky or puff pastry uses a larger proportion of fat to flour and relies on the folding and rolling during making to ensure that the pastry rises and flakes well.

Flour

Flour Types

We can buy a wide range of flour all designed for specific jobs. Strong ('bread') flour, which is rich in gluten, whether it is white or brown (this includes granary and stoneground), is best kept for bread and Yorkshire pudding. It is also recommended for steamed suet puddings as well as puff pastry. '00' flour is designed for pasta making and there is no substitute for this flour. Ordinary flour or weak flour is best for cakes, biscuits and sauces as it absorbs the fat easily and gives a soft light texture. This flour comes in plain white/all-purpose, self-raising (which has the raising agent already incorporated) and wholemeal/whole-wheat varieties. Plain flour can be used for all types of baking and sauces.

Flour and Raising Agents

If using plain flour for scones or cakes and puddings, unless otherwise stated in the recipe, use 1 teaspoon baking powder to 225 g/8 oz/1¾ cups plain flour. With sponge cakes and light fruit cakes, where it is important that an even rise is achieved, it is best to

use self-raising flour because, since the raising agent has already been added, there is no danger of using too much – which can result in a sunken cake with a sour taste. There are other raising agents that are also used. Some cakes use bicarbonate of soda/baking soda with or without cream of tartar (both these compounds are typical ingredients in baking powder), blended with warm or sour milk. Whisked eggs also act as a raising agent as the air trapped in the egg ensures that the mixture rises. Generally, no other raising agent is required.

Other Flours

Flour also comes ready sifted. There is even a special sponge flour designed especially for whisked sponges. Also, it is possible to buy flours that contain no gluten and so cater for coeliacs. Buckwheat, soya and chick pea flours are also available.

Eggs

When a recipe states 1 egg, it is generally accepted this refers to a medium ('large' in the USA) egg. Over the past few years, the grading of eggs has changed. For years, in the UK, eggs were sold as small, standard and large, then this method changed and they were graded in numbers with 1 being the largest. The general feeling by the public was that this system was misleading, so now we buy our eggs as small, medium and large. Due to the slight risk of salmonella, all eggs are now sold date stamped to ensure that the eggs are used in their prime. This applies even to farm eggs, which are no longer allowed to be sold straight from the farm. Look for the lion quality

stamp (on 85% of all eggs sold in the UK) which guarantees that the eggs come from hens vaccinated against salmonella, have been laid in the UK and are produced to the highest food safety and standards. All of these eggs carry a best before date.

Sizes

The sizing of eggs in the USA does not quite match that of the UK: a small egg in the UK is anything under 53 g/1.8 oz, which covers 'peewee' and 'small' in the USA and, at a push, 'medium'; a medium egg in the UK most closely corresponds to a 'large' in the USA, and a large UK egg is equivalent to an 'extra-large' American egg – hence our use of 'small', 'medium/large' and 'large/extra-large' for the recipes in this book, where the first word refers to the UK and the second to the USA.

Types

There are many types of eggs sold and it is a question of personal preference which you chose. All offer the same nutritional benefits. More than half the eggs sold in the UK are from caged hens, though this looks set to change. These are the cheapest eggs and the hens have been fed on a manufactured mixed diet. Barn eggs are from hens kept in barns who are free to roam within the barn. However, their diet is similar to caged hens and barns may be overcrowded.

Free-range

It is commonly thought that free-range eggs are from hens that lead a much more natural life and are fed natural foods. This, however, is not always the case and in some instances they may still live in a crowded environment and be fed the same foods as caged and barn hens. However, it is good that the production of eggs from caged hens is steadily decreasing in favour of free-range eggs – with more and more shops selling only free-range.

Four-grain and Organic

Four-grain eggs are from hens that have been fed on grain and no preventative medicines have been included in their diet. Organic eggs are from hens that live in a flock, whose beaks are not clipped and who are completely free to roam. Obviously, these eggs are much more expensive than the others.

Storage

Store eggs in the refrigerator with the round end uppermost (as packed in the egg boxes). Allow to come to room temperature before using. Do remember, raw or semi-cooked eggs should not be given to babies, toddlers, pregnant women, the elderly and those suffering from a recurring illness.

Sugar

Sugar not only offers taste to baking but also adds texture and volume to the mixture. It is generally accepted that caster/superfine sugar is best for sponge cakes, puddings and meringues. Its fine granules disperse evenly when creaming or whisking. Granulated sugar is used for more general cooking, such as stewing fruit, whereas demerara/turbinado sugar, with its toffee taste and crunchy texture, is good for sticky puddings and cakes such as flapjacks. For rich fruit cakes, Christmas puddings and cakes, use the muscovado sugars (dark brown or golden brown) which give a rich intense molasses or treacle flavour.

Icing/confectioners' (powdered) sugar is used primarily for icings and can be used in meringues and in fruit sauces when the sugar needs to dissolve quickly. For a different flavour, try flavouring your own sugar. Place a vanilla pod in a screw-top jar, fill with caster sugar, screw down the lid and leave for 2–3 weeks before using. Top up after use or use thinly pared lemon or orange rind in the same manner.

Reducing Sugar Intake

If trying to reduce sugar intake, then use the unrefined varieties, such as golden/unrefined granulated, golden caster/unrefined superfine, unrefined demerara and the muscovado sugars. All of these are a little sweeter than their refined counterparts, so less is required. Alternatively, clear honey or fructose (fruit sugar) can reduce sugar intake as they have similar calories to sugar, but are twice as sweet. Also, they have a slow release, so their effect lasts longer. Dried fruits can also be included in the diet to top up sugar intake.

Yeast

There is something very comforting about the aroma of freshly baked bread and the taste is far different and superior to commercially made bread. Bread making is regarded by some as being a time-consuming process but, with the advent of fast-acting yeast, this no longer applies. There are three types of yeast available: fresh yeast, which can now be bought in the instore bakery department of many supermarkets (fresh yeast freezes well), dried yeast (which is available in tins) and quick-acting yeast, which comes in packets.

Fresh

Fresh yeast should be bought in small quantities; it has a putty-like colour and texture with a slight wine smell. It should be creamed with a little sugar and some warm liquid before being added to the flour.

Dried

Dried yeast can be stored for up to six months and comes in small hard granules. It should be sprinkled onto warm liquid with a little sugar, then left to stand, normally between 15–20 minutes, until the mixture froths. When replacing the fresh yeast with dried yeast, use 1 tablespoon dried yeast for 25 g/1 oz fresh yeast.

Quick-acting

Quick-acting yeast cuts down the time of bread making, as it eliminates the need for proving the bread twice and can be added straight to the flour without it needing to be activated. When replacing quick-acting yeast for dried yeast, you will need double the amount. When using yeast, the most important thing to remember is that yeast is a living plant and needs food, water and warmth to work.

Equipment

Nowadays, you can get lost in the cookware sections of some of the larger stores – they really are a cook's paradise with gadgets, cooking tools and state-of-the-art electronic blenders, mixers and liquidizers. A few, well-picked, high-quality utensils and pieces of equipment will be frequently used and will therefore be a much wiser buy than cheaper gadgets.

Cooking equipment not only assists in the kitchen, but can make all the difference between success and failure. Take the humble cake tin/pan: although a very basic piece of cooking equipment, it plays an essential role in baking. Using the incorrect size can mean disaster – a tin that is too large, for example, will spread the mixture too thinly and the result will be a flat, limp-looking cake. On the other hand, cramming the mixture into a tin which is too small will result in the mixture rising up and out of the tin.

Baking Tins & Utensils

To ensure successful baking, it is worth investing in a selection of high-quality tins, which, if looked after properly, should last for many years. Follow the manufacturer's instructions when first using and ensure that the tins are thoroughly washed and dried after use and before putting away.

Deep Cake Tins

With these, it is personal choice whether you buy round or square tins and they vary in size from 12.5–35.5 cm/5–14 inches (a useful size is 20.5 cm/8 inches), with a depth of between 12.5–15 cm/5–6 inches. A deep cake tin, for everyday fruit or Madeira cake, is a must.

Sandwich/layer-cake Tins

Perhaps the most useful of tins for baking are sandwich/layer-cake tins, ideal for classics such as Victoria sponge, Genoese and coffee and walnut cake. You will need two tins, normally 18 cm/7 inches or 20.5 cm/8 inches in diameter and about 5–7.5 cm/2–3 inches deep. They are often nonstick.

Loaf Tins

Loaf tins are used for bread, fruit or tea breads and terrines and normally come in two sizes: 450 g/1 lb and 900 g/2 lb.

Baking Sheets and Trays

Good baking sheets and trays are a must for all cooks. Dishes that are too hot to handle, such as apple pies, should be placed directly onto a baking sheet. Meringues, biscuits and cookies are cooked on the sheet. Though the terms are often used interchangeably, the difference between baking 'sheets' and baking 'trays', or specific Swiss/jelly-roll tins, is that the latter have sides all around, whereas a sheet only has one raised side, or none.

Other Tins and Dishes

Square or oblong shallow baking tins are also very useful for making traybakes, fudge brownies, flapjacks and shortbread. Then there are patty tins, which are ideal for making small buns, jam tarts or mince pies; and individual Yorkshire pudding tins, muffin tins or flan tins/tart pans. They are available in a variety of sizes.

There are plenty of other tins to choose from, ranging from themed tins, such as Christmas tree shapes, numbers from 1–9 and tins shaped as petals, to ring-mould tins (tins with a hole in the centre) and springform tins, where the sides release after cooking, allowing the finished cake to be removed easily.

A selection of different-sized roasting tins (i.e. deep baking trays) are also a worthwhile investment, as they can double up as a bain marie, or for cooking larger quantities of cakes such as gingerbread. A few different tins and dishes are required if baking crumbles, soufflés and pies. Ramekin dishes and small pudding basins can be used for a variety of different recipes, as can small tartlet tins and dariole moulds.

Cooling Racks

Another piece of equipment which is worth having is a wire cooling rack. It is essential when baking to allow biscuits and cakes to cool (either in their tins and/or after being removed from their tins), and a wire rack protects your kitchen surfaces from the heat as well as allowing air to circulate around the goodies, speeding cooling and preventing soggy bottoms.

Rolling Pin

When purchasing your implements for baking, perhaps the rolling pin is one of the most important. Ideally it should be long and thin, and heavy enough to roll the pastry out easily, but not so heavy that it is uncomfortable to use. Pastry needs to be rolled out on a flat surface and, although a lightly floured flat surface will do, a marble slab will ensure that the pastry is kept cool and ensures that the fats do not melt while being rolled. This helps to keep the pastry light, crisp and flaky rather than heavy and stodgy, which happens if the fat melts before being baked.

Other Tools

Other useful basic pastry implements are tools such as a pastry brush (which can be used to wet pastry or brush on a glaze), a pastry wheel

for cutting and a sieve to remove impurities and also to sift air into the flour, encouraging the pastry or mixture to be lighter in texture.

Basic mixing cutlery is also essential, such as a wooden spoon (for mixing and creaming), a spatula (for transferring the mixture from the mixing bowl to the baking tins and spreading the mixture once it is in the tins) and a palette knife (to ease cakes and breads out of their tins before placing them on the wire rack to cool). Scales and measuring jugs, or measuring spoons and cups, are essential for accurate measuring of both dry and wet ingredients. Three to four different sizes of mixing bowls are also very useful.

Electrical Equipment

Nowadays, help from time-saving gadgets and electrical equipment make baking far easier and quicker. Equipment can be used for creaming, mixing, beating, whisking, kneading, grating and chopping. There is a wide choice of machines available, from the most basic to the very sophisticated.

Food Processors

First decide what you need your processor to do when choosing a machine. If you are a novice to baking, it may be a waste to start with a machine that offers a wide range of implements and functions. This can be off-putting and result in you not using the machine to its fullest. In general, while styling and product design play a role in the price, the more you pay, the larger the machine will be, with a bigger bowl capacity and many more gadgets attached. Nowadays, you can chop, shred, slice, chip, blend, purée, knead, whisk and cream anything. However, just what basic features should you ensure your machine has before buying it?

Food Mixers

These are ideally suited to mixing cakes and kneading dough, either as a table-top mixer or a hand-held mixer. Both are extremely useful and based on the same principle of mixing or whisking in an open bowl to allow more air to get to the mixture and therefore give a lighter texture.

The table-top mixers are freestanding and are capable of dealing with fairly large quantities of mixture. They are robust machines, capable of easily dealing with kneading dough and heavy cake mixing as well as whipping cream, whisking egg whites or making one-stage cakes. These mixers also offer a wide range of attachments ranging from liquidizers, mincers, juicers, can openers and many more and varied attachments.

Hand-held mixers are smaller than freestanding mixers and often come with their own bowl and stand from which they can be lifted off and used as hand-held devices. They have a motorized head with detachable twin whisks. These mixers are particularly versatile as they do not need a specific bowl in which to whisk. Any suitable mixing bowl can be used.

When buying a food processor, look for measurements on the side of the processor bowl and machines with a removable feed tube which allows food or liquid to be added while the motor is still running. Look out for machines that have the facility to increase the capacity of the bowl (ideal when making soup) and have a pulse button for controlled chopping. For many, storage is also an issue, so reversible discs and flex storage or, on more advanced models, a blade storage compartment or box, can be advantageous.

It is also worth thinking about machines that offer optional extras that can be bought as your cooking requirements change. Mini-chopping bowls are available for those wanting to chop small quantities of food. If time is an issue, dishwasher-friendly attachments may be vital. Citrus presses, liquidizers and whisks may all be useful attachments for the individual cook.

Blenders

Blenders often come as attachments to food processors and are generally used for liquidizing and puréeing foods. There are two main types of blender. The first is known as a goblet blender. The blades of this blender are at the bottom of the goblet with measurements up the sides. The second blender is portable. It is hand-held and should be placed in a bowl to blend.

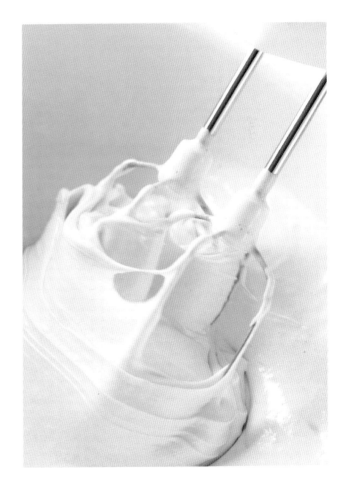

Basic Techniques

There is no mystery to successful baking. It really is easy providing you follow a few simple rules and guidelines. First, read the recipe right through before commencing. There is nothing more annoying than getting to the middle of a recipe and discovering that you are minus one or two of the ingredients. Until you are confident, follow a recipe, do not try a short cut, otherwise you may find that you have left out a vital step which means that the recipe really cannot work. Most of all, have patience, baking is easy – if you can read, you can bake.

Working with Pastry

Pastry dough needs to be kept as cool as possible throughout. Cool hands help, but are not essential. Use cold or iced water, but not too much as pastry does not need to be wet. Make sure that your fat is not runny or melted but firm (this is why block fat is the best). Avoid using too much flour when rolling out as this alters the proportions, and also avoid handling the dough too much. Roll in one direction as this helps to ensure that the pastry does not shrink. Allow the pastry to rest, preferably in the refrigerator, after rolling. If you follow these guidelines but your pastry is still not as good as you would like it to be, then make in a processor instead.

Lining a Flan Dish

It is important to choose the right dish or tin/pan to bake with. You will often find that a loose–bottomed metal flan tin is the best option, as it conducts heat more efficiently and evenly than a ceramic dish. It also has the added advantage of a removable base which makes the transfer of the final flan or tart a much simpler process; it simply lifts out, keeping the pastry intact.

Roll the pastry dough out on a lightly floured surface, ensuring that it is a few inches larger than the flan tin. Wrap the pastry round the rolling pin, lift and place in the tin. Carefully ease the pastry into the base and sides of the tin, ensuring that there are no gaps or tears in the pastry. Allow to rest for a few minutes, then trim the edge either with a sharp knife or by rolling a rolling pin across the top of the flan tin.

Baking Blind

The term 'baking blind' means cooking the pastry case/pie crust without the filling, resulting in a crisp pastry shell that is either partially or fully cooked, depending on whether the filling needs any cooking. Pastry shells can be prepared ahead of time as they last for several days if stored correctly in an airtight container, or longer if frozen.

To bake blind, line a tin or dish with the prepared pastry dough and allow to rest in the refrigerator for 30 minutes. This will help to minimize shrinkage while it is being cooked. Remove from the refrigerator and lightly prick the base all over with a fork (do not do this if the filling is runny). Brush with a little beaten egg if desired or simply line the case with a large square of greaseproof/wax paper, big enough to cover both the base and sides of the pastry case. Fill with ceramic baking beans/pie weights, dried beans or rice. Place on a baking sheet and bake in a preheated oven, generally at 200°C/400°F/Gas Mark 6, remembering that ovens can take at least 15 minutes to reach this heat (unless they are fan/convection ovens, *see* page 16). Cook for 10–12 minutes, then remove from the oven, discard the paper and beans. Return to the oven and continue to cook for a further 5–10 minutes, depending on whether the filling needs cooking. Normally, unless otherwise stated, individual pastry tartlet cases also benefit from baking blind.

Covering a Pie with a Pastry Lid

To cover a pie, roll out the pastry dough until it is about 5 cm/ 2 inches larger than the circumference of the dish. Cut a 2.5 cm/1 inch strip from around the outside of the pastry and then moisten the edge of the pie dish you are using. Place the strip on the edge of the dish and brush with water or beaten egg. Generously fill the pie dish until the surface is slightly rounded. Using the rolling pin, lift the remaining pastry and cover the pie dish. Press together, then seal. Using a sharp knife, trim off any excess pastry from around the edges. Try to avoid brushing the edges of the pastry, especially puff pastry, as this prevents the pastry rising evenly. Before placing in the oven, make a small hole in the centre of the pie to allow the steam to escape.

The edges of the pie can be forked by pressing the back of a fork around the edge of the pie or instead crimp by pinching the edge crust, holding the thumb and index finger of your right (or left) hand against the edge while gently pushing with the index finger of your left (or right) hand. Other ways of finishing the pie are to knock up

(achieved by gently pressing your index finger down onto the rim and, at the same time, tapping a knife horizontally along the edge, giving it a flaky appearance), or fluting the edges by pressing your thumb down on the edge of the pastry while drawing the blunt edge of a knife inwards, against your thumb for about 1 cm/^{1}/$_2$ inch, and repeating around the rim. Experiment by putting leaves and berries made out of leftover pastry on top, to finish off the pie, then brush the top of the pie with beaten egg.

Lining Cake Tins

If a recipe states that the tin needs lining, do not be tempted to ignore this. Rich fruit cakes and other cakes that take a long time to cook benefit from the tin being lined so that the edges and base do not burn or dry out. Greaseproof paper or baking parchment is ideal for this. It is a good idea to have the paper at least double thickness, or preferably 3–4 thicknesses. Sponge cakes and other cakes that are cooked in 30 minutes or less are also better if the bases are lined, as it is far easier to remove them from the tin.

The best way to line a round or square tin is to lightly draw around the base and then cut just inside the markings, making it easy to sit in the tin. Next, lightly oil the paper so that it will easily peel away from the cake. If the sides of the tin also need to be lined, then cut a strip of paper long enough for the tin. This can be measured by wrapping a piece of string around the rim of the tin. Once again, lightly oil the paper, push against the tin and oil once more, as this will hold the paper to the sides of the tin. Steamed puddings usually need only a disc of greaseproof paper at the bottom of the dish, as the sides come away easily.

Hints for Successful Baking

Measurements

Ensure that the ingredients are accurately measured. A cake that has too much flour or insufficient egg will be dry and crumbly. Take care when measuring the raising agent if used, as too much will mean that the cake will rise too quickly and then sink. Insufficient raising agent means the cake will not rise in the first place.

Oven Temperature

Ensure that the oven is preheated to the correct temperature; it can take 10 minutes to reach 180°C/350°F/Gas Mark 4. You may find that an oven thermometer is a good investment. Cakes are best if cooked in the centre of the preheated oven. Do try to avoid the temptation of opening the oven door at the beginning of cooking, as a draught can make the cake sink. *Important:* If using a fan/convection oven, then refer to the manufacturer's instructions, as they normally cook 10–20 degrees hotter than conventional ovens and often do not need preheating.

Testing for Doneness

Check that the cake is thoroughly cooked by removing from the oven and inserting a clean skewer into the cake. Leave for just 30 seconds and then remove. If the skewer is completely clean, then the cake is cooked; if there is a little mixture left on the skewer, then return to the oven for a few minutes.

Problems

Other problems that you may encounter while cake making are insufficient creaming of the fat and sugar or a curdled creamed mixture (which will result in a densely textured and often fairly solid cake). Flour that has not been folded in carefully enough or has not been mixed with enough raising agent may also result in a fairly heavy consistency. It is very important to try to ensure that the correct size of tin is used, as you may end up either with a flat, hard cake or one which has spilled over the edge of the tin. Another tip to be aware of (especially when cooking with fruit) is that, if the consistency is too soft, the cake will not be able to support the fruit.

Cooling and Storing

Finally, when you take your cake out of the oven, unless the recipe states that it should be left in the tin until cold, leave for a few minutes, then loosen the edges and turn out onto a wire rack to cool. Cakes which are left in the tin for too long, unless otherwise stated, tend to sink or slightly overcook. Make sure the cake is completely cold before storing an airtight tin or plastic container.

Equipment for Chocolate

Chocolate has a reputation for being difficult to work with but a few pieces of well-chosen equipment make the job much easier. Although you can get by with just a selection of basic items, the following list provides a more comprehensive set of equipment for the serious chocolatier.

Bowls Bowls in a variety of sizes in glass, ceramic and metal are all suitable for working with chocolate, as these materials distribute the heat well and are suitable for use on the hob and over hot water. Glass and ceramic can be used in the microwave too. Plastic is less versatile, as it can only be used in the microwave.

Saucepans All kitchens will have a set of saucepans, but for chocolate cooking they need to be fairly small so that a bowl can sit snugly on top without touching the bottom of the pan. Alternatively, glass double boilers are very useful. The top pan sits in the bottom one, with a large gap for water between them. They were designed for making sauces such as hollandaise which did not require the bottom of the pan to get any direct heat and so are perfect for melting chocolate.

Microwave oven This is very good for melting chocolate. Most packets of chocolate will have instructions for melting using a microwave, but you will need to know the power of your oven. This is usually indicated on the door panel or on the control panel and will either be a letter rating or a number indicating wattage. It is important, as with all methods, not to overheat the chocolate, so the best method is to use the microwave in bursts of about 30 seconds, stirring well between bursts.

Candy thermometer This is very useful, especially if tempering chocolate (*see* Working with Chocolate, page 19).

Cake-cooling rack As we have seen, this has a multitude of uses, not just for chocolate, and is essential if you are going to do any kind of baking. If items are left to cool in tins or on baking sheets, they are likely to create steam as they cool, which will be trapped by the tin or baking sheet. Biscuits and cookies will not be crisp and cakes may become soggy.

Fine-mesh cooling rack This is great for setting dipped items. Put coated items on it to drain and set, putting the rack over a plate or tray to catch any drips. Larger-meshed cake-cooling racks are not really suitable but can be adapted by being covered with nonstick baking parchment.

Kitchen forks/skewers These are a much more affordable alternative to specialist chocolate forks. Kitchen forks and skewers can both be used to handle dipped items. Using skewers, items can be speared before being dipped (fruit or truffles, for example). Harder items such as biscuits/cookies should be dipped using two kitchen forks. Both items are more likely to leave marks on the chocolate than specialist forks.

Chocolate forks These are very fine forks, similar to fondue forks, but with longer prongs. Sometimes the points of the prongs are joined and curved. They are very useful for coating truffles and handling chocolate-dipped items. They are also very expensive, however, and are really only for the dedicated chocolate maker.

Large sharp knife Good for cutting shapes out of a set sheet of chocolate or for making chocolate caraque.

Paint scraper A clean paint scraper is the best tool for making chocolate curls. It is worth purchasing one and keeping it specially for the purpose.

Vegetable peeler This is excellent for making chocolate curls quickly from a bar of chocolate. They will be smaller and coarser than curls made using set chocolate, but can be an effective decoration on top of a cake.

Pastry cutters These are mainly useful for cutting shapes out of chocolate that has set in a sheet. These can then be used for sandwiching a filling or for decorating cakes.

Petit-four cutters As with pastry cutters, these are very useful for making small shapes for use as decorations.

Grater The coarser side of a box grater is very useful for making chocolate decorations.

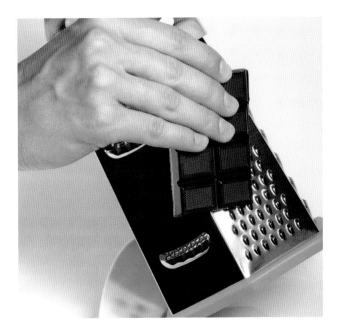

Small paintbrush/pastry brush Brushes are most useful for making moulded chocolates in unusual shapes, but are also good for painting the insides of pastry cases with chocolate before filling with fruit or cream.

Greaseproof/wax paper and nonstick baking parchment As we have seen, these are both essential items for baking, to line cake tins. Also available are reusable nonstick mats which can be cut to size and used again and again. Nonstick baking parchment is good for making small disposable decorating bags, which are perfect for drizzling chocolate or icing onto cakes and biscuits. Take a piece of paper, about 20.5 cm/8 inches square, and fold it in half diagonally to make a double triangle. Fold the paper round to form a cone. Tighten the cone until all the points meet, then fold the points of paper down into the top of the cone. You can now fill the cone and then snip off the bottom to make a decorating bag.

Decorating bag with tip This is a small nylon decorating bag with a variety of tips that is very useful for decorating cakes and, when fitted with a plain tip, for drizzling chocolate.

Marble slab This is also useful in pastry making, as it stays cool regardless of the kitchen temperature. Melted chocolate can be poured directly onto the marble, either in a sheet for making curls or caraque, or for making shapes.

Metal spatulas These are long thin blades with rounded ends, though they come in different sizes. The blades are flexible and are very useful for spreading melted chocolate, either onto cakes or biscuits/cookies or onto marble slabs for making chocolate decorations.

Rubber spatulas These are available in small, medium and large sizes, including one that is spoon shaped.

Moulds A large variety of moulds for making chocolates is available from specialist shops and by mail order. Sometimes made of rigid material, flexible plastic moulds are the easiest to use. There are three methods for using the moulds, depending on the desired result. Method 1 is to pour melted chocolate into the mould and leave until set. This is the best method for making small chocolate shapes. Method 2 is to pour chocolate into the mould until about one-third full, then tilt the mould until the inside is completely coated with a layer of chocolate, then pour off any excess. This is the best method for making large hollow shapes, such as Easter eggs. Method 3 is to use a paintbrush dipped in melted chocolate to paint the inside of the mould with a thin layer. Repeat the process using thin layers until the chocolate is set firm. This is the best method to use if your mould is unconventional, a paper fairy cake case, for example. The plastic moulds can then simply be bent and flexed until the chocolate comes loose. These produce excellent results and the chocolate emerges from the mould with a beautiful shiny surface. If using something like a paper fairy cake case, it will need to be removed carefully, possibly in strips.

Petit-four cases These are available in supermarkets and kitchenware shops and come in a variety of sizes and colours. They are perfect for displaying handmade chocolates, especially if they are being packed in a box.

Sifter This is useful for sifting cocoa powder and icing sugar, both of which are a bit sticky and may have lumps that need removing.

Dredger This is useful both for icing sugar and cocoa powder and is less messy than using a sieve. Dredgers are also good for dusting finished chocolates or cakes.

Working with Chocolate & Caramel

There are a few useful techniques for working with chocolate. None of them is very complicated and all can be mastered easily with a little practice. These general guidelines apply equally for all types of chocolate.

Melting Chocolate

All types of chocolate are sensitive to temperature, so care needs to be taken during the melting process. It is also worth noting that different brands of chocolate have different consistencies when melting and when melted. Experiment with different brands to find one that you prefer.

No Water

As a general rule, it is important not to allow any water to come into contact with the chocolate. In fact, a drop or two of water is more dangerous than larger amounts, which may blend in. The melted chocolate will seize and it will be impossible to bring it back to a smooth consistency.

Gently Does It

Do not overheat chocolate or melt it by itself in a pan over a direct heat. Always use either a double boiler or a heatproof bowl set over a saucepan of water, but do not allow the bottom of the bowl to come into contact with the water, as this would overheat the chocolate. Keep an eye on the chocolate, checking it every couple of minutes and reducing or extinguishing the heat under the saucepan, as necessary. Stir the chocolate once or twice during

melting until it is smooth and no lumps remain. Do not cover the bowl once the chocolate has melted or condensation will form, water will drop into it and it will be ruined. If the chocolate turns from a glossy, liquid mass into a dull, coarse, textured mess, you will have to start again.

Microwaving

Microwaving is another way of melting chocolate but, again, caution is required. Follow the oven manufacturer's instructions together with the instructions on the chocolate and proceed with care. Melt the chocolate in bursts of 30 or so seconds, stirring well between bursts, until the chocolate is smooth. If possible, stop microwaving before all the chocolate has melted and allow the residual heat in the chocolate to finish the job. The advantage of microwaving is that you do not need to use a saucepan, making the whole job quicker and neater.

Making Chocolate Decorations

Curls and caraque Chocolate curls are made using a clean paint scraper. They are usually large, fully formed curls which are useful for decorating gateaux and cakes. Caraque are long thin curls which can be used in the same way, but are less dramatic. To make either shape, melt the chocolate following your preferred method and then spread it in a thin layer over a cool surface, such as a marble slab, ceramic tile or piece of granite. Leave until just set but not hard.

To make curls, take a clean paint scraper and set it at an angle to the surface of the chocolate, then push, taking a layer off the surface. This will curl until you release the pressure. Alternatively, you can make curled shapes by painting melted chocolate onto pieces of kitchen foil, shaping accordingly and chilling until set.

To make caraque, use a large sharp knife and hold it at about a 45-degree angle to the chocolate. Hold the handle and the tip and scrape the knife towards you, pulling the handle but keeping the tip more or less in the same place. This method makes thinner, tighter, longer curls.

Shaved chocolate Using a vegetable peeler, shave a thick block of chocolate to make mini-curls. These are best achieved if the chocolate is a little soft, otherwise it has a tendency to break into little flakes.

Chocolate shapes Spread a thin layer of chocolate, as described in the instructions for chocolate curls, and allow to set as before. Use shaped cutters or a sharp knife to cut out shapes. Use to decorate cakes.

Chocolate leaves Many types of leaf are suitable, but ensure they are not poisonous before using. Rose leaves are easy to find and make good shapes. Wash and dry the leaves carefully before using. Melt chocolate following the instructions given at the beginning of the section. Using a small paintbrush, paint a thin layer of chocolate onto the back of the leaf. Allow to set before adding another thin layer. When set, carefully peel off the leaf. Chocolate leaves are also very attractive when made using two different types of chocolate, white and dark chocolate, for example. Paint half the leaf first with one type of chocolate and allow to set before painting the other half with the second chocolate. Leave to set, then peel off the leaf as above.

Chocolate lace Make a nonstick baking parchment decorating bag (*see* Equipment for Chocolate, page 18). Draw an outline of the required shape onto some nonstick baking parchment, a triangle, for example. Pipe chocolate evenly onto the outline, fill in the centre with lacy squiggles and leave until set. Remove the paper to use.

Chocolate squiggles Use a teaspoon of melted chocolate to drizzle random shapes onto nonstick baking parchment. Leave to set and remove the paper to use. Alternatively, pipe a zigzag line about 5 cm/2 inches long onto a piece of nonstick baking parchment. Pipe a straight line slightly longer at either end down the middle of the zigzag.

Chocolate butterflies Draw a butterfly shape on a piece of nonstick baking parchment. Fold the paper down the middle of the body of the butterfly to make a crease, then open the paper out flat. Pipe chocolate onto the outline of the butterfly, then fill in the wings with loose zigzag lines. Carefully fold the paper so the wings are at right-angles, supporting them from underneath in the corner of a large tin or with some other support, and leave until set. Peel away the paper to use.

Chocolate modelling paste To make chocolate modelling paste (very useful for cake coverings and for making heavier shapes, such as ribbons) put 200 g/7 oz dark chocolate in a bowl and add 3 tablespoons liquid glucose. Set the bowl over a pan of gently simmering water. Stir until the chocolate is just melted, then remove from the heat. Beat until smooth and leave the mixture to cool. When cool enough to handle, knead to a smooth paste on a clean work surface. The mixture can now be rolled and cut to shape. If the paste hardens, wrap it in plastic wrap and warm it in the microwave for a few seconds on low.

Caramel-dipped nuts Make the caramel, remove the pan from the heat and plunge into cold water as described earlier. Using two skewers or two forks, dip individual nuts into the hot caramel, lift out carefully, allowing excess to run off, then transfer to a foil-covered tray until set. If the caramel becomes too sticky or starts making a lot of sugar strands, reheat gently until liquid again.

Caramel shapes Make the caramel, remove the pan from the heat and plunge into cold water as described earlier. Using a teaspoon, drizzle or pour spoonfuls of caramel onto an oiled baking sheet. Leave to set before removing from the tray. Do not refrigerate caramel shapes as they will liquefy.

Caramel lace Follow the method for caramel shapes, but use the teaspoon to drizzle threads in a random pattern onto an oiled tray. When set, break into pieces for decorations. Do not refrigerate.

Praline

To make praline, follow the instructions as for caramel, but do not plunge the pan into cold water. Add nuts to the caramel mixture. Do not stir, but pour immediately onto an oiled baking sheet. Leave to set at room temperature. Once cold, the praline can be chopped or broken into pieces as required. Keep leftover praline in a sealed container. It will keep for several months stored this way.

Caramel and Praline Decorations

Caramel

To make caramel, put 75 g/3 oz/¹⁄₃ cup granulated sugar into a heavy-based saucepan with about 3 tablespoons cold water. Over a low heat, stir well until the sugar has dissolved completely. If any sugar clings to the pan, brush it down using a wet brush. Bring the mixture to the boil and cook, without stirring, until the mixture turns golden. You may need to tilt the pan carefully to ensure the sugar colours evenly. As soon as the desired colour is reached, remove the pan from the heat and plunge the base of the pan into cold water to stop it from cooking further.

Basic Recipes: Pastry

Shortcrust Pastry

Makes 225 g/8 oz

225 g/8 oz/2 cups plain/all-purpose white flour
pinch salt
50 g/2 oz/4 tbsp white vegetable fat/shortening or lard
50 g/2 oz/4 tbsp butter or block margarine

Sift the flour and salt into a mixing bowl. Cut the fats into small
pieces and add to the bowl. Rub the fats into the flour using your
fingertips until the mixture resembles fine breadcrumbs. Add 1–2
tablespoons cold water and, using a knife or your hands if easier,
mix to form a soft, pliable dough. Knead gently on a lightly floured
surface until smooth and free from cracks, then wrap and chill for
30 minutes before rolling out on a lightly floured surface. Use as
required. Cook in a preheated hot oven (200°C/400°F/Gas Mark 6).

Sweet Shortcrust Pastry (Pâte Sucrée)

Makes 225 g/8 oz

225 g/8 oz/2 cups plain/all-purpose white flour
150 g/5 oz/²/₃ cups (1¼ sticks) unsalted butter, softened
2 tbsp caster/superfine sugar
1 egg yolk

Sift the flour into a mixing bowl, cut the fat into small pieces, add to
the bowl and rub into the flour. Stir in the sugar, then mix to form a
pliable dough with the egg yolk and about 1 tablespoon cold water.
Wrap, chill and use as required.

Cheese Pastry

Follow the recipe for sweet shortcrust pastry, but omit the sugar and
add 1 teaspoon dried mustard powder and 50 g/2 oz/¹/₂ cup mature
grated Cheddar cheese.

Rough Puff Pastry

Makes 225 g/8 oz

225 g/8 oz/2 cups plain/all-purpose white flour
pinch salt
150 g/5 oz/²/₃ cups (1¼ sticks) butter, block margarine or lard
squeeze lemon juice

Sift the flour and salt together in a mixing bowl. Cut up the fat, add
to the bowl. Add the lemon juice and 6–7 tablespoons cold water.
Mix with a fork until it is a fairly stiff mixture. Turn out onto a lightly
floured surface. Roll into an oblong. Fold the bottom third up to the
centre, bring the top third down to the centre. Gently press the
edges together. Give the pastry a half turn, roll the pastry out again
into an oblong. Repeat the folding, turning and rolling at least four
times. Wrap. Leave to rest in a cool place for at least 30 minutes.
Cook as directed by your recipe, in a preheated oven at
220°C/425°F/Gas Mark 7.

Choux Pastry

Makes 225 g/8 oz

50 g/2 oz/4 tbsp butter
75 g/3 oz/³/₄ cup plain/all-purpose white flour
pinch salt
2 eggs, beaten

Place the butter and 150 ml/5 fl oz/²/₃ cup water in a heavy-based saucepan. Heat gently, stirring until the butter has melted, and bring to the boil. Draw off the heat and add the flour and salt all at once. Beat with a wooden spoon until the mixture forms a ball in the centre. Cool for 5 minutes. Gradually add the eggs, beating well after each addition, until a stiff mixture is formed. Either place in a decorating bag fitted with a large tip, or shape using two spoons. Cook in a preheated oven at 200°C/400°F/Gas Mark 6 for 15–25 minutes, depending on size. Remove and make a small slit in the side, then return to the oven and cook for a further 5 minutes. Remove and cool before filling.

Hot Water Crust Pastry

Makes 450 g/1 lb

450 g/1 lb/4 cups plain/all-purpose white flour
1 tsp salt
125 g/4 oz/7 tbsp lard or white vegetable fat/shortening
150 ml/¹/₄ pt/²/₃ cup milk and water, mixed

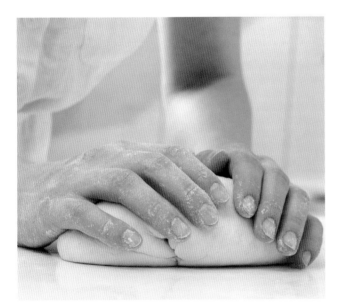

Sift the flour and salt together and reserve. Heat the lard or white vegetable fat/shortening until melted. Bring to the boil. Pour immediately into the flour along with some of the milk and water and, using a wooden spoon, mix together and beat until the mixture comes together and forms a ball, using more milk and water as needed. When cool enough to handle, knead lightly until smooth and pliable. Use as required, covering the dough with a clean cloth before use. Bake in a preheated oven at 220°C/425°F/Gas Mark 7, or as directed.

Basic Recipes: Batters

Pouring Batter for Yorkshire Puddings and Pancakes

125 g/4 oz/1 cup plain/all-purpose white flour
pinch salt
2 eggs
300 ml/¹/₂ pint/1¹/₄ cups whole milk and water, mixed
1 tbsp vegetable oil

Sift the flour and salt into a mixing bowl and make a well in the centre. Drop the eggs into the well with a little milk. Beat the eggs into the flour, gradually drawing the flour in from the sides of the bowl. Once half the milk has been added, beat well until smooth and free from lumps. Stir in the remaining milk and leave to stand for 30 minutes. Stir before using. Heat 1 tablespoon oil in a roasting tin/pan or individual Yorkshire pudding tins/pans in an oven preheated to 220°C/425°F/Gas Mark 7. When the oil is almost smoking, stir the batter, then pour it into the hot oil. Cook for 30–40 minutes for a large pudding and 18–20 minutes for individual puddings. This batter can also be used for pancakes and, if liked, 2 tbsp caster/superfine sugar can be added.

Coating Batter for Fritters

125 g/4 oz/1 cup plain/all-purpose white flour
pinch salt
1 tbsp sunflower/corn oil
2 egg whites

Sift the flour and salt into a mixing bowl and make a well in the centre. Add the oil and 75 ml/2 ¹/₂ fl oz/ 5 tbsp water and beat until smooth and free from lumps. Gradually beat in the 75 ml/2 ¹/₂ fl oz/ 5 tbsp water. Just before using, whisk the egg whites until stiff, then stir into the batter and use immediately.

ready. Slowly add half the sugar, 1 teaspoon at a time, whisking well after each addition. Once half the sugar has been added, add the remaining sugar and gently stir it in with a metal spoon. Take care not to over-mix.

Spoon the meringue onto a baking sheet lined with nonstick baking parchment. Shape the meringue according to preference or the recipe – such as in a round 'case' – and typically bake in a preheated oven at 150°C/300°F/Gas Mark 2 for 1½ hours, or until set and firm to the touch. Remove from the oven, leave until cold before using or storing in an airtight container.

Basic Recipes: Meringues

Meringue is made from egg whites and caster/superfine sugar. As a general rule, allow 1 egg white to 50 g/2 oz/¼ cup caster sugar. If liked, add a pinch of salt at the start of whisking.

Making Meringue

Place the egg whites in a clean mixing bowl (any grease in the bowl will prevent the egg white from whisking). Use a balloon or wire whisk if whisking by hand, or an electric mixer fitted with a balloon whisk if not. Whisk the egg whites until stiff. To test if they are stiff enough, turn the bowl upside down – if the egg white does not move, it is

Whipped Cream
(to accompany the meringues)

Whipping cream, double/heavy cream or a combination of single/light cream and double cream will all whip. For the combination option, use one third single cream and two thirds double cream.

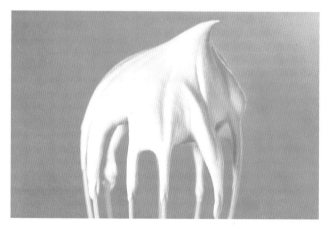

Place the cream in a mixing bowl and use a balloon whisk, wire whisk or electric mixer fitted with the balloon whisk attachment. Place the bowl on a damp cloth if whipping by hand. Whip until thickened and soft peaks are formed – this is when the whisk, if dragged gently through the cream and lifted out, leaves soft peaks in the cream. Whipped cream is ideal for using in soufflés, mousses and other cream desserts. For decorating and to use as a filling, whip for a little longer until the cream is slightly stiffer. If using only double cream, take care that you do not over-whip, as it will curdle.

Basic Recipes: Fruit & Icings

Poaching Fruit

This method is suitable for plums, apricots, damsons, greengages, peaches, nectarines, cherries, raspberries, strawberries, blackberries and currants, cored and sliced cooking apples, peeled and cored pears and rhubarb. Poached fruit can be used in pies or wrapped in pastry, but is also delicious served with cream or sauce.

Place 75 g/3 oz/$^1/_3$ cup sugar in a heavy-based saucepan with 150 ml/$^1/_4$ pint/$^2/_3$ cup water. Place over a gentle heat and stir occasionally until the sugar has dissolved. Bring to the boil and boil steadily for 5 minutes, or until a syrup is formed. Pour into a frying pan, or, if the pan is large enough, keep the syrup in the pan. Prepare the fruit to be poached by rinsing and cutting in half and discarding the stones. Add to the syrup and poach gently for 8–10 minutes until just cooked. Remove from the heat and gently transfer to a serving dish.

Alternatively, the fruits can be gently poached without sugar. Prepare as required and rinse lightly. Half-fill a frying pan with water or a mixture of orange juice and water and bring to the boil. Reduce the heat to a simmer, then add the fruits and cook for 5–10 minutes until just tender.

Icings

Butter Cream

125 g/4 oz/$^1/_2$ cup (1 stick) unsalted butter or margarine, softened
1 tsp vanilla extract
225 g/8 oz/2 cups icing/confectioners' sugar, sifted

Cream the butter or margarine with the vanilla extract until soft and creamy. Add the icing/confectioners' sugar, 1 tablespoon at a time, and beat well. Continue until all the icing sugar is incorporated. Beat in 1–2 tablespoons slightly cooled boiled water or fruit juice to give a smooth, spreadable consistency.

Chocolate butter cream Melt 50 g/2 oz dark/bittersweet chocolate. Stir into the prepared butter cream, omitting the hot water. Or, if preferred, replace 1 tablespoon of the icing/confectioners' sugar with 1 tablespoon cocoa.

Orange/lemon butter cream Beat 1 tablespoon finely grated orange or lemon zest into the butter cream and replace the water with fruit juice.

Coffee butter cream Dissolve 1 tablespoon coffee granules in a little very hot water. Omit the vanilla extract and stir in the coffee in place of the hot water.

Mocha butter cream Make the coffee butter cream as above and replace 1 tablespoon of the icing sugar with 1 tablespoon unsweetened cocoa powder, or use melted chocolate.

Glacé Icing

Sift 225 g/8 oz/2 cups icing/confectioners' sugar into a mixing bowl, then slowly stir in 2–3 tablespoons hot water. Blend to form a spreadable consistency – the icing should coat the back of a wooden spoon. Other flavours can be made by adding 1 tablespoon cocoa to the sugar or 1 tablespoon coffee granules, dissolved in hot water. Or use orange or lemon juice, such as with Bakewell Tart. For a coloured icing, add a few drops of food colouring.

Culinary Terms Explained

At a glance, here are some of the key terms you will come across when baking. Some we may have discussed already, some may be new to you.

Baking parchment Sometimes called 'baking parchment paper' or just 'baking paper'. Used for wrapping food to be cooked (en papillote) and for lining cake tins/pans to prevent sticking. Usually comes as nonstick, in theory avoiding the need to grease or oil the paper.

Greaseproof/wax paper Paper that tends to be relatively nonstick and which is used to line tins/pans to prevent cakes and puddings from sticking, and for wrapping food such as packed lunches or fatty foods. Historically, unlike baking parchment, if greaseproof paper was used in the oven, it would smoke, so the batter or cake mixture had to cover it entirely. However, today, greaseproof paper and baking parchment are often able to be used in the same way – check the packaging.

En papillote A French term used to describe food which is baked, but is wrapped in baking parchment before cooking. This works well with fish, as the aroma from the different herbs or spices and the fish are contained during cooking and not released until the paper parcel is opened.

Rice paper This edible paper is made from the pith of a Chinese tree and can be used as a base on which to bake sticky cakes and biscuits such as almond macaroons.

Centigrade This is a metric scale for measuring the temperature within the oven (usually known as Celsius).

Baking blind The method often used for cooking the pastry case/pie crust of flans and tarts before the filling is added. After lining the tin/pan with the uncooked pastry, it is then covered with a sheet of greaseproof/wax paper or baking parchment and weighed down with either ceramic baking beans/pie weights, dried beans or rice and is baked in the oven as directed in the recipe.

Baking powder A raising agent which works by producing carbon dioxide as a consequence of a reaction caused by the acid and alkali ingredients, which expand during the baking process and make the breads and cakes rise.

Bicarbonate of soda/baking soda This alkali powder acts as a raising agent in baking when combined with an acid or acid liquid (cream of tartar, lemon juice, yogurt, buttermilk, cocoa or vinegar, for example).

Cream of tartar An acid raising agent (potassium hydrogen tartrate) often present in both self-raising flour and baking powder. Activates the alkali component of baking powder.

Fermenting A term used during bread, beer or wine making to note the chemical change brought about through the use of a fermenting or leavening agent, such as yeast.

Unleavened Often refers to bread which does not use a raising agent and is therefore flat, such as Indian naan bread.

Cornflour/cornstarch Used to thicken consistency and can also be used in meringue making to prevent the meringue becoming hard and brittle and to enhance its chewiness.

Pasteurizing The term given when milk and eggs are heated to destroy bacteria.

Curdling When the milk separates from a sauce through acidity or excessive heat. This can also happen to creamed cake mixtures that have separated due to the eggs being too cold or added too quickly.

Sifting The shaking of dry ingredients (primarily flour) through a metal or nylon sieve to remove impurities before using in baking.

Binding Adding liquid or egg to bring a dry mixture together. Normally, this entails using either a fork, spoon or your fingertips.

Blending When two or more ingredients are thoroughly mixed together.

Creaming The method by which fat and sugar are beaten together until lighter in colour and fluffy. By creaming the fat in cake mixtures, air is incorporated into the fairly high fat content. It thus lightens the texture of cakes and puddings.

Folding A method of combining creamed fat and sugar with flour in cake and pudding mixes, usually by carefully mixing with a large metal spoon, either by cutting and folding, or by doing a figure of eight in order to maintain a light texture.

Rubbing in The method of combining fat into flour for crumble toppings, shortcrust pastry, biscuits/cookies and scones.

Beating The method by which air is introduced into a mixture using a fork, wooden spoon, whisk or electric mixer. Beating is also used as a method to soften ingredients.

Whipping/whisking The term given to incorporating air rapidly into a mixture (either through the use of a manual whisk or an electric whisk).

Dropping consistency The consistency that a cake or pudding mixture reaches before being cooked. It tends to be fairly soft (but not runny) and should drop off a spoon in around five seconds when tapped lightly on the side of a bowl.

Grinding Reducing hard ingredients, such as nuts, to crumbs, normally by the use of a grinder or a pestle and mortar.

Blender An electric machine with rotating blades used mainly with soft and wet ingredients to purée and liquidize, although it can grind dry ingredients such as nuts and breadcrumbs.

Dough A dense mixture of flour, water and, often, yeast. Also used to describe raw pastry, scones and biscuit/cookie mixtures.

Knead The process of pummelling and working dough in order to strengthen the gluten in the flour and make the dough more elastic, thus giving a good rise. Also applies to pastry making; the dough is kneaded on a lightly floured surface to give a smooth and elastic pastry, making it easier to roll and ensuring an even texture after baking. In both cases, the outside of the dough is drawn into the centre.

Proving The term used in bread making when the bread is allowed to rise a second time after it has been kneaded once and then shaped before it is baked.

Knock back The term used for a second kneading after the dough has been allowed to rise. This is done to ensure an even texture and to disperse any large pockets of air.

Crumb The internal texture of a cake or bread as defined by the air pockets.

En croûte Used to describe food which is covered with raw pastry and then baked.

Vol-au-vent Meaning 'flying' or 'floating' on the wind, this small and usually round or oval puff pastry case is first baked and then filled with savoury meat, seafood or vegetable filling in a sauce.

Choux A type of pastry, whose uncooked dough is rather like a glossy batter, which is piped into small balls onto a baking sheet and baked until light and airy. They can then be filled with cream or savoury fillings.

Filo/Phyllo A type of pastry that is wafer–thin. Three to four sheets are usually used at a time in baking.

Puff pastry Probably the richest of pastries. When making from the beginning, it requires the lightest of handling.

Brioche A traditional bread eaten in France for breakfast, usually served warm. Brioche has a rich but soft texture, made from a very light yeast dough, and is baked in the shape of a small cottage loaf. A delicious substitute for bread in bread and butter pudding.

Caramel Obtained by heating sugar at a very low heat until it turns liquid and deep brown in colour. This is used in dishes such as crème caramel, which is, in turn, baked in a *bain marie*.

Bain marie A French term, meaning water bath. A shallow tin/pan, often a roasting tin, is half–filled with water; smaller dishes of food are then placed in it, allowing them to cook at lower temperatures without over–heating. This method is often used to cook custards and other egg dishes or to keep some dishes warm.

Ramekin An ovenproof, earthenware dish which provides an individual serving.

Cocotte Another name for a ramekin.

Dariole A small narrow mould with sloping sides used for making Madeleines. Darioles can also be used for individual steamed or baked puddings and jellies.

Crimping The fluted effect used for the decoration on pies or tarts, created by pinching the edge crust with the thumb and index finger of your right (or left) hand and gently pushing against them with the index finger of your other hand.

Scalloping The term given to a type of pie decoration achieved by horizontal cuts made in the pastry which is then pulled back with the knife to produce a scalloped effect.

Dusting To sprinkle lightly, often with flour, sugar or icing/confectioners' sugar.

Dredging The sprinkling of food with a coating (generally of flour or sugar). A board may be dredged with flour before the pastry is rolled out and cakes and biscuits/cookies can be dredged with sugar or icing/confectioners' sugar after baking.

Glacé A French term meaning glossy or iced. Glacé icing is a quick icing often used to decorate cakes and biscuits. It is made using icing/confectioners' sugar and warm water.

Piping A way in which cakes and desserts are decorated, or the method by which choux pastry is placed onto a baking sheet. This is achieved by putting cream, icing or mixture in a nylon bag (with a tip attached), or an improvised decorating bag made from a cone of greaseproof/wax paper, and then slowly forcing through the tip and piping it onto the cake or baking sheet.

Zest This can refer to the outer, coloured part of an orange, lemon or lime peel, or the very thin, long pieces of that peel. The zest contains the fruit oil, which is responsible for the citrus flavour. Normally, a zester is used to create the strips, as it removes the zest without any of the bitter white pith. Zest can also be grated on a grater into very small pieces, again taking care to only remove the very outer layer.

Useful Conversions

Liquid Measures
Metric, Imperial and US Cups/Quarts

2.5 ml	½ tsp		
5 ml	1 tsp		
15 ml	1 tbsp		
25 ml	1 fl oz	⅛ cup	2 tbsp
50 ml	2 fl oz	¼ cup	3–4 tbsp
65 ml	2½ fl oz	⅓ cup	5 tbsp
85 ml	3 fl oz	⅓ cup	6 tbsp
100 ml	3½ fl oz	⅓ cup	7 tbsp
125 ml	4 fl oz	½ cup	8 tbsp
135 ml	4½ fl oz	½ cup	9 tbsp
150 ml	5 fl oz	¼ pint	⅔ cup
175 ml	6 fl oz	⅓ pint	scant ¾ cup
200 ml	7 fl oz	⅓ pint	¾ cup
250 ml	8 fl oz	⅜ pint	1 cup
275 ml	9 fl oz	½ pint	1⅛ cups
300 ml	10 fl oz	½ pint	1¼ cups
350 ml	12 fl oz	⅔ pint	1½ cups
400 ml	14 fl oz	⅝ pint	1⅔ cups
450 ml	15 fl oz	¾ pint	1¾ cups
475 ml	16 fl oz	⅞ pint	scant 2 cups
500 ml	18 fl oz	⅞ pint	2 cups
600 ml	20 fl oz	1 pint	2½ cups
750 ml	26 fl oz	1¼ pints	3¼ cups
900 ml		1½ pints	scant 1 quart
1 litre		2 pints	1 quart
1.25 litres		2¼ pints	1¼ quarts
1.3 litres		2⅓ pints	1⅓ quarts
1.5 litres		2½ pints	1½ quarts
1.6 litres		2¾ pints	1¾ quarts
1.7 litres		3 pints	1¾ quarts
1.8 litres		3⅛ pints	1⅞ quarts
1.9 litres		3⅓ pints	2 quarts
2 litres		3½ pints	2 quarts
2.25 litres		4 pints (½ gal)	2¼ quarts
2.5 litres		4¼ pints	2½ quarts
2.75 litres		5 pints	3 quarts
3 litres		5¼ pints	3 quarts
4.5 litres		8 pints (1 gal)	scant 5 quarts

Temperature Conversion

−4°F	−20°C
5°F	−15°C
14°F	−10°C
23°F	−5°C
32°F	0°C
41°F	5°C
50°F	10°C
59°F	15°C
68°F	20°C
77°F	25°C
86°F	30°C
95°F	35°C
104°F	40°C
113°F	45°C
122°F	50°C
212°F	100°C

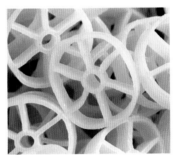

Dry Weights
Metric/Imperial

10 g	¼ oz
15 g	½ oz
20 g	¾ oz
25 g	1 oz
40 g	1½ oz
50 g	2 oz
65 g	2½ oz
75 g	3 oz
100 g	3½ oz
125 g	4 oz
150 g	5 oz
165 g	5½ oz
175 g	6 oz
185 g	6½ oz
200 g	7 oz
225 g	8 oz
250 g	9 oz
275 g	10 oz
300 g	11 oz
325 g	11½ oz
350 g	12 oz
375 g	13 oz
400 g	14 oz
425 g	15 oz
450 g	1 lb

Oven Temperatures
Bear in mind that if using a fan oven you should reduce the stated temperature by around 20°C – check the manufacturer's instructions.

110°C	225°F	Gas Mark ¼	Very slow (low) oven
120/130°C	250°F	Gas Mark ½	Very slow oven
140°C	275°F	Gas Mark 1	Slow oven
150°C	300°F	Gas Mark 2	Slow oven
160/170°C	325°F	Gas Mark 3	Moderate oven
180°C	350°F	Gas Mark 4	Moderate oven
190°C	375°F	Gas Mark 5	Moderately hot oven
200°C	400°F	Gas Mark 6	Moderately hot oven
220°C	425°F	Gas Mark 7	Hot oven
230°C	450°F	Gas Mark 8	Hot oven
240°C	475°F	Gas Mark 9	Very hot oven

Puddings, Pies & Tarts

This section includes a wide range of classic desserts. There are several traditional puddings, all perfect warm comfort food for a rainy day. The Steamed Chocolate Chip Pudding and Spotted Dick are sure to be a delight. There are also many different pie and tart recipes, from fruit-filled classics such as Apple Pie and Strawberry Tartlets to more unusual fillings such as Chocolate Mallow Pie or Fudgy Mocha Pie with Espresso Custard Sauce.

Rice Pudding

Serves 4

Ingredients

65 g/2¹/₂ oz/¹/₃ cup pudding rice
50 g/2 oz/¹/₄ cup granulated sugar
410 g/14 oz can light evaporated milk
300 ml/¹/₂ pint/1¹/₄ cups semi-skimmed/low-fat milk
pinch freshly grated nutmeg
25 g/1 oz/2 tbsp butter
jam/jelly, to decorate

Preheat the oven to 150 C/300 F/Gas Mark 2, 10 minutes before baking. Lightly oil a large ovenproof dish. Sprinkle the rice and the sugar into the dish and mix.

Bring the evaporated milk and milk to the boil in a small pan, stirring occasionally. Stir the milks into the rice and mix well until the rice is coated thoroughly.

Sprinkle over the nutmeg, cover with kitchen foil and bake in the preheated oven for 30 minutes.

Remove the pudding from the oven and stir well, breaking up any lumps. Cover with the same kitchen foil. Bake in the preheated oven for a further 30 minutes. Remove from the oven and stir well again.

Dot the pudding with butter and bake for a further 45–60 minutes until the rice is tender and the skin is browned.

Divide the pudding into four individual serving bowls. Top with a large spoonful of the jam/jelly. Serve immediately.

Difficulty Rating: 2 points

Lemon Meringue Pie

Serves 4–6

Ingredients

175 g/6 oz/1$^1/_3$ cups plain/all-purpose flour

pinch salt

40 g/1$^1/_2$ oz/3 tbsp lard or white vegetable fat/shortening

40 g/1$^1/_2$ oz/3 tbsp butter or block margarine

For the filling:

grated zest and juice of 2 lemons

75 g/3 oz/$^1/_3$ cup granulated sugar

40 g/1$^1/_2$ oz/$^1/_3$ cup cornflour/cornstarch

2 large/extra large egg yolks

For the topping:

2 large/extra large egg whites

125 g/4 oz/$^2/_3$ cup caster/superfine sugar

Preheat the oven to 200 C/400 F/Gas Mark 6 and place a baking sheet in the oven to heat. Sift the flour and salt in a bowl or a food processor and rub in the fats with your fingertips, or process, until the mixture looks like fine crumbs. Mix in 2–3 tablespoons cold water to form a soft dough. Knead until smooth. Grease a 20.5 cm/8 inch round flan tin. Roll out the pastry and line the tin. Chill for 30 minutes while making the filling.

Put the zest and granulated sugar in a pan with 300 ml/$^1/_2$ pint/1$^1/_4$ cups water in a heavy-based pan over a low heat and stir until the sugar dissolves. Blend the cornflour/cornstarch with the lemon juice, add to the pan and bring to the boil, stirring all the time. Boil for 2 minutes, then remove from the heat and beat in the egg yolks. Set aside to cool.

Prick the pastry case/pie crust, line with greaseproof/wax paper and pour in baking beans/pie weights. Place on the baking sheet and bake for 10 minutes. Remove from the oven and lift out the paper and beans. Bake the pastry for a further 10 minutes. Remove from the oven, spoon in the lemon filling and set aside. Reduce the oven temperature to 150 C/300 F/Gas Mark 2.

Then whisk the egg whites until stiff. Whisk in half the caster/ superfine sugar a little at a time, then fold in the remainder.

Spread over the lemon filling. Bake for 30 minutes until the meringue is golden. Leave to 'settle' for 20 minutes before serving.

Difficulty Rating: 4 points

Nutty Date Pudding with Chocolate Sauce

Serves 6-8

Ingredients

125 g/4 oz/¹/₂ cup (1 stick) butter, softened

125 g/4 oz/¹/₂ cup golden caster/unbleached superfine sugar

3 medium/large eggs, beaten

175 g/6 oz/1¹/₂ cups sifted self-raising flour

50 g/2 oz dark/semisweet chocolate, grated

3 tbsp milk

75 g/3 oz/³/₄ cup hazelnuts, roughly chopped

75 g/3 oz/¹/₂ cup stoned dates, roughly chopped

chopped toasted hazelnuts, to serve

For the chocolate sauce:

50 g/2 oz/4 tbsp unsalted butter

50 g/2 oz dark/semisweet chocolate, broken into pieces

50 g/2 oz/¹/₄ cup soft light brown sugar

125 ml/4 fl oz/¹/₂ cup double/heavy cream

Lightly oil a 1.1 litre/2 pint pudding basin/heatproof bowl and line the base with baking parchment. Cream the butter and sugar together in a bowl. Add the beaten eggs a little at a time, adding 1 tablespoon of the flour after each addition. When all the eggs have gone in, stir in the remaining flour.

Add the grated chocolate and mix in lightly, then stir in the milk together with the hazelnuts and dates. Stir lightly until mixed together well. Spoon the mixture into the pudding basin and level. Cover with a double sheet of baking parchment with a pleat in the centre, allowing for expansion, then cover either with a pudding cloth or a double sheet of kitchen foil, again with a central pleat. Tie with string.

Steam for 2 hours, or until cooked and firm to the touch. Remove the pudding from the saucepan and leave to rest for 5 minutes, before turning out onto a serving plate. Discard the small circle of baking parchment, then sprinkle with the chopped toasted hazelnuts.

Keep warm while you make the sauce. Place the butter, chocolate and sugar in a saucepan and heat until the chocolate has melted. Stir in the cream and simmer for 3 minutes until thickened. Pour over the pudding and serve.

Difficulty Rating: 2 points

Mocha Pie

Serves 4–6

Ingredients

1 x 23 cm/9 inch ready-made sweet pastry case/shell

For the filling:
125 g/4½ oz dark/semisweet chocolate, broken into pieces
175 g/6 oz/¾ cup (1½ sticks) unsalted butter
225 g/8 oz/1 cup soft brown sugar
1 tsp vanilla extract
3 tbsp strong black coffee

For the topping:
600 ml/1 pint/2 cups double/heavy cream
50 g/2 oz/½ cup icing/confectioners' sugar
2 tsp vanilla extract
1 tsp instant coffee dissolved in 1 tsp boiling water, cooled
grated dark/semisweet and white chocolate, to decorate

Place the prepared pastry case/shell on a large serving plate and reserve. Melt the chocolate in a heatproof bowl over simmering water. Ensure the water is not touching the base of the bowl. Remove from the heat, stir until smooth and leave to cool.

Cream the butter, soft brown sugar and vanilla extract until light and fluffy, then beat in the cooled chocolate. Add the black coffee, pour into the pastry case and chill in the refrigerator for 30 minutes. For the topping, whip the cream until it thickens, then whip in the sugar and vanilla extract. Continue to whip until softly peaking. Spoon half the cream into a separate bowl and fold in the dissolved coffee.

Spread the remaining cream over the filling in the pastry case. Spoon the coffee-flavoured whipped cream evenly over the top, swirling it decoratively with a palette knife. Sprinkle with grated chocolate and chill in the refrigerator until ready to serve.

Difficulty Rating: 3 points

Chocolate Brioche Bake

Serves 6

Ingredients

200 g/7 oz dark/semisweet chocolate, broken
    into pieces
75 g/3 oz/6 tbsp unsalted butter
225 g/8 oz/1 large brioche, sliced
1 tsp pure orange oil or 1 tbsp grated orange zest
$^{1}/_{2}$ tsp freshly grated nutmeg
3 eggs, beaten
2 tbsp golden caster/unrefined superfine sugar
600 ml/1 pint/2$^{1}/_{2}$ cups milk
cocoa powder (unsweetened) and icing/confectioners' sugar,
    for dusting

Preheat the oven to 180°C/350°F/Gas Mark 4, 10 minutes
before baking. Lightly oil or butter a 1.7 litre/3 pint/1$^{3}/_{4}$ quart
ovenproof dish. Melt the chocolate with 25 g/1 oz/2 tbsp of the
butter in a heatproof bowl set over a saucepan of simmering
water. Stir until smooth.

Arrange half of the sliced brioche in the ovenproof dish,
overlapping the slices slightly, then pour over half of the melted
chocolate. Repeat the layers, finishing with a layer of chocolate.

Melt the remaining butter in a saucepan. Remove from the
heat and stir in the orange oil or zest, the nutmeg and the
beaten eggs. Continuing to stir, add the sugar and finally the
milk. Beat thoroughly and pour over the brioche. Leave to
stand for 30 minutes before baking. Bake on the centre shelf
in the preheated oven for 45 minutes, or until the custard is
set and the topping is golden brown. Leave to stand for
5 minutes, then dust with cocoa powder and icing/
confectioners' sugar. Serve warm.

Difficulty Rating: 2 points

Apple Pie

Serves 6–8

Ingredients

175 g/6 oz/1$^{1}/_{3}$ cups plain/all-purpose flour
pinch salt
40 g/1$^{1}/_{2}$ oz/3 tbsp lard or white vegetable fat
40 g/1$^{1}/_{2}$ oz/3 tbsp butter or block margarine
1 tbsp caster/superfine sugar

For the filling:
500 g/1$^{1}/_{4}$ lb/5$^{1}/_{3}$ cups cooking apples, peeled, cored and sliced
125 g/4 oz/$^{2}/_{3}$ cup caster sugar
1 tsp ground cinnamon
$^{1}/_{3}$ tsp ground nutmeg
50 g/2 oz/$^{1}/_{3}$ cup sultanas/golden raisins
15 g/$^{1}/_{2}$ oz/1 tbsp butter
milk, for glazing
caster sugar, for sprinkling

Sift the flour and salt into a bowl or a food processor and add
the fats. Rub in with your fingers, or process. Mix in the sugar
and add 2–3 tablespoons cold water to form a soft dough, then
knead lightly. Wrap and chill for 30 minutes.

Preheat the oven to 220°C/425°F/Gas Mark 7 and grease a
1.2 litre/2$^{1}/_{4}$ pint/5 cup pie dish. Roll out the pastry. Turn the dish
top down onto the pastry and cut round it for the lid. Roll the
trimmings into a strip and press around the edge of the dish.

Mix together the apples, sugar, spices and sultanas/golden
raisins. Place in the dish and dot with butter. Put on the pastry
lid. Make a hole in the centre for steam to escape, then
decorate with trimmings. Brush with milk, and sprinkle with caster
sugar. Bake for 10 minutes, then reduce the oven temperature
to 190°C/375°F/Gas Mark 5 and bake for a further 25–30
minutes. Serve hot.

Difficulty Rating: 3 points

Individual Steamed Chocolate Puddings

Serves 8

Ingredients

150 g/5 oz/²/₃ cup (1¹/₄ sticks) unsalted butter, softened

175 g/6 oz/1 scant cup light muscovado/golden brown sugar

¹/₂ tsp freshly grated nutmeg

3 tbsp sifted plain/all-purpose white flour

4 tbsp sifted cocoa powder (unsweetened)

5 eggs, separated

125 g/4 oz/1¹/₃ cups ground almonds

50 g/2 oz/1 cup fresh white breadcrumbs

To serve:

Greek yogurt

orange-flavoured chocolate curls

Preheat the oven to 180°C/350°F/Gas Mark 4. Lightly oil and line the bases of eight individual 175 ml/6 fl oz/²/₃ cup pudding basins/heatproof bowls with nonstick baking parchment. Cream the butter with 50 g/2 oz/¹/₄ cup of the sugar and the nutmeg until fluffy. Sift the flour and cocoa powder together, then stir into the creamed mixture. Beat in the egg yolks and mix well. Fold in the almonds and breadcrumbs.

Whisk the egg whites until standing in peaks, then whisk in the remaining sugar gradually. Using a metal spoon, fold the egg whites into the chocolate mixture and mix well. Spoon the mixture into the prepared basins, filling them two-thirds full to allow for expansion. Cover with a double sheet of kitchen foil and secure tightly with string. Stand the pudding basins in a roasting tin with water halfway up the sides of the basins. Bake in the centre of the oven for 30 minutes, or until the puddings are firm to the touch. Remove from the oven and turn onto warmed plates. Serve with Greek yogurt and chocolate curls.

Difficulty Rating: 2 points

Rhubarb & Raspberry Cobbler

Serves 4

Ingredients

325 g/11½ oz rhubarb, cut into chunks
175 g/6 oz raspberries
50 g/2 oz/¼ cup golden caster/superfine sugar
1 orange

For the topping:
225 g/8 oz/1⅔ plain/all-purpose flour
1 tbsp baking powder
50 g/2 oz/4 tbsp butter, diced
50 g/2 oz/¼ cup caster/superfine sugar
150 ml/¼ pint/⅔ cup milk
custard or double/heavy cream, to serve

Preheat the oven to 220°C/425°F/Gas Mark 7. Butter a 1.7 litre/3 pint ovenproof dish. Mix the rhubarb chunks with the raspberries and sugar and place in the buttered dish. Finely grate the zest from the orange and set aside. Squeeze out the juice and add to the dish with the rhubarb. Cover the dish with a piece of foil and bake for 20 minutes.

To make the topping, sift the flour and baking powder into a bowl and stir in the grated orange zest. Rub in the butter with your fingertips until the mixture resembles fine crumbs. Stir in the caster/superfine sugar and quickly add the milk. Mix with a fork to make a soft dough. (The mixture has to be made quickly as the raising agent – baking powder – starts to activate as soon as liquid is added.)

Take the dish out of the oven and discard the foil. Break off rough tablespoons of the dough and drop them on top of the fruit filling. Bake for about 25 minutes until the topping is firm and golden. Serve immediately while hot with custard or double/heavy cream.

Difficulty Rating: 2 points

Chocolate Pear Pudding

Serves 6

Ingredients

140 g/4½ oz/½ cup plus 1 tbsp (1⅛ sticks) butter, softened

2 tbsp soft brown sugar

400 g/14 oz can pear halves, drained and juice reserved

25 g/1 oz/¼ cup walnut halves

125 g/4 oz/⅔ cup golden caster/unrefined superfine sugar

2 medium/large eggs, beaten

75 g/3 oz/½ cup sifted self-raising flour

50 g/2 oz/½ cup cocoa powder (unsweetened)

1 tsp baking powder

prepared chocolate custard, to serve

Preheat the oven to 190°C/375°F/Gas Mark 5. 10 minutes before baking. Butter a 20.5 cm/8 inch sandwich tin with 1 tablespoon of the butter and sprinkle the base with the soft brown sugar. Arrange the drained pear halves on top of the sugar, cut-side down. Fill the spaces between the pears with the walnut halves, flat-side upwards.

Cream the remaining butter with the caster/superfine sugar, then stir in the eggs in batches, adding 1 tablespoon of the flour after each addition. When all the eggs are in, stir in the remaining flour.

Sift the cocoa powder and baking powder together, then stir into the creamed mixture with 1–2 tablespoons of the reserved pear juice to give a smooth dropping consistency. Spoon the mixture over the pear halves, smoothing the surface. Bake in the oven for 20–25 minutes until well risen and the surface springs back when lightly pressed.

Remove from the oven and leave to cool for 5 minutes. Using a palette knife, loosen the sides and invert onto a serving plate. Serve with custard.

Difficulty Rating: 2 points

Peach & Chocolate Bake

Serves 6

Ingredients

200 g/7 oz dark/semisweet chocolate

125 g/4 oz/^{1}/$_2$ cup (1 stick) unsalted butter

4 medium/large eggs, separated

125 g/4 oz/^{2}/$_3$ cup caster/superfine sugar

425 g/15 oz can peach slices, drained

^{1}/$_2$ tsp ground cinnamon

1 tbsp sifted icing/confectioners' sugar, to decorate

crème fraîche/sour cream, to serve

Preheat the oven to 170˚C/325˚F/Gas Mark 3, 10 minutes before baking. Lightly oil a 1.7 litre/3 pint ovenproof dish. Break the chocolate and butter into small pieces and place in a small heatproof bowl over gently simmering water. Ensure the water is not touching the base of the bowl. Once melted, remove from the heat and stir until smooth.

Whisk the egg yolks with the sugar until very thick and creamy, then stir the melted chocolate and butter into the whisked egg yolk mixture and mix together lightly.

Place the egg whites in a clean, grease–free bowl and whisk until stiff, then fold 2 tablespoons of the whisked egg whites into the chocolate mixture. Mix well, then add the remaining egg white and fold in very lightly.

Fold the peach slices and the cinnamon into the mixture, then spoon into the prepared dish. Do not level the mixture, leave a little uneven. Bake in the preheated oven for 35–40 minutes until risen and just firm to the touch. Sprinkle with the icing/confectioners' sugar and serve immediately with spoonfuls of crème fraîche/sour cream.

Difficulty Rating: 2 points

Sticky Chocolate Surprise Pudding

Serves 6–8

Ingredients

150 g/5 oz/1 heaped cup self-raising flour
25 g/1 oz/¼ cup cocoa powder (unsweetened)
200 g/7 oz/1 cup caster/superfine sugar
75 g/3 oz mint-flavoured chocolate, chopped
175 ml/6 fl oz/scant ¾ cup whole milk
2 tsp vanilla extract
50 g/2 oz/4 tbsp unsalted butter, melted
1 egg
fresh mint sprig, to decorate

For the sauce:
175 g/6 oz/¾ cup muscovado/dark brown sugar
125 g/4 oz/1⅓ cups cocoa powder (unsweetened)

Preheat the oven to 180°C/350°F/Gas Mark 4. Lightly oil a 1.5 litre/2½ pint/1½ quart ovenproof soufflé dish. Sift the flour and cocoa powder into a large bowl and stir in the caster/superfine sugar and the chocolate and make a well in the centre.

Whisk the milk, vanilla extract and the melted butter together, then beat in the egg. Pour into the well in the dry ingredients and mix together thoroughly, drawing the dry ingredients in from the sides of the bowl. Spoon into the prepared soufflé dish.

To make the sauce, blend the muscovado/dark brown sugar and the cocoa powder together and mix with 600 ml/1 pint/2½ cups hot water until the sugar and cocoa have dissolved. Carefully pour over the top of the pudding, but do not stir in. Bake in the preheated oven for 35–40 minutes until firm to the touch and the mixture has formed a sauce underneath. Decorate with mint and serve immediately.

Difficulty Rating: 2 points

Steamed Chocolate Chip Pudding

Serves 6

Ingredients

175 g/6 oz/1¹/₂ cups self-raising flour

¹/₂ tsp baking powder

75 g/3 oz/1¹/₄ cups fresh white breadcrumbs

125 g/4¹/₂ oz/1 cup shredded suet

125 g/4¹/₂ oz/²/₃ cup golden caster/unrefined superfine sugar

2 eggs, lightly beaten

1 tsp vanilla extract

125 g/4¹/₂ oz/²/₃ cup chocolate chips

150 ml/¹/₄ pint/²/₃ cup cold milk

grated chocolate, to decorate

For the chocolate custard:

300 ml/¹/₂ pint/1¹/₄ cups milk

1 tbsp cornflour/cornstarch

1 tbsp (unsweetened) cocoa powder

1 tbsp caster/superfine sugar

¹/₂ tsp vanilla extract; 1 egg yolk

Oil a 1.2 litre/2 pint/1¹/₄ quart pudding basin and line the base with nonstick baking parchment. Sift the flour and baking powder into a bowl, add the breadcrumbs, suet and sugar, and mix.

Stir in the eggs and vanilla extract with the chocolate chips and mix with sufficient cold milk to form a smooth dropping consistency.

Spoon the mixture into the basin and cover with a double sheet of baking parchment and then a double sheet of kitchen foil or a pudding cloth, with a pleat in the centre to allow for expansion. Tie with string.

Cook in a steamer for 1¹/₂–2 hours until the pudding is cooked and firm to touch – replenish the water as necessary. Remove and leave to rest for 5 minutes, then turn out on to a warmed plate.

Meanwhile, make the custard/custard sauce. Blend a little of the milk with the cornflour/cornstarch and cocoa powder to form a paste. Stir in the remaining milk with the sugar and vanilla extract. Pour into a saucepan and bring to the boil, stirring. Whisk in the egg yolk and cook for 1 minute. Decorate the pudding with grated chocolate and serve with the sauce.

Difficulty Rating: 2 points

Chocolate Meringue Nests with Fruity Filling

Serves 8

Ingredients

125 g/4 oz/1²/₃ cups toasted hazelnuts

125 g/4 oz/²/₃ cup golden caster/unrefined superfine sugar

75 g/3 oz dark/semisweet chocolate, broken
   into pieces

2 medium/large egg whites

pinch salt

1 tsp cornflour/cornstarch

¹/₂ tsp white wine vinegar

chocolate curls, to decorate

For the filling:

150 ml/¹/₄ pint/²/₃ cup double/heavy cream

150 g/5 oz/²/₃ cup mascarpone cheese

prepared summer fruits, such as strawberries, raspberries
   and redcurrants

Preheat the oven to 110°C/225°F/Gas Mark ¹/₄ 5 minutes before baking and line a baking sheet with nonstick baking parchment. Place the hazelnuts and 2 tablespoons of the caster/superfine sugar in a food processor and blend to a powder. Add the chocolate and blend again until the chocolate is roughly chopped.

Whisk the egg whites and salt until soft peaks form. Gradually whisk in the remaining sugar a teaspoonful at a time and continue to whisk until the meringue is stiff and shiny. Fold in the cornflour/cornstarch and the white wine vinegar with the chocolate and hazelnut mixture.

Spoon the mixture into eight mounds, about 10 cm/4 inches in diameter, on the baking parchment. Do not worry if not perfect shapes. Make a hollow in each mound, then place in the preheated oven. Cook for 1¹/₂ hours, then switch the oven off and leave in the oven until cool.

To make the filling, whip the cream until soft peaks form. In another bowl, beat the mascarpone cheese until it is softened, then mix with the cream. Spoon the mixture into the meringue nests and top with the fresh fruits. Add chocolate curls and serve.

Difficulty Rating: 2 points

Triple Chocolate Cheesecake

Serves 6

Ingredients

For the base:
150 g/5 oz/2 cups digestive biscuits/Graham crackers, crushed
50 g/2 oz/4 tbsp butter, melted

For the cheesecake:
75 g/3 oz white chocolate, roughly chopped
300 ml/½ pint/1¼ cups double/heavy cream
50 g/2 oz/¼ cup caster/superfine sugar
3 eggs, beaten
400 g/14 oz/1¾ cups full-fat soft cream cheese
2 tbsp cornflour/cornstarch
75 g/3 oz each dark/semisweet chocolate
and milk chocolate, roughly chopped
fromage frais/sour cream, to serve

Preheat the oven to 180°C/350°F/Gas Mark 4. Lightly oil a 23 x 7.5 cm/9 x 3 inch springform tin/pan. To make the base, mix together the crushed biscuits/crackers and the melted butter. Press into the base of the tin and chill in the refrigerator. Gently heat the white chocolate and cream in a small, heavy-based saucepan until the chocolate melts. Stir until smooth and reserve.

Beat the sugar and eggs together, add the cream cheese and then beat until smooth. Stir the reserved white chocolate cream and the cornflour/cornstarch into the cream cheese mixture.

Blend the dark/semisweet and milk chocolate into the cream cheese mixture. Spoon over the chilled base. Place on a baking sheet and bake for 1 hour. Leave the cheesecake to cool, then chill in the refrigerator for at least 6 hours before removing from the tin and serving with fromage frais/sour cream.

Difficulty Rating: 2 points

Chocolate Mallow Pie

Serves 6

Ingredients

200 g/7 oz digestive biscuits/Graham crackers
75 g/3 oz/6 tbsp butter
175 g/6 oz dark/semisweet chocolate
20 marshmallows
1 medium/large egg, separated
300 ml/¹⁄₂ pint/1¹⁄₄ cups double/heavy cream

Lightly oil an 18 cm/7 inch flan tin/tart pan. Place the biscuits/crackers in a plastic bag and crush with a rolling pin. Alternatively, place in a food processor and blend until fine crumbs are formed.

Melt the butter in a medium-sized saucepan, add the crushed biscuits and mix together. Press into the base of the prepared tin and leave to cool in the refrigerator.

Melt 125 g/4 oz of the chocolate with the marshmallows and 2 tablespoons of water in a saucepan over a gentle heat, stirring constantly. Leave to cool slightly, then stir in the egg yolk, beat well, then return to the refrigerator until cool.

Whisk the egg white until stiff and standing in peaks, then fold into the chocolate mixture.

Lightly whip the cream and fold three-quarters of the cream into the chocolate mixture. Reserve the remainder. Spoon the chocolate cream into the flan case/pie crust and chill in the refrigerator until set.

When ready to serve, spoon the remaining cream over the chocolate pie, swirling in a decorative pattern. Grate the remaining dark chocolate and sprinkle over the cream, then serve.

Difficulty Rating: 2 points

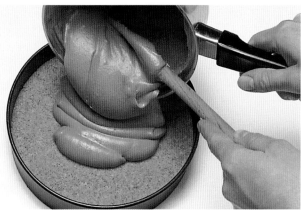

Fruity Chocolate Pudding with Sticky Chocolate Sauce

Serves 4

Ingredients

125 g/4 oz/^{1}/$_2$ cup dark muscovado/brown sugar

1 orange, peeled and segmented

75 g/3 oz/^{3}/$_4$ cup cranberries, fresh or thawed if frozen

125 g/4 oz/^{1}/$_2$ cup soft margarine/butter

2 medium/large eggs

75 g/3 oz/^{3}/$_4$ cup plain/all purpose flour

^{1}/$_2$ tsp baking powder

3 tbsp cocoa powder (unsweetened)

chocolate curls, to decorate

For the sticky chocolate sauce:

175 g/6 oz dark/bittersweet chocolate, broken into pieces

50 g/2 oz/4 tbsp butter

50 g/2 oz/^{1}/$_4$ cup caster/superfine sugar

2 tbsp golden/light corn syrup

200 ml/7 fl oz/^{3}/$_4$ cup milk

Lightly oil 4 x 200 ml/7 fl oz individual pudding basins/ heatproof bowls and sprinkle with a little of the muscovado/ brown sugar. Place a few orange segments in each basin followed by a spoonful of the cranberries.

Cream the remaining muscovado sugar with the margarine until light and fluffy, then gradually beat in the eggs a little at a time, adding 1 tablespoon of the flour after each addition. Sift the remaining flour, baking powder and cocoa powder together, then stir into the creamed mixture with 1 tablespoon of cooled boiled water to give a soft dropping consistency. Spoon the mixture into the basins.

Cover each pudding with a double sheet of nonstick baking parchment with a pleat in the centre and secure tightly with string. Cover with a double sheet of kitchen foil with a pleat in the centre to allow for expansion and secure tightly with string. Place in the top of a steamer, set over a saucepan of gently simmering water and steam steadily for 45 minutes, or until firm to the touch. Remember to replenish the water if necessary. Remove the puddings from the steamer and leave to rest for about 5 minutes before running a knife around the edges of the puddings and turning out onto individual plates.

Meanwhile, make the chocolate sauce. Melt the chocolate and butter in a pudding basin set over a saucepan of gently simmering water. Add the sugar and golden/corn syrup and stir until dissolved, then stir in the milk and continue to cook, stirring often, until the sauce thickens. Decorate the puddings with a few chocolate curls and serve with the sauce.

Difficulty Rating: 3 points

Baked Lemon & Sultana Cheesecake

Cuts into 10 slices

Ingredients

275 g/9½ oz/1⅓ cups caster/superfine sugar

50 g/2 oz/4 tbsp butter

50 g/2 oz/½ cup self-raising flour

½ level tsp baking powder

5 large/extra-large eggs

450 g/1 lb/2 cups cream cheese

40 g/1½ oz/⅓ cup plain/all-purpose flour

grated zest of 1 lemon

3 tbsp fresh lemon juice

150 ml/¼ pint/½ cup crème fraîche/sour cream

75 g/3 oz/½ cup sultanas/golden raisins

To decorate:

1 tbsp icing/confectioners' sugar

fresh blackcurrants or blueberries

mint leaves

Preheat the oven to 170°C/325°F/Gas Mark 3. Oil a 20.5 cm/ 8 inch loose-bottomed round cake tin/pan with nonstick baking parchment.

Beat 50 g/2 oz/¼ cup of the sugar and the butter together until light and creamy, then stir in the self-raising flour, baking powder and 1 egg. Mix together lightly until well blended. Spoon into the prepared tin and spread the mixture over the base. Separate the 4 remaining eggs and reserve.

Blend the cheese in a food processor until soft. Gradually add the egg yolks and sugar and blend until smooth. Turn into a bowl and stir in the plain/all-purpose flour, lemon zest and juice. Mix lightly before adding the crème fraîche/sour cream and sultanas/golden raisins, stirring well.

Whisk the egg whites until stiff, fold into the cheese mixture and pour into the tin. Tap lightly on the work surface to remove any air bubbles. Bake in the preheated oven for about 1 hour, or

until golden and firm. Cover lightly if browning too much. Switch the oven off and leave in the oven to cool for 2–3 hours. Remove the cheesecake from the oven. When completely cold, remove from the tin. Sprinkle with icing/ confectioners' sugar, decorate with the blackcurrants or blueberries and mint and serve.

Difficulty Rating: 2 points

Crunchy Rhubarb Crumble

Serves 4

Ingredients

100 g/3½ oz/1 scant cup plain/all-purpose flour
50 g/2 oz/4 tbsp butter, softened
50 g/2 oz/⅔ cup rolled oats
50 g/2 oz/¼ cup demerara/turbinado sugar
1 tbsp sesame seeds
½ tsp ground cinnamon
450 g/1 lb/3¾ cups (prepared as below) fresh rhubarb
50 g/2 oz/¼ cup caster/superfine sugar, plus extra, for sprinkling
custard or cream, to serve

Preheat the oven to 180 C/350 F/Gas Mark 4. Place the flour in a large bowl and add the butter in cubes. Rub in with the fingertips until the mixture looks like fine breadcrumbs, or blend for a few seconds in a food processor. Stir in the oats, demerara/turbinado sugar, sesame seeds and cinnamon. Mix well and reserve.

Prepare the rhubarb by removing the thick ends of the stalks and cut diagonally into 2.5 cm/1 inch chunks. Wash thoroughly and pat dry with a clean dishtowel. Place the rhubarb in a 1.1 litre/2 pint/1¼ quart pie dish.

Sprinkle the caster/superfine sugar over the rhubarb and top with the reserved crumble/crisp mixture. Level the top of the crumble so that all the fruit is well covered and press down firmly. If liked, sprinkle the top with a little extra caster sugar.

Place on a baking sheet and bake in the preheated oven for 40–50 minutes until the fruit is soft and the topping is golden brown. Sprinkle with caster sugar and serve hot with custard or cream.

Difficulty Rating: 1 point

Classic Apple Strudel

Serves 8

Ingredients

700 g/1½ lb cooking apples

zest and juice of 1 orange

50 g/2 oz/¼ cup natural caster/superfine sugar

75 g/3 oz/½ cup raisins

125 g/4 oz/½ cup (1 stick) butter

50 g/2 oz/1 cup fresh white breadcrumbs

40 g/1½ oz/⅓ cup flaked almonds

½ tsp ground cinnamon

350 g/12 oz filo/phyllo pastry sheets

icing/confectioners' sugar, for dusting

whipped cream, crème fraîche/sour cream or natural/plain
   yogurt, to serve

Difficulty Rating: 2 points

Preheat the oven to 190°C/375°F/Gas Mark 5 and butter a large baking sheet. Peel, core and slice the apples, finely grate the orange zest and squeeze out the juice. Put in a pan with caster/superfine sugar and cook for 10 minutes until the apples are tender. Pour into a bowl, stir in the raisins and leave to cool.

Melt 25 g/1 oz of the butter in a frying pan and add the breadcrumbs. Cook for a minute to brown, add the almonds and cook for a further minute. Take off the heat, stir in the cinnamon and leave to cool.

Melt the remaining butter and brush and layer the filo/phyllo sheets, reserving 1 sheet for decoration. Sprinkle half the breadcrumb mixture over the filo sheets, leaving a 5 cm/2 inch border. Top with the cooked apples, then more breadcrumb mixture. Fold in the sides, then roll to encase the filling. Place on the greased baking sheet seam–side down. Arrange the reserved sheet on top in ruffles and brush all over with butter. Bake for 20–30 minutes until crisp and light golden. Dust with icing/confectioners' sugar, serve with cream, crème fraîche/sour cream or natural/plain yogurt.

Iced Bakewell Tart

Cuts into 8 slices

Ingredients

For the pastry:
175 g/6 oz/1½ cups plain/all-purpose flour
pinch salt
65 g/2½ oz/5 tbsp butter, cut into small pieces
50 g/2 oz/4 tbsp white vegetable fat/shortening, cut into small pieces
2 small egg yolks, beaten

For the filling:
125 g/4 oz/½ cup (1 stick) butter, melted
125 g/4 oz/⅔ cup caster/superfine sugar
125 g/4 oz/1⅓ cups ground almonds
2 large/extra-large eggs, beaten
few drops almond extract
2 tbsp seedless raspberry jam/jelly

For the icing:
125 g/4 oz/1 cup icing/confectioners' sugar, sifted
6–8 tsp fresh lemon juice
25 g/1 oz/¼ cup toasted flaked/slivered almonds

Preheat the oven to 200°C/400°F/Gas Mark 6, 15 minutes before baking. Place the flour and salt in a bowl and rub in the butter and vegetable fat/shortening until the mixture resembles breadcrumbs. Alternatively, blend in short bursts in a food processor. Add the eggs with sufficient water to make a soft, pliable dough. Knead lightly on a floured board, then chill in the refrigerator for about 30 minutes. Roll out the dough and use to line a 23 cm/9 inch loose–bottomed flan tin/tart pan.

For the filling, mix together the butter, sugar, almonds and beaten eggs and add a few drops of almond extract. Spread the base of the pastry case/pie crust with the raspberry jam/jelly and spoon over the egg mixture. Bake in the oven for 30 minutes, or until the filling is firm and golden brown. Remove from the oven and leave to cool.

When the tart is cold, make the icing by mixing together the icing/confectioners' sugar and lemon juice, a little at a time, until the icing is smooth and of a spreadable consistency. Spread the icing over the tart, leave to set for 2–3 minutes and sprinkle with the almonds. Chill in the refrigerator for about 10 minutes and then serve.

Difficulty Rating: 3 points

Queen of Puddings

Serves 4

Ingredients

75 g/3 oz/1²/₃ cups fresh white breadcrumbs
2 tbsp granulated sugar
450 ml/³/₄ pt/1³/₄ cups whole milk
25 g/1 oz/2 tbsp butter
grated zest of 1 small lemon
2 medium/large eggs, separated
2 tbsp seedless raspberry jam/jelly
50 g/2 oz/¹/₄ cup caster/superfine sugar

Preheat the oven to 170°C/325°F/Gas Mark 3. Oil a 900 ml/
1¹/₂ pint/1 scant quart ovenproof baking dish and reserve. Mix
the breadcrumbs and sugar together in a bowl.

Pour the milk into a small saucepan and heat gently with the
butter and lemon zest until the butter has melted. Allow the
mixture to cool a little, then pour over the breadcrumbs. Stir
well and leave to soak for 30 minutes.

Whisk the egg yolks into the cooled breadcrumb mixture and
pour into the prepared dish. Place the dish on a baking sheet
and bake in the preheated oven for about 30 minutes, or until
firm and set. Remove from the oven. Allow to cool slightly, then
spread the jam/jelly over the pudding.

Whisk the egg whites until stiff and standing in peaks. Gently
fold in the caster/superfine sugar with a metal spoon or rubber
spatula. Pile the meringue over the top of the pudding. Return
the dish to the oven for a further 25–30 minutes until the
meringue is crisp and just slightly coloured. Serve hot or cold.

Difficulty Rating: 3 points

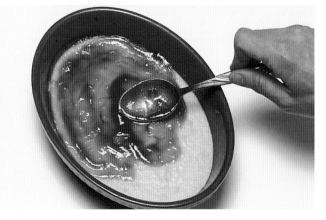

Chocolate Sponge Pudding with Fudge Sauce

Serves 4

Ingredients

75 g/3 oz/6 tbsp

75 g/3 oz/¹/₃ cup caster/superfine sugar

50 g/2 oz dark/semisweet chocolate, melted

50 g/2 oz/¹/₃ cup self-raising flour

25 g/1 oz/¹/₃ cup drinking chocolate/sweetened cocoa powder

1 large/extra-large egg

1 tbsp icing/confectioners' sugar, for dusting

crème fraîche/sour cream, to serve

For the fudge sauce:

50 g/2 oz/¹/₄ cup soft light brown sugar

1 tbsp cocoa powder (unsweetened)

40 g/1¹/₂ oz/¹/₃ cup pecan nuts, roughly chopped

2 tbsp caster/superfine sugar

300 ml/¹/₂ pint/1¹/₄ cups hot, strong black coffee

Preheat the oven to 170˚C/325˚F/Gas Mark 3. Oil a 900 ml/ 1¹/₂ pint/1 quart pie dish. Cream the butter and sugar together in a large bowl. Mix in the melted chocolate, flour, drinking chocolate and egg. Turn the mixture into the pie dish and level.

To make the fudge sauce, blend the brown sugar, cocoa powder and pecan nuts together and sprinkle evenly over the top of the pudding.

Stir the caster/superfine sugar into the hot black coffee until it has dissolved. Pour this over the top of the pudding. Bake in the oven for 50–60 minutes. There will be a rich sauce underneath the sponge. Dust with icing/confectioners' sugar and serve hot with crème fraîche/sour cream.

Difficulty Rating: 2 points

Eve's Pudding

Serves 6

Ingredients

450 g/1 lb cooking apples

175 g/6 oz/1¹/₂ cups blackberries

75 g/3 oz/¹/₃ cup demerara/turbinado sugar

grated zest of 1 lemon

125 g/4 oz/²/₃ cup caster/superfine sugar

125 g/4 oz/¹/₂ cup (1 stick) butter

few drops vanilla extract

2 medium/large eggs, beaten

125 g/4 oz/1 cup self-raising flour

1 tbsp icing/confectioners' sugar

ready-made custard, to serve

Difficulty Rating: 1 point

Preheat the oven to 180°C/350°F/Gas Mark 4. Oil a 1.2 litre/2 pint/1¹/₄ quart baking dish. Peel, core and slice the apples and place a layer in the base of the prepared dish. Sprinkle over some blackberries, a little demerara/turbinado sugar and lemon zest. Continue to layer the apple and blackberries in this way until all the ingredients have been used.

Cream the sugar and butter together until light and fluffy. Beat in the vanilla extract and then the eggs, a little at a time, adding a spoonful of flour after each addition. Fold in the extra flour with a metal spoon or rubber spatula and mix well.

Spread the mixture over the top of the fruit and level. Place the dish on a baking sheet and bake in the oven for 35–40 minutes until well risen and golden brown. To test if the pudding is cooked, press the cooked sponge with a finger – if it springs back, the sponge is cooked. Dust the pudding with icing/confectioners' sugar and serve with custard.

Lemon & Apricot Pudding

Serves 4

Ingredients

125 g/4 oz/1 cup dried apricots

3 tbsp warmed orange juice

50 g/2 oz/4 tbsp butter

125 g/4 oz/^{2}/$_3$ cup caster/superfine sugar

juice and grated zest of 2 lemons

2 medium/large eggs, separated

100 g/3^1/$_2$ oz/1 scant cup self-raising flour

300 ml/^{1}/$_2$ pint/1^1/$_4$ cups milk

custard or fresh cream, to serve

Preheat the oven to 180°C/350°F/Gas Mark 4. Oil a 1.2 litre/ 2 pint/1^1/$_4$ quart pie dish. Soak the apricots in the orange juice for 10–15 minutes, or until most of the juice has been absorbed, then place in the base of the pie dish.

Cream the butter and sugar together with the lemon zest until light and fluffy. Beat the egg yolks into the creamed mixture with a spoonful of flour after each addition. Add the remaining flour and beat well until smooth. Stir the milk and lemon juice into the creamed mixture.

Whisk the egg whites in a grease–free mixing bowl until stiff and standing in peaks. Fold into the mixture using a metal spoon or rubber spatula. Pour into the prepared dish and place in a baking tray filled with enough cold water to come halfway up the sides of the dish.

Bake in the preheated oven for about 45 minutes until the sponge is firm and golden brown. Remove from the oven. Serve immediately with the custard or fresh cream.

Difficulty Rating: 2 points

Rich Double-crust Plum Pie

Serves 6

Ingredients

For the pastry:
75 g/3 oz/6 tbsp butter
75 g/3 oz/¹⁄₃ cup white vegetable fat/shortening
225 g/8 oz/2 cups plain/all-purpose flour
2 egg yolks
1 tbsp milk
a little extra caster/superfine sugar

For the filling:
450 g/1 lb/3 cups fresh plums
50 g/2 oz/¹⁄₄ cup caster/superfine sugar

Preheat the oven to 200˚C/400˚F/Gas Mark 6, 15 minutes before baking. Make the pastry dough by rubbing the butter and white vegetable fat/shortening into the flour until it resembles fine breadcrumbs or blend in a food processor. Add the egg yolks and enough water to make a soft dough. Knead lightly, then wrap and leave in the refrigerator for about 30 minutes.

Meanwhile, prepare the fruit. Rinse and dry the plums, then cut in half and remove the stones. Slice the plums into chunks and cook in a saucepan with 25 g/1 oz/2 tablespoons of the sugar and 2 tablespoons water for 5–7 minutes, or until slightly softened. Remove from the heat and add the remaining sugar to taste and leave to cool.

Roll out half the chilled pastry dough on a lightly floured surface and use to line the base and sides of a 1.2 litre/2 pint/1¹⁄₄ quart pie dish. Allow the dough to hang over the edge of the dish. Spoon in the prepared plums. Roll out the remaining dough to use as the lid and brush the edge with a little water. Wrap the dough around the rolling pin and place over the plums. Press the edges together to seal and mark a decorative edge around the rim by pinching with the thumb and forefinger or using the back of a fork. Brush the lid with milk and make a few slits in the top.

Use any trimmings to decorate the top of the pie with dough leaves. Place on a baking sheet and bake in the oven for 30 minutes, or until golden brown. Sprinkle with a little caster/superfine sugar. Serve hot or cold.

Difficulty Rating: 3 points

Spotted Dick

Serves 6

Ingredients

125 g/4 oz/1 cup self-raising flour
125 g/4 oz/1 cup fresh white breadcrumbs
125 g/4 oz vegetable suet
juice and grated zest of 1 large lemon, preferably unwaxed
50 g/2 oz/¼ cup caster/superfine sugar
175 g/6 oz/1½ cups currants
85–125 ml/3–4 fl oz/½ cup semi-skimmed/low-fat milk
custard, to serve

Mix together the flour, breadcrumbs, suet, lemon zest and caster/superfine sugar in a large bowl and then add the currants. Slowly add the lemon juice with sufficient milk to make a soft, but not sticky, dough.

Flour a board well and place the dough on top. Shape it into a roll about 18 cm/7 inches in length. Wrap in a well-floured pudding cloth or double piece of muslin, or in greaseproof/wax paper and then kitchen foil.

Secure firmly with, then place in the top of a steamer standing over a saucepan of gently boiling water. Steam steadily for 1½–2 hours until the roll feels firm when pushed with your finger.

When the pudding is finished, remove from the steamer and unwrap carefully. Place it on a warm serving dish and serve immediately with custard.

Difficulty Rating: 2 points

Baked Apple Dumplings

Serves 4

Ingredients

225 g/8 oz/1¾ cups self-raising flour

¼ tsp salt

125 g/4 oz/1 cup shredded suet

4 medium cooking apples

4–6 tsp luxury mincemeat/mince pie filling

1 medium/large egg white, beaten

2 tsp caster/superfine sugar

custard or vanilla sauce, to serve

Preheat the oven to 200°C/400°F/Gas Mark 6. Lightly oil a baking tray. Place the flour and salt in a bowl and stir in the suet. Add just enough water to the mixture to mix to a soft but not sticky dough, using the fingertips.

Turn the dough onto a lightly floured board and knead lightly into a ball. Divide the dough into four pieces and roll out each piece into a thin square, large enough to encase the apples.

Peel and core the apples and place an apple in the centre of each square of dough. Fill the centre of each apple with mincemeat/mince pie filling, brush the edges of the pastry squares with water and draw the corners up to meet over each apple. Press the edges of the dough firmly together and decorate with leaves and shapes made from the extra dough trimmings.

Place the apples on the prepared baking tray, brush with the egg white and sprinkle with the sugar. Bake in the preheated oven for 30 minutes, or until golden and the pastry and apples are cooked. Serve the dumplings hot with the custard or vanilla sauce.

Difficulty Rating: 2 points

Jam Roly Poly

Serves 4

Ingredients

225 g/8 oz/1³/₄ cups self-raising flour
¹/₄ tsp salt
125 g/4 oz/1 cup shredded suet
3 tbsp strawberry jam/jelly
1 tbsp milk, for glazing
1 tsp caster/superfine sugar
ready-made jam/jelly sauce, to serve

Preheat the oven to 200°C/400°F/Gas Mark 6. Make the pastry by sifting the flour and salt into a large bowl. Add the suet and mix, then mix in about 150 ml/¹/₄ pint/²/₃ cup water a little at a time to form a soft and pliable dough. (Try to ensure the dough is not too wet.)

Turn the dough out onto a lightly floured board and knead gently until smooth. Roll the dough out into a 23 x 28 cm/ 9 x 11 inch rectangle.

Spread the jam/jelly over the dough, leaving a border of 1 cm/¹/₂ inch all round. Fold the border over the jam and brush the edges with water. Lightly roll the rectangle up from one of the short sides, seal the top edge and press the ends together. (Do not roll the pudding up too tightly.)

Turn the pudding upside down onto a large piece of greaseproof/wax paper large enough to come halfway up the sides. (If not using nonstick paper, then oil lightly.) Tie the ends of the paper to make a boat–shaped paper case for the pudding to sit in, leaving plenty of room for the roly poly to expand.

Brush the pudding lightly with milk and sprinkle with the sugar. Bake in the preheated oven for 30–40 minutes until well risen and golden. Serve immediately with the jam sauce.

Difficulty Rating: 2 points

Egg Custard Tart

Serves 6

Ingredients

For the sweet pastry:
50 g/2 oz/4 tbsp butter
50 g/2 oz/^{1}/$_4$ cup white vegetable fat/shortening
175 g/6 oz/^{1}/$_3$ cups plain/all-purpose flour
1 egg yolk, beaten
2 tsp caster/superfine sugar

For the filling:
300 ml/^{1}/$_2$ pint/1^1/$_4$ cups milk
2 medium/large eggs, plus 1 egg yolk
2 tbsp caster/superfine sugar
^{1}/$_2$ tsp freshly grated nutmeg

Preheat the oven to 200°C/400°F/Gas Mark 6, 15 minutes before baking. Oil a 20.5 cm/8 inch flan tin/tart pan. Make the pastry by cutting the butter and vegetable fat/shortening into small cubes. Add to the flour in a large bowl and rub in until it looks like fine breadcrumbs. Add the egg yolk, sugar and enough water to form a soft and pliable dough. Turn onto a lightly floured surface and knead. Wrap and chill in the refrigerator for 30 minutes.

Roll the dough out onto a lightly floured surface and use to line the oiled flan tin. Place in the refrigerator to chill. Then warm the milk in a small saucepan. Briskly whisk together the eggs, egg yolk and sugar. Pour the milk into the egg mixture and whisk until blended. Strain through a sieve into the pastry case/pie crust. Place the flan tin on a baking sheet.

Sprinkle the top of the tart with nutmeg and bake in the preheated oven for about 15 minutes. Turn the oven down to 170°C/325°F/Gas Mark 3 and bake for a further 30 minutes, or until the custard has set. Serve hot or cold.

Difficulty Rating: 3 points

Strawberry Flan

Serves 6

Ingredients

For the sweet pastry:
175 g/6 oz/1^1/$_3$ cups plain/all-purpose flour
50 g/2 oz/4 tbsp butter
50 g/2 oz/^{1}/$_4$ cup white vegetable fat/shortening
2 tsp caster/superfine sugar
1 medium/large egg yolk, beaten

For the filling:
1 medium/large egg, plus 1 extra egg yolk
50 g/2 oz/^{1}/$_4$ cup caster/superfine sugar
25 g/1 oz/3 heaped tbsp plain/all-purpose flour
300 ml/^{1}/$_2$ pint/1^1/$_4$ cups milk
few drops vanilla extract
450 g/1 lb/3 heaped cups fresh strawberries, cleaned and hulled
   mint leaves, to decorate

Preheat the oven to 200°C/400°F/Gas Mark 6. Blend the flour, butter and vegetable fat in a food processor until they resemble fine breadcrumbs. Stir in the sugar, then, with the machine running, add the egg yolk and enough water to make a stiff dough. Knead lightly and chill in the refrigerator for 30 minutes. Roll out the dough and use to line a 23 cm/9 inch loose-bottomed flan tin/tart pan. Place greaseproof/wax paper in the pastry case/pie crust and cover with baking beans/pie weights or rice. Bake in the oven for 15–20 minutes. Reserve until cool.

For the filling, whisk the eggs and sugar together. Stir in the flour and the milk, then simmer in a saucepan for 3–4 minutes, stirring throughout. Add the vanilla to taste, pour into a bowl and leave to cool. Cover with greaseproof paper to stop a skin forming.

When the filling is cold, whisk until smooth, then pour into the cooked flan case. Arrange the sliced strawberries and mint leaves on the top and leave to set.

Difficulty Rating: 3 points

Golden Castle Pudding

Serves 4–6

Ingredients

125 g/4 oz/¹⁄₂ cup (1 stick) butter

125 g/4 oz/²⁄₃ cup caster/superfine sugar

few drops vanilla extract

2 medium/large eggs, beaten

125 g/4 oz/1 cup self-raising flour

4 tbsp golden/light corn syrup

crème fraîche/sour cream or ready-made custard, to serve

Preheat the oven to 180°C/350°F/Gas Mark 4. Lightly oil four to six individual pudding/heatproof bowls and place a small circle of lightly oiled greaseproof/wax paper or baking parchment in the base of each one. Place the butter and caster/superfine sugar in a large bowl, then beat together until the mixture is pale and creamy. Stir in the vanilla extract and gradually add the beaten eggs, a little at a time. Add a tablespoon of flour after each addition of egg and beat well.

When the mixture is smooth, add the remaining flour and fold in gently. Add a tablespoon of water and mix to form a soft mixture that will drop easily off a spoon. Spoon enough mixture into each bowl to come halfway up, allowing enough space for the puddings to rise. Place on a baking sheet and bake in the preheated oven for about 25 minutes until firm and golden brown.

Leave the puddings to stand for 5 minutes. Discard the paper circle and turn out onto individual serving plates.

Warm the golden/light corn syrup in a small saucepan and pour a little over each pudding. Serve hot with the crème fraîche/sour cream or custard.

Difficulty Rating: 1 point

Banoffee Pie

Serves 6–8

Ingredients

175 g/6 oz/1⅓ cups plain/all-purpose flour

pinch salt

1 tbsp caster/superfine sugar

75 g/3 oz/6 tbsp butter, diced

1 egg yolk

For the filling and topping:

75 g/3 oz/6 tbsp butter

50 g/2 oz/¼ cup soft light brown sugar

225 g/8 oz canned condensed milk

2 tbsp milk

3 bananas, peeled and sliced

150 ml/¼ pint/scant ⅔ cup double/heavy cream, whipped

25 g/1 oz dark/semisweet chocolate, grated, to decorate

Difficulty Rating: 3 points

Sift the flour and salt into a bowl or a food processor, then rub in, or process, the sugar and butter until it resembles fine crumbs. Add the egg yolk and a few drops of cold water and mix to a dough. Knead, wrap in plastic wrap and chill for 30 minutes.

Preheat the oven to 200°C/400°F/Gas Mark 6 and grease a 20.5 cm/8 inch round flan tin/tart pan. Roll out the pastry on a lightly floured surface and use to line the tin. Press the pastry into the sides of the tin and prick the base with a fork. Line the pastry case with greaseproof/wax paper and baking beans/pie weights and bake for 10 minutes. Remove the beans and bake for a further 5–10 minutes. Place the tin/pan on a wire rack to cool.

For the filling, heat the butter and sugar in a pan so the butter melts and the sugar dissolves. Leave to boil for 1 minute. Remove from the heat and add the condensed milk and the milk. Stirring constantly, allow to boil for 2 minutes. Remove from the heat. Place the bananas in the pastry case/pie crust and pour in the warm toffee. Leave to cool for 1 hour. Spread the whipped cream over the cold banoffee filling and sprinkle with the grated chocolate.

College Pudding

Serves 4

Ingredients

125 g/4 oz/1 cup shredded suet
125 g/4 oz/2¾ cups fresh white breadcrumbs
50 g/2 oz/⅓ cup sultanas/golden raisins
50 g/2 oz/⅓ cup seedless raisins
½ tsp ground cinnamon
¼ tsp freshly grated nutmeg
¼ tsp mixed/pumpkin pie spice
50 g/2 oz/¼ cup caster/superfine sugar
½ tsp baking powder
2 medium/large eggs, beaten
orange zest, to decorate

Preheat the oven to 180°C/350°F/Gas Mark 4. Lightly oil an ovenproof 900 ml/1½ pint/1 scant quart ovenproof pudding basin/heatproof bowl and place a small circle of greaseproof/wax paper in the base.

Mix the shredded suet and breadcrumbs together and rub lightly together with the fingertips to remove any lumps. Stir in the dried fruit, spices, sugar and baking powder. Add the eggs and beat lightly together until the mixture is well blended and the fruit is evenly distributed.

Spoon the mixture into the prepared pudding basin and level the surface. Place on a baking sheet and cover lightly with some greaseproof paper. Bake in the preheated oven for 20 minutes, then remove the paper and continue to bake for a further 10–15 minutes until the top is firm.

When the pudding is cooked, remove from the oven and carefully turn out onto a warmed serving dish. Decorate with the orange zest and serve immediately.

Difficulty Rating: 1 point

Lattice Treacle Tart

Serves 6–8

Ingredients

For the pastry:
175 g/6 oz/1⅓ cups plain/all-purpose flour
40 g/1½ oz/3 tbsp butter
40 g/1½ oz/3 tbsp white vegetable fat/shortening
1 small egg, beaten, for brushing

For the filling:
225 g/8 oz/¾ cup golden/light corn syrup
finely grated zest and juice of 1 lemon
75 g/3 oz/1½ cups fresh white breadcrumbs

Preheat the oven to 190°C/375°F/Gas Mark 5. Make the pastry by placing the flour, butter and white vegetable fat/shortening in a food processor. Blend in short, sharp bursts until the mixture resembles fine breadcrumbs. Remove from the processor and place on a pastry board or in a large bowl. Stir in enough cold water to make a dough and knead until smooth and pliable. Roll out the dough and use to line a 20.5 cm/8 inch loose-bottomed fluted flan dish or tin/tart pan. Reserve the dough trimmings for decoration. Chill for 30 minutes.

To make the filling, place the golden/light corn syrup in a saucepan and warm gently with the lemon zest and juice. Tip the breadcrumbs into the pastry case/pie crust and pour over the syrup mixture.

Roll the dough trimmings out on a lightly floured surface and cut into 6–8 thin strips. Lightly dampen the edge of the tart, then place the strips across the filling in a lattice pattern. Brush the ends of the strips with water and seal to the edge of the tart. Brush a little beaten egg over the pastry and bake in the oven for 25 minutes, or until the filling is just set. Serve hot or cold.

Difficulty Rating: 2 points

Apple & Cinnamon Brown Betty

Serves 2

Ingredients

450 g/1 lb cooking apples, peeled, cored and sliced
50 g/2 oz/¹/₄ cup caster/superfine sugar
finely grated zest of 1 lemon
125 g/4 oz/2³/₄ cups fresh white breadcrumbs
125 g/4 oz/²/₃ cup demerara/turbinado sugar
¹/₂ tsp ground cinnamon
25 g/1 oz/2 tbsp butter

For the custard:

3 egg yolks
1 tbsp caster/superfine sugar
500 ml/18 fl oz/2¹/₂ cups milk
1 tbsp cornflour/cornstarch
few drops vanilla extract

Preheat the oven to 180°C/350°F/Gas Mark 4. Lightly oil a 900 ml/1¹/₂ pint/1 scant quart ovenproof dish. Place the apples in a saucepan with the caster/superfine sugar, lemon zest and 2 tablespoons water. Simmer for 10–15 minutes until the apples are soft.

Mix the breadcrumbs with the sugar and the cinnamon. Place half the sweetened apples in the base of the prepared dish and spoon over half of the crumb mixture. Place the remaining apples on top and cover with the rest of the crumb mixture. Melt the butter and pour over the surface of the dessert. Cover the dish with nonstick baking parchment and bake in the preheated oven for 20 minutes. Remove the paper and bake for a further 10–15 minutes until golden.

Make the custard by whisking the egg yolks and sugar together until creamy. Mix 1 tablespoon of the milk with the cornflour/cornstarch until a paste forms and reserve. Warm the rest of the milk until nearly boiling and pour over the egg mixture with the paste and vanilla extract.

Place the bowl over a saucepan of gently simmering water. Stir over the heat until the custard is thickened and can coat the back of a spoon. Strain into a jug and serve hot, poured over the dessert.

Difficulty Rating: 3 points

Cherry Batter Pudding

Serves 4

Ingredients

450 g/1 lb/3 cups fresh cherries (or 425 g/15 oz can
   pitted cherries)
50 g/2 oz/scant ½ cup plain/all-purpose flour
pinch salt
3 tbsp caster/superfine sugar
2 eggs
300 ml/½ pint/1¼ cups milk
40 g/1½ oz/3 tbsp butter
1 tbsp rum
extra caster/superfine sugar, to decorate
double/heavy cream, to serve

Preheat the oven to 220°C/425°F/Gas Mark 7. Lightly oil a
shallow casserole dish. Rinse the cherries and remove the
stones (using a cherry stoner/pitter, if possible). If using canned
cherries discard the juice and place in the prepared dish.

Sift the flour and salt into a large bowl. Stir in 2 tablespoons of
the caster/superfine sugar and make a well in the centre. Beat
the eggs, then pour into the well. Warm the milk and slowly
pour into the well, beating throughout and gradually drawing in
the flour from the sides of the bowl. Continue until a smooth
batter has formed.

Melt the butter in a small saucepan over a low heat, then stir
into the batter with the rum. Reserve for 15 minutes, then beat
again until smooth and easy to pour. Pour into the prepared
baking dish and bake in the preheated oven for 30–35 minutes
until golden brown and set. Remove the pudding from the
oven, sprinkle with the remaining sugar and serve hot with
plenty of double/heavy cream.

Difficulty Rating: 2 points

Chocolate, Orange & Pine Nut Tart

Cuts into 8–10 slices

Ingredients

For the sweet shortcrust pastry:
150 g/5 oz/1 heaped cup plain/all-purpose flour
$\frac{1}{2}$ tsp salt
3–4 tbsp icing/confectioners' sugar
125 g/4 oz/$\frac{1}{2}$ cup (1 stick) unsalted butter, diced
2 medium/large egg yolks, beaten
$\frac{1}{2}$ tsp vanilla extract

For the filling:
125 g/4 oz dark/semisweet chocolate, chopped
65 g/2$\frac{1}{2}$ oz/scant $\frac{1}{2}$ cup lightly toasted pine nuts
2 large/extra-large eggs
grated zest of 1 orange
1 tbsp Cointreau
250 ml/8 fl oz/1 cup whipping cream
2 tbsp orange marmalade

Preheat the oven to 200°C/400°F/Gas Mark 6. Place the flour, salt and sugar in a food processor with the butter and blend briefly. Add the egg yolks, 2 tablespoons iced water and the vanilla extract and blend until a soft dough is formed. Remove and knead until smooth, wrap in plastic wrap and chill in the refrigerator for 1 hour.

Lightly oil a 23 cm/9 inch loose-based flan tin/tart pan. Roll the dough out on a lightly floured surface to a 28 cm/11 inch round and use to line the tin. Press into the sides of the tin/pan, crimp the edges, prick the base with a fork and chill in the refrigerator for 1 hour. Bake blind in the preheated oven for 10 minutes. Remove and place on a baking sheet. Reduce the oven temperature to 190°C/375°F/Gas Mark 5.

To make the filling, sprinkle the chocolate and the pine nuts evenly over the base of the pastry case/pie crust. Beat the eggs, orange zest, Cointreau and cream in a bowl until well blended, then pour over the chocolate and pine nuts.

Bake in the oven for 30 minutes, until the pastry is golden and the custard mixture set. Cool on a wire rack. Heat the marmalade with 1 tablespoon water and brush over the tart. Serve warm.

Difficulty Rating: 3 points

Chocolate Pecan Pie

Cuts into 8–10 slices

Ingredients

225 g/8 oz prepared sweet shortcrust pastry dough (*see page 22*)

200 g/7 oz/2 cups pecan halves

125 g/4 oz dark/semisweet chocolate, chopped

25 g/1 oz/2 tbsp butter, diced

3 eggs

125 g/4 oz/²/₃ cup light brown sugar

175 ml/6 fl oz/scant ³/₄ cup golden/light corn syrup

2 tsp vanilla extract

vanilla ice cream, to serve

Difficulty Rating: 2 points

Preheat the oven to 180°C/350°F/Gas Mark 4. Roll the prepared pastry dough out on a lightly floured surface and use to line a 25.5 cm/10 inch pie tin/plate. Roll the trimmings out and use for a decorative edge around the pie. Chill for 1 hour.

Reserve enough pecan halves to cover the top of the pie, then coarsely chop the remainder and reserve. Melt the chocolate and butter in a small saucepan over a low heat or in the microwave and reserve.

Beat the eggs and brush the base and sides of the pastry with a little of the egg. Beat the sugar, golden/light corn syrup and vanilla extract into the eggs. Add the pecans, then beat in the chocolate mixture.

Pour the filling into the pastry case/pie crust and arrange the reserved pecan halves over the top. Bake in the preheated oven for 45–55 minutes until the filling is well risen and just set. If the edge browns too quickly, cover with strips of kitchen foil. Remove from the oven. Serve with ice cream.

Osborne Pudding

Serves 4

Ingredients

8 slices white bread
50 g/2 oz/4 tbsp butter
2 tbsp marmalade
50 g/2 oz/^{1}/₃ cup mixed dried fruit
2 tbsp fresh orange juice
3 tbsp caster/superfine sugar
2 large/extra-large eggs
450 ml/^{3}/₄ pint/1^1/₄ cups milk
150 ml/^{1}/₄ pint/^{2}/₃ cup whipping cream

For the marmalade sauce:

zest and juice of 1 orange
2 tbsp thick-cut orange marmalade
1 tbsp brandy (optional)
2 tsp cornflour/cornstarch

Preheat the oven to 170°C/325°F/Gas Mark 3. Lightly oil a 1.2 litre/2 pint/1^1/₄ quart baking dish. Remove the crusts from the bread and spread thickly with butter and marmalade. Cut the bread into small triangles. Place half the bread in the dish and sprinkle over the dried mixed fruit, 1 tablespoon orange juice and half the caster/superfine sugar. Top with the remaining bread, buttered side up, and pour over remaining orange juice and sugar. Whisk the eggs with the milk and cream and pour over the pudding. Reserve for about 30 minutes to allow the bread to absorb the liquid, then place in a roasting tin/pan and pour in boiling water to halfway up the sides of the dish. Bake for 50–60 minutes.

Meanwhile, make the sauce. Heat the orange zest and juice with the marmalade and brandy. Mix 1 tablespoon water with the cornflour/cornstarch and mix together well. Add to the saucepan and cook over a low heat, stirring until warmed through and thickened. Serve the pudding hot with the sauce.

Difficulty Rating: 1 point

Mini Strawberry Tartlets

Makes 12 tartlets

Ingredients

225 g/8 oz/1^3/₄ cups plain/all-purpose flour
25 g/1 oz/3^1/₂ tbsp icing/confectioners' sugar
125 g/4 oz/^{1}/₂ cup (1 stick) butter, diced
25 g/1 oz/^{1}/₄ cup ground almonds
1 egg yolk

For the filling:

85 ml/3 fl oz/6 tbsp double/heavy cream
175 g/6 oz/^{3}/₄ cup full-fat cream cheese
25 g/1 oz/2 tbsp vanilla caster/superfine sugar
2 tbsp amaretto almond-flavoured liqueur
250 g/9 oz fresh strawberries, hulled, and halved if large
2 tbsp sieved raspberry jam
small mint leaves, to decorate

Sift the flour and icing/confectioners' sugar into a bowl, or food processor, and add the butter. Rub, or process, the butter into the flour until the mixture resembles fine crumbs. Stir in the almonds and egg yolk and mix with 1 tablespoon cold water to form a soft dough. Cover with plastic wrap and chill for 30 minutes.

Preheat the oven to 200°C/400°F/Gas Mark 6 and grease a 12-hole muffin tin/pan. Roll out the dough to 6 mm/^{1}/₄ inch thickness and cut out twelve 10 cm/4 inch circles. Place the circles into the tin, fluting up the edges. Prick the bases with a fork and bake for 12–15 minutes until light golden. Leave to cool in the tins for 3 minutes, then cool on a wire rack.

To make the filling, whip the cream until stiff then mix with the cream cheese, sugar and liqueur. Chill until needed and then spoon into the pastry cases/shells. Arrange the fresh strawberries on top and brush with a little jam. Decorate with mint leaves and serve.

Difficulty Rating: 2 points

Pear & Chocolate Custard Tart

Cuts into 6–8 slices

Ingredients

For the chocolate pastry:
125 g/4 oz/¹/₂ cup (1 stick) unsalted butter, softened
65 g/2¹/₂ oz/¹/₃ cup caster/superfine sugar
2 tsp vanilla extract
175 g/6 oz/1¹/₃ cups sifted plain/all-purpose flour
40 g/1¹/₂ oz/¹/₂ cup cocoa powder (unsweetened)
whipped cream, to serve

For the filling:
125 g/4 oz dark/semisweet chocolate, chopped
250 ml/8 fl oz/1 cup whipping cream
50 g/2 oz/¹/₄ cup caster/superfine sugar
1 large/extra-large egg; 1 large/extra-large egg yolk
1 tbsp crème de cacao (chocolate crème liqueur)
3 ripe pears

Preheat the oven to 190°C/375°F/Gas Mark 5. Process the butter, sugar and vanilla extract. Add the flour and cocoa powder and process until a soft dough forms. Remove the dough, wrap in plastic wrap and chill for at least 1 hour. Roll out the dough between two sheets of plastic wrap to a 28 cm/11 inch round. Peel off the top sheet of plastic wrap and invert the pastry round into a lightly oiled 23 cm/9 inch loose-based flan tin/tart pan, easing the dough into the base and sides. Prick the base with a fork, then chill in the refrigerator for 1 hour. Place baking parchment and baking beans/pie weights in the case and bake blind for 10 minutes. Remove the parchment and beans and bake for a further 5 minutes. Remove and cool.

For the filling, heat the chocolate, cream and half the sugar in a saucepan over a low heat, stirring until melted and smooth. Remove from the heat and cool slightly before beating in the egg, egg yolk and crème de cacao. Spread over the pastry pie case.

Peel the pears, cut into thin slices and arrange over the custard, gently fanning them towards the centre and pressing into the custard. Bake in the oven for 10 minutes. Reduce the

temperature to 180°C/350°F/Gas Mark 4 and sprinkle the surface evenly with the remaining sugar. Bake for 20–25 minutes. Remove from the oven and leave to cool slightly. Cut into slices, then serve with whipped cream.

Difficulty Rating: 4 points

Double Chocolate Truffle Slice

Cuts into 12–14 slices

Ingredients

1 quantity chocolate pastry dough (*see* page 72)
300 ml/¹⁄₂ pint/1¹⁄₄ cups double/heavy cream
300 g/11 oz dark/semisweet chocolate, chopped
25–40 g/1–1¹⁄₂ oz/2–3 tbsp unsalted butter, diced
50 ml/2 fl oz/¹⁄₄ cup brandy or liqueur
icing/confectioners' sugar or cocoa powder (unsweetened),
   for dusting
chocolate leaves, caraques or curls, to decorate

Preheat the oven to 200°C/400°F/Gas Mark 6. Prepare the chocolate pastry dough and chill. Roll the dough out to a rectangle about 38 x 15 cm/15 x 6 inches and use to line a rectangular loose-based flan tin/tart pan and trim. Chill for 1 hour.

Place a sheet of nonstick baking parchment and baking beans/pie weights in the pastry case/pie crust. Bake blind for 20 minutes. Remove the baking parchment and beans and bake for a further 10 minutes. Leave to cool.

Bring the cream to the boil. Remove from the heat and add the chocolate all at once, stirring until melted and smooth. Beat in the butter, then stir in the brandy or liqueur. Leave to cool slightly, then pour into the cooked pastry case. Refrigerate until set.

Cut out 2.5 cm/1 inch strips of nonstick baking parchment. Place over the tart in a crisscross pattern and dust with icing/confectioners' sugar or cocoa powder. Arrange chocolate leaves, caraques or curls around the edges of the tart. Refrigerate until ready to serve. Leave to soften at room temperature for 15 minutes before serving.

Difficulty Rating: 3 points

Autumn Tart

Serves 6–8

Ingredients

175 g/6 oz/1⅓ cups plain flour

pinch salt

1 tbsp caster/superfine sugar

75 g/3 oz/6 tbsp butter, diced

1 egg yolk

For the filling:

50 g/2 oz/4 tbsp butter

50 g/2 oz/¼ cup caster/superfine sugar

50 g/2 oz/½ cup ground almonds

1 egg yolk

2 dessert apples, peeled, cored and sliced

4 plums, pitted and sliced

2 tbsp lemon juice

2 tbsp caster/superfine sugar

milk, for brushing

crème fraîche/sour cream, to serve

Sift the flour and salt into a bowl or a food processor, add the sugar and butter and rub in or process until the mixture resembles fine crumbs. Add the egg yolk and 1 tablespoon cold water and mix to a dough. Knead until smooth, then wrap in plastic wrap and chill for 30 minutes.

Preheat the oven to 180°C/350°F/Gas Mark 4 and grease a 20.5 cm/8 inch round flan tin/tart pan. Roll the pastry out on a lightly floured surface and use to line the tin/pan. Trim the top and reserve the trimmings for use later as decoration. Press the pastry well into the sides of the tin and prick the base with a fork.

To make the filling, put the butter and sugar in a bowl and beat until fluffy. Beat in the ground almonds and egg yolk and spoon into the pastry case/pie crust. Arrange the sliced fruit over the filling. Mix the lemon juice and caster/superfine sugar together and brush over the top of the fruit filling.

Roll out the pastry trimmings and cut out leaf shapes and mark veins on. Brush the edge of the tart with milk, place the leaves round the edge and brush with milk. Bake for 30 minutes, or until the pastry is golden and the fruit is tender and golden. Serve with crème fraîche/sour cream.

Difficulty Rating: 3 points

Double Chocolate Banoffee Tart

Cuts into 8 slices

Ingredients

2 x 400 g/14 oz cans sweetened condensed milk

175 g/6 oz dark/semisweet chocolate, chopped

600 ml/1 pint/2½ cups whipping cream

1 tbsp golden/light corn syrup

25 g/1 oz/2 tbsp butter, diced

150 g/5 oz white chocolate, grated or finely chopped

1 tsp vanilla extract

2–3 ripe bananas

cocoa powder (unsweetened), for dusting

For the ginger crumb crust:

24–26 gingernut biscuits/ginger snap cookies, roughly crushed

100 g/3½ oz/7 tbsp butter, melted

1–2 tbsp sugar, or to taste

½ tsp ground ginger

Preheat the oven to 190°C/375°F/Gas Mark 5. Place the condensed milk in a heavy-based saucepan over a gentle heat. Allow to boil, stirring constantly, for about 3–5 minutes until golden. Remove from the heat and leave to cool.

For the crust, place the biscuits/cookies with the melted butter, sugar and ground ginger in a food processor and blend together. Press into the sides and base of a 23 cm/9 inch loose-based flan tin/tart pan with the back of a spoon. Chill for 15–20 minutes, then bake in the oven for 5–6 minutes. Remove from the oven and leave to cool.

Melt the dark/semisweet chocolate in a medium-sized saucepan with 150 ml/¼ pint/⅔ cup of the whipping cream, the golden/light corn syrup and the butter over a low heat. Stir until smooth. Carefully pour into the crumb crust, tilting the tin to distribute the chocolate layer evenly. Chill in the refrigerator for at least 1 hour, or until set.

Heat 150 ml/¼ pint/⅔ cup of the remaining cream until hot, then add all the white chocolate and stir until melted and smooth. Stir in the vanilla extract and strain into a bowl. Leave to cool to room temperature.

Scrape the cooked condensed milk into a bowl and whisk until smooth, adding a little of the remaining cream if too thick. Spread over the chocolate layer, then slice the bananas and arrange evenly over the top.

Whip the remaining cream until peaks form. Stir a spoonful of cream into the white chocolate mixture, then fold in the remaining cream. Spread over the bananas, swirling to the edge. Dust with cocoa powder and chill until ready to serve.

Difficulty Rating: 3 points

Chocolate Apricot Linzer Torte

Cuts into 10–12 slices

Ingredients

For the chocolate almond pastry:
75 g/3 oz/¹/₂ cup whole blanched almonds
125 g/4 oz/²/₃ cup caster/superfine sugar
215 g/7¹/₂ oz/1²/₃ cups plain/all-purpose flour
2 tbsp cocoa powder (unsweetened)
1 tsp ground cinnamon
¹/₂ tsp salt
grated zest of 1 orange
225 g/8 oz/1 cup (2 sticks) unsalted butter, diced
2–3 tbsp iced water

For the filling:
350 g/12 oz apricot jam/jelly
75 g/3 oz milk chocolate, chopped
icing/confectioners' sugar, for dusting

Preheat the oven to 190°C/375°F/Gas Mark 5. Lightly oil a 28 cm/11 inch flan tin/tart pan. Place the almonds and half the sugar into a food processor and blend until finely ground. Add the remaining sugar, flour, cocoa powder, cinnamon, salt and orange zest and blend again. Add the diced butter and blend in short bursts to form coarse crumbs. Add the water 1 tablespoon at a time until the mixture starts to come together.

Turn onto a lightly floured surface and knead lightly, roll out, then, using your fingertips, press half the dough into the base and sides of the tin. Prick the base with a fork and chill. Roll out the remaining dough between two pieces of plastic wrap to a 28–30.5 cm/11–12 inch round. Slide the round onto a baking sheet and chill for 30 minutes.

For the filling, spread the apricot jam/jelly evenly over the chilled pastry base and sprinkle with the chopped chocolate.

Slide the remaining dough round onto a lightly floured surface and peel off the top layer of plastic wrap. Using a straight edge, cut the round into 1 cm/¹/₂ inch strips; allow to soften until

slightly flexible. Place the strips across the torte, about 1 cm/¹/₂ inch apart, to create a lattice pattern. Bake for 35 minutes, or until cooked. Let cool then dust with icing/confectioners' sugar and serve in slices.

Difficulty Rating: 3 points

Chocolate Peanut Butter Pie

Cuts into 8 slices

Ingredients

22–24 chocolate wafers or peanut butter cookies

100 g/3^1/$_2$ oz/7 tbsp butter, melted

1–2 tbsp sugar

1 tsp vanilla extract

1^1/$_2$ tbsp gelatine

100 g/3^1/$_2$ oz/^{1}/$_2$ cup caster/superfine sugar

1 tbsp cornflour/cornstarch

^{1}/$_2$ tsp salt

225 ml/8 fl oz/1 cup milk

2 large/extra large eggs, separated

2 large/extra large egg yolks

100 g/3^1/$_2$ oz dark/semisweet chocolate, chopped

2 tbsp rum or 2 tsp vanilla extract

125 g/4 oz/^{1}/$_2$ cup smooth peanut butter

300 ml/^{1}/$_2$ pint/1 cup whipping cream

chocolate curls, to decorate

Place the wafers or cookies with the melted butter, sugar and vanilla into a food processor and blend together. Press into the base of a 23 cm/9 inch pie plate or flat tin. Chill for 15–20 minutes. Then, place 3 tablespoons cold water into a bowl and sprinkle over the powdered gelatine; leave until softened.

Blend half the sugar with the cornflour/cornstarch and salt in a saucepan and gradually whisk in the milk. Boil gently for 1–2 minutes, or until smooth, stirring constantly. Beat all the egg yolks together, then whisk in half the hot milk mixture and whisk until blended. Whisk in the remaining milk mixture, return to a clean saucepan and cook gently until the mixture comes to the boil and thickens. Boil, stirring vigorously, for 1 minute, then pour a quarter of the custard into a bowl. Add the chopped chocolate and rum or vanilla extract and stir until the chocolate has melted and the mixture is smooth. Pour onto the crust and chill until set.

Whisk the gelatine into the remaining custard until dissolved. Then whisk in the peanut butter. Next, whisk the egg whites until stiff, then whisk in the remaining sugar, 1 tablespoon at a time.

Whip the cream, then fold 125 ml/4 fl oz/^{1}/$_2$ cup into the custard, and then fold in the egg whites. Spread the peanut butter cream mixture over the chocolate layer. Pipe the cream on top. Decorate with chocolate curls and chill until ready to serve.

Difficulty Rating: 4 points

Mini Pistachio & Chocolate Strudels

Makes 24

Ingredients

5 large sheets ready-made filo/phyllo pastry
50 g/2 oz/4 tbsp butter, melted
1–2 tbsp caster/superfine sugar, for sprinkling
50 g/2 oz white chocolate, melted, to decorate

For the filling:
125 g/4 oz/1 cup finely chopped unsalted pistachios
3 tbsp caster/superfine sugar
50 g/2 oz dark/semisweet chocolate, finely chopped
1–2 tsp rosewater
1 tbsp icing/confectioners' sugar, for dusting

Preheat the oven to 170°C/325°F/Gas Mark 3. Lightly oil two large baking sheets. For the filling, mix the pistachios, sugar and dark chocolate in a bowl. Sprinkle with the rosewater, then reserve.

Cut each filo/phyllo pastry sheet into four to make 23 x 18 cm/9 x 7 inch rectangles. Place one rectangle on the work surface and brush with a little melted butter. Place another rectangle on top and brush with a little more butter. Sprinkle with a little caster/superfine sugar and spread about 1 dessertspoon of the filling along one short end. Fold the short end over the filling, then fold in the long edges and roll up. Place on the baking sheet seam-side down, then repeat.

Brush each strudel with the remaining melted butter and sprinkle with a little caster sugar. Bake for 20 minutes. Remove from the oven and leave on the baking sheet for 2 minutes, transfer to a wire rack. Dust with icing/confectioners' sugar. Place the white chocolate in a small decorating bag and pipe squiggles over the strudels. Leave to set, then serve.

Difficulty Rating: 1 point

'Mars' Bar Mousse in Filo Cups

Serves 6

Ingredients

6 large sheets ready-made filo/phyllo pastry, thawed if frozen

40 g/1½ oz/3 tbsp unsalted butter, melted

1 tbsp caster/superfine sugar

3 x 58 g/2 oz 'Mars' bars/caramel nougat chocolate bars, coarsely chopped

1½ tbsp milk

300 ml/½ pint/1¼ cups double/heavy cream

1 large/extra-large egg white

1 tsp cocoa powder (unsweetened)

1 tbsp dark/semisweet grated chocolate

chocolate sauce (see page 34), to serve (optional)

For the topping:

300 ml/½ pint/1¼ cups whipping cream

125 g/4 oz white chocolate, grated

1 tsp vanilla extract

Preheat the oven to 180°C/350°F/Gas Mark 4. Lightly oil six 150 ml/¼ pint ramekins. Cut the filo/phyllo pastry into 15 cm/6 inch squares, place one square on the work surface, then brush with the melted butter, sprinkle with a little caster/superfine sugar. Butter a second square and lay it over the first at an angle, sprinkle with a little more caster sugar, repeat with two more pastry squares. Press the pastry well into the oiled ramekins, then bake on a baking sheet for 10–15 minutes. Leave to cool, then remove the filo cups from the ramekins. Leave until cold.

Melt the 'Mars' bars/caramel nougat chocolate bars and milk in a saucepan, stirring constantly. Leave to cool for 10 minutes. Whip the cream and stir a spoonful into the melted 'Mars' bar mixture, then fold in the remaining cream. Whisk the egg white until stiff and fold into the 'Mars' bar mixture together with the cocoa powder. Chill the mousse for 2–3 hours. For the topping, boil 125 ml/4 fl oz/½ cup of the whipping cream, add the white chocolate and vanilla extract and stir until smooth, then strain into a bowl and leave to cool.

Whip the remaining cream, then fold into the cream mixture. Spoon the mousse into the filo cups, cover with the cream mixture and sprinkle with grated chocolate. Chill before serving with chocolate sauce, if liked.

Difficulty Rating: 3 points

Raspberry Chocolate Ganache & Berry Tartlets

Serves 8

Ingredients

1 quantity chocolate pastry dough (*see* page 72)
600 ml/1 pint/2¹/₂ cups whipping cream
275 g/10 oz/1 cup seedless raspberry jam/jelly
225 g/8 oz dark/semisweet chocolate, chopped
700 g/1¹/₂ lb/5³/₄ cups raspberries or other summer berries
50 ml/2 fl oz/¹/₄ cup framboise liqueur
1 tbsp caster/superfine sugar
crème fraîche/sour cream, to serve

Preheat the oven to 200°C/400°F/Gas Mark 6. Use the chocolate pastry dough to line eight 7.5 cm/3 inch tartlet tins/pans. Bake blind for 12 minutes.

Place 400 ml/14 fl oz/1²/₃ cups of the whipping cream and half the raspberry jam/jelly in a saucepan and boil, whisking constantly to dissolve the jam. Remove from the heat and add the chocolate, stirring until the chocolate melts. Pour into the tartlet tins, shaking gently to distribute the ganache evenly. Chill in the refrigerator for 1 hour, or until set.

Place the berries in a large shallow bowl. Heat the remaining raspberry jam with half the framboise liqueur over a medium heat until melted and bubbling. Drizzle over the berries. Divide the berries among the tartlets. Chill until ready to serve.

Remove the tartlets from the refrigerator 30 minutes before serving. Whip the remaining cream with the caster/superfine sugar and the remaining framboise liqueur until it is softly peaking. Serve with the tartlets and crème fraîche/sour cream.

Difficulty Rating: 3 points

Chocolate Melting Pots

Serves 4

Ingredients

125 g/4 oz good-quality dark/semisweet chocolate
1 tbsp cocoa powder (unsweetened)
125 g/4 oz/¹/₂ cup (1 stick) unsalted butter
2 medium eggs
2 medium egg yolks
150 g/5 oz/³/₄ cup caster/superfine sugar
150 g/5 oz/1¹/₄ cups plain/all purpose flour
1 tbsp ground almonds
icing/confectioners' sugar, for dusting (optional)
fresh raspberries, fresh mint sprigs and whipped/whipping cream, to serve

Preheat the oven to 160°C/325°F/Gas Mark 3. Lightly butter four individual pudding basins/heatproof bowls or four 150 ml/¹/₄ pint ramekins, then dust the inside of each with a little of the cocoa powder.

Break the chocolate into small pieces and place in a heatproof bowl set over a pan of gently simmering water. Leave until softened, then remove from the heat. Add the butter and stir until smooth. Reserve. Place a large mixing bowl over a pan of gently simmering water and add the eggs, egg yolks and sugar. Whisk until thick and creamy. Remove from the heat, stir in the melted chocolate and leave to cool for 5 minutes.

Sift the flour over the mixture and gently fold in together with the ground almonds. Spoon into the prepared pudding basins or ramekins, filling them three-quarters full.

Place on a baking sheet and bake in the oven for 12 minutes. Remove from the oven and invert onto serving plates. Dust with a little icing/confectioners' sugar, if using, and serve with raspberries, fresh mint sprigs and whipped/whipping cream.

Difficulty Rating: 2 points

White Chocolate & Macadamia Tartlets

Makes 10

Ingredients

1 quantity sweet shortcrust pastry (*see* page 22)
2 medium/large eggs
50 g/2 oz/¹/₄ cup caster/superfine sugar
250 ml/8 fl oz/1 cup golden/light corn syrup
40 g/1¹/₂ oz/3 tbsp butter, melted
50 ml/2 fl oz/¹/₄ cup whipping cream
1 tsp vanilla or almond extract
225 g/8 oz/1²/₃ cups coarsely chopped unsalted macadamia nuts
150 g/5 oz white chocolate, coarsely chopped

Preheat the oven to 200˚C/400˚F/Gas Mark 6. Roll out the pastry and use to line ten 7.5–9 cm/3–3¹/₂ inch tartlet tins/pans. Line each tin with kitchen foil and fill with baking beans/pie weights. Arrange on a baking sheet and bake blind for 10 minutes. Remove the foil and beans and leave to cool.

Beat the eggs with the sugar until light and creamy, then beat in the golden/light corn syrup, the butter, cream and vanilla or almond extract. Stir in the macadamia nuts. Sprinkle 100 g/3¹/₂ oz/³/₄ cup of the chopped white chocolate equally over the bases of the tartlet cases and divide the mixture evenly among them.

Reduce the oven temperature to 180˚C/ 350˚F/Gas Mark 4 and bake the tartlets for 20 minutes, or until golden and the filling set. Remove from the oven and leave to cool on a wire rack.

Remove the tartlets from their tins and arrange on a wire rack. Melt the remaining white chocolate and, using a teaspoon or a small paper decorating bag, drizzle the melted chocolate over the surface of the tartlets in a zigzag pattern. Serve slightly warm.

Difficulty Rating: 3 points

Rice Pudding & Chocolate Tart

Serves 8

Ingredients

1 quantity chocolate pastry dough (*see* page 72)

1 tsp cocoa powder (unsweetened), for dusting

few fresh blueberries and fresh mint sprigs, to decorate

For the chocolate ganache:

200 ml/7 fl oz/³⁄₄ cup double/heavy cream

1 tbsp golden/light corn syrup

175 g/6 oz dark/semisweet chocolate, chopped

1 tbsp butter; 1 tsp vanilla extract

For the rice pudding:

1 litre/1³⁄₄ pints/4 cups milk

¹⁄₂ tsp salt; 1 vanilla pod/bean

100 g/3¹⁄₂ oz/¹⁄₂ cup long-grain white rice

1 tbsp cornflour/cornstarch; 2 tbsp sugar

Preheat the oven to 200°C/400°F/Gas Mark 6. Roll the chocolate pastry dough out and use to line a 23 cm/9 inch flan tin/tart pan. Place a sheet of nonstick baking parchment and baking beans/pie weights in the tin and bake blind for 15 minutes.

For the ganache, place the cream and golden/light corn syrup in a saucepan and bring to the boil. Remove from the heat and add the chocolate, stirring until smooth. Beat in the butter and vanilla extract, pour into the baked pastry case/pie crust and reserve.

For the rice pudding, bring the milk and salt to the boil in a medium-sized saucepan. Split the vanilla pod/bean and scrape the seeds into the milk and add the vanilla pod. Sprinkle in the rice, then bring to the boil. Reduce the heat and simmer until the rice is tender and the milk is creamy. Remove from the heat. Blend the cornflour/cornstarch and sugar together, then stir in

2 tablespoons water to make a paste. Stir a little of the rice mixture into the cornflour mixture, then stir into the rice. Bring to the boil and cook, stirring constantly, until thickened. Set the base of the saucepan into iced water and stir until cooled and thickened. Spoon the rice pudding into the tart, level and leave to set. Dust with cocoa powder and decorate with blueberries and fresh mint to serve.

Difficulty Rating: 4 points

Chocolate Fruit Pizza

Serves 8

Ingredients

1 quantity sweet shortcrust pastry dough (*see page 22?*)

2 tbsp chocolate spread

1 small peach, very thinly sliced

1 small nectarine, very thinly sliced

150 g/5 oz/1 cup halved or quartered strawberries

75 g/3 oz/²⁄₃ cup raspberries

75 g/3 oz blueberries

75 g/3 oz dark/semisweet chocolate, coarsely chopped

15 g/¹⁄₂ oz/1 tbsp butter, melted

2 tbsp sugar

75 g/3 oz white chocolate, chopped

1 tbsp toasted and chopped hazelnuts

fresh mint sprigs, to decorate

Preheat the oven to 200°C/400°F/Gas Mark 6. Lightly oil a large baking sheet. Roll the prepared pastry out to a 23 cm/9 inch round, place the pastry round onto the baking sheet and crimp the edges. Using a fork, prick the base all over and chill in the refrigerator for 30 minutes.

Line the pastry with kitchen foil and weigh down with an ovenproof flat dinner plate or base of a large flan tin/tart pan and bake blind in the oven until the edges begin to colour. Remove from the oven and discard the weight and foil.

Carefully spread the chocolate spread over the pizza base and arrange the peach and nectarine slices around the outside edge in overlapping circles. Toss the berries with the dark/semisweet chocolate and arrange in the centre. Drizzle with the melted butter and sprinkle with the sugar.

Bake in the preheated oven for 10–12 minutes until the fruit begins to soften. Transfer the pizza to a wire rack. Sprinkle the white chocolate and hazelnuts over the surface and return to the oven for 1 minute, or until the chocolate begins to soften.

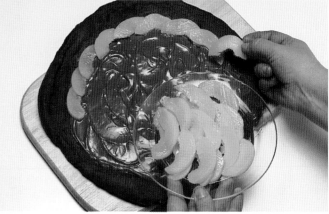

If the pastry starts to darken too much, cover the edge with strips of foil. Remove to a wire rack and leave to cool. Decorate with sprigs of fresh mint and serve warm.

Difficulty Rating: 2 points

Chocolate Lemon Tartlets

Makes 10

Ingredients

1 quantity sweet shortcrust pastry dough (*see* page 22)
175 ml/6 fl oz/scant ¾ cup double/heavy cream
175 g/6 oz dark/semisweet chocolate, chopped
25 g/1 oz/2 tbsp butter, diced
1 tsp vanilla extract
350 g/12 oz/1 cup lemon curd
250 ml/8 fl oz/1 cup prepared custard
250 ml/8 fl oz/1 cup single/light cream
½–1 tsp almond extract
grated chocolate, toasted flaked/slivered almonds, to decorate

Preheat the oven to 200°C/400°F/Gas Mark 6. Roll out the prepared pastry dough and use to line ten 7.5 cm/3 inch tartlet tins/pans. Place a small piece of crumpled kitchen foil in each and bake blind in the preheated oven for 12 minutes. Remove from the oven and leave to cool.

Bring the cream to the boil, then remove from the heat and add the chocolate. Stir until smooth and melted. Beat in the butter and vanilla extract, pour into the tartlets and leave to cool.

Beat the lemon curd until soft and spoon a thick layer over the chocolate in each tartlet, spreading gently to the edges. Do not chill in the refrigerator or the chocolate will be too firm.

Place the prepared custard into a large bowl and gradually whisk in the cream and almond extract until smooth and runny. To serve, spoon a little custard sauce onto a plate and place a tartlet in the centre. Sprinkle with grated chocolate and almonds, then serve.

Difficulty Rating: 2 points

Fudgy Mocha Pie with Espresso Custard Sauce

Cuts into 10 slices

Ingredients

125 g/4 oz dark/semisweet chocolate, chopped
125 g/4 oz/¹/₂ cup (1 stick) butter, diced
1 tbsp instant espresso powder
4 large/extra-large eggs
1 tbsp golden/light corn syrup
125 g/4 oz/²/₃ cup sugar
1 tsp ground cinnamon
3 tbsp milk
icing/confectioners' sugar, for dusting
few fresh strawberries, to serve

For the espresso custard sauce:
2–3 tbsp instant espresso powder, or to taste
250 ml/8 fl oz/1 cup prepared custard
250 ml/8 fl oz/1 cup single/light cream
2 tbsp coffee-flavoured liqueur (optional)

Preheat the oven to 180°C/350°F/Gas Mark 4. Line with a 23 cm/ 9 inch pie plate with kitchen foil. Melt the chocolate and butter and reserve. Dissolve the espresso powder in 1–2 tablespoons hot water and reserve.

Beat the eggs with the golden/corn syrup, sugar, dissolved espresso powder, cinnamon and milk until blended. Whisk in the melted chocolate mixture. Pour into the pie plate. Bake for 20–25 minutes. Leave to cool, then dust with icing/ confectioners' sugar.

For the custard sauce, dissolve the instant espresso powder with 2–3 tablespoons hot water, whisk into the prepared custard. Whisk in the single/light cream, stir in the coffee-flavoured liqueur. Serve pie slices with the espresso custard and strawberries.

Difficulty Rating: 1 point

Chocolate Pecan Angel Pie

Cuts into 8–10 slices

Ingredients

4 large/extra-large egg whites

¹⁄₄ tsp cream of tartar

225 g/8 oz/1 heaping cup caster/superfine sugar

3 tsp vanilla extract

100 g/3¹⁄₂ oz/1 cup lightly toasted and chopped pecans

75 g/3 oz/¹⁄₂ cup dark/semisweet chocolate chips

150 ml/¹⁄₄ pint/²⁄₃ cup double/heavy cream

150 g/5 oz white chocolate, grated

fresh raspberries, dark chocolate curls, few fresh mint sprigs to
    decorate

Preheat the oven to 110°C/225°F/Gas Mark ¹⁄₄. Lightly oil a
23 cm/9 inch pie plate. Using an electric mixer, whisk the egg
whites and cream of tartar on a low speed until foamy, then
increase the speed and beat until soft peaks form. Gradually
beat in the sugar, 1 tablespoon at a time, beating well after
each addition, until stiff glossy peaks form and the sugar is
completely dissolved. (Test by rubbing a bit of meringue
between your fingers – if gritty, continue beating.) This will take
about 15 minutes. Beat in 2 teaspoons of the vanilla extract,
then fold in the nuts and the chocolate chips.

Spread the meringue evenly in the pie plate, making a shallow
well in the centre and slightly building up the sides. Bake in the
preheated oven for 1–1¹⁄₄ hours until a golden creamy colour.
Reduce the oven temperature if the meringue colours too
quickly. Turn the oven off, but do not remove the meringue.
Leave the oven door ajar (about 5 cm/2 inches) for about
1 hour. Transfer to a wire rack until cold.

Pour the double/heavy cream into a small saucepan and bring
to the boil. Remove from the heat, add the grated white
chocolate and stir until melted. Add the remaining vanilla
extract and leave to cool, then whip until thick. Spoon the white
chocolate whipped cream into the meringue shell, piling it high
and swirling decoratively.

Decorate with fresh raspberries and chocolate curls. Chill in the
refrigerator for 2 hours before serving. When ready to serve,
add sprigs of fresh mint on the top and cut into slices.

Difficulty Rating: 2 points

Frozen Mississippi Mud Pie

Cuts into 6–8 slices

Ingredients

24–26 gingernut biscuits/cookies, roughly crushed
100 g/3½ oz/7 tbsp butter, melted
1–2 tbsp sugar, or to taste
½ tsp ground ginger
600 ml/1 pint/2 cups chocolate ice cream
600 ml/1 pint/2 cups coffee-flavoured ice cream

For the chocolate topping:
175 g/6 oz dark/semisweet chocolate, chopped
50 ml/2 fl oz/¼ cup single/light cream
1 tbsp golden/light corn syrup
1 tsp vanilla extract
50 g/2 oz white and milk/semisweet chocolate, coarsely grated

For the crust, place the biscuits/cookies with the melted butter, sugar and ginger in a food processor and blend. Press into the sides and base of a 23 cm/9 inch loose–based flan tin/tart pan and freeze for 30 minutes. Soften the ice creams at room temperature for about 25 minutes. Spoon the chocolate ice cream into the crumb crust, spreading it evenly over the base, then spoon the coffee ice cream on top. Return to the freezer to re–freeze the ice cream.

For the topping, heat the chocolate with the cream, golden/light corn syrup and vanilla extract in a saucepan. Stir until the chocolate has melted and is smooth. Pour into a bowl. Chill in the refrigerator, stirring occasionally until cold but not set.

Spread the cooled chocolate mixture over the top of the frozen pie. Sprinkle with the chocolate and return to the freezer for 1½ hours, or until firm. Serve at room temperature.

Difficulty Rating: 1 point

Luxury Mince Pies

Makes 20

Ingredients

275 g/10 oz/2¼ cups plain/all-purpose flour
25 g/1 oz/¼ cup ground almonds
175 g/6 oz/¾ cup (1½ sticks) butter, diced
75 g/3 oz/⅓ cup icing/confectioners' sugar
finely grated zest of 1 lemon
1 egg yolk
3 tbsp milk

For the filling:
225 g/8 oz/1¼ cups mincemeat
1 tbsp dark rum or orange juice
finely grated zest of 1 orange
75 g/3 oz/⅔ cup dried cranberries
icing/confectioners' sugar, for dusting

Difficulty Rating: 2 points

Sift the flour and ground almonds into a bowl or a food processor and add the butter. Rub in, or process, until the mixture resembles fine crumbs. Sift in the icing/confectioners' sugar and stir in the lemon zest. Whisk the egg yolk and milk together in a separate bowl and stir into the mixture until a soft dough forms. Wrap the pastry in plastic wrap and chill for 30 minutes.

Preheat the oven to 200°C/400°F/Gas Mark 6. Grease two 12-hole shallow bun tins/muffin pans. Roll out the pastry on a lightly floured surface to 3 mm/⅛ inch thickness. Cut out 20 rounds using a 7.5 cm/3 inch fluted round pastry cutter. Re-roll the trimmings into thin strips.

Mix the filling ingredients together in a bowl. Place 1 tablespoon of the filling in each pastry case/pie crust, then dampen the edges of each case with a little water. Put four strips of pastry over the top of each case to form a lattice.

Bake for 10–15 minutes until the pastry is crisp. Dust with icing sugar and serve hot or cold.

White Chocolate Mousse & Strawberry Tart

Cuts into 10 slices

Ingredients

1 quantity sweet shortcrust pastry dough (*see page 22*)
65 g/2½ oz/¼ cup strawberry jam/jelly
1–2 tbsp kirsch or framboise liqueur
450–700 g/1–1½ lb/4–6 cups ripe strawberries, sliced lengthways

For the white chocolate mousse:
250 g/9 oz white chocolate, chopped
350 ml/12 fl oz/1½ cups double/heavy cream
3 tbsp kirsch or framboise liqueur
1–2 large/extra-large egg whites (optional)

Preheat the oven to 200°C/400°F/Gas Mark 6. Roll the pastry dough out and use to line a 25 cm/10 inch flan tin/tart pan. Line with kitchen foil or nonstick baking parchment and baking beans/pie weights, then bake blind for 15–20 minutes. Remove the kitchen foil or baking parchment and beans and return to the oven for 5 minutes.

To make the mousse, place the white chocolate with 2 tablespoons water and 125 ml/4 fl oz/½ cup of the cream in a saucepan and heat gently, stirring, until the chocolate has melted and is smooth. Remove from the heat, stir in the kirsch or framboise liqueur and cool.

Whip the remaining cream until soft peaks form. Fold a spoonful of the cream into the cooled white chocolate mixture, then fold in the remaining cream. If using, whisk the egg whites until stiff and gently fold into the white chocolate cream mixture to make a softer, lighter mousse. Chill in the refrigerator for 15–20 minutes. Heat the strawberry jam/jelly with the kirsch or framboise liqueur and brush or spread half the mixture onto the pastry base. Leave to cool. Spread the chilled chocolate mousse over the jam and arrange the sliced strawberries in

concentric circles over the mousse. Reheat the remaining jam, if necessary, and glaze the strawberries lightly. Chill the tart for about 3–4 hours, or until the chocolate mousse has set. Cut into slices and serve.

Difficulty Rating: 4 points

Chocolate & Saffron Cheesecake

Serves 6

Ingredients

¹/₄ tsp saffron threads

175 g/6 oz/1¹/₃ cups plain/all-purpose flour

pinch salt

75 g/3 oz/6 tbsp butter

1 tbsp caster/superfine sugar

1 medium/large egg yolk

350 g/12 oz/1¹/₂ cups curd cheese/sieved cottage cheese

75 g/3 oz/¹/₃ cup golden/unrefined granulated sugar

125 g/4 oz dark/semisweet chocolate, melted and cooled

6 tbsp milk

3 medium/large eggs

1 tbsp icing/confectioners' sugar, sifted, to decorate

Preheat the oven to 200°C/400°F/Gas Mark 6. Lightly oil a 20.5 cm/8 inch fluted flan tin/tart pan. Soak the saffron threads in 1 tablespoon hot water for 20 minutes. Sift the flour and salt into a bowl. Cut the butter into small cubes, add to the flour and, using your fingertips, rub in the butter until it resembles breadcrumbs. Stir in the sugar.

Beat the egg yolk with 1 tablespoon cold water, add to the mixture and mix together until a pliable dough is formed. Knead until free from cracks, wrap in plastic wrap and chill for 30 minutes.

Roll the out the pastry dough and use it to line the tin. Prick the pastry base and sides with a fork and line with nonstick baking parchment and baking beans/pie weights. Bake blind for 12 minutes. Take out the beans and baking parchment and bake blind for a further 5 minutes. Beat together the curd cheese/sieved cottage cheese and granulated sugar, then beat in the melted chocolate, saffron liquid, milk and eggs, until blended. Pour the mixture into the pastry case/pie crust and place on a baking sheet.

Reduce the oven temperature to 190°C/375°F/ Gas Mark 5 and bake for 15 minutes, then reduce the temperature to 180°C/350°F/Gas Mark 4 and bake for 20–30 minutes more until set.

Remove from the oven and leave for 10 minutes before removing from the tin, if serving warm. If serving cold, leave in the tin to cool before removing. Sprinkle with icing/confectioners' sugar before serving.

Difficulty Rating: 3 points

Caramelized Chocolate Tartlets

Serves 6

Ingredients

350 g/12 oz/1½ cups ready-made shortcrust pastry dough,
   thawed if frozen
150 ml/¼ pint/⅔ cup coconut milk
3 tbsp demerara/turbinado sugar
50 g/2 oz dark/bittersweet chocolate, melted
1 egg, beaten
few drops vanilla extract
1 small mango, peeled, stoned and sliced
1 small papaya, peeled, deseeded and chopped
1 star fruit, sliced
1 kiwi, peeled and sliced, or use fruits of your choice

Preheat the oven to 200°C/400°F/Gas Mark 6. Lightly oil six individual tartlet tins/pans. Roll out the ready-made pastry dough and use to line the oiled tins. Prick the bases and sides with a fork and line with nonstick baking parchment and baking beans/pie weights. Bake blind for 10 minutes, then remove from the oven and discard the baking beans and the baking parchment.

Reduce the oven temperature to 180°C/350°F/Gas Mark 4. Heat the coconut milk and a tablespoon of the sugar in a saucepan, stirring constantly, until the sugar dissolves. Remove from the heat and leave to cool. Stir the melted chocolate, beaten egg and vanilla extract into the coconut milk. Mix well, then strain into the cooked pastry cases/pie crusts. Place on a baking sheet and bake for 25 minutes, or until set. Remove and leave to cool, then chill.

Preheat the grill/broiler, then decorate each tartlet with the fruits. Sprinkle with the remaining sugar and grill/broil for 2 minutes. Turn the tartlets so as not to burn the sugar. Remove from the grill, cool and serve.

Difficulty Rating: 2 points

Bread & Butter Pudding

Serves 4–6

Ingredients

2–3 tbsp unsalted butter, softened
4–6 slices white bread
75 g/3 oz mixed dried fruits
25 g/1 oz/2 tbsp caster/superfine sugar, plus extra for sprinkling
2 medium/large eggs
450 ml/¾ pint/2 cups semi-skimmed/low-fat milk, warmed
freshly grated nutmeg
custard, to serve

Preheat the oven to 180°C/350°F/Gas Mark 4, 10 minutes before cooking. Lightly butter a 1.1 litre/2 pint ovenproof dish. Butter the bread and cut into quarters. Arrange half the bread in the dish and scatter over two-thirds of the dried fruit and sugar. Repeat the layering, finishing with the dried fruits.

Beat the eggs and milk together and pour over the bread and butter. Leave to stand for 30 minutes.

Sprinkle with the remaining sugar and a little nutmeg and carefully place in the oven. Cook for 40 minutes, or until the pudding has lightly set and the top is golden.

Remove and sprinkle with a little extra caster/superfine sugar, if liked. Serve with custard.

Difficulty Rating: 1 point

Topsy Turvy Pudding

Serves 6

Ingredients

For the topping:
175 g/6 oz demerara/turbinado sugar
2 oranges

For the sponge:
175 g/6 oz/³⁄₄ cup (1¹⁄₂ sticks) butter, softened
175 g/6 oz/1 scant cup caster/superfine sugar
3 medium/large eggs, beaten
175 g/6 oz/1¹⁄₃ cups sifted self-raising flour
50 g/2 oz dark/semisweet chocolate, melted
grated zest of 1 orange
25 g/1 oz/¹⁄₄ cup sifted cocoa powder (unsweetened)
custard or sour cream, to serve

Preheat the oven to 180°C/350°F/Gas Mark 4. Lightly oil a 20.5 cm/8 inch deep round loose-based cake tin/pan. Place the demerara/turbinado sugar and 3 tablespoons water in a saucepan and heat until the sugar has dissolved, then boil rapidly until a golden caramel is formed. Pour into the base of the tin and let cool. Cream the butter and sugar together until light and fluffy. Beat in the eggs gradually, adding a spoonful of flour after each addition to prevent curdling. Add the melted chocolate and stir well. Fold in the orange zest, self-raising flour and sifted cocoa powder and mix well.

Remove the peel from both oranges. Thinly slice the peel into strips and then slice the oranges. Arrange the peel and then the orange slices over the caramel. Top with the sponge mixture and level the top. Place the tin on a baking sheet and bake for 40–45 minutes. Remove from the oven, leave for 5 minutes, invert onto a serving plate and sprinkle with cocoa powder. Serve with custard or sour cream.

Difficulty Rating: 4 points

Orange Chocolate Cheesecake

Serves 8

Ingredients

225 g/8 oz/1¹⁄₂ cups plain chocolate-coated digestive
   biscuits/Graham crackers
50 g/2 oz/4 tbsp butter
450 g/1 lb/4 cups mixed fruits, such as blueberries and
   raspberries
1 tbsp sifted icing/confectioners' sugar
few fresh mint sprigs, to decorate

For the filling:
450 g/1 lb soft cream cheese
1 tbsp powdered gelatine
350 g/12 oz orange chocolate,
   broken into segments
600 ml/1 pint/2¹⁄₂ cups double/heavy cream

Lightly oil and line a 20.5 cm/8 inch round loose-based cake tin/pan with nonstick baking parchment. Place the biscuits/cookies in a plastic bag and crush with a rolling pin, or use a food processor. Melt the butter in a saucepan, add the crushed biscuits/cookies and mix well. Press the biscuit mixture into the base of the lined tin and chill for 20 minutes.

For the filling, remove the cream cheese from the refrigerator at least 20 minutes before using, to allow it to come to room temperature. Place the cream cheese in a bowl, beat until smooth. Reserve. Pour 4 tablespoons water into a small bowl and sprinkle over the gelatine. Leave to stand for 5 minutes until spongy. Place the bowl over a saucepan of simmering water and allow to dissolve, stirring occasionally. Leave to cool slightly.

Melt the orange chocolate in a heatproof bowl set over a saucepan of simmering water, then leave to cool slightly. Whip the cream until soft peaks form. Beat the gelatine and chocolate into the cream cheese. Fold in the cream. Spoon into the tin and level the surface. Chill in the refrigerator for 4 hours until set.

Remove the cheesecake from the tin and place on a serving plate. Top with the fruits, dust with icing/confectioners' sugar and decorate with fresh mint sprigs.

Difficulty Rating: 3 points

Fruity Chocolate Bread Pudding

Serves 4

Ingredients

175 g/6 oz dark/semisweet chocolate

1 small fruit loaf

125 g/4 oz/1 cup roughly chopped, ready-to-eat dried apricots

450 ml/³/₄ pint/1³/₄ cups single/light cream

300 ml/¹/₂ pint/1¹/₄ cups milk

1 tbsp caster/superfine sugar

3 medium/large eggs

3 tbsp demerara/turbinado sugar, for sprinkling

Preheat the oven to 180°C/350°F/Gas Mark 4. Lightly butter a shallow ovenproof dish. Break the chocolate into small pieces, then place in a heatproof bowl set over gently simmering water. Heat gently, stirring frequently, until the chocolate has melted and is smooth. Remove from the heat and leave for about 10 minutes, or until the chocolate begins to thicken slightly.

Cut the fruit loaf into medium to thick slices, then spread with the melted chocolate. Leave until almost set, then cut each slice in half to form triangles. Layer the chocolate-coated bread slices and the chopped apricots in the prepared ovenproof dish.

Stir the cream and milk together, then stir in the caster/superfine sugar. Beat the eggs, then gradually beat in the cream and milk mixture until well blended. Carefully pour over the bread slices and apricots and leave to stand for 30 minutes.

Sprinkle with the demerara/turbinado sugar and place in a roasting tin/pan half filled with boiling water. Bake for 45 minutes, or until golden and the custard is lightly set. Serve immediately.

Difficulty Rating: 2 points

Puff Pastry Jalousie

Serves 6–8

Ingredients

2 large dessert apples, peeled and cored

4 tbsp mincemeat

finely grated zest of 1 orange

1 tbsp orange marmalade

350 g/12 oz puff pastry

1 medium/large egg, beaten

caster/superfine sugar, for sprinkling

custard or double/heavy cream, to serve

Preheat the oven to 200°C/400°F/Gas Mark 6 and grease a large baking sheet. Grate the apples coarsely, then mix together with the mincemeat, orange zest and the marmalade, then reserve.

Place the pastry on a lightly floured surface and cut it in half. Roll each piece into an 18 x 25 cm/7 x 10 inch rectangle. Place one of the rectangles on the baking sheet.

Spoon the filling down the middle, leaving a 2.5 cm/1 inch edge all round. Brush the pastry edges with the beaten egg. Score thin lines across the middle of the remaining pastry rectangle right through the pastry, leaving a plain narrow 2.5 cm/1 inch rim all round. Lift the scored pastry on top of the filling and press the edges together to seal. Place on the baking sheet.

Brush the pastry with the beaten egg and bake for about 30 minutes until golden and crisp. Sprinkle generously with caster/superfine sugar and return to the oven for 5 minutes. Serve hot with custard or double/heavy cream.

Difficulty Rating: 1 point

Raspberry & Almond Tart

Serves 6–8

Ingredients

For the pastry:
225 g/8 oz/2 cups plain/all-purpose flour
pinch salt
125 g/4 oz/¹/₂ cup (1 stick) butter, cut into pieces
50 g/2 oz/¹/₄ cup caster/superfine sugar
grated zest of ¹/₂ lemon
1 egg yolk

For the filling:
75 g/3 oz/6 tbsp butter
75 g/3 oz/¹/₃ cup caster/superfine sugar
75 g/3 oz/³/₄ cup ground almonds
2 eggs
225 g/8 oz/2 cups raspberries, thawed if frozen
2 tbsp flaked/slivered almonds
icing/confectioners' sugar, for dusting

Preheat the oven to 200°C/400°F/Gas Mark 6. Blend the flour, salt and butter in a food processor until the mixture resembles breadcrumbs. Add the sugar and lemon zest and blend again for 1 minute. Mix the egg yolk with 2 tablespoons cold water and add to the mixture. Blend until the mixture starts to come together, adding a little more water if necessary, then tip out onto a lightly floured surface. Knead until smooth, wrap in plastic wrap and chill in the refrigerator for 30 minutes.

Roll the dough out thinly and use to line a 23 cm/9 inch fluted tart tin/pan. Chill in the refrigerator for 10 minutes. Line the pastry case/shell with greaseproof/wax paper and baking beans/pie weights. Bake for 10 minutes, remove the paper and beans and return to the oven for a further 10–12 minutes. Leave to cool slightly, then reduce the oven temperature to 190°C/375°F/Gas Mark 5. Blend together the butter, sugar, ground almonds and eggs until smooth. Spread the raspberries over the base of the pastry, then cover with the almond mixture. Bake for 15 minutes.

Remove from the oven. Sprinkle with the flaked/slivered almonds and dust generously with icing/confectioners' sugar. Bake for 15–20 minutes until firm and golden brown. Leave to cool, then serve.

Difficulty Rating: 3 points

Goat's Cheese & Lemon Tart

Serves 4

Ingredients

For the pastry:
125 g/4 oz/$\frac{1}{2}$ cup (1 stick) butter, cut into small pieces
225 g/8 oz/2 cups plain/all-purpose flour
pinch salt
50 g/2 oz/$\frac{1}{4}$ cup sugar
1 egg yolk

For the filling:
350 g/12 oz/1$\frac{1}{2}$ cups mild fresh goat's cheese
3 eggs, beaten
150 g/5 oz/$\frac{3}{4}$ cup sugar
grated zest and juice of 3 lemons
450 ml/$\frac{3}{4}$ pint/1$\frac{3}{4}$ cups double/heavy cream
fresh raspberries, to decorate

Preheat the oven to 200°C/400°F/Gas Mark 6. Rub the butter into the plain/all-purpose flour and salt until the mixture resembles breadcrumbs, then stir in the sugar. Beat the egg yolk with 2 tablespoons cold water and add to the mixture. Mix together until a dough is formed, then turn the dough out onto a lightly floured surface and knead until smooth. Chill for 30 minutes.

Roll the dough out thinly and use to line a 4 cm/1$\frac{1}{2}$ inch deep 23 cm/9 inch fluted flan tin/tart pan. Chill in the refrigerator for 10 minutes. Line the pastry case/pie crust with greaseproof/wax paper and baking beans/pie weights or kitchen foil and bake blind in the preheated oven for 10 minutes. Remove the paper and beans or foil.

Return to the oven for a further 12–15 minutes until cooked. Leave to cool slightly, then reduce the oven temperature to 150°C/300°F/Gas Mark 2. Beat the goat's cheese until smooth. Whisk in the eggs, sugar, lemon zest and juice. Add the cream and mix well. Carefully pour the cheese mixture into the pastry case and return to the oven.

Bake in the oven for 35–40 minutes until just set. If it begins to brown or swell, open the oven door for 2 minutes. Reduce the oven temperature to 120°C/ 250°F/Gas Mark $\frac{1}{2}$ and leave the tart to cool in the oven. Chill until cold, then decorate with raspberries.

Difficulty Rating: 3 points

Passion Fruit & Pomegranate Citrus Tart

Serves 4

Ingredients

For the pastry:
175 g/6 oz/1⅓ cups plain/all-purpose flour
pinch salt
125 g/4 oz/½ cup (1 stick) butter
4 tsp caster/superfine sugar
1 small egg, separated

For the filling:
2 passion fruit
175 g/6 oz/1 scant cup caster/superfine sugar
4 large/extra-large eggs
175 ml/6 fl oz/scant ¾ cup double/heavy cream
3 tbsp lime juice
1 pomegranate
icing/confectioners' sugar, for dusting

Preheat the oven to 200°C/400°F/Gas Mark 6. Sift the flour and salt into a bowl, rub in the butter until it resembles fine breadcrumbs. Stir in the sugar.

Whisk the egg yolk and add to the dry ingredients. Mix well to form a pliable dough. Knead gently, wrap the pastry in plastic wrap and leave in the refrigerator for 30 minutes.

Roll out the pastry and use to line a 25.5 cm/10 inch loose-based flan tin/tart pan. Line the pastry case/pie crust with greaseproof/wax paper and baking beans/pie weights. Brush the edges with the egg white and bake blind for 15 minutes. Remove the paper and beans and bake for a further 5 minutes. Remove and reduce the oven temperature to 180°C/350°F/Gas Mark 4.

Halve the passion fruit and spoon the flesh into a bowl. Whisk the sugar and eggs together in a bowl. When mixed thoroughly, stir in the double/heavy cream with the passion fruit juice and flesh and the lime juice. Pour the mixture into the pastry case and bake for 30–40 minutes until the filling is just set. Remove

and cool slightly, then chill in the refrigerator for 1 hour. Cut the pomegranate in half and scoop the seeds into a sieve. Spoon the drained seeds over the top and, just before serving, dust with icing/confectioners' sugar.

Difficulty Rating: 3 points

Almond & Pine Nut Tart

Serves 6

Ingredients

250 g/9 oz/1¼ cups ready-made sweet shortcrust pastry dough
  (*see* page 22)

75 g/3 oz/¾ cup blanched almonds

75 g/3 oz/⅓ cup caster/superfine sugar

pinch salt

2 eggs

1 tsp vanilla extract

2–3 drops almond extract

125 g/4 oz/½ cup (1 stick) unsalted butter, softened

2 tbsp plain/all-purpose flour

½ tsp baking powder

3–4 tbsp raspberry jam/jelly

50 g/2 oz/½ cup pine nuts

icing/confectioners' sugar, to decorate

whipped/whipping cream, to serve

Preheat the oven to 200°C/400°F/Gas Mark 6. Roll out the pastry dough and use to line a 23 cm/9 inch fluted flan tin/tart pan. Chill for 10 minutes, then line with greaseproof/wax paper and baking beans/pie weights. Bake blind for 10 minutes. Remove the paper and beans. Bake for a further 10–12 minutes until cooked. Leave to cool. Reduce the oven temperature to 190°C/375°F/Gas Mark 5.

Grind the almonds in a food processor until fine. Add the sugar, salt, eggs, vanilla and almond extracts and blend. Add the butter, flour and baking powder and blend until smooth. Spread a thick layer of the raspberry jam/jelly over the cooled pastry case/pie crust, then pour in the almond filling. Sprinkle the pine nuts evenly over the top and bake for 30 minutes. Remove from the oven and leave to cool. Dust with icing/confectioners' sugar and serve cut into wedges with whipped cream.

Difficulty Rating: 2 points

Creamy Puddings with Mixed Berry Compote

Serves 6

Ingredients

300 ml/¹/₂ pint/1²/₃ cups half-fat double/heavy cream

1 x 250 g carton/1 cup ricotta cheese

50 g/2 oz/¹/₄ cup caster/superfine sugar

125 g/4 oz white chocolate, broken into pieces

350 g/12 oz mixed summer fruits such as strawberries, blueberries and raspberries

2 tbsp Cointreau

Set the freezer to rapid freeze. Whip the cream until soft peaks form. Fold in the ricotta cheese and half the sugar.

Place the chocolate in a bowl set over a saucepan of simmering water. Stir until melted. Remove from the heat and leave to cool, stirring occasionally. Stir into the cheese mixture until well blended.

Spoon the mixture into 6 individual pudding moulds and level the surface of each pudding with the back of a spoon. Place in the freezer and freeze for 4 hours.

Place the fruits and the remaining sugar in a pan and heat gently, stirring occasionally until the sugar has dissolved and the juices are just beginning to run. Stir in the Cointreau to taste.

Dip the pudding moulds in hot water for 30 seconds and invert on to 6 serving plates. Spoon the fruit compote over the puddings and serve immediately. Remember to return the freezer to its normal setting.

Difficulty Rating: 2 points

Freeform Fruit Pie

Serves 6

Ingredients

175 g/6 oz/1¹/₃ cups plain/all-purpose flour

40 g/1¹/₂ oz/3 tbsp lard or white vegetable fat/shortening

40 g/1¹/₂ oz/3 tbsp butter

1 tbsp caster/superfine sugar

1 medium/large egg, separated

2 tbsp semolina

For the filling:

600 g/1¹/₄ lb/3³/₄ cups gooseberries

75 g/3 oz/¹/₃ cup caster/superfine sugar

finely grated zest of 1 orange

1 egg, separated

2 tbsp caster/superfine sugar

vanilla ice cream, to serve

Sift the flour into a bowl or a food processor and add the fats in small pieces. Rub in with the fingers, or process, until fine crumbs form. Stir in the sugar and the egg yolk and mix with a few drops of cold water to make a soft dough. Knead lightly, then wrap in plastic wrap and chill for 30 minutes.

Preheat the oven to 190°C/375°F/Gas Mark 5 and grease a large baking sheet. Roll out the pastry to a circle approximately 30 cm/12 inches wide. Lift the pastry onto a rolling pin and place on the baking sheet. Beat the egg yolk and brush over the pastry. Sprinkle the semolina lightly over the egg yolk.

Mix the gooseberries with the sugar and zest and pile into the centre of the pastry circle, leaving a border of 8 cm/3¹/₄ inches all round. Gather the pastry edges up over the filling. Press the edges together, leaving the centre exposed. Beat the egg whites until foaming, then brush over the pastry. Scatter over the caster/superfine sugar and bake for about 30 minutes until golden. Serve with vanilla ice cream.

Difficulty Rating: 2 points

Lemon Surprise

Serves 4

Ingredients

75 g/3 oz/¹⁄₃ cup low-fat margarine/spread

175 g/6 oz/³⁄₄ cup caster/superfine sugar

3 eggs, separated

75 g/3 oz/²⁄₃ cup self-raising flour

450 ml/³⁄₄ pint/2 cups semi-skimmed/low-fat milk

juice of 2 lemons

juice of 1 orange

2 tsp icing/confectioners' sugar

lemon slices, to decorate

sliced fresh strawberries, to serve

Preheat the oven to 190°C/375°F/Gas Mark 5. Lightly oil a deep ovenproof dish.

Beat together the margarine/spread and sugar until pale and fluffy. Add the egg yolks, one at a time, with 1 tablespoon of the flour and beat well after each addition. Once all the egg yolks are added, stir in the remaining flour. Stir in the milk, 4 tablespoons of the lemon juice and 3 tablespoons of the orange juice.

Whisk the egg whites until stiff and fold into the pudding mixture with a metal spoon or rubber spatula until well combined. Pour into the prepared dish.

Stand the dish in a roasting tin/pan and pour in just enough boiling water to come halfway up the sides of the dish. Bake in the preheated oven for 45 minutes, or until well risen and the top is spongy to the touch.

Remove the pudding from the oven and sprinkle with the icing/confectioners' sugar. Decorate with the lemon slices and serve immediately with the sliced strawberries.

Difficulty Rating: 2 points

Orange Curd & Plum Pie

Serves 4

Ingredients

700 g/1¹⁄₂ lb/4¹⁄₄ cups stoned and quartered plums
2 tbsp light brown sugar
grated zest of ¹⁄₂ lemon
25 g/1 oz/2 tbsp butter, melted
1 tbsp olive oil
6 sheets filo/phyllo pastry, plus 1 for decoration
¹⁄₂ x 411 g/14 oz jar luxury orange (or lemon) curd
50 g/2 oz/¹⁄₃ cup sultanas/golden raisins
icing/confectioners' sugar, to decorate
Greek/plain yogurt, to serve

Preheat the oven to 200°C/400°F/Gas Mark 6. Lightly oil a 20.5 cm/8 inch round cake tin/pan. Cook the plums with the brown sugar for 8–10 minutes to soften. Remove from the heat and reserve.

Mix together the lemon zest, butter and oil. Lay one of the sheets of filo/phyllo pastry in the prepared cake tin and brush with the lemon zest mixture. Cut four of the remaining pastry sheets in half and then place them one at a time in the cake tin, brushing each time with the lemon zest mixture. Fold each sheet in half lengthways so that they line the sides of the tin at the same time as lining the bottom, to make a filo case.

Mix together the plums, orange curd and sultanas/golden raisins. Spoon into the pastry case/pie crust. Draw the pastry edges up over the filling to enclose. Brush the extra remaining pastry sheet with the lemon zest mixture. Cut into thick strips. Scrunch each strip of pastry and arrange on top of the pie. Bake in the preheated oven for 25 minutes, or until golden. Sprinkle with icing/confectioners' sugar and serve with the Greek/plain yogurt.

Difficulty Rating: 3 points

Oaty Fruit Puddings

Serves 4

Ingredients

125 g/4 oz/1¼ cups rolled oats
50 g/2 oz/¼ cup low-fat spread, melted
2 tbsp chopped almonds
1 tbsp clear honey
pinch of ground cinnamon
2 pears, peeled, cored and finely chopped
1 tbsp marmalade
orange zest, to decorate
low-fat custard or low-fat fruit-flavoured yogurt, to serve

Preheat the oven to 200°C/ 400°F/Gas Mark 6. Lightly oil and line the bases of four individual pudding bowls or muffin tins with a small circle of greaseproof paper.

Mix together the oats, low-fat spread, nuts, honey and cinnamon in a small bowl. Using a spoon, spread two thirds of the oaty mixture over the base and around the sides of the pudding bowls or muffin tins.

Toss together the pears and marmalade and spoon into the oaty cases. Scatter over the remaining oaty mixture to cover the pears and marmalade.

Bake in the preheated oven for 15–20 minutes until cooked and the tops of the puddings are golden and crisp.

Leave for 5 minutes before removing the pudding bowls or the muffin tins. Decorate with orange zest and serve hot with low-fat custard or low-fat fruit-flavoured yogurt.

Difficulty Rating: 1 point

Summer Pudding

Serves 6–8

Ingredients

450 g/1 lb/4 cups redcurrants

125 g/4½ oz/⅔ cup caster/superfine sugar

350 g/12 oz/3 cups hulled and halved fresh strawberries

125 g/4½ oz/1 cup raspberries

2 tbsp Grand Marnier or Cointreau

8–10 slices white bread, crusts removed

fresh mint sprigs, to decorate

Greek/plain yogurt or low-fat fromage frais/
    reduced-fat sour cream, to serve

Place the redcurrants, sugar and 1 tablespoon water in a large saucepan. Heat gently until the sugar has just dissolved and the juices have just begun to run. Remove the saucepan from the heat and stir in the strawberries, raspberries and the Grand Marnier or Cointreau.

Line the base and sides of a 1.1 litre/2 pint/1¼ quart pudding basin/heatproof bowl with two-thirds of the bread, making sure that the slices overlap each other slightly.

Spoon the fruit with their juices into the bread-lined pudding basin, then top with the remaining bread slices.

Place a small plate on top of the pudding inside the pudding basin. Ensure the plate fits tightly, then weigh down with a clean can or some weights and chill in the refrigerator overnight.

When ready to serve, remove the weights and plate. Carefully loosen round the sides of the basin with a round-bladed knife. Invert the pudding on to a serving plate, decorate with the mint sprigs and serve with the yogurt or fromage frais/reduced-fat sour cream.

Difficulty Rating: 1 point

Everyday Desserts & Cakes

Although these desserts are familiar classics for any day of the week, it certainly does not mean they are boring! The wide selection of desserts, from cakes, crumbles and trifles to ice creams or buns, in this chapter, means that you won't run out of options in a hurry and these desserts are sure to put a smile on anyone's face!

Chocolate Fudge Sundae 110
Hot Cross Buns 111
Chocolate Ice Cream 112
White Chocolate Trifle 113
Chocolate Roulade 114
Drop Scones 114
Chocolate Pancakes 116
Apricot & Almond Slice 117
Easy Victoria Sponge 118
Apple & Cinnamon Crumble-top Cake 119
Chocolate & Coconut Cake 120
Citrus Cake 121
Victoria Sponge with Mango & Mascarpone 122
Almond Cake 123
Lemon Drizzle Cake 124
Double Chocolate Cake with Cinnamon 125
Swiss Roll 126
Toffee Apple Cake 127
Fruit Cake 128
Dundee Cake 128
Cappuccino Cakes 130
Honey Cake 131
Banana Cake 132
Coffee & Pecan Cake 133
Gingerbread 134
Carrot Cake 135
Whisked Sponge Cake 136
Easy Chocolate Cake 136
Marble Cake 138
Chocolate Creams 139
Hazelnut Meringues with Chocolate Sauce 140
Iced Chocolate & Raspberry Mousse 141
White Chocolate Terrine with Red Fruit Compote 142
Chocolate Fruit Tiramisu 143
Buttery Passion Fruit Madeira Cake 144
Butterscotch Loaf 144
Chocolate & Fruit Crumble 146
Brandied Raisin Chocolate Mousse 147
Poached Pears with Chocolate Sauce 148
Chocolate Trifle 149
Moist Mincemeat Tea Loaf 150
Maple, Pecan & Lemon Loaf 150
Chocolate Chip Ice Cream 152

Autumn Bramley Apple Cake 153
Marbled Chocolate & Orange Loaf 154
Banana & Honey Tea Bread 154
Chunky Chocolate Muffins 156
Fudgy & Top Hat Chocolate Buns 157
Chocolate & Orange Rock Buns 158
Chocolate Madeleines 159
Fruit & Spice Chocolate Slice 160
Chocolate Pecan Traybake 161
Fruity Apple Tea Bread 162
Marmalade Loaf Cake 162
Chocolate Brazil & Polenta Squares 164
Moist Mocha & Coconut Cake 165
Chocolate Walnut Squares 166
Indulgent Chocolate Squares 167
Crunchy-topped Citrus Chocolate Slices 168
All-in-one Chocolate Fudge Cakes 169
Marbled Chocolate Traybake 170
Triple Chocolate Brownies 171
Chocolate Nut Brownies 172
Chocolate Fudge Brownies 172
Light White Chocolate & Walnut Blondies 174
Apple & Cinnamon Crumble Bars 175
Lemon Bars 176
Lemon-iced Ginger Squares 177
Coconut Sorbet with Mango Sauce 178
Chocolate & Lemon Grass Mousse 179
Grape & Almond Layer 180
Caramelized Oranges in an Iced Bowl 180
Maple Pears with Pistachios & Simple Chocolate Sauce 182
Hot Cherry Fritters 183
Easy Danish Pastries 184
Raspberry Sorbet Crush 185
Coffee & Peach Creams 186
Summer Pavlova 186
Autumn Fruit Layer 188
Chocolate Brandy Dream 189
Sweet-stewed Dried Fruits 190
Fruity Roulade 190
Fruit Salad 192
Orange Freeze 193
Chocolate Mousse 194
Fat Free Sponge 194

Chocolate Fudge Sundae

Serves 2

Ingredients

75 g/3 oz dark/semisweet chocolate, broken into pieces
450ml/³/₄ pint/1³/₄ cups double/heavy cream
175g/6 oz/³/₄ cup golden caster/unrefined superfine sugar
25 g/1 oz/¹/₄ cup plain/all-purpose flour
pinch salt
15 g/¹/₂ oz/1 tbsp unsalted butter
1 tsp vanilla extract

For the sundae:
125 g/4¹/₂ oz/1 cup raspberries, fresh, or thawed if frozen
4 scoops vanilla ice cream
2 scoops chocolate ice cream
2 tbsp toasted flaked/slivered almonds
2 wafers, to serve

To make the chocolate fudge sauce, place the chocolate and cream in a heavy–based saucepan and heat gently until the chocolate has melted into the cream. Stir until smooth. Mix the sugar with the flour and salt, then stir in sufficient chocolate mixture to make a smooth paste. Gradually blend the remaining melted chocolate mixture into the paste, then pour into a clean saucepan. Cook over a low heat, stirring frequently, until smooth and thick. Remove from the heat and add the butter and vanilla extract. Stir until smooth, then cool slightly.

To make the sundae, lightly crush the raspberries and reserve. Spoon some of the chocolate sauce into the sundae glasses. Add some of the crushed raspberries, then a scoop each of vanilla and chocolate ice cream. Top each one with a scoop of the vanilla ice cream. Pour over the sauce, sprinkle on the almonds and serve with a wafer.

Difficulty Rating: 1 point

Hot Cross Buns

Makes 12

Ingredients

500 g/1 lb 2 oz/3²/₃ cups strong white bread flour

1 tsp salt

2 tsp mixed spice/allspice

50 g/2 oz/¹/₄ cup soft light brown sugar

7 g sachet fast-action dried/active dry yeast

275 ml/9 fl oz/1 cup plus 1 tbsp milk

1 medium/large egg, beaten

50 g/2 oz/4 tbsp butter, melted and cooled

225 g/8 oz/1¹/₄ cups mixed dried fruit

To decorate:

1 medium/large egg, beaten

75 g/3 oz shortcrust pastry/prepared pastry dough (*see* page 22)

50 g/2 oz/¹/₄ cup caster/superfine sugar

Sift the flour, salt and spice into a bowl and then stir in the sugar and yeast. In a jug/pitcher, whisk together the milk and the egg. Add the liquid to the flour in the bowl with the cooled melted butter and mix to a soft dough. Knead for 10 minutes by hand, or for 5 minutes using a tabletop mixer fitted with a dough hook, until smooth and elastic.

Knead in the fruit and place the dough in a bowl. Cover it with oiled plastic wrap. Leave in a warm place for about 1 hour until doubled in size. Butter a large 32 x 23 cm/12 x 9 inch baking tray or a roasting tin/pan. Cut the dough into 12 chunks and roll each one into a ball. Place in the tray, leaving enough space for the buns to rise and spread out. Cover with the oiled plastic wrap and leave for about 45 minutes until doubled in size.

Preheat the oven to 200°C/400°F/Gas Mark 6. Discard the plastic wrap and brush the buns with the beaten egg. Roll the pastry into long thin strips. Place the pastry strips over each bun to make crosses. Repeat until all the buns are topped with pastry crosses. Bake for 20–25 minutes until the buns have risen and are golden.

Heat 2 tablespoons water and add the caster/superfine sugar, continuing to heat gently until the sugar is completely dissolved. While still hot, turn the buns out of the tray and place on a wire rack. Brush the sugar glaze over the warm buns and leave to cool. These are best eaten on the day of baking. Split and toast any leftovers and serve with butter.

Difficulty Rating: 3 points

Chocolate Ice Cream

Makes 1 litre/1¾ pints/4 cups

Ingredients

450 ml/¾ pint/2 cups single/light cream

200 g/7 oz dark/semisweet chocolate

2 medium/large eggs

2 medium/large egg yolks

125 g/4 oz/½ cup caster/superfine sugar

1 tsp vanilla extract

300 ml/½ pint/1 cup double/heavy cream

To serve:

chopped nuts

coarsely grated white and dark chocolate

few physalis

Set the freezer to rapid freeze, 2 hours before freezing. Place the single/light cream and chocolate in a heavy-based saucepan and heat gently until the chocolate has melted. Stir until smooth. Take care not to let the mixture boil. Remove from the heat. Whisk the eggs, egg yolks and all but 1 tablespoon of the sugar together in a bowl until thick and pale. Whisk the warmed single cream and chocolate mixture with the vanilla extract into the custard mixture. Place the bowl over a saucepan of simmering water and continue whisking until the mixture thickens and will coat the back of a spoon. To test, lift the spoon out of the mixture and draw a clean finger through the mixture coating the spoon, if it leaves a clean line, then it is ready.

Stand the bowl in cold water to cool. Sprinkle the surface with the reserved sugar to prevent a skin forming while it is cooling. Whip the double/heavy cream until soft peaks form, then whisk into the cooled chocolate custard. Turn the ice cream mixture into a rigid container and freeze for 1 hour. Beat the ice cream with a wooden spoon to break up all the ice crystals, then return to the freezer.

Continue to freeze the ice cream for a further hour, then remove and beat again. Repeat this process once or twice more, then leave the ice cream in the freezer until firm. Leave to soften in the

refrigerator for at least 30 minutes before serving. Remove from the refrigerator, then sprinkle over the chopped nuts and grated chocolate and serve with physalis. Turn the freezer back to its normal setting.

Difficulty Rating: 3 points

White Chocolate Trifle

Serves 6

Ingredients

1 homemade or bought chocolate Swiss/jelly roll, sliced

4 tbsp brandy

2 tbsp Irish cream liqueur

425 g/15 oz can black cherries, drained and pitted, with 3 tbsp of the juice reserved

900 ml/1½ pints/scant 1 quart double/heavy cream

125 g/4 oz white chocolate, broken into pieces

6 medium/large egg yolks

50 g/2 oz/¼ cup caster/superfine sugar

2 tsp cornflour/cornstarch

1 tsp vanilla extract

50 g/2 oz dark/semisweet chocolate, grated

50 g/2 oz milk chocolate, grated

Place the Swiss/jelly roll slices in the bottom of a trifle dish and pour over the brandy, Irish cream liqueur and some reserved black cherry juice to moisten the Swiss roll. Arrange the cherries on top.

Pour 600 ml/1 pint/2½ cups of the cream into a saucepan and add the white chocolate. Heat gently to just below simmering point. Whisk together the egg yolks, caster/superfine sugar, cornflour/cornstarch and vanilla extract in a small bowl. Whisk the egg mixture into the hot cream, then strain into a clean saucepan and return to the heat.

Cook the custard gently, stirring throughout, until it is thick and coats the back of a spoon. Leave to cool slightly, then pour over the trifle. Leave the trifle to chill in the refrigerator for at least 3–4 hours. Before serving, lightly whip the remaining cream until soft peaks form, then spoon the cream over the set custard, swirling the cream in a decorative pattern. Sprinkle with grated plain and milk chocolate and serve.

Difficulty Rating: 2 points

Chocolate Roulade

Cuts into 8 slices

Ingredients

200 g/7 oz dark/semisweet chocolate
7 medium/large eggs, separated
200 g/7 oz/1 cup caster/superfine sugar
4 tbsp icing/confectioners' sugar, for dusting
300 ml/¹/₂ pint/1¹/₄ cups double/heavy cream
3 tbsp Cointreau or Grand Marnier
fresh raspberries and fresh mint sprigs to decorate

Preheat the oven to 180°C/350°F/Gas Mark 4. Lightly oil and line a 33 x 23 cm/13 x 9 inch Swiss roll tin/jelly roll pan with baking parchment. Break the chocolate into small pieces into a heatproof bowl set over simmering water. Leave until almost melted, stirring occasionally. Remove from the heat and leave to stand for 5 minutes. Whisk the egg yolks with the sugar until pale and creamy and the whisk leaves a trail in the mixture when lifted, then fold in the melted chocolate.

Whisk the egg whites until stiff, then fold 1 large spoonful into the chocolate mixture. Mix lightly, then gently fold in the remaining egg whites. Pour the mixture into the prepared tin and level the surface. Bake in the preheated oven for 20–25 minutes. Remove the cake from the oven, leave in the tin and cover with a wire rack and a damp dish towel. Leave for 8 hours, or overnight.

Dust a large sheet of baking parchment with 2 tablespoons of the icing/confectioners' sugar. Unwrap the cake and turn out onto the paper. Remove the lining paper. Whip the cream with the liqueur until soft peaks form. Spread over the cake, leaving a 2.5 cm/1 inch border all round. Using the paper, roll the cake from a short end. Transfer to a serving plate, seam–side down, and dust with the remaining icing sugar. Decorate with the raspberries and the mint and serve.

Difficulty Rating: 4 points

Drop Scones

Makes 18 scones

Ingredients

175 g/6 oz/1¹/₂ cups self-raising flour
1 tsp baking powder
40 g/1¹/₂ oz/3 tbsp caster sugar
1 medium/large egg
200 ml/7 fl oz/1 cup milk
butter and golden/light corn or maple syrup, to serve

Grease a heavy–based nonstick frying pan or a flat griddle pan with white vegetable fat and heat gently.

Sift the flour and baking powder into a bowl, stir in the sugar and make a well in the centre. Add the egg and half the milk and beat to a smooth thick batter. Beat in enough of the remaining milk to give the consistency of thick cream.

Drop the mixture onto the hot pan 1 heaping tablespoon at a time, spacing them well apart. When small bubbles rise to the surface of each scone, flip them over with a palette knife and cook for about 1 minute until golden brown.

Place on a serving dish and keep warm, covered with a clean cloth, while you cook the remaining mixture. Serve warm with butter and golden/light corn and maple syrup and eat on the day of making.

Difficulty Rating: 1 point

Chocolate Pancakes

Serves 6

Ingredients

For the pancakes/crepes:
75 g/3 oz/²⁄₃ cup plain/all-purpose flour
1 tbsp cocoa powder (unsweetened)
1 tsp caster/superfine sugar
¹⁄₂ tsp freshly grated nutmeg
2 medium/large eggs
175 ml/6 fl oz/³⁄₄ cup milk
75 g/3 oz/6 tbsp unsalted butter, melted

For the mango sauce:
1 ripe mango, peeled and diced
50 ml/2 fl oz/¹⁄₄ cup white wine
2 tbsp golden caster/unrefined superfine sugar
2 tbsp rum

For the filling:
225 g/8 oz dark/semisweet chocolate
75 ml/3 fl oz/¹⁄₃ cup double/heavy cream
3 medium/large eggs, separated
2 tbsp golden caster/unrefined superfine sugar

Preheat the oven to 200˚C/400˚F/Gas Mark 6, 15 minutes before cooking. To make the pancakes/crepes, sift the flour, cocoa powder, sugar and nutmeg into a bowl and make a well in the centre. Beat the eggs and milk together, then beat into the flour mixture to form a batter. Stir in 50 g/2 oz/¹⁄₄ cup of the melted butter and stand for 1 hour.

Heat an 18 cm/7 inch nonstick frying pan and brush with a little melted butter. Add about 3 tablespoons of the batter and swirl to cover the base of the pan. Cook over a medium heat for 1–2 minutes, flip over and cook for a further 40 seconds. Repeat with the remaining batter. Stack the pancakes interleaving with greaseproof/wax paper.

To make the sauce, place the mango, white wine and sugar in a saucepan and bring to the boil over a medium heat, then simmer for 2–3 minutes, stirring constantly. When the mixture has thickened, add the rum. Chill in the refrigerator while making the filling and baking. For the filling, melt the chocolate and cream in a small heavy-based saucepan over a medium heat. Stir until smooth, then leave to cool. Beat the egg yolks with the sugar for 3–5 minutes, or until the mixture is pale and creamy, then beat in the chocolate mixture.

Beat the egg whites until stiff, then add a little to the chocolate mixture. Stir in the remainder. Spoon a little of the mixture on to a pancake. Fold in half, then fold in half again, forming a triangle. Repeat with the remaining pancakes. Brush the pancakes with a little melted butter. Bake in the preheated oven for 15–20 minutes until the filling is set. Serve hot or cold with the mango sauce.

Difficulty Rating: 4 points

Apricot & Almond Slice

Cuts into 10 slices

Ingredients

2 tbsp demerara/turbinado sugar

25 g/1 oz/¼ cup flaked/slivered almonds

400 g/14 oz can apricot halves, drained

225 g/8 oz/1 cup (2 sticks) butter, softened

225 g/8 oz/1 heaping cup caster/superfine sugar

4 medium/large eggs

200 g/7 oz/1½ cups self-raising flour

25 g/1 oz/1¼ cup ground almonds

½ tsp almond extract

50 g/2 oz/⅓ cup chopped ready-to-eat dried apricots

3 tbsp clear honey

3 tbsp chopped almonds, toasted

Preheat the oven to 180°C/350°F/Gas Mark 4. Oil a 20.5 cm/ 8 inch square cake tin/pan and line with nonstick baking parchment. Sprinkle the sugar and the flaked/slivered almonds over the paper, then arrange the apricot halves cut-side down on top.

Cream the butter and sugar together in a large bowl until light and fluffy. Gradually beat the eggs into the butter mixture, adding a spoonful of flour after each addition of egg. When all the eggs have been added, stir in the remaining flour and the ground almonds and mix thoroughly. Add the almond extract and the dried apricots and stir well. Spoon the mixture into the prepared tin, taking care not to dislodge the apricot halves. Bake in the preheated oven for 1 hour, or until golden and firm to touch.

Remove from the oven and allow to cool slightly for 15–20 minutes. Turn out carefully, discard the lining paper and transfer to a serving dish. Pour the honey over the top of the cake, sprinkle on the toasted almonds and serve.

Difficulty Rating: 2 points

Easy Victoria Sponge

Serves 8

Ingredients

225 g/8 oz/1 cup soft margarine

225 g/8 oz/1¹⁄₈ cup caster/superfine sugar

4 medium/large eggs

1 tsp vanilla extract

225 g/8 oz/2 cups self-raising flour

1 tsp baking powder

4 tbsp seedless raspberry jam

100 ml/3¹⁄₂ fl oz/¹⁄₂ cup double/heavy cream

icing/confectioners' sugar, for dusting

Difficulty Rating: 1 point

Preheat the oven to 180°C/350°F/Gas Mark 4. Grease two 20.5 cm/8 inch sandwich tins/layer-cake pans and line the bases with nonstick baking parchment.

Place the margarine, caster/superfine sugar, eggs and vanilla extract in a large bowl and sift in the flour and baking powder. Beat for about 2 minutes until smooth and blended, then divide between the tins and smooth level.

Bake for about 25 minutes until golden, well risen and the tops of the cakes spring back when lightly touched with a fingertip. Leave to cool in the tins for 2 minutes, then turn out onto a wire rack to cool. When cold, peel away the baking parchment.

When completely cold, spread one cake with jam and place on a serving plate. Whip the cream until it forms soft peaks, then spread on the underside of the other cake. Sandwich the two cakes together and sift a little icing/confectioners' sugar over the top.

Apple & Cinnamon Crumble–top Cake

Cuts into 8 slices

Ingredients

For the topping:
350 g/12 oz/³⁄₄ lb eating apples, peeled
1 tbsp lemon juice
125 g/4 oz/1 cup self-raising flour
1 tsp ground cinnamon
75 g/3 oz/6 tbsp butter or margarine
75 g/3 oz/¹⁄₃ cup demerara/turbinado sugar
1 tbsp milk

For the base:
125 g/4 oz/¹⁄₂ cup (1 stick) butter or margarine
125 g/4 oz/²⁄₃ cup caster/superfine sugar
2 medium/large eggs
150 g/5 oz/1 heaping cup self-raising flour
cream or custard, to serve

Preheat the oven to 180°C/350°F/Gas Mark 4, 10 minutes before baking. Lightly oil and line the base of a 20.5 cm/8 inch deep round cake tin/pan with greaseproof/wax paper or baking parchment.

Finely chop the apples and mix with the lemon juice. Reserve while making the cake.

For the crumble topping, sift the flour and cinnamon together into a large bowl. Rub the butter or margarine into the flour and cinnamon until the mixture resembles coarse breadcrumbs. Stir the sugar into the breadcrumbs and reserve.

For the base, cream the butter or margarine and sugar together until light and fluffy. Gradually beat the eggs into the sugar and butter mixture a little at a time until all the egg has been added. Sift the flour and gently fold in with a metal spoon or rubber spatula. Spoon into the base of the prepared cake tin. Arrange the apple pieces on top. Lightly stir the milk into the crumble

mixture. Scatter the crumble mixture over the apples and bake in the preheated oven for 1¹⁄₂ hours. Serve cold with cream or custard.

Difficulty Rating: 3 points

Chocolate & Coconut Cake

Cuts into 8 slices

Ingredients

125 g/4 oz dark/semisweet chocolate, roughly chopped

175 g/6 oz/³/₄ cup (1¹/₂ sticks) butter or margarine

175 g/6 oz/1 scant cup caster/superfine sugar

3 medium/large eggs, beaten

175 g/6 oz/1¹/₃ cups self-raising flour

1 tbsp cocoa powder (unsweetened)

50 g/2 oz/²/₃ cup desiccated/shredded coconut

For the icing:

125 g/4 oz/¹/₂ cup (1 stick) butter or margarine

2 tbsp creamed coconut, grated (or ¹/₂ tbsp coconut cream)

225 g/8 oz/2¹/₄ cups icing/confectioners' sugar

25 g/1 oz/¹/₃ cup desiccated/shredded coconut, lightly toasted

Preheat the oven to 180°C/350°F/Gas Mark 4, 10 minutes before baking. Melt the chocolate in a small bowl placed over a saucepan of gently simmering water, ensuring that the base of the bowl does not touch the water. When the chocolate has melted, stir until smooth and leave to cool.

Lightly oil and line the bases of two 18 cm/7 inch sandwich tins/layer-cake pans with greaseproof/wax paper or baking parchment. In a large bowl, beat the butter or margarine and sugar together with a wooden spoon until light and creamy. Beat in the eggs a little at a time, then stir in the melted chocolate. Sift the flour and cocoa powder together and gently fold into the chocolate mixture with a metal spoon or rubber spatula. Add the desiccated/shredded coconut and mix lightly. Divide between the two prepared tins and level the tops.

Bake in the preheated oven for 25–30 minutes until a skewer comes out clean when inserted into the centre of the cake. Leave to cool in the tin for 5 minutes, then turn out, discard the lining paper and leave on a wire rack until cold. Beat together the butter or margarine and creamed coconut. Add the icing/confectioners' sugar and mix well.

Spread half of the icing on one cake and press the cakes together. Spread the remaining icing over the top, sprinkle with coconut and serve.

Difficulty Rating: 2 points

Citrus Cake

Cuts into 6 slices

Ingredients

175 g/6 oz/1 scant cup golden caster/superfine sugar

175 g/6 oz/³⁄₄ cup (1¹⁄₂ sticks) butter or margarine

3 medium/large eggs

2 tbsp orange juice

175 g/6 oz/1¹⁄₃ cups self-raising flour

finely grated zest of 2 oranges

5 tbsp lemon curd

125 g/4 oz icing/confectioners' sugar

finely grated zest of 1 lemon

1 tbsp freshly squeezed lemon juice

Preheat the oven to 190˚C/375˚F/Gas Mark 5. Lightly oil and line the base of a round 20.5 cm/8 inch deep cake tin/pan with baking parchment.

In a large bowl, cream the sugar and butter or margarine together until light and fluffy. Whisk the eggs together and beat into the creamed mixture a little at a time. Beat in the orange juice with 1 tablespoon of the flour.

Sift the remaining flour onto a large plate several times, then, with a metal spoon or rubber spatula, fold into the creamed mixture. Spoon into the prepared cake tin. Stir the finely grated orange zest into the lemon curd and dot randomly across the top of the mixture.

Using a fine skewer, swirl the lemon curd through the cake mixture. Bake in the preheated oven for 35 minutes, or until risen and golden. Leave to cool for 5 minutes in the tin, then turn out carefully onto a wire rack. Sift the icing/confectioners' sugar into a bowl, add the grated lemon zest and juice and stir well to mix. When the cake is cold, cover the top with the icing and serve.

Difficulty Rating: 2 points

Victoria Sponge with Mango & Mascarpone

Cuts into 8 slices

Ingredients

175 g/6 oz/³/₄ cup caster/superfine sugar, plus extra for dusting
175 g/6 oz/1¹/₂ cups self-raising flour, plus extra for dusting
175 g/6 oz/³/₄ cup (1¹/₂ sticks) butter or margarine
3 large/extra-large eggs
1 tsp vanilla extract
25 g/1 oz/¹/₄ cup icing/confectioners' sugar
250 g/9 oz tub mascarpone cheese
1 large ripe mango, peeled

Preheat the oven to 190°C/375°F/Gas Mark 5. Lightly oil two 18 cm/7 inch sandwich tins/layer–cake pans. Lightly dust with caster/superfine sugar and flour, tapping the tins to remove any excess.

In a large bowl, cream the butter or margarine and sugar together. In another bowl, mix the eggs and vanilla extract. Sift the flour several times onto a plate. Beat a little egg into the butter and sugar, then a little flour, and beat well. Continue gradually adding the flour and eggs until the mixture is well mixed and smooth; divide between the prepared cake tins, level, then, with the back of a spoon, make a dip in the centre of each cake. Bake for 25–30 minutes. Turn out onto a wire rack and leave to cool.

Beat the icing/confectioners' sugar and mascarpone cheese together, then chop the mango into cubes. Use half the mascarpone and mango to sandwich the cakes together. Spread the rest of the mascarpone on top, decorate with the remaining mango and serve, or use within 3–4 days.

Difficulty Rating: 2 points

Almond Cake

Cuts into 8 slices

Ingredients

225 g/8 oz/1 cup (2 sticks) butter or margarine

225 g/8 oz/1 heaping cup caster/superfine sugar

3 large/extra-large eggs

1 tsp vanilla extract

1 tsp almond extract

125 g/4 oz/1 cup self-raising flour

175 g/6 oz/2 scant cups ground almonds

50 g/2 oz/⅓ cup blanched whole almonds

25 g/1 oz/1 square dark/semisweet chocolate

Difficulty Rating: 1 point

Preheat the oven to 150°C/300°F/Gas Mark 2. Lightly oil and line the base of a 20.5 cm/8 inch deep round cake tin/pan with greaseproof/wax paper or baking parchment.

Cream together the butter or margarine and sugar with a wooden spoon until light and fluffy. Beat the eggs and extracts together. Gradually add to the sugar and butter mixture and mix well between each addition. Sift the flour and mix with the ground almonds. Beat into the egg mixture until well mixed and smooth. Pour into the prepared cake tin.

Roughly chop the almonds and scatter over the cake. Bake in the preheated oven for 45 minutes, or until golden and risen and a skewer inserted into the centre of the cake comes out clean. Remove from the tin and leave to cool on a wire rack. Melt the chocolate in a small bowl placed over a saucepan of gently simmering water, stirring until smooth. Drizzle the melted chocolate over the cooled cake and serve once the chocolate has set.

Lemon Drizzle Cake

Cuts into 16 squares

Ingredients

125 g/4 oz/¹/₂ cup (1 stick) butter or margarine

175 g/6 oz/1 scant cup caster/superfine sugar

2 large/extra-large eggs

175 g/6 oz/1¹/₂ cups self-raising flour

2 lemons

50 g/2 oz/¹/₄ cup granulated sugar

Preheat the oven to 180 C/350 F/Gas Mark 4, 10 minutes before baking. Lightly oil and line the base of an 18 cm/7 inch square cake tin/pan with baking parchment.

In a large bowl, cream the butter or margarine and caster/superfine sugar together until soft and fluffy. Beat the eggs, then gradually add a little of the egg to the creamed mixture, adding 1 tablespoon of flour after each addition. Finely grate the zest from one of the lemons and stir into the creamed mixture, beating well until smooth. Squeeze the juice from the lemon, strain, then stir into the mixture. Spoon into the prepared tin, level the surface and bake in the preheated oven for 25–30 minutes.

Using a zester, remove the zest from the last lemon and mix with 25 g/1 oz of the granulated sugar and reserve. Squeeze the juice into a small saucepan. Add the rest of the granulated sugar to the lemon juice and heat gently, stirring occasionally. When the sugar has dissolved, simmer gently for 3–4 minutes until syrupy.

Prick the cake all over with a cocktail stick/toothpick or fine skewer, to allow the syrup to soak in. Sprinkle the lemon zest and sugar over the top of the cake, drizzle over the syrup and leave to cool in the tin. Cut the cake into squares and serve.

Difficulty Rating: 2 points

Double Chocolate Cake with Cinnamon

Cuts into 10 slices

Ingredients

50 g/2 oz/²/₃ cup cocoa powder (unsweetened)

1 tsp ground cinnamon

225 g/8 oz/1³/₄ cups self-raising flour

225 g/8 oz/1 cup (2 sticks) unsalted butter or margarine

225 g/8 oz/1 heaping cup caster/superfine sugar

4 large/extra-large eggs

For the filling:

125 g/4 oz white chocolate

50 ml/2 fl oz/¹/₄ cup double/heavy cream

25 g/1 oz/1 square dark/semisweet chocolate

Preheat the oven to 190°C/375°F/Gas Mark 5. Lightly oil and line the base of two 20.5 cm/8 inch sandwich tins/layer–cake pans with greaseproof/wax paper or baking parchment. Sift the cocoa powder, cinnamon and flour together and reserve.

In a large bowl, cream the butter or margarine and sugar. Beat in the eggs a little at a time until the mixture is smooth. Using a rubber spatula or metal spoon, fold the sifted flour and cocoa powder into the egg mixture until well mixed. Divide between the cake tins. Bake for 25–30 minutes until springy to the touch and a skewer inserted into the cake comes out clean. Leave to cool on a wire rack.

For the filling, break the white chocolate and heat the cream in a saucepan; add the white chocolate, stirring until melted. Leave to cool, then, use half the cooled white chocolate to sandwich the cakes together. Top the cake with the remaining cooled white chocolate. Grate over the dark chocolate and serve.

Difficulty Rating: 2 points

Swiss Roll

Cuts into 8 slices

Ingredients

75 g/3 oz/¹/₂ cup self-raising flour

3 large/extra-large eggs

1 tsp vanilla extract

100 g/3¹/₂ oz/scant ¹/₂ cup caster/superfine sugar

25 g/1 oz/¹/₄ cup toasted and finely chopped hazelnuts

3 tbsp apricot jam/jelly

300 ml/¹/₂ pint/1¹/₄ cups double/heavy cream, lightly whipped

Preheat the oven to 220°C/425°F/Gas Mark 7. Lightly oil and line the base of a 23 x 33 cm/9 x 13 inch Swiss roll tin/jelly roll pan with a single sheet of greaseproof/wax paper or baking parchment. Sift the flour several times, then reserve on top of the oven to warm a little.

Place a mixing bowl with the eggs, vanilla extract and sugar over a saucepan of hot water, with the base of the bowl not touching the water. With the saucepan off the heat, whisk until the mixture is pale and mousse–like and has increased in volume. Remove the bowl from the saucepan and continue to whisk for a further 2–3 minutes. Sift in the flour and gently fold in using a spoon or rubber spatula. Pour into the prepared tin, ensuring the mixture is evenly distributed. Bake for 10–12 minutes until well risen, golden brown and the top springs back when touched lightly.

Sprinkle the hazelnuts over a sheet of greaseproof paper. When the cake has cooked, turn out onto the hazelnut–covered paper and trim the edges of the cake. Holding an edge of the paper with the short side of the cake nearest you, roll the cake up. When fully cold, carefully unroll and spread with the jam/jelly and then the cream. Roll back up and serve, or store in the refrigerator and eat within two days.

Difficulty Rating: 4 points

Toffee Apple Cake

Cuts into 6–8 slices

Ingredients

2 small eating apples, peeled

50 g/2 oz/¼ cup soft dark brown sugar

175 g/6 oz/¾ cup (1½ sticks) butter or margarine

175 g/6 oz/1 scant cup caster/superfine sugar

3 medium/large eggs

175 g/6 oz/1½ cups self-raising flour

150 ml/¼ pint/⅔ cup double/heavy cream

2 tbsp icing/confectioners' sugar

½ tsp vanilla extract

½ tsp ground cinnamon

Preheat the oven to 180°C/350°F/Gas Mark 4, 10 minutes before baking. Lightly oil and line the bases of two 20.5 cm/8 inch sandwich tins/layer-cake pans with greaseproof/wax paper or baking parchment. Thinly slice the apples, toss them in the brown sugar and arrange in the prepared tins. Reserve.

Cream together the butter or margarine and caster/superfine sugar until light and fluffy. Beat the eggs together in a small bowl. Gradually beat them into the creamed mixture, beating well between each addition.

Sift the flour into the mixture. With a metal spoon or rubber spatula, fold in. Divide the mixture between the two cake tins and level the surface. Bake in the preheated oven for 25–30 minutes until golden and well risen. Leave to cool.

Lightly whip the cream with 1 tablespoon of the icing/confectioners' sugar and vanilla extract. Sandwich the cakes together with the cream. Mix the remaining icing sugar and the ground cinnamon together, sprinkle over the top of the cake and serve.

Difficulty Rating: 2 points

Fruit Cake

Cuts into 10 slices

Ingredients

225 g/8 oz/1 cup (2 sticks) butter or margarine

200 g/7 oz/1 scant cup brown sugar

finely grated zest of 1 orange

1 tbsp black treacle/molasses

3 large/extra-large eggs, beaten

275 g/10 oz/2¹⁄₂ cups plain/all-purpose flour

¹⁄₄ tsp ground cinnamon

¹⁄₂ tsp mixed/pumpkin pie spice

pinch freshly grated nutmeg

¹⁄₄ tsp bicarbonate of soda/baking soda

75 g/3 oz/¹⁄₂ cup mixed peel/candied peel

50 g/2 oz/¹⁄₄ cup glacé/candied cherries

125 g/4 oz/²⁄₃ cup raisins

125 g/4 oz/²⁄₃ cup sultanas/golden raisins

125 g/4 oz/²⁄₃ cup chopped ready-to-eat dried apricots

Preheat the oven to 150°C/300°F/Gas Mark 2. Lightly oil and line a 23 cm/9 inch deep round cake tin/pan with a double thickness of greaseproof/wax paper. In a large bowl, cream together the butter or margarine, sugar and orange zest until light and fluffy, then beat in the treacle/molasses. Beat in the eggs a little at a time, beating well between each addition. Reserve 1 tablespoon of the flour. Sift the remaining flour, the spices and bicarbonate of soda/baking soda into the mixture.

Mix all the fruits and the reserved flour together, then stir into the cake mixture. Turn into the prepared tin and level the top, making a small hollow in the centre of the cake mixture.

Bake for 1 hour, then reduce the temperature to 140°C/275°F/Gas Mark 1. Bake for a further 1¹⁄₂ hours, or until and a skewer inserted into the centre comes out clean. Leave to cool in the tin, then turn out and serve. Store in an airtight tin when cold.

Difficulty Rating: 1 point

Dundee Cake

Serves 8–10

Ingredients

400 g/14 oz mixed dried fruit

50 g/2 oz/¹⁄₂ cup ground almonds

finely grated zest and juice of 1 lemon

150 g/5 oz/²⁄₃ cup (1¹⁄₄ sticks) butter, at room temperature

150 g/5 oz/³⁄₄ cup natural golden caster/superfine sugar

3 medium/large eggs, beaten

125 g/4 oz/1 cup plain/all-purpose flour

40 g/1¹⁄₂ oz/¹⁄₃ cup whole blanched almonds

Preheat the oven to 180°C/350°F/Gas Mark 4. Grease and line the base of an 18 cm/7 inch deep round cake tin with nonstick baking parchment.

Place the dried fruits in a bowl and stir in the ground almonds to coat the dried fruit.

Put the finely grated lemon zest into the bowl, and then add 1 tablespoon of the lemon juice to the same bowl. In another bowl, beat the butter and sugar together until light and fluffy. Whisk in the eggs a little at a time, adding 1 teaspoon of flour with each addition.

Sift in the remaining flour, then add the fruit and almond mixture. Fold together with a large metal spoon until smooth. Spoon the mixture into the tin and make a dip in the centre with the back of a spoon. Arrange the almonds over the top in circles.

Bake for 1 hour, then reduce the temperature to 150°C/300°F/Gas Mark 2 and bake for a further 1 hour or until a skewer inserted into the centre comes out clean. Cool in the tin for 5 minutes, then turn out to cool on a wire rack.

Difficulty Rating: 1 point

Cappuccino Cakes

Makes 6

Ingredients

125 g/4 oz/¹/₂ cup (1 stick) butter or margarine

125 g/4 oz/²/₃ cup caster/superfine sugar

2 medium/large eggs

1 tbsp strong black coffee

150 g/5 oz/scant 1¹/₄ cups self-raising flour

125 g/4 oz/¹/₂ cup mascarpone cheese

1 tbsp sifted icing/confectioners' sugar

1 tsp vanilla extract

sifted cocoa powder (unsweetened), for dusting

Difficulty Rating: 1 point

Preheat the oven to 190°C/375°F/Gas Mark 5. Place six paper muffin cases/baking cups into a muffin tin/pan or, alternatively, onto a baking sheet.

Cream the butter or margarine and caster/superfine sugar together until light and fluffy. Break the eggs into a small bowl and beat lightly with a fork. Using a wooden spoon, beat the eggs into the butter and sugar mixture a little at a time until they are all incorporated. If the mixture looks curdled, beat in a spoonful of the flour to return the mixture to a smooth consistency. Finally beat in the black coffee.

Sift the flour into the mixture, then, with a metal spoon or rubber spatula, fold in the flour. Place spoonfuls of the mixture into the muffin cases and bake for 20–25 minutes until risen and springy to the touch. Cool on a wire rack.

Beat together the mascarpone cheese, icing/confectioners' sugar and vanilla extract. When the cakes are cold, spoon the vanilla mascarpone onto the top of each one. Dust with cocoa powder and serve. Store in the refrigerator, eat within 24 hours.

Honey Cake

Cuts into 6 slices

Ingredients

50 g/2 oz/4 tbsp butter

2 tbsp caster/superfine sugar

125 g/4 oz/¹⁄₃ cup clear honey

175 g/6 oz/1¹⁄₃ cups plain/all-purpose flour

¹⁄₂ tsp bicarbonate of soda/baking soda

¹⁄₂ tsp mixed/pumpkin pie spice

1 medium/large egg

2 tbsp milk

25 g/1 oz/¹⁄₄ cup flaked/slivered almonds

1 tbsp clear honey, for drizzling

Preheat the oven to 180°C/350°F/Gas Mark 4. Lightly oil and line the base of an 18 cm/7 inch deep round cake tin/pan with lightly oiled greaseproof/wax paper or baking parchment.

In a saucepan, gently heat the butter, sugar and honey until the butter has just melted. Sift the flour, bicarbonate of soda/baking soda and mixed/pumpkin pie spice together into a bowl. Beat the egg and the milk until mixed thoroughly. Make a well in the centre of the sifted flour and pour in the melted butter and honey. Using a wooden spoon, beat well, gradually drawing in the flour from the sides of the bowl.

When all the flour has been beaten in, add the egg mixture and mix thoroughly. Pour into the prepared tin and sprinkle with the flaked/slivered almonds. Bake in the preheated oven for 30–35 minutes until well risen and golden brown and a skewer inserted into the centre of the cake comes out clean.

Remove from the oven, and cool for a few minutes in the tin before turning out and leaving to cool on a wire rack. Drizzle with the remaining tablespoon of honey and serve.

Difficulty Rating: 1 point

Banana Cake

Cuts into 8 slices

Ingredients

3 medium-sized ripe bananas
1 tsp lemon juice
150 g/5 oz/³⁄₄ cup brown sugar
75 g/3 oz/6 tbsp butter or margarine
250 g/9 oz/2 cups self-raising flour
1 tsp ground cinnamon
3 medium/large eggs
50 g/2 oz/¹⁄₃ cup walnuts, chopped
1 tsp each ground cinnamon and caster/superfine sugar
cream, to serve

Preheat the oven to 190°C/375°F/Gas Mark 5, 10 minutes before baking. Lightly oil and line the base of an 18 cm/7 inch deep round cake tin/pan with greaseproof/wax paper or baking parchment.

Mash two of the bananas in a small bowl, sprinkle with the lemon juice and a heaping tablespoon of the brown sugar. Mix together lightly and reserve.

Gently heat the remaining brown sugar and butter or margarine in a small saucepan until the butter has just melted. Pour into a small bowl, then leave to cool slightly. Sift the flour and cinnamon into a large bowl and make a well in the centre.

Beat the eggs into the cooled sugar mixture, pour into the well of flour and mix thoroughly. Gently stir in the mashed banana mixture. Pour half of the mixture into the prepared tin. Thinly slice the remaining banana and arrange over the cake mixture. Sprinkle over the chopped walnuts, then cover with the remaining cake mixture.

Bake in the preheated oven for 50–55 minutes until well risen and golden brown. Leave to cool in the tin, turn out and sprinkle with the ground cinnamon and caster/superfine sugar. Serve hot or cold with a jug/pitcher of cream for pouring.

Difficulty Rating: 2 points

Coffee & Pecan Cake

Cuts into 8 slices

Ingredients

175 g/6 oz/1⅓ cups self-raising flour

125 g/4 oz/½ cup (1 stick) butter or margarine

175 g/6 oz/1 scant cup golden caster/superfine sugar

1 tbsp instant coffee powder or granules

2 large/extra-large eggs

50 g/2 oz/½ cup roughly chopped pecans

For the icing:

1 tsp instant coffee powder or granules

1 tsp cocoa powder (unsweetened)

75 g/3 oz/6 tbsp unsalted butter, softened

175 g/6 oz/1¾ cups icing/confectioners' sugar, sifted

whole pecans, to decorate

Preheat the oven to 190°C/375°F/Gas Mark 5, 10 minutes before baking. Lightly oil and line the bases of two 18 cm/ 7 inch sandwich tins/layer–cake pans with greaseproof/wax paper or baking parchment. Sift the flour and reserve.

Beat the butter or margarine and caster/superfine sugar together until light and creamy. Dissolve the coffee in 2 tablespoons hot water and leave to cool. Lightly mix the eggs with the coffee liquid.

Gradually beat into the creamed butter and sugar, adding a little of the sifted flour with each addition. Fold in the pecans, then divide the mixture between the prepared tins and bake in the preheated oven for 20–25 minutes until well risen and firm to the touch. Leave to cool in the tins for 5 minutes before turning out and cooling on a wire rack.

To make the icing, blend together the coffee and cocoa powder with enough boiling water to make a stiff paste. Beat into the butter and icing/confectioners' sugar.

Sandwich the two cakes together using half of the icing. Spread the remaining icing over the top of the cake and decorate with the whole pecans to serve. Store in an airtight container.

Difficulty Rating: 2 points

Gingerbread

Cuts into 8 slices

Ingredients

175 g/6 oz/³/₄ cup (1¹/₂ sticks) butter or margarine

225 g/8 oz/²/₃ cup black treacle/molasses

50 g/2 oz/¹/₄ cup dark muscovado/dark brown sugar

350 g/12 oz/3 cups plain/all-purpose flour

2 tsp ground ginger

150 ml/¹/₄ pint/²/₃ cup milk, warmed

2 medium/large eggs

1 tsp bicarbonate of soda/baking soda

1 piece stem preserved ginger in syrup

1 tbsp stem preserved ginger syrup

Difficulty Rating: 1 point

Preheat the oven to 150°C/300°F/Gas Mark 2, 10 minutes before baking. Lightly oil and line the base of a 20.5 cm/8 inch deep round cake tin/pan with greaseproof/wax paper or baking parchment.

In a saucepan, gently heat the butter or margarine, black treacle/molasses and sugar, stirring occasionally, until the butter melts. Leave to cool slightly.

Sift the flour and ground ginger into a large bowl. Make a well in the centre, then pour in the treacle mixture. Reserve 1 tablespoon of the milk, then pour the rest into the treacle mixture. Stir together lightly until mixed.

Beat the eggs together, then stir into the mixture. Dissolve the bicarbonate of soda/baking soda in the remaining 1 tablespoon of warmed milk and add to the mixture. Beat the mixture until well combined and free of lumps. Pour into the prepared tin and bake in the preheated oven for 1 hour, or until well risen and a skewer inserted into the centre comes out clean. Cool in the tin, then remove. Slice the stem preserved ginger into thin slivers and sprinkle over the cake. Drizzle with the syrup and serve.

Carrot Cake

Cuts into 8 slices

Ingredients

200 g/7 oz/1½ cups plain/all-purpose flour

½ tsp ground cinnamon

½ tsp freshly grated nutmeg

1 tsp baking powder

1 tsp bicarbonate of soda/baking soda

150 g/5 oz/¾ cup muscovado/dark brown sugar

200 ml/7 fl oz/1 scant cup vegetable oil

3 medium/large eggs

225 g/8 oz/1¾ cups peeled and roughly grated carrots

50 g/2 oz/½ cup chopped walnuts

For the icing:

175 g/6 oz/¾ cup cream cheese

finely grated zest of 1 orange; 1 tbsp orange juice

1 tsp vanilla extract

125 g/4 oz/1 cup icing/confectioners' sugar

Preheat the oven to 150 C/300 F/Gas Mark 2, 10 minutes before baking. Lightly oil and line the base of a 15 cm/6 inch deep square cake tin/pan with greaseproof/wax paper or baking parchment. Sift the flour, spices, baking powder and bicarbonate of soda/baking soda together into a large bowl. Stir in the muscovado/dark brown sugar and mix together.

Lightly whisk the oil and eggs together, then gradually stir into the flour and sugar mixture. Stir well. Add the carrots and walnuts. Mix thoroughly, then pour into the prepared cake tin. Bake in the preheated oven for 1¼ hours, or until light and springy to the touch and a skewer inserted into the centre of the cake comes out clean. Remove from the oven and leave to cool in the tin for 5 minutes before turning out onto a wire rack. Leave until cold.

To make the icing, beat together the cream cheese, orange zest and juice and vanilla extract. Sift the icing/confectioners' sugar and stir into the cream cheese mixture. When cold, discard the lining paper, spread the cream cheese icing over the top and serve cut into squares.

Difficulty Rating: 1 point

Whisked Sponge Cake

Cuts into 6 slices

Ingredients

125 g/4 oz/1 cup plain/all-purpose flour, plus 1 tsp
175 g/6 oz/1 scant cup caster/superfine sugar, plus 1 tsp
3 medium/large eggs
1 tsp vanilla extract
4 tbsp raspberry jam/jelly
50 g/2 oz (about 25) fresh raspberries, crushed
icing/confectioners' sugar, for dredging

Preheat the oven to 200°C/400°F/Gas Mark 6, 15 minutes before baking. Mix 1 teaspoon of the flour and 1 teaspoon of the sugar together. Lightly oil two 18 cm/7 inch sandwich tins/layer-cake pans and dust lightly with the sugar and flour.

Place the eggs in a large heatproof bowl. Add the sugar, then place over a saucepan of gently simmering water, ensuring that the base of the bowl does not touch the hot water. Using an electric whisk, beat the sugar and eggs until they become light and fluffy. (The whisk should leave a trail in the mixture when it is lifted out.)

Remove the bowl from the saucepan of water, add the vanilla extract and continue beating for 2–3 minutes. Sift the flour gently into the egg mixture and, using a metal spoon or rubber spatula, carefully fold in, taking care not to overmix and remove all the air that has been whisked in.

Divide the mixture between the two prepared cake tins. Tap lightly on the work surface to remove any air bubbles. Bake in the preheated oven for 20–25 minutes until golden. Test that the cake is ready by gently pressing the centre with a clean finger – it should spring back.

Leave to cool in the tins for 5 minutes, then turn out onto a wire rack. Blend the jam/jelly and the crushed raspberries together. When the cakes are cold, spread over the jam mixture and sandwich together. Dredge the top with icing/confectioners' sugar and serve.

Difficulty Rating: 4 points

Easy Chocolate Cake

Serves 8–10

Ingredients

75 g/3 oz dark/semisweet chocolate, broken into squares
200 ml/7 fl oz/1 scant cup milk
250 g/9 oz/1 heaping cup dark muscovado/packed dark brown sugar
75 g/3 oz/6 tbsp butter, softened
2 medium/large eggs, beaten
150 g/5 oz/1¼ cups plain/all-purpose flour
½ tsp vanilla extract
1 tsp bicarbonate of soda/baking soda
25 g/1 oz/¼ cup unsweetened cocoa powder

For the topping and filling:
125 g/4 oz/½ cup (1 stick) unsalted butter
225 g/8 oz/2 scant cups icing/confectioners' sugar, sifted
175 g/6 oz/1¼ cups fresh strawberries, halved
tiny fresh mint sprigs, to decorate

Preheat the oven to 180°C/350°F/Gas Mark 4. Grease two 20.5 cm/8 inch round sandwich tins/layer-cake pans and line the bases with nonstick baking parchment. Place the chocolate, milk and 75 g/3 oz/⅓ cup of the sugar in a heavy-based saucepan. Heat gently until the mixture has melted, then leave to cool.

Place the butter and remaining sugar in a large bowl and whisk with an electric mixer until light and fluffy. Gradually whisk in the eggs, adding 1 teaspoon flour with each addition. Stir in the cooled melted chocolate mixture along with the vanilla extract. Sift in the flour, bicarbonate of soda/baking soda and cocoa powder, then fold into the mixture until smooth. Spoon the batter into the tins and level. Bake for about 30 minutes until a skewer inserted in the centre comes out clean. Turn out to cool on a wire rack.

To decorate, beat the butter with the icing/confectioners' sugar and 1 tablespoon warm water. Place half in a decorating bag fitted with a star tip. Spread half the buttercream over one sponge layer and scatter half the strawberries over it. Top with the other cake, spread the remaining buttercream over the top. Pipe stars around the edge. Decorate with the remaining strawberries and mint sprigs.

Difficulty Rating: 3 points

Marble Cake

Cuts into 8 slices

Ingredients

225 g/8 oz/1 cup (2 sticks) butter or margarine

225 g/8 oz/1 cup caster/superfine sugar

4 medium/large eggs

225 g/8 oz/2 cups sifted self-raising flour

finely grated zest and juice of 1 orange

25 g/1 oz/¼ cup sifted cocoa powder (unsweetened)

For the topping:

zest and juice of 1 orange

1 tbsp caster/superfine sugar

Preheat the oven to 190°C/375°F/Gas Mark 5, 10 minutes before baking. Lightly oil and line the base of a 20.5 cm/8 inch deep round cake tin/pan with greaseproof/wax paper or baking parchment.

In a large bowl, cream the butter or margarine and sugar together until light and fluffy. Beat the eggs together. Beat into the creamed mixture a little at a time, beating well between each addition. When all the egg has been added, fold in the flour with a metal spoon or rubber spatula. Divide the mixture equally between two bowls. Beat the grated orange zest into one of the bowls with a little of the orange juice. Mix the cocoa with the remaining orange juice until smooth, then add to the other bowl and beat well. Spoon the mixture into the prepared tin, in alternate spoonfuls. When all the cake mixture is in the tin, take a skewer and swirl it in the two mixtures. Tap the base of the tin on the work surface to level the mixture. Bake in the preheated oven for 50 minutes, or until cooked and a skewer inserted into the centre of the cake comes out clean. Remove from the oven and leave in the tin for a few minutes before cooling on a wire rack. Discard the lining paper.

For the topping, place the orange zest and juice with the caster/superfine sugar in a small saucepan and heat gently until the sugar has dissolved. Bring to the boil and simmer gently for 3–4 minutes until the juice is syrupy. Pour over the cooled cake and serve when cool. Otherwise, store the marble cake in an airtight tin.

Difficulty Rating: 2 points

Chocolate Creams

Serves 4

Ingredients

125 g/4 oz plain dark/semisweet chocolate

1 tbsp brandy

4 medium/large eggs, separated

200 ml/7 fl oz pint/1 cup double/heavy cream

1 tbsp caster/superfine sugar

grated rind of 1 orange

2 tbsp Cointreau

25 g/1 oz white chocolate

8 physalis, to decorate

Break the chocolate into small pieces, then place in a heatproof bowl set over a saucepan of gently simmering water. Add the brandy and heat gently, stirring occasionally until the chocolate has melted and is smooth. Remove from the heat and leave to cool slightly, then beat in the egg yolks, one at a time, beating well after each addition. Reserve.

Whisk the egg whites until stiff but not dry and then stir 1 tablespoon into the chocolate mixture. Add the remainder and stir in gently. Chill in the refrigerator while preparing the cream.

Whip the cream until just beginning to thicken, then stir in the sugar, orange rind and Cointreau and continue to whisk together until soft peaks form. Spoon the chocolate mousse into the cream mixture and using a metal spoon, fold the two mixtures together to create a marbled effect. Alternatively, continue folding the two mixtures together until mixed thoroughly. Spoon into four individual glass dishes, cover each dessert with plastic wrap and chill in the refrigerator for 2 hours.

Using a potato peeler, shave the white chocolate into curls. Uncover the desserts and scatter over the shavings. Peel the husks back from the physalis berries and pinch together for decoration. Top each dessert with 2 berries and chill in the refrigerator until ready to serve.

Difficulty Rating: 2 points

Hazelnut Meringues with Chocolate Sauce

Serves 6

Ingredients

4 medium/large egg whites
225 g/8 oz/1 heaping cup caster/superfine sugar
125 g/4 oz/1²/₃ cups ground hazelnuts
50 g/2 oz/¹/₃ cup toasted hazelnuts
sliced fresh berries, such as raspberries, strawberries and
   blueberries, to serve

For the chocolate sauce:
225 g/8 oz dark/semisweet chocolate, broken into pieces
50 g/2 oz/4 tbsp butter
300 ml/¹/₂ pint/1¹/₄ cups double/heavy cream
1 tbsp golden/light corn syrup

Preheat the oven to 150°C/300°F/Gas Mark 2, 10 minutes
before baking. Line two baking sheets with nonstick baking
parchment. Whisk the egg whites in a large grease-free bowl
until stiff, then add the caster/superfine sugar, 1 teaspoonful at
a time, whisking well after each addition. Continue to whisk
until the mixture is stiff and dry, then, using a metal spoon, fold
in the ground hazelnuts.

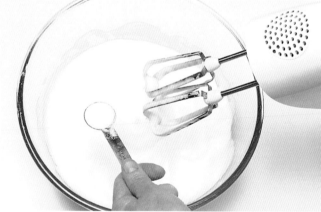

Using two dessertspoons, spoon the mixture into 12 quenelle
shapes onto the baking parchment. Sprinkle over the toasted
hazelnuts and bake in the preheated oven for 1¹/₂–2 hours until
dry and crisp. Switch the oven off and leave to cool in the oven.

To make the chocolate sauce, place the chocolate with the
butter and 4 tablespoons of the cream and the golden/light corn
syrup in a heavy-based saucepan and heat, stirring occasionally,
until the chocolate has melted and the mixture is blended. Do
not boil. Whip the remaining cream until soft peaks form.

Sandwich the meringues together with the whipped cream and
place on serving plates. Spoon over the sauce and serve with a
few fresh berries.

Difficulty Rating: 2 points

Iced Chocolate & Raspberry Mousse

Serves 4

Ingredients

12 sponge finger biscuits/ladyfingers
juice of 2 oranges
2 tbsp Grand Marnier/orange-flavoured liqueur
300 ml/½ pint/1 cup double/heavy cream
175 g/6 oz dark/semisweet chocolate,
   broken into small pieces
225 g/8 oz/2 cups frozen raspberries
6 tbsp sifted icing/confectioners' sugar
cocoa powder (unsweetened), for dusting

To decorate:
few fresh whole raspberries
few fresh mint sprigs
grated white chocolate

Break the sponge finger biscuits/ladyfingers into small pieces and divide between four individual glass dishes. Blend together the orange juice and Grand Marnier, then drizzle evenly over the sponge fingers/ladyfingers. Cover with plastic wrap and chill in the refrigerator for 30 minutes.

Place the cream in a small, heavy-based saucepan and heat gently, stirring occasionally until boiling. Remove the saucepan from the heat then add the pieces of dark/semisweet chocolate and leave to stand untouched for about 7 minutes. Using a whisk, whisk the chocolate and cream together, until the chocolate has melted and is well blended and completely smooth. Leave to cool slightly.

Place the frozen raspberries and icing/confectioners' sugar into a food processor or blender, and blend until roughly crushed. Fold the crushed raspberries into the cream and chocolate mixture and mix lightly until well blended. Spoon over the chilled sponge fingers/ladyfingers. Lightly dust with a little cocoa and decorate with whole raspberries, mint sprigs and grated white chocolate. Serve immediately.

Difficulty Rating: 2 points

White Chocolate Terrine with Red Fruit Compote

Serves 4

Ingredients

225 g/8 oz white chocolate
300 ml/¹/₂ pint/1¹/₄ cups double/heavy cream
225 g/8 oz/1 cup full fat soft cream cheese
2 tbsp finely grated orange rind
125 g/4¹/₂ oz/²/₃ cup sugar
350 g/12 oz/3 cups mixed summer
fruits, such as strawberries, blueberries and raspberries
1 tbsp Cointreau or orange-flavoured liqueur
fresh mint sprigs, to decorate

Set the freezer to rapid freeze at least 2 hours before required. Lightly oil and line a 450 g/1 lb loaf tin/pan with plastic wrap, taking care to keep it as wrinkle free as possible. Break the white chocolate into small pieces and place in a heatproof bowl set over a saucepan of gently simmering water. Leave for 20 minutes or until melted, then remove from the heat and stir until smooth. Leave to cool.

Whip the cream until soft peaks form. Beat the cream cheese until soft and creamy, then beat in the grated orange rind and 50 g/2 oz/¹/₄ cup of the sugar. Mix well. Fold in the whipped cream and then the cooled melted white chocolate.

Spoon the mixture into the prepared loaf tin/pan and level the surface. Place in the freezer and freeze for at least 4 hours, or until frozen. Once frozen, remember to return the freezer to its normal setting.

Place the fruits with the remaining sugar in a heavy-based saucepan and heat gently, stirring occasionally, until the sugar has dissolved and the juices from the fruits are just beginning to run. Add the Cointreau. Dip the loaf tin/pan into hot water for 30 seconds and invert onto a serving plate. Carefully remove the tin/pan and plastic wrap. Decorate the terrine with sprigs of mint, and serve sliced with the prepared red fruit compote.

Difficulty Rating: 2 points

Chocolate Fruit Tiramisu

Serves 4

Ingredients

2 ripe passion fruit

2 nectarines or peaches

75 g/3 oz/¼ cup sponge finger/ladyfingers

125 g/4½ oz/1 cup amaretti biscuits/cookies

5 tbsp amaretto/liqueur

6 tbsp prepared black coffee

250 g tub/1 cup mascarpone cheese

450 ml/¾ pint/2 cups fresh custard

200 g/7 oz dark/semisweet chocolate, finely chopped
    or grated

2 tbsp sifted cocoa powder (unsweetened)

Cut the passion fruit, scoop out the seeds and reserve. Plunge the nectarines or peaches into boiling water and leave for 2–3 minutes. Carefully remove the nectarines or peaches from the water, cut in half and remove the stones. Peel off the skin, chop the flesh finely and reserve.

Break the sponge finger/ladyfinger biscuits/cookies and amaretti biscuits in half. Place the amaretto liqueur and prepared black coffee into a shallow dish and stir well. Place half the sponge fingers and amaretti biscuits into the amaretto and coffee mixture and soak for 30 seconds. Lift out the biscuits from the liquor and arrange in the bases of four deep individual glass dishes.

Cream the mascarpone cheese until soft and creamy, then slowly beat in the fresh custard/custard sauce and mix well together. Spoon half the mascarpone mixture over the biscuits in the dishes and sprinkle with 125 g/4½ oz of the finely chopped or grated dark chocolate.

Arrange half the passion fruit seeds and the chopped nectarine or peaches over the chocolate and sprinkle with half the sifted cocoa powder.

Place the remaining biscuits in the remaining coffee liqueur mixture and soak for 30 seconds, then arrange on top of the fruit and cocoa powder.

Top with the remaining chopped or grated chocolate, the nectarines or peaches and the mascarpone cheese mixture, piling the mascarpone high in the dishes.

Chill in the refrigerator for 1½ hours, then spoon the remaining passion fruit seeds and cocoa powder over the desserts. Chill in the refrigerator for 30 minutes and serve.

Difficulty Rating: 3 points

Buttery Passion Fruit Madeira Cake

Cuts into 8–10 slices

Ingredients

210 g/7$\frac{1}{2}$ oz/1$\frac{2}{3}$ cups plain/all-purpose flour

1 tsp baking powder

175 g/6 oz/$\frac{3}{4}$ cup (1$\frac{1}{2}$ sticks) unsalted butter, softened

250 g/9 oz/1$\frac{1}{4}$ cups, plus 1 tsp caster/superfine sugar

grated zest of 1 orange

1 tsp vanilla extract

3 medium/large eggs, beaten

2 tbsp milk

6 ripe passion fruits

50 g/2 oz/$\frac{1}{2}$ cup icing/confectioners' sugar,
   plus extra for dusting

Preheat the oven to 180°C/350°F/Gas Mark 4, 10 minutes before baking. Lightly oil and line the base of a 23 x 12.5 cm/ 9 x 5 inch loaf tin/pan with greaseproof/wax paper. Sift the flour and baking powder into a bowl and reserve.

Beat the butter, sugar, zest and vanilla extract until light and fluffy, then gradually beat in the eggs, 1 tablespoon at a time, beating well after each addition. If the mixture appears to curdle or separate, beat in a little of the flour mixture. Fold in the flour mixture with the milk until just blended. Do not overmix. Spoon lightly into the prepared tin and level the top evenly. Sprinkle lightly with the teaspoon of caster/superfine sugar. Bake in the oven for 55 minutes, or until well risen and golden brown. Remove from the oven and leave to cool for 15–20 minutes.

Cut the passion fruits in half and scoop out the pulp into a sieve set over a bowl. Press the juice through using a spatula or spoon. Add the icing/confectioners' sugar and stir to dissolve, adding a little extra sugar if necessary. Using a skewer, pierce holes all over the cake. Slowly spoon the passion fruit glaze over the cake and allow to seep in. Gently turn the cake out of the tin onto a wire rack and turn it back the right way up, discarding the lining paper. Dust with icing sugar and cool completely. Serve cold.

Difficulty Rating: 2 points

Butterscotch Loaf

Serves 8

Ingredients

1 banana, peeled, weighing about 100 g/3$\frac{1}{2}$ oz

125 g/4 oz/$\frac{1}{2}$ cup soft margarine

125 g/4 oz/$\frac{2}{3}$ cup golden caster/superfine sugar

2 medium/large eggs

1 tsp almond extract

$\frac{1}{2}$ tsp vanilla extract

125 g/4 oz/1 cup self-raising flour

75 g/3 oz/$\frac{1}{2}$ cup dark/semisweet chocolate chips

75 g/3 oz/$\frac{2}{3}$ cup walnuts, chopped

To decorate:

50 g/2 oz/$\frac{1}{3}$ cup natural icing/confectioners' sugar

25 g/1 oz/8 cubes golden/unbleached lump sugar

Preheat the oven to 170°C/325°F/Gas Mark 3. Grease and line the base of a 1 kg/2 lb 3 oz loaf tin/pan with a long thin strip of nonstick baking parchment.

Place the banana in a bowl and mash. Add the margarine, sugar and eggs along with the extracts and sift in the flour. Beat until smooth, then stir in the chocolate chips and add half the chopped walnuts. Stir until smooth, then spoon into the prepared tin and spread level.

Bake for about 45 minutes until a skewer inserted into the centre comes out clean. Leave in the tin for 5 minutes, then turn out to cool on a wire rack, peel away the paper and leave to cool.

To decorate, make the icing/confectioners' sugar into a runny consistency with 2 teaspoons water. Drizzle over the cake and sprinkle over the remaining walnuts and the sugar lumps. Leave to set for 30 minutes, then serve sliced.

Difficulty Rating: 2 points

Chocolate & Fruit Crumble

Serves 4

Ingredients

For the crumble/crisp:
100 g/4 oz/1 cup plain/all-purpose flour
125 g/4 oz/¹⁄₂ cup (1 stick) butter
75 g/3 oz/¹⁄₃ cup soft light brown/golden brown sugar
50 g/2 oz/¹⁄₂ cup rolled porridge oats
50 g/2 oz/¹⁄₂ cup hazelnuts, chopped

For the filling:
450 g/1 lb Bramley/tart cooking apples
1 tbsp lemon juice
50 g/2 oz/¹⁄₄ cup sultanas/golden raisins
50 g/2 oz/¹⁄₄ cup seedless raisins
50 g/2 oz/¹⁄₄ cup firmly packed soft light brown/golden brown sugar
350 g/12 oz pears, peeled, cored and chopped
1 tsp ground cinnamon
125 g/4 oz dark/semisweet chocolate, very
   roughly chopped
2 tsp caster/superfine sugar, for sprinkling

Preheat the oven to 190°C/375°F/Gas Mark 5, 10 minutes before baking. Lightly oil an ovenproof dish.

For the crumble/crisp, sift the flour into a large bowl. Cut the butter into small cubes and add to the flour. Rub the butter into the flour until the mixture resembles fine breadcrumbs. Stir the sugar, porridge oats and the chopped hazelnuts into the mixture and reserve.

For the filling, peel the apples, core and slice thickly. Place in a large heavy-based saucepan with the lemon juice and 3 tablespoons water. Add the sultanas/golden raisins, raisins and the soft brown sugar. Bring slowly to the boil, cover and simmer over a gentle heat for 8–10 minutes, stirring occasionally, or until the apples are slightly softened. Remove the saucepan from the heat and leave to cool slightly before stirring in the pears, ground cinnamon and the chopped chocolate.

Spoon into the prepared ovenproof dish. Sprinkle the crumble/crisp evenly over the top, then bake in the preheated oven for 35–40 minutes until the top is golden.

Remove from the oven, sprinkle with the caster/superfine sugar and serve immediately.

Difficulty Rating: 1 point

Brandied Raisin Chocolate Mousse

Serves 4

Ingredients

125 g/4 oz/²/₃ cup raisins
1 tsp soft brown sugar
3 tbsp brandy
200 g/7 oz dark/semisweet chocolate
150 ml/¹/₄ pint/²/₃ cup ready-made custard
300 ml/¹/₂ pint/1¹/₄ cups double/heavy cream
1 tbsp strong black coffee
1 medium/large egg white
50 ml/2 fl oz/¹/₄ cup freshly whipped cream
chocolate curls, to decorate

Place the raisins in a bowl together with the sugar, then pour over the brandy. Stir well and cover with plastic wrap. Leave to marinate overnight or until the raisins have absorbed most, or all of the brandy. Stir occasionally during marinating.

Break the chocolate into small pieces and place in a small heatproof bowl set over a saucepan of gently simmering water. Heat gently, stirring occasionally, until the chocolate has melted and is smooth. Remove the bowl from the heat and leave to stand for about 10 minutes, or until the chocolate cools and begins to thicken. Using a metal spoon or rubber spatula, carefully fold in the prepared custard.

Whip the cream until soft peaks form and fold into the chocolate custard mixture together with the coffee. Gently stir in the brandy–soaked raisins with any remaining brandy left in the bowl.

Whisk the egg white in a clean, grease–free bowl, until stiff but not dry, then fold 1 tablespoon into the chocolate mixture and mix together lightly. Add the remaining egg white and stir lightly until well mixed. Spoon into four tall glasses and chill in the refrigerator for up to 2 hours. Just before serving, pipe a swirl of whipped cream on the top of each mousse and decorate with the chocolate curls, then serve.

Difficulty Rating: 2 points

Poached Pears with Chocolate Sauce

Serves 4

Ingredients

300 ml/½ pint/1¼ cups red wine

125 g/4 oz/½ cup caster/superfine sugar

grated rind and juice of 1 small orange

2 cm/1 inch piece fresh root ginger, peeled and chopped

4 firm pears, such as Williams or Conference

175 g/6 oz dark/semisweet chocolate

150 ml/¼ pint/⅔ cup double/heavy cream

25 g/1 oz/2 tbsp golden granulated sugar

Pour the red wine with 150 ml/¼ pint/⅔ cup of water into a heavy-based saucepan and stir in the sugar, the orange rind and juice with the ginger. Place over a gentle heat and bring slowly to the boil, stirring occasionally until the sugar has dissolved. Once the sugar has dissolved, boil steadily for 5 minutes, then remove from the heat.

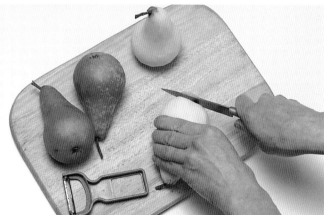

Using a potato peeler, carefully peel the pears, leaving the stalks intact. If preferred, gently remove the cores from the base of each pear. (You can, if you prefer, leave the cores intact for a neater finish.) If necessary, cut a very thin slice off the base of each pear so they sit upright.

Carefully stand the pears in the hot syrup, return to the heat, cover with a lid and simmer gently for 20 minutes or until tender, turning the pears occasionally. Remove from the heat and leave to cool in the syrup, turning occasionally. Using a slotted spoon, transfer the pears to a large dish.

Strain the syrup, then bring back to the boil and boil rapidly until reduced and syrupy. Add the chocolate, cream and sugar to the saucepan and bring very slowly to the boil, stirring constantly until the chocolate has melted. Arrange the pears on serving plates and carefully spoon over the chocolate sauce. Serve immediately.

Difficulty Rating: 2 points

Chocolate Trifle

Serves 4

Ingredients

1½ homemade or bought chocolate Swiss/jelly rolls

4 tbsp strawberry jam

3 tbsp medium sherry

3 tbsp brandy

350 g/12 oz/3 cups fresh strawberries

2 small mangos, peeled, stoned and diced

200 g/7 oz dark/semisweet chocolate

2 tbsp custard powder/vanilla pudding mix

2 tbsp granulated sugar

300 ml/½ pint/1¼ cups whole milk

250 g/9 oz/1 cup mascarpone cheese

300 ml/½ pint/1¼ cups double/heavy cream

15 g/½ oz/3 tbsp toasted flaked/slivered almonds

Slice the chocolate Swiss roll thickly and spread each slice with a little strawberry jam. Place the Swiss roll slices in the base of a trifle dish or glass bowl. Sprinkle over the sherry and brandy and leave to stand for 10 minutes to let the sherry and brandy soak into the Swiss roll. Slice half the strawberries and scatter evenly over the Swiss roll with half the diced mangos.

Break the chocolate into small pieces and place in a small heatproof bowl set over a saucepan of gently simmering water. Heat gently, stirring occasionally until the chocolate has melted and is smooth and free from lumps.

Blend the custard powder/vanilla pudding mix, sugar and milk to a smooth paste in a bowl, then pour into a heavy-based saucepan. Place over a gentle heat and cook, stirring constantly, until smooth and thick. Add the melted chocolate and stir until blended. Take off the heat and leave to cool. Stir in the mascarpone cheese.

Spoon the custard mixture over the fruit and chill in the refrigerator for 1 hour. Whip the cream until soft peaks form and pile over the top of the set custard. Sprinkle over the toasted flaked/slivered almonds and decorate with the remaining whole strawberries and diced mango.

Difficulty Rating: 2 points

Moist Mincemeat Tea Loaf

Cuts into 10 slices

Ingredients

225 g/8 oz/2 cups self-raising flour
½ tsp ground mixed spice
125 g/4 oz/½ cup (1 stick) cold butter, cubed
75 g/3 oz/¾ cup flaked/slivered almonds
25 g/1 oz/¼ cup rinsed, dried and quartered glacé/
  candied cherries,
75 g/3 oz/⅓ cup light muscovado/golden brown sugar
2 medium/large eggs
250 g/9 oz/2 cups prepared mincemeat/mince pie filling
1 tsp lemon zest
2 tsp brandy or milk

Preheat the oven to 180°C/350°F/Gas Mark 4, 10 minutes before cooking. Oil and line the base of a 900 g/2 lb loaf tin/pan with nonstick baking parchment.

Sift the flour and mixed spice into a large bowl. Add the butter and rub in until the mixture resembles breadcrumbs. Reserve 2 tablespoons of the flaked/slivered almonds and stir in the rest with the glacé/candied cherries and sugar.

Lightly whisk the eggs, then stir in the mincemeat/mince pie filling, lemon zest and brandy or milk. Make a well in the centre of the dry ingredients, add the egg mixture and fold together until blended. Spoon into the prepared loaf tin, level the top with the back of a spoon, then sprinkle over the reserved flaked almonds. Bake on the middle shelf of the preheated oven for 30 minutes. Cover with kitchen foil to prevent the almonds browning too much. Bake for a further 30 minutes, or until well risen and a skewer inserted into the centre comes out clean.

Leave the tea loaf in the tin for 10 minutes before removing and cooling on a wire rack. Remove the lining paper, slice thickly and serve.

Difficulty Rating: 2 points

Maple, Pecan & Lemon Loaf

Cuts into 12 slices

Ingredients

350 g/12 oz/2¾ cups plain/all-purpose flour
1 tsp baking powder
175 g/6 oz/¾ cup (1½ sticks) butter, cubed
75 g/3 oz/⅓ cup caster/superfine sugar
125 g/4 oz/1¼ cups roughly chopped pecan nuts
3 medium/large eggs
1 tbsp milk
finely grated zest of 1 lemon
5 tbsp maple syrup

For the icing:
75 g/3 oz/¾ cup icing/confectioners' sugar
1 tbsp lemon juice
25 g/1 oz/¼ cup pecans, roughly chopped

Preheat the oven to 170°C/325°F/Gas Mark 3, 10 minutes before baking. Lightly oil and line the base of a 900 g/2 lb loaf tin/pan with nonstick baking parchment.

Sift the flour and baking powder into a large bowl. Rub in the butter until the mixture resembles fine breadcrumbs. Stir in the caster/superfine sugar and pecan nuts. Beat the eggs together with the milk and lemon zest. Stir in the maple syrup. Add to the dry ingredients and stir in until mixed thoroughly.

Spoon the mixture into the prepared tin and level the top with the back of a spoon. Bake on the middle shelf of the preheated oven for 50–60 minutes until the cake is risen and lightly browned, and a skewer inserted into the centre comes out clean. Leave the cake in the tin for about 10 minutes, then turn out and leave to cool on a wire rack. Carefully remove the lining paper.

Sift the icing/confectioners' sugar into a bowl and stir in lemon juice to make a smooth icing. Drizzle the icing over the loaf, scatter with the chopped pecans. Leave to set, slice and serve.

Difficulty Rating: 2 points

Chocolate Chip Ice Cream

Serves 4

Ingredients

350 g/12 oz/3 cups fresh raspberries, or thawed if frozen

25 g/1 oz/¼ cup icing/confectioners' sugar, or to taste

2 tbsp lemon juice

600 ml/1 pint/2½ cups milk

1 vanilla pod/bean, seeds removed

6 medium/large egg yolks

125 g/4 oz/½ cup caster/superfine sugar

450 g/1 lb/16 oz dark/semisweet chocolate

150 ml/¼ pint/⅔ cup double/heavy cream

fresh fruit of your choice, to serve

Set the freezer to rapid freeze. Simmer the raspberries with the sugar and lemon juice for 5 minutes. Leave to cool, then purée in a food processor. Press through a fine sieve to remove the pips. Reserve the coulis.

Pour the milk into a heavy-based saucepan and add the vanilla pod/bean. Bring slowly to the boil, then remove from the heat and leave to infuse for 30 minutes. Remove the pod.

Whisk the egg yolks and caster/superfine sugar together until pale and creamy, then gradually whisk in the infused milk. Strain the mixture into a clean saucepan, place over a gentle heat and bring slowly to the boil. Cook over a gentle heat, stirring constantly, until the mixture thickens and coats the back of a wooden spoon. Do not let the mixture boil otherwise it will curdle. Once thickened, cover with plastic wrap and leave the custard to cool completely.

Break half the chocolate into small pieces and place in a heatproof bowl set over a saucepan of gently simmering water. Heat gently, stirring frequently, until the chocolate has melted and smooth. Remove from the heat and leave to cool.

Whip the cream until soft peaks form and fold into the cooled custard. Roughly chop the remaining chocolate and stir into the custard mixture together with the melted chocolate. Spoon into a suitable container and freeze for 1 hour.

Remove from the freezer and beat well to break up all the ice crystals. Repeat the beating and freezing process twice more, then freeze for 4 hours or until the ice cream is solid. Leave to soften in the refrigerator for 30 minutes before serving with fresh fruit and the raspberry coulis. Remember to return the freezer to its normal setting.

Difficulty Rating: 3 points

Autumn Bramley Apple Cake

Cuts into 8–10 slices

Ingredients

225 g/8 oz/2 cups self-raising flour

1½ tsp baking powder

150 g/5 oz/½ cup plus 2 tbsp margarine, softened

150 g/5 oz/¾ cup caster/superfine sugar, plus extra for sprinkling

1 tsp vanilla extract

2 large/extra-large eggs, beaten

1.1 kg/2½ lb Bramley apples/tart cooking apples, peeled, cored and sliced

1 tbsp lemon juice

½ tsp ground cinnamon

custard or cream, to serve

Preheat the oven to 170°C/325°F/Gas Mark 3, 10 minutes before baking. Lightly oil and line the base of a 20.5 cm/8 inch deep cake tin/pan with nonstick baking parchment or greaseproof/wax paper. Sift the flour and baking powder into a small bowl. Beat the margarine, sugar and vanilla extract in a larger bowl until light and fluffy. Gradually beat in the eggs a little at a time, beating well after each addition. Stir in the flour. Spoon about one third of the mixture into the tin, levelling the surface.

Toss the apple slices in the lemon juice and cinnamon and spoon over the cake mixture, making a thick even layer. Spread the remaining mixture over the apple layer to the edge of the tin, making sure the apples are covered. Level the top with the back of a wet spoon and sprinkle generously with sugar. Bake in the preheated oven for 1½ hours, or until well risen and golden, the apples are tender and the centre of the cake springs back when lightly pressed. If the top browns too quickly, reduce the oven temperature slightly and cover the cake loosely with kitchen foil. Transfer to a wire rack and cool for about 20 minutes in the tin. Run a thin knife blade between the cake and the tin to loosen the cake and invert onto a paper-lined rack. Turn the cake the right way up and cool. Serve with the custard or cream.

Difficulty Rating: 2 points

Marbled Chocolate & Orange Loaf

Cuts into 6 slices

Ingredients

50 g/2 oz dark/semisweet chocolate, broken into squares,
or ⅓ cup semisweet chocolate chips
125 g/4 oz/½ cup (1 stick) butter, softened
125 g/4 oz/⅔ cup caster/superfine sugar
zest of 1 orange
2 medium/large eggs, beaten
125 g/4 oz/1 cup self-raising flour
2 tsp orange juice
1 tbsp sifted cocoa powder (unsweetened)

To finish:
1 tbsp icing/confectioners' sugar
1 tsp cocoa powder (unsweetened)

Preheat the oven to 180°C/350°F/Gas Mark 4. Lightly oil a 450 g/1 lb loaf tin/pan and line the base with a layer of nonstick baking parchment. Put the chocolate in a bowl over a saucepan of very hot water. Stir occasionally until melted. Remove and leave until just cool, but not starting to reset.

Cream together the butter, sugar and orange zest until pale and fluffy. Gradually add the beaten eggs, beating well after each addition. Sift in the flour, add the orange juice and fold with a metal spoon or rubber spatula. Divide the mixture in half into two separate bowls. Gently fold the cocoa powder and chocolate into one half of the mixture. Drop tablespoonfuls of each cake mixture into the prepared tin, alternating between the orange and chocolate mixtures. Briefly swirl the colours together with a knife to give a marbled effect. Bake for 40 minutes, or until firm and a fine skewer inserted into the centre comes out clean.

Leave in the tin for 5 minutes, then turn out and cool on a wire rack. Carefully remove the lining paper. Dust the cake with the icing/confectioners' sugar and then with the cocoa powder. Cut into thick slices and serve.

Difficulty Rating: 2 points

Banana & Honey Tea Bread

Makes one 900 g/2 lb loaf

Ingredients

2 large bananas, about 225 g/8 oz
1 tbsp fresh orange juice
125 g/4 oz/½ cup soft margarine
125 g/4 oz/½ cup soft light brown sugar
125 g/4 oz/6 tbsp honey
2 medium/large eggs, beaten
225 g/8 oz/2 cups wholemeal self-raising flour
½ tsp ground cinnamon
75 g/3 oz/½ cup sultanas/golden raisins

Preheat the oven to 180°C/350°F/Gas Mark 4. Grease a 900 g/ 2 lb loaf tin and line the base with a strip of nonstick baking parchment. Mash the bananas together in a large bowl with the orange juice.

Place the soft margarine, sugar and honey in the bowl and add the eggs. Sift in the flour and cinnamon, adding any bran left behind in the sieve. Beat everything together until light and fluffy and then fold in the sultanas/golden raisins.

Spoon the mixture into the prepared tin and level the top. Bake for about 1 hour until golden, well risen and a skewer inserted into the centre comes out clean. Cool in the tin for 5 minutes, then turn out on a wire rack.

Difficulty Rating: 1 points

Chunky Chocolate Muffins

Makes 7

Ingredients

50 g/2 oz dark/semisweet chocolate, roughly chopped

50 g/2 oz/¹/₄ cup light muscovado/golden brown sugar

25 g/1 oz/2 tbsp butter, melted

125 ml/4 fl oz/¹/₂ cup milk, at room temperature

¹/₂ tsp vanilla extract

1 medium/large egg, lightly beaten

150 g/5 oz/1¹/₄ cups self-raising flour

¹/₂ tsp baking powder

pinch salt

75 g/3 oz white chocolate, chopped

2 tsp icing/confectioners' sugar (optional)

Preheat the oven to 200°C/400°F/Gas Mark 6, 15 minutes before baking. Line a muffin tin/pan with seven paper muffin cases/baking cups, or else oil the individual compartments well. Place the dark/semisweet chocolate in a large heatproof bowl set over a saucepan of very hot water. Stir occasionally until melted. Remove the bowl and leave to cool for a few minutes.

Stir the sugar and butter into the melted chocolate, then add the milk, vanilla extract and egg. Sift the flour, baking powder and salt in together. Add the chopped white chocolate. Using a metal spoon, fold together quickly, taking care not to overmix.

Divide the mixture between the paper cases, piling it up in the centre. Bake on the centre shelf of the preheated oven for 20–25 minutes or until well risen and firm to the touch.

Lightly dust the tops of the muffins with icing/confectioners' sugar as soon as they come out of the oven, if wanted. Leave the muffins in the tray for a few minutes, then transfer to a wire rack. Serve either warm or cold.

Difficulty Rating: 2 points

Fudgy & Top Hat Chocolate Buns

Makes 12

Ingredients

50 g/2 oz/¹/₂ cup self-raising flour

25 g/1 oz/¹/₄ cup cocoa powder (unsweetened)

¹/₂ tsp baking powder

75 g/3 oz/6 tbsp butter, softened

75 g/3 oz/¹/₃ cup demerara/turbinado sugar

1 medium/large egg, lightly beaten

1 tbsp milk

For the fudgy icing:

15 g/¹/₂ oz/1 tbsp unsalted butter, melted

1 tbsp milk

15 g/¹/₂ oz/2 tbsp cocoa powder (unsweetened), sifted

3 tbsp icing/confectioners' sugar, sifted

25 g/1 oz dark/semisweet chocolate, coarsely grated

For the top hat filling:

150 ml/¹/₄ pint/²/₃ cup whipping cream

2 tsp orange liqueur

1 tbsp icing/confectioners' sugar, sifted

Preheat the oven to 190 C/375 F/Gas Mark 5, 10 minutes before baking. Sift the flour, cocoa powder and baking powder into a bowl. Add the butter, sugar, egg and milk and beat for 2–3 minutes until light and fluffy.

Divide the mixture equally between 12 paper cases/baking cups arranged in a muffin tin/pan. Bake on the shelf above the centre in the preheated oven for 15–20 minutes until well risen and firm to the touch. Leave in the tin for a few minutes, then transfer to a wire rack and leave to cool completely.

For the fudgy icing, mix together the melted butter, milk, cocoa powder and icing/confectioners' sugar. Place a spoonful of icing on the top of six of the cakes, spreading out to a circle with the back of the spoon. Sprinkle with grated chocolate.

To make the top hats, use a sharp knife to cut and remove a circle of sponge, about 3 cm/1¹/₄ inch across from each of the six remaining cakes. Whip the cream, orange liqueur and 1 teaspoon icing sugar together until soft peaks form. Spoon the filling into a decorating bag fitted with a large star tip and pipe a swirl in the centre of each cake. Replace the tops, then dust with the remaining icing sugar and serve with the other buns.

Difficulty Rating: 2 points

Chocolate & Orange Rock Buns

Makes 12

Ingredients

200 g/7 oz/1³/₄ cups self-raising flour

25 g/1 oz/¹/₄ cup cocoa powder (unsweetened)

¹/₂ tsp baking powder

125 g/4 oz/¹/₂ cup (1 stick) butter

3 tbsp granulated sugar

50 g/2 oz/¹/₃ cup chopped glacé/candied pineapple

50 g/2 oz/¹/₃ cup chopped ready-to-eat dried apricots

50 g/2 oz/2 tbsp quartered glacé/candied cherries

1 medium/large egg

finely grated zest of ¹/₂ orange

1 tbsp orange juice

2 tbsp demerara/turbinado sugar

Preheat the oven to 200°C/400°F/Gas Mark 6, 15 minutes before baking. Lightly oil two baking sheets, or line with nonstick baking parchment. Sift the flour, cocoa powder and baking powder into a bowl. Cut the butter into squares, add to the dry ingredients. Rub in until the mixture resembles fine breadcrumbs. Add the granulated sugar, pineapple, apricots and cherries and stir to mix.

Lightly beat the egg together with the grated orange zest and juice. Drizzle the egg mixture over the dry ingredients. Stir to combine. The mixture should be fairly stiff but not too dry – add a little more orange juice if necessary.

Using two teaspoons, shape the mixture into 12 rough heaps on the prepared baking sheets. Sprinkle generously with the demerara/turbinado sugar. Bake in the preheated oven for 15 minutes, switching the baking sheets around after 10 minutes. Leave on the baking sheets for 5 minutes to cool slightly, then transfer to a wire rack to cool. Serve warm or cold.

Difficulty Rating: 2 points

Chocolate Madeleines

Makes 10

Ingredients

125 g/4 oz/¹/₂ cup (1 stick) butter

125 g/4 oz/²/₃ cup soft light brown sugar

2 medium/large eggs, lightly beaten

1 drop almond extract

1 tbsp ground almonds

75 g/3 oz/²/₃ cup self-raising flour

20 g/³/₄ oz/¹/₄ cup cocoa powder (unsweetened)

1 tsp baking powder

To finish:

5 tbsp apricot conserve

1 tbsp amaretto liqueur, brandy or orange juice

50 g/2 oz/²/₃ cup desiccated/shredded coconut

10 large chocolate buttons (optional)

Preheat the oven to 180°C/350°F/Gas Mark 4, 10 minutes before baking. Lightly oil 10 dariole moulds and line the bases of each with a small circle of nonstick baking parchment. Stand the moulds on a baking sheet. Cream the butter and sugar together until light and fluffy. Gradually add the eggs, beating well between each addition. Beat in the almond extract and ground almonds.

Sift the flour, cocoa powder and baking powder over the creamed mixture. Gently fold in using a metal spoon. Divide the mixture equally between the prepared moulds; each should be about half full. Bake on the centre shelf of the preheated oven for 20 minutes, or until well risen and firm to the touch. Leave in the moulds for a few minutes, then run a small palette knife round the edge and turn out onto a wire rack to cool. Remove the paper circles from the sponges.

Heat the conserve with the liqueur, brandy or juice in a small saucepan. Sieve to remove any lumps. If necessary, trim the sponge bases, so they are flat. Brush the tops and sides with warm conserve, then roll in the coconut. Top each with a chocolate button, fixed by brushing its base with conserve.

Difficulty Rating: 3 points

Fruit & Spice Chocolate Slice

Makes 10 slices

Ingredients

350 g/12 oz/2³/₄ cups self-raising flour

1 tsp mixed/pumpkin pie spice

175 g/6 oz/³/₄ cup (1¹/₂ sticks) butter, chilled

125 g/4 oz dark/semisweet chocolate, roughly chopped

125 g/4 oz/1 scant cup dried mixed fruit

75 g/3 oz/¹/₂ cup dried apricots, chopped

75 g/3 oz/¹/₂ cup chopped mixed nuts

175 g/6 oz/1 scant cup demerara/turbinado sugar

2 medium/large eggs, lightly beaten

150 ml/¹/₄ pint/²/₃ cup milk

Preheat the oven to 180°C/350°F/Gas Mark 4. Oil and line a deep 18 cm/7 inch square tin/pan with nonstick baking parchment. Sift the flour and mixed/pumpkin pie spice into a large bowl. Cut the butter into small squares and, using your hands, rub in until the mixture resembles fine breadcrumbs.

Add the chocolate, dried mixed fruit, apricots and nuts to the dry ingredients. Reserve 1 tablespoon of the sugar, then add the rest to the bowl and stir together. Add the eggs and half of the milk and mix together, then add enough of the remaining milk to give a soft dropping consistency.

Spoon the mixture into the prepared tin, level the surface with the back of a spoon and sprinkle with the reserved demerara/turbinado sugar. Bake on the centre shelf of the preheated oven for 50 minutes. Cover the top with kitchen foil to prevent the cake from browning too much and bake for a further 30–40 minutes or until it is firm to the touch and a skewer inserted into the centre of the cake comes out clean.

Leave the cake in the tin for 10 minutes to cool slightly, then turn out onto a wire rack and leave to cool completely. Cut into 10 slices and serve. Store in an airtight container.

Difficulty Rating: 1 point

Chocolate Pecan Traybake

Makes 12 squares

Ingredients

175 g/6 oz/³/₄ cup (1¹/₂) sticks butter
75 g/3 oz/³/₄ cup icing/confectioners' sugar, sifted
175 g/6 oz/1¹/₃ cups plain/all-purpose flour
3 tbsp self-raising flour
5 tbsp cocoa powder (unsweetened)

For the pecan topping:
75 g/3 oz/6 tbsp butter
50 g/2 oz/¹/₄ cup light muscovado/golden brown sugar
2 tbsp golden/light corn syrup
2 tbsp milk
1 tsp vanilla extract
2 medium/large eggs, lightly beaten
125 g/4 oz/1¹/₄ cups pecan halves

Preheat the oven to 180°C/350°F/Gas Mark 4, 10 minutes before baking. Lightly oil and line a 28 x 18 x 2.5 cm/11 x 7 x 1 inch cake tin/pan with nonstick baking parchment. Beat the butter and sugar together until light and fluffy. Sift in the flours and cocoa powder and mix together to form a soft dough.

Press the mixture evenly over the base of the prepared tin. Prick all over with a fork, then bake on the shelf above the centre of the preheated oven for 15 minutes.

Put the butter, sugar, golden/light corn syrup, milk and vanilla extract in a small saucepan and heat gently until melted. Remove from the heat and leave to cool for a few minutes, then stir in the eggs and pour over the base. Sprinkle with the nuts.

Bake in the preheated oven for 25 minutes, or until dark golden brown but still slightly soft. Leave to cool in the tin. When cool, carefully remove from the tin, then cut into 12 squares and serve. Store in an airtight container.

Difficulty Rating: 1 point

Fruity Apple Tea Bread

Cuts into 12 slices

Ingredients

125 g/4 oz/^{1}/$_2$ cup (1 stick) 1 tbsp butter
125 g/4 oz/^{2}/$_3$ cup soft light brown sugar
275 g/10 oz/2 cups sultanas/golden raisins
150 ml/^{1}/$_4$ pint/^{2}/$_3$ cup apple juice
1 eating apple, peeled, cored and chopped
2 medium/large eggs, beaten
275 g/10 oz/2^1/$_2$ cups plain/all-purpose flour
^{1}/$_2$ tsp ground cinnamon
^{1}/$_2$ tsp ground ginger
2 tsp bicarbonate of soda/baking soda
butter curls, to serve

To decorate:
1 eating apple, cored, sliced
1 tsp lemon juice
1 tbsp warmed golden/light corn syrup

Preheat the oven to 180°C/350°F/Gas Mark 4. Oil and line the base of a 900 g/2 lb loaf tin/pan with nonstick baking parchment.

Put the butter, sugar, sultanas/golden raisins and apple juice in a small saucepan. Heat gently, stirring occasionally, until the butter has melted. Tip into a bowl and leave to cool.

Stir in the chopped apple and beaten eggs. Sift the flour, spices and bicarbonate of soda/baking soda over the apple mixture. Stir into the sultana mixture, spoon into the prepared loaf tin and smooth the top level with the back of a spoon. Toss the apple slices in lemon juice and arrange on top.

Bake in the preheated oven for 50 minutes, or until a skewer inserted into the centre comes out clean. Cover with kitchen foil to prevent the top from browning too much. Leave in the tin for 10 minutes before turning out onto a wire rack to cool.

Brush the top with golden/light corn syrup and leave to cool. Remove the lining paper, slice and serve with curls of butter.

Difficulty Rating: 2 points

Marmalade Loaf Cake

Serves 8–10

Ingredients

175 g/6 oz/^{3}/$_4$ cup plus 2 tbsp natural golden caster/superfine sugar
175 g/6 oz/^{3}/$_4$ cup (1^1/$_2$ sticks) butter, softened
3 medium/large eggs, beaten
175 g/6 oz/1^1/$_3$ cups self-raising flour
finely grated zest and juice of 1 orange
100 g/3^1/$_2$ oz/^{1}/$_3$ cup orange marmalade

For the topping:
zest and juice of 1 orange
125 g/4 oz/1 cup icing/confectioners' sugar

Preheat the oven to 180°C/350°F/Gas Mark 4. Grease and line a 1 kg/2 lb 3 oz loaf tin with a long thin strip of nonstick baking parchment.

Place the sugar and butter in a bowl and whisk until light and fluffy. Add the beaten eggs a little at a time, adding 1 teaspoon flour with each addition.

Add the remaining flour to the bowl with the orange zest, 2 tablespoons orange juice and the marmalade. Using a large metal spoon, fold the mixture together using a figure-of-eight movement until all the flour is incorporated. Spoon the batter into the tin and smooth level.

Bake for about 40 minutes until firm in the centre and a skewer inserted into the centre comes out clean. Cool in the tin for 5 minutes, then turn out to cool on a wire rack.

To make the topping, peel more thin strips of zest away from the orange and set aside. Squeeze more juice from the orange. Sift the icing/confectioners' sugar into a bowl and mix with 1 tablespoon orange juice until a thin smooth consistency forms. Drizzle over the top of the cake, letting it run down the sides. Scatter over the orange zest and leave to set for 1 hour.

Difficulty Rating: 2 points

Chocolate Brazil & Polenta Squares

Makes 9 squares

Ingredients

125 g/4 oz/1 cup shelled Brazil nuts

150 g/5 oz/²⁄₃ cup (1¼ sticks) butter, softened

150 g/5 oz/³⁄₄ cup soft light brown sugar

2 medium/large eggs, lightly beaten

75 g/3 oz/²⁄₃ cup plain/all-purpose flour

25 g/1 oz/¼ cup cocoa powder (unsweetened)

¼ tsp ground cinnamon

1 tsp baking powder

pinch salt

5 tbsp milk

65 g/2½ oz/¹⁄₃ cup instant polenta

Preheat the oven to 180°C/350°F/Gas Mark 4, 10 minutes before baking. Oil and line a deep 18 cm/7 inch square tin/pan with nonstick baking parchment. Finely chop half of the Brazil nuts and reserve. Roughly chop the remainder. Cream the butter and sugar together until light and fluffy. Gradually add the eggs, beating well between each addition.

Sift the flour, cocoa powder, cinnamon, baking powder and salt into the creamed mixture and gently fold in using a large metal spoon or spatula. Add the milk, polenta and the roughly chopped Brazil nuts. Fold into the mixture.

Turn the mixture into the prepared tin, levelling the surface with the back of a spoon. Sprinkle the reserved finely chopped Brazil nuts over the top. Bake the cake on the centre shelf of the preheated oven for 45–50 minutes until well risen and lightly browned and when a clean skewer inserted into the centre of the cake for a few seconds comes out clean.

Leave the cake in the tin for 10 minutes to cool slightly, then turn out onto a wire rack and leave to cool completely. Cut the cake into nine equal squares and serve. Store in an airtight container.

Difficulty Rating: 2 points

Moist Mocha & Coconut Cake

Makes 9 squares

Ingredients

3 tbsp ground coffee; 5 tbsp hot milk

75 g/3 oz/6 tbsp butter

175 g/6 oz/½ cup golden/light corn syrup

2 tbsp soft light brown sugar

40 g/1½ oz/½ cup desiccated/shredded coconut

150 g/5 oz/scant 1¼ cups plain/all-purpose flour

25 g/1 oz/¼ cup cocoa powder (unsweetened)

½ tsp bicarbonate of soda/baking soda

2 medium/large eggs, lightly beaten

2 chocolate flakes, to decorate

For the coffee icing:

225 g/8 oz/2¼ cups sifted icing/confectioners' sugar

125 g/4 oz/½ cup (1 stick) butter, softened

Preheat the oven to 170°C/325°F/Gas Mark 3, 10 minutes before baking. Lightly oil and line a deep 20.5 cm/8 inch square tin/pan with nonstick baking parchment. Place the ground coffee in a small bowl and pour over the hot milk. Leave to infuse for 5 minutes, then strain through a tea-strainer or a sieve lined with muslin/cheesecloth. You will end up with about 4 tablespoons of liquid. Reserve.

Put the butter, golden/light corn syrup, sugar and coconut in a small heavy-based saucepan and heat gently until the butter has melted and the sugar dissolved. Sift the flour, cocoa powder and bicarbonate of soda/baking soda together and stir into the melted mixture with the eggs and 3 tablespoons of the coffee-infused milk. Pour the mixture into the prepared tin. Bake on the centre shelf of the preheated oven for 45 minutes, or until the cake is well risen and firm to the touch. Leave in the tin for 10 minutes to cool slightly, then turn out onto a wire rack to cool completely.

For the icing, gradually add the icing/confectioners' sugar to the softened butter and beat together well. Add the remaining 1 tablespoon of coffee-infused milk and beat until light and fluffy. Carefully spread the icing over the top of the cake, then cut into squares. Decorate with pieces of chocolate flake and serve.

Difficulty Rating: 2 points

Chocolate Walnut Squares

Makes 24 squares

Ingredients

125 g/4 oz/^{1}/$_2$ cup (1 stick) butter

150 g/5 oz dark/semisweet chocolate, broken into pieces

450 g/1 lb/2^1/$_4$ cups caster/superfine sugar

^{1}/$_2$ tsp vanilla extract

200 g/7 oz/1^1/$_2$ cups plain/all-purpose flour

75 g/3 oz/^{1}/$_3$ cup self-raising flour

50 g/2 oz/^{1}/$_2$ cup cocoa powder (unsweetened)

225 g/8 oz/1 cup mayonnaise, at room temperature

For the chocolate glaze/to decorate:

125 g/4 oz dark/semisweet chocolate, broken into pieces

40 g/1^1/$_2$ oz/3 tbsp unsalted butter

24 walnut halves

1 tbsp icing/confectioners' sugar, for dusting

Preheat the oven to 170°C/325°F/Gas Mark 3, 10 minutes before baking. Oil and line a 28 x 18 x 5 cm/11 x 7 x 2 inch cake tin/pan with nonstick baking parchment. Place the butter, chocolate, sugar, vanilla extract and 250 ml/8 fl oz/1 cup cold water in a heavy–based saucepan. Heat gently, stirring occasionally, until the chocolate and butter have melted, but do not boil.

Sift the flours and cocoa powder into a large bowl and make a well in the centre. Add the mayonnaise and about one third of the chocolate mixture and beat until smooth. Gradually beat in the remaining chocolate mixture. Pour into the prepared tin and bake on the centre shelf of the preheated oven for 1 hour, or until slightly risen and firm to the touch. Place the tin on a wire rack and leave to cool. Remove the cake from the tin and peel off the parchment.

To make the chocolate glaze, place the chocolate and butter in a small saucepan with 1 tablespoon water and heat very gently, stirring occasionally, until melted and smooth. Leave to cool until thickened, then spread evenly over the cake.

Chill the cake in the refrigerator for about 5 minutes, then mark into 24 squares. Lightly dust the walnut halves with a little icing/confectioners' sugar and place one on the top of each square. Cut into pieces and store in an airtight container until ready to serve.

Difficulty Rating: 2 points

Indulgent Chocolate Squares

Makes 16 squares

Ingredients

350 g/12 oz dark/semisweet chocolate
175 g/6 oz/³/₄ cup (1¹/₂ sticks) butter, softened
175 g/6 oz/1 scant cup soft light brown sugar
175 g/6 oz/2 scant cups ground almonds
6 large/extra-large eggs, separated
3 tbsp sifted cocoa powder (unsweetened)
75 g/3 oz/1²/₃ cups fresh brown breadcrumbs
125 ml/4 fl oz/¹/₂ cup double/heavy cream
50 g/2 oz white chocolate, chopped
50 g/2 oz milk chocolate, chopped
few sliced strawberries, to decorate

Preheat the oven to 180°C/350°F/Gas Mark 4. Oil and line a deep 20.5 cm/8 inch square cake tin/pan with nonstick baking parchment. Melt 225 g/8 oz of the dark/bittersweet chocolate in a heatproof bowl set over a saucepan of almost boiling water. Stir until smooth, then leave until just cool, but not beginning to set.

Beat the butter and sugar until light and fluffy. Stir in the melted chocolate, ground almonds, egg yolks, cocoa powder and breadcrumbs. Whisk the egg whites until stiff peaks form, then stir a large spoonful into the chocolate mixture. Gently fold in the rest, then pour the mixture into the prepared tin. Bake on the centre shelf in the preheated oven for 1¹/₄ hours, or until firm, covering the top with foil after 45 minutes, to prevent it over-browning. Leave in the tin for 20 minutes, then turn out onto a wire rack and leave to cool.

Melt the remaining 125 g/4 oz dark chocolate with the cream in a heatproof bowl set over a saucepan of almost boiling water, stirring occasionally. Leave to cool for 20 minutes, or until thickened slightly. Spread the topping over the cake. Scatter over the white and milk chocolate and leave to set. Cut into 16 squares and serve decorated with a few sliced strawberries, then serve.

Difficulty Rating: 3 points

Crunchy-topped Citrus Chocolate Slices

Makes 12 slices

Ingredients

175 g/6 oz/³/₄ cup (1¹/₂ sticks) butter
175 g/6 oz/³/₄ cup firmly packed muscovado/dark brown sugar
finely grated zest of 1 orange
3 medium/large eggs, lightly beaten
1 tbsp ground almonds
175 g/6 oz/1¹/₂ cups self-raising flour
¹/₄ tsp baking powder
125 g/4 oz dark/semisweet chocolate, coarsely grated
2 tsp milk

For the crunchy topping:
125 g/4 oz/²/₃ cup caster/superfine sugar
juice of 2 limes
juice of 1 orange

Preheat the oven to 170°C/325°F/Gas Mark 3, 10 minutes before baking. Oil and line a 28 x 18 x 2.5 cm/11 x 7 x 1 inch cake tin/pan with nonstick baking parchment. Place the butter, sugar and orange zest into a large bowl and cream together until light and fluffy. Gradually add the eggs, beating after each addition, then beat in the ground almonds. Sift the flour and baking powder into the creamed mixture. Add the grated chocolate and milk, then gently fold in using a metal spoon. Spoon the mixture into the prepared tin.

Bake on the centre shelf of the preheated oven for 35–40 minutes until well risen and firm to the touch. Leave in the tin for a few minutes to cool slightly. Turn out onto a wire rack and remove the baking parchment.

For the topping, place the sugar and fruit juices into a small jug. Stir together. Drizzle over the hot cake, covering the whole surface. Leave until completely cold, then cut into 12 slices to serve.

Difficulty Rating: 2 points

All-in-one Chocolate Fudge Cakes

Makes 15 squares

Ingredients

175 g/6 oz/1 scant cup soft dark brown sugar

175 g/6 oz/³/₄ cup (1¹/₂ sticks) butter, softened

150 g/5 oz/scant 1¹/₄ cups self-raising flour

25 g/1 oz/¹/₄ cup cocoa powder (unsweetened)

¹/₂ tsp baking powder

pinch salt

3 medium/large eggs, lightly beaten

1 tbsp golden/light corn syrup

For the fudge topping:

75 g/3 oz/heaping ¹/₃ cup granulated sugar

150 ml/¹/₄ pint/²/₃ cup evaporated milk

175 g/6 oz dark/semisweet chocolate, roughly chopped

40 g/1¹/₂ oz/3 tbsp unsalted butter, softened

125 g/4 oz soft fudge sweets, finely chopped

Preheat the oven to 180°C/350°F/Gas Mark 4, 10 minutes before baking. Oil and line a 28 x 18 x 2.5 cm/11 x 7 x 1 inch cake tin/pan with nonstick baking parchment.

Place the soft brown sugar and butter in a bowl and sift in the flour, cocoa powder, baking powder and salt. Add the eggs and golden/light corn syrup, then beat with an electric whisk for 2 minutes, before adding 2 tablespoons warm water and beating for a further 1 minute. Turn the mixture into the prepared tin and level the top with the back of a spoon. Bake on the centre shelf of the preheated oven for 30 minutes, or until firm to the touch. Turn the cake out onto a wire rack and leave to cool before removing the baking parchment.

To make the topping, gently heat the sugar and evaporated milk in a saucepan, stirring frequently, until the sugar has dissolved. Bring the mixture to the boil and simmer for 6 minutes without stirring.

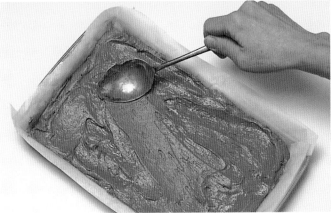

Remove the mixture from the heat. Add the chocolate and butter and stir until melted and blended. Pour into a bowl and chill in the refrigerator for 1–2 hours until thickened. Spread the topping over the cake, then sprinkle with the chopped fudge. Cut the cake into 15 squares before serving.

Difficulty Rating: 1 point

Marbled Chocolate Traybake

Makes 18 squares

Ingredients

175 g/6 oz/³/₄ cups (1½ sticks) butter

175 g/6 oz/1 scant cup caster/superfine sugar

1 tsp vanilla extract

3 medium/large eggs, lightly beaten

200 g/7 oz/1½ cups self-raising flour

½ tsp baking powder

1 tbsp milk

1½ tbsp cocoa powder (unsweetened)

For the chocolate icing:

75 g/3 oz dark/semisweet chocolate, broken into pieces

75 g/3 oz white chocolate, broken into pieces

Preheat the oven to 180°C/350°F/Gas Mark 4, 10 minutes before baking. Oil and line a 28 x 18 x 2.5 cm/11 x 7 x 1 inch cake tin/pan with nonstick baking parchment. Cream the butter, sugar and vanilla extract until light and fluffy. Gradually add the eggs, beating well after each addition. Sift in the flour and baking powder and fold in with the milk. Spoon half the mixture into the prepared tin, spacing the spoonfuls apart and leaving gaps in between. Blend the cocoa powder to a smooth paste with 2 tablespoons warm water. Stir this into the remaining cake mixture. Drop small spoonfuls between the vanilla cake mixture to fill in all the gaps. Use a knife to swirl the mixtures together a little.

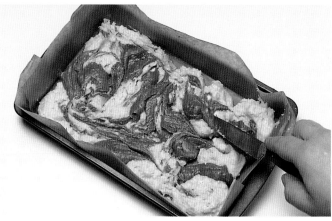

Bake on the centre shelf of the preheated oven for 35 minutes, or until well risen and firm to the touch. Leave in the tin for 5 minutes to cool, then turn out onto a wire rack and leave to cool. Remove the parchment.

For the icing, place the dark/semisweet and white chocolate in separate heatproof bowls and melt each over a saucepan of almost boiling water. Spoon into separate nonstick baking parchment decorating bags, snip off the tips and drizzle over the top. Leave to set before cutting into squares.

Difficulty Rating: 2 points

Triple Chocolate Brownies

Makes 15 squares

Ingredients

350 g/12 oz dark/semisweet chocolate, broken
  into pieces
225 g/8 oz/1 cup (2 sticks) butter, cubed
225 g/8 oz/1 heaping cup caster/superfine sugar
3 large/extra-large eggs, lightly beaten
1 tsp vanilla extract
2 tbsp very strong black coffee
100 g/3½ oz/¾ cup self-raising flour
125 g/4 oz/1 cup roughly chopped pecans
75 g/3 oz white chocolate, roughly chopped
75 g/3 oz milk chocolate, roughly chopped

Preheat the oven to 190°C/375°F/Gas Mark 5, 10 minutes before baking. Oil and line a 28 x 18 x 2.5 cm/11 x 7 x 1 inch cake tin/pan with nonstick baking parchment. Place the dark/semisweet chocolate in a heatproof bowl with the butter over a saucepan of almost boiling water. Stir occasionally until melted. Remove from the heat and leave until just cool, but not beginning to set.

Place the caster/superfine sugar, eggs, vanilla extract and coffee in a large bowl and beat together until smooth. Gradually beat in the chocolate mixture. Sift the flour into the chocolate mixture. Add the pecans and the white and milk chocolate. Gently fold in until mixed thoroughly. Spoon the mixture into the prepared tin and level the top.

Bake on the centre shelf of the preheated oven for 45 minutes, or until just firm to the touch in the centre and crusty on top. Leave to cool in the tin, then turn out onto a wire rack. Trim off the crusty edges and cut into 15 squares. Store in an airtight container.

Difficulty Rating: 2 points

Chocolate Nut Brownies

Makes 16 squares

Ingredients

125 g/4 oz/^{1}⁄$_2$ cup (1 stick) butter
150 g/5 oz/^{3}⁄$_4$ cup demerara/turbinado sugar
50 g/2 oz dark/semisweet chocolate, roughly
 chopped or broken
2 tbsp smooth peanut butter
2 medium/large eggs
50 g/2 oz/^{1}⁄$_2$ cup finely chopped unsalted roasted peanuts
100 g/3^1⁄$_2$ oz/1 scant cup self-raising flour

For the topping:
125 g/4 oz dark/semisweet chocolate, roughly
 chopped or broken
50 ml/2 fl oz/^{1}⁄$_4$ cup sour cream

Preheat the oven to 180°C/350°F/Gas Mark 4, 10 minutes before baking. Lightly oil and line a 20.5 cm/8 inch square cake tin/pan with greaseproof/wax paper or baking parchment. Combine the butter, sugar and chocolate in a small saucepan and heat gently until the sugar and chocolate have melted, stirring constantly. Reserve and cool slightly.

Mix together the peanut butter, eggs and peanuts in a large bowl. Stir in the cooled chocolate mixture. Sift in the flour and fold together with a metal spoon or rubber spatula until combined. Pour into the prepared tin and bake in the preheated oven for about 30 minutes, or until just firm. Cool for 5 minutes in the tin before turning out onto a wire rack to cool.

To make the topping, melt the chocolate in a heatproof bowl over a saucepan of simmering water, making sure that the base of the bowl does not touch the water. Cool slightly, then stir in the sour cream until smooth and glossy. Spread the topping over the brownies, refrigerate until set, then cut into squares. Serve the brownies cold.

Difficulty Rating: 2 points

Chocolate Fudge Brownies

Makes 16 squares

Ingredients

125 g/4 oz/^{1}⁄$_2$ cup (1 stick) butter
175 g/6 oz dark/semisweet chocolate, roughly
 chopped or broken
225 g/8 oz/1 heaping cup caster/superfine sugar
2 tsp vanilla extract
2 medium/large eggs, lightly beaten
150 g/5 oz/1 heaping cup plain/all-purpose flour
175 g/6 oz/1^1⁄$_2$ cups icing/confectioners' sugar
2 tbsp cocoa powder (unsweetened)
1 tbsp butter

Preheat the oven to 180°C/350°F/Gas Mark 4, 10 minutes before baking. Lightly oil and line a 20.5 cm/8 inch square cake tin/pan with greaseproof/wax paper or baking parchment.

Slowly melt the butter and chocolate together in a heatproof bowl set over a saucepan of simmering water. Transfer the mixture to a large bowl. Stir in the sugar and vanilla extract, then stir in the eggs. Sift over the flour and fold together well with a metal spoon or rubber spatula. Pour into the prepared tin.

Transfer to the preheated oven and bake for 30 minutes until just set. Remove the cooked mixture from the oven. Leave to cool in the tin before turning it out onto a wire rack.

Sift the icing/confectioners' sugar and cocoa into a small bowl and make a well in the centre. Place the butter in the well, then gradually add about 2 tablespoons hot water. Mix to form a smooth, spreadable icing.

Pour the icing over the cooked mixture. Leave the icing to set before cutting into squares. Serve the brownies when they are cold, or store in an airtight container.

Difficulty Rating: 2 points

Light White Chocolate & Walnut Blondies

Makes 15 blondies

Ingredients

75 g/3 oz/6 tbsp unsalted butter

200 g/7 oz/1 cup demerara/turbinado sugar

2 large/extra-large eggs, lightly beaten

1 tsp vanilla extract

2 tbsp milk

125 g/4 oz/1 cup, plus 1 tbsp plain/all-purpose flour

1 tsp baking powder

pinch salt

75 g/3 oz/²⁄₃ cup roughly chopped walnuts

125 g/4 oz/³⁄₄ cup white chocolate drops

1 tbsp icing/confectioners' sugar

Preheat the oven to 190°C/375°F/Gas Mark 5, 10 minutes before baking. Oil and line a 28 x 18 x 2.5 cm/11 x 7 x 1 inch cake tin/pan with nonstick baking parchment. Place the butter and demerara/turbinado sugar into a heavy-based saucepan and heat gently until the butter has melted and the sugar has started to dissolve. Remove from the heat and leave to cool.

Place the eggs, vanilla extract and milk in a large bowl and beat together. Stir in the butter and sugar mixture, then sift in the 125 g/4 oz/³⁄₄ cup of flour, the baking powder and salt. Gently stir the mixture twice.

Toss the walnuts and chocolate drops in the remaining 1 tablespoon of flour to coat. Add to the bowl and stir the ingredients together gently.

Spoon the mixture into the prepared tin and bake on the centre shelf of the preheated oven for 35 minutes, or until the top is firm and slightly crusty. Place the tin on a wire rack and leave to cool.

When completely cold, remove the cake from the tin and lightly dust the top with icing/confectioners' sugar. Cut into 15 blondies, using a sharp knife, and serve.

Difficulty Rating: 2 points

Apple & Cinnamon Crumble Bars

Makes 16 bars

Ingredients

450 g/1 lb apples (ideally Bramley cooking apples),
   roughly chopped
50 g/2 oz/¹⁄₃ cup raisins
50 g/2 oz/¹⁄₄ cup caster/superfine sugar
1 tsp ground cinnamon
zest of 1 lemon
200 g/7 oz/1³⁄₄ cups plain/all-purpose flour
250 g/9 oz/1¹⁄₄ cups demerara/turbinado sugar
¹⁄₂ tsp bicarbonate of soda/baking soda
150 g/5 oz/2 cups rolled oats
150 g/5 oz/²⁄₃ cup (1¹⁄₄ sticks) butter, melted
crème fraîche or whipped cream, to serve

Preheat the oven to 190°C/375°F/Gas Mark 5, 10 minutes before baking. Place the apples, raisins, sugar, cinnamon and lemon zest into a saucepan over a low heat. Cover and cook for about 15 minutes, stirring occasionally, until the apple is cooked through. Remove the cover and stir well with a wooden spoon to break up the apple completely. Cook for a further 15–30 minutes over a very low heat until reduced, thickened and slightly darkened. Leave to cool.

Lightly oil and line a 20.5 cm/8 inch square cake tin/pan with greaseproof/wax paper or baking parchment.

Mix together the flour, sugar, bicarbonate of soda/baking soda, oats and melted butter until well combined and crumbly. Spread half of the flour mixture into the bottom of the prepared tin and press down. Pour over the apple mixture. Sprinkle over the remaining flour mixture and press down lightly. Bake in the preheated oven for 30–35 minutes until golden brown.

Remove from the oven and leave to cool before cutting into slices. Serve the bars warm or cold with crème fraîche or whipped cream.

Difficulty Rating: 3 points

Lemon Bars

Makes 24 bars

Ingredients

175 g/6 oz/1¹⁄₂ cups plain/all-purpose flour

125 g/4 oz/¹⁄₂ cup (1 stick) butter

50 g/2 oz/¹⁄₄ cup caster/superfine sugar

2 tbsp plain/all-purpose flour

¹⁄₂ tsp baking powder

¹⁄₄ tsp salt

2 medium/large eggs, lightly beaten

juice and finely grated zest of 1 lemon

sifted icing/confectioners' sugar, to decorate

Preheat the oven to 170°C/325°F/Gas Mark 3, 10 minutes before baking. Lightly oil and line a 20.5 cm/8 inch square cake tin/pan with greaseproof/wax paper or baking parchment.

Rub together the flour and butter until the mixture resembles breadcrumbs. Stir in 4 tablespoons of the caster/superfine sugar and mix. Turn the mixture into the prepared tin and press down firmly. Bake in the preheated oven for 20 minutes until pale golden.

Meanwhile, in a food processor, mix together the remaining sugar, the flour, baking powder, salt, eggs, lemon juice and zest until smooth. Pour over the prepared base.

Transfer to the oven and bake for a further 20–25 minutes until nearly set but still a bit wobbly in the centre. Remove from the oven and cool in the tin/pan on a wire rack. Dust with icing/confectioners' sugar and cut into squares. Serve cold and store in an airtight container.

Difficulty Rating: 2 points

Lemon–iced Ginger Squares

Makes 12 squares

Ingredients

225 g/8 oz/1 heaping cup caster/superfine sugar

50 g/2 oz/4 tbsp butter, melted

2 tbsp black treacle/molasses

2 egg whites, lightly whisked

225 g/8 oz/2 cups plain/all-purpose flour

1 tsp bicarbonate of soda/baking soda

$^1/_2$ tsp ground cloves

1 tsp ground cinnamon

$^1/_4$ tsp ground ginger

pinch salt

250 ml/8 fl oz/1 cup buttermilk

175 g/6 oz/1$^1/_2$ cups icing/confectioners' sugar

lemon juice

Preheat the oven to 200°C/400°F/Gas Mark 6, 15 minutes before baking. Lightly oil a 20.5 cm/8 inch square cake tin/pan and sprinkle with a little flour.

Mix together the caster/superfine sugar, butter and treacle/molasses. Stir in the egg whites.

Mix together the flour, bicarbonate of soda/baking soda, cloves, cinnamon, ginger and salt. Stir the flour mixture and buttermilk alternately into the butter mixture until well blended. Spoon into the prepared tin and bake in the preheated oven for 35 minutes, or until a skewer inserted into the centre of the cake comes out clean. Remove from the oven and leave to cool for 5 minutes in the tin before turning out onto a wire rack over a large plate. Using a cocktail stick/toothpick, make holes on the top of the cake.

Mix together the icing/confectioners' sugar with enough lemon juice to make a smooth, pourable icing. Carefully pour the icing over the hot cake, then leave until cold. Cut the ginger cake into squares and serve.

Difficulty Rating: 3 points

Coconut Sorbet with Mango Sauce

Serves 4

Ingredients

2 sheets gelatine
250 g/9 oz/1⅓ cups caster/superfine sugar
600 ml/1 pint/2½ cups coconut milk
2 mangoes, peeled, pitted, sliced
2 tbsp icing/confectioners' sugar
zest and juice of 1 lime

Set the freezer to rapid freeze 2 hours before freezing the sorbet. Place the sheets of gelatine in a shallow dish, pour over cold water to cover and leave for 15 minutes. Squeeze out excess moisture before use.

Place the caster/superfine sugar and 300 ml/½ pint/1¼ cups of the coconut milk in a heavy–based saucepan and heat gently, stirring occasionally, until the sugar has dissolved. Remove from the heat.

Add the soaked gelatine to the saucepan. Stir gently until dissolved. Stir in the remaining coconut milk and leave until cold.

Pour the gelatine and coconut mixture into a freezable container and place in the freezer. Leave for at least 1 hour, or until the mixture has started to form ice crystals. Remove and beat with a spoon, then return to the freezer and continue to freeze until the mixture is frozen, beating at least twice more during this time.

Meanwhile, make the sauce. Place the sliced mango, icing/ confectioners' sugar and the lime zest and juice in a food processor and blend until smooth. Spoon into a small jug/pitcher.

Leave the sorbet to soften in the refrigerator for at least 30 minutes before serving. Serve scoops of sorbet on individual plates with a little of the mango sauce poured over. Remember to return the freezer to its normal setting.

Difficulty Rating: 3 points

Chocolate & Lemon Grass Mousse

Serves 4

Ingredients

3 lemon grass stalks, outer leaves removed

200 ml/7 fl oz/³⁄₄ cup milk

2 sheets gelatine

150 g/5 oz milk chocolate, broken into small pieces

2 egg yolks

50 g/2 oz/¹⁄₄ cup caster/superfine sugar

150 ml/¹⁄₄ pint/²⁄₃ cup double/heavy cream

juice of 2 lemons

1 tbsp caster/superfine sugar

lemon zest, to decorate

Use a wooden spoon to bruise the lemon grass, then cut in half. Pour the milk into a large, heavy-based saucepan, add the lemon grass and bring to the boil. Remove from the heat, leave to infuse for 1 hour, then strain. Place the gelatine in a shallow dish, pour over cold water to cover and leave for 15 minutes. Squeeze out excess moisture before use.

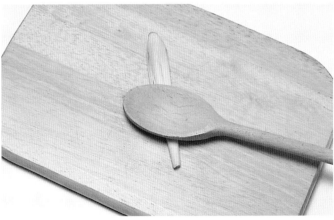

Place the chocolate in a small bowl set over a saucepan of gently simmering water and leave until melted. Make sure the water does not touch the bowl. Whisk the egg yolks and sugar together until thick, then whisk in the flavoured milk. Pour into a clean saucepan and cook gently, stirring continuously, until the mixture starts to thicken. Remove from the heat, stir in the melted chocolate and gelatine and leave to cool for a few minutes. Whip the double/heavy cream until soft peaks form, then stir into the cooled milk mixture to form a mousse. Spoon into individual ramekins or moulds and leave in the refrigerator for 2 hours or until set.

Just before serving, pour the lemon juice into a small saucepan, bring to the boil, then simmer for 3 minutes or until reduced. Add the sugar and heat until dissolved, stirring continuously. Serve the mousse drizzled with the lemon sauce and decorated with lemon zest.

Difficulty Rating: 3 points

Grape & Almond Layer

Serves 4

Ingredients

300 ml/½ pint/1¼ cups fromage frais/reduced-fat sour cream

300 ml/½ pint/1¼ cups Greek yogurt

3 tbsp icing/confectioners' sugar, sifted

2 tbsp crème de cassis

450 g/1 lb/3 cups red grapes

175 g/6 oz (about 30) amaretti biscuits/cookies

2 ripe passion fruit

To decorate:

extra grapes (optional)

icing/confectioners' sugar

Mix together the fromage frais/reduced-fat sour cream and yogurt in a bowl. Lightly fold in the sifted icing/confectioners' sugar and crème de cassis with a large metal spoon or rubber spatula until lightly blended.

Using a small knife, remove the seeds from the grapes, if necessary. Rinse lightly and pat dry on absorbent paper towels. Place the deseeded grapes in a bowl and stir in any juice from the grapes from deseeding.

Place the amaretti biscuits/cookies in a plastic bag and crush roughly with a rolling pin, or use a food processor.

Cut the passion fruit in half, scoop out the seeds with a teaspoon and reserve.

Divide the yogurt mixture between four tall glasses, then layer alternately with grapes, crushed biscuits and most of the passion fruit seeds. Top with the yogurt mixture and the remaining passion fruit seeds. Chill for 1 hour and decorate with extra grapes. Lightly dust with icing sugar and serve.

Difficulty Rating: 2 points

Caramelized Oranges in an Iced Bowl

Serves 4

Ingredients

For the iced bowl:

about 36 ice cubes

fresh flowers and fruits

For the caramelized oranges:

8 oranges

225 g/8 oz/1 cup sugar

4 tbsp Grand Marnier or Cointreau

Set the freezer to rapid freeze. Place a few ice cubes in the base of a 1.7 litre/3 pint/1¾ quart freezable glass bowl. Place a 900 ml /1½ pint/1 quart glass bowl on top of the ice cubes. Arrange the flower heads and fruits in between the two bowls, wedging in position with the ice cubes. Weigh down the smaller bowl with some heavy weights, then pour cold water between the two bowls, covering the flowers and the fruit. Freeze for 6 hours.

Remove the weights and using a hot, damp cloth rub the inside of the smaller bowl with the cloth until it loosens sufficiently for you to remove the bowl. Place the larger bowl in the sink or washing-up bowl, half filled with very hot water. Leave for about 30 seconds or until the ice loosens. Take care not to leave the bowl in the water for too long or the ice will melt. Remove the bowl and leave in the refrigerator. Return the freezer to its normal setting.

Thinly pare the rind from 2 oranges and then cut into julienne strips. Using a sharp knife, cut away the rind and pith from all the oranges. Slice the oranges and reform each orange back to its original shape. Secure with cocktail sticks/toothpicks.

Heat 300 ml/½ pint/1¼ cups water with the orange rind and sugar in a pan. Dissolved the sugar and bring to the boil. Boil for 15 minutes until a caramel colour and remove from the heat. Stir in the liqueur and pour over the oranges. Leave to cool. Chill for 3 hours, turning the oranges occasionally. Serve in the ice bowl.

Difficulty Rating: 3 points

Maple Pears with Pistachios & Simple Chocolate Sauce

Serves 4

Ingredients

25 g/1 oz/2 tbsp unsalted butter

50 g/2 oz/¹/₂ cup unsalted pistachios

4 medium-ripe firm pears, peeled, quartered and cored

2 tsp lemon juice

pinch of ground ginger (optional)

6 tbsp maple syrup

For the chocolate sauce:

150 ml/¹/₄ pint/²/₃ cup double/heavy cream

2 tbsp milk

¹/₂ tsp vanilla extract

150 g/5 oz dark/semisweet chocolate, broken into squares and roughly chopped

Melt the butter in a wok over a medium heat until sizzling. Reduce the heat a little, add the pistachios and stir–fry for 30 seconds.

Add the pears to the wok and continue cooking for about 2 minutes, turning frequently and carefully, until the nuts are beginning to brown and the pears are tender.

Add the lemon juice, ground ginger if using, and maple syrup. Cook for 3–4 minutes until the syrup has reduced slightly. Spoon the pears and the syrup into a serving dish and leave to cool for 1–2 minutes while making the chocolate sauce.

Pour the cream and milk into the wok. Add the vanilla extract and heat just to boiling point. Remove the wok from the heat.

Add the chocolate to the wok and leave for 1 minute to melt, then stir until the chocolate is evenly mixed with the cream. Pour into a jug/pitcher and serve while still warm, with the pears.

Difficulty Rating: 2 points

Hot Cherry Fritters

Serves 4

Ingredients

50 g/2 oz/4 tbsp butter

pinch salt

2 tbsp caster/superfine sugar

100 g/3½ oz/¾ cup sifted plain/all-purpose flour

¼ tsp ground cinnamon

25 g/1 oz/¼ cup ground almonds

3 medium/large eggs, lightly beaten

175 g/6 oz cherries, stoned

sunflower/corn oil for frying

2 tbsp icing/confectioners' sugar

1 tsp cocoa powder (unsweetened)

fresh mint sprigs, to decorate

Place the butter, salt and sugar in a small saucepan with 250 ml/8 fl oz/1 cup water. Heat gently until the butter has melted, then add the flour and ground cinnamon and beat over a low heat until the mixture leaves the sides of the pan.

Remove the saucepan from the heat and beat in the ground almonds. Gradually add the eggs, beating well after each addition. Finally stir in the cherries.

Pour 5 cm/2 inches depth of oil in a wok and heat until it reaches 180°C/350°F on a sugar thermometer. Drop in heaping teaspoons of the mixture, cooking 4 or 5 at a time for about 2 minutes, or until lightly browned and crisp. Remove the fritters from the pan with a slotted spoon and drain on paper towels. Keep warm in a low oven while cooking the remaining fritters. Arrange on a warmed serving plate, dust with the icing/confectioners' sugar and cocoa powder. Decorate with mint and serve hot.

Difficulty Rating: 3 points

Easy Danish Pastries

Makes 16

Ingredients

500 g/1 lb 2 oz/3²/₃ cups strong white/bread flour

¹/₂ tsp salt

350 g/12 oz/1¹/₂ cups (3 sticks) butter

7 g sachet/1¹/₂ tsp fast-action yeast

50 g/2 oz/¹/₄ cup caster/superfine sugar

150 ml/¹/₄ pint/²/₃ cup lukewarm milk

2 medium/large eggs, beaten

For the filling and topping:

225 g/8 oz almond paste, grated

8 canned apricot halves, drained

1 medium/large egg, beaten

125 g/4 oz/1 cup fondant icing/confectioners' sugar

50 g/2 oz/¹/₄ cup glacé cherries

50 g/2 oz/¹/₂ cup flaked/slivered almonds

Sift the flour and salt into a bowl, add 50 g/2 oz/4 tablespoons of the butter and rub in until the mixture resembles fine crumbs, then stir in the yeast and sugar. Stir in the milk and beaten eggs and mix to a soft dough. Knead by hand for 10 minutes until smooth or place in a tabletop mixer fitted with a dough hook and knead for 5 minutes. Cover with oiled plastic wrap and leave for about 1 hour in a warm place or until doubled in size. Place the dough on a floured surface and knead to knock out the air for about 4 minutes until smooth. Roll out into a rectangle 20 x 35 cm/8 x 14 inches. Dot two thirds of the dough with half the remaining butter, leaving one third plain. Fold the plain third up over the buttered section, then fold the top third over this to form a square parcel. Press the edges to seal, then turn the dough, with the fold to the left. Roll out again to a rectangle and dot with the remaining butter as before. Chill for 15 minutes, then roll out and fold again. Roll, fold and chill once more.

Preheat the oven to 220°C/425°F/Gas Mark 7. Roll out the dough into a 55 cm/22 inch square and cut into 16 squares. Put 25 g/1 oz of the grated almond paste in the centre of each. Take eight of the squares and cut the corners almost to the middle and fold over the alternate points. Top each of the remaining squares with an apricot half and fold the opposite corners over to cover the apricots.

Arrange all the pastries on buttered baking sheets and leave to rise for 20 minutes until puffy. Brush with beaten egg and bake for 15 minutes until golden. When cold, mix the fondant icing sugar with enough water to make a smooth icing. Drizzle over the pastries and place a halved cherry on the windmill shapes. Scatter the apricot–filled pastries with flaked/slivered almonds and leave to set for 30 minutes.

Difficulty Rating: 4 points

Raspberry Sorbet Crush

Serves 4

Ingredients

225 g/8 oz/2 cups raspberries, thawed if frozen
grated rind and juice of 1 lime
300 ml/½ pint/1¼ cups orange juice
225 g/8 oz/1 cup sugar
2 medium/large egg whites

Set the freezer to rapid freeze. If using fresh raspberries pick over and lightly rinse. Place the raspberries in a dish and, using a masher, mash to a chunky purée. Place the lime rind and juice, orange juice and half the sugar in a large, heavy-based saucepan.

Heat gently, stirring frequently until the sugar is dissolved. Bring to the boil and boil rapidly for about 5 minutes.

Remove the pan from the heat and pour carefully into a freezable container. Leave to cool, then place in the freezer and freeze for 2 hours, stirring occasionally to break up the ice crystals. Fold the ice mixture into the raspberry purée with a metal spoon and freeze for a further 2 hours, stirring occasionally.

Whisk the egg whites until stiff. Then gradually whisk in the remaining sugar a tablespoonful at a time until the egg white mixture is stiff and glossy.

Fold into the raspberry sorbet with a metal spoon and freeze for 1 hour. Spoon into tall glasses and serve immediately. Remember to return the freezer to its normal setting.

Difficulty Rating: 3 points

Coffee & Peach Creams

Serves 4

Ingredients

4 peaches
50 g/2 oz/¼ cup caster/superfine sugar
2 tbsp coffee extract
200 g/7 oz/¾ cup carton half-fat Greek set yogurt
300 g/11 oz/1¼ cup carton half-fat ready-made custard

To decorate:
peach slices
fresh mint sprigs
low-fat crème fraîche

Cut the peaches in half and remove the stones. Place the peaches in a large bowl, cover with boiling water and leave for 2–3 minutes.

Drain the peaches, then carefully remove the skin. Using a sharp knife, halve the peaches.

Place the caster/superfine sugar in a saucepan and add 50 ml/2 fl oz/¼ cup water. Bring the sugar mixture to the boil, stirring occasionally, until the sugar has dissolved. Boil rapidly for about 2 minutes.

Add the peaches and coffee extract to the pan. Remove from the heat and leave the peach mixture to cool.

Meanwhile, mix together the Greek yogurt and custard until well combined. Divide the peaches between the four glass dishes. Spoon over the custard mixture then top with remaining peach mixture.

Chill for 30 minutes and then serve, decorated with peach slices, mint sprigs and a little crème fraîche.

Difficulty Rating: 2 points

Summer Pavlova

Serves 6–8

Ingredients

4 egg whites
225 g/8 oz/1 cup caster/superfine sugar
1 tsp vanilla extract
2 tsp white wine vinegar
1½ tsp cornflour/cornstarch
300 ml/½ pint/1¼ cup Greek yogurt
2 tbsp honey
225 g/8 oz/2 cups fresh hulled strawberries
125 g/4½ oz/1 cup fresh raspberries
125 g/4½ oz/1 cup fresh blueberries
4 kiwis, peeled and sliced
icing/confectioners' sugar, to decorate

Preheat the oven to 150°C/300°F/Gas Mark 2. Line a baking tray with a sheet of greaseproof/wax paper or baking parchment.

Place the egg whites in a clean, grease-free bowl and whisk until very stiff. Whisk in half the sugar, vanilla extract, vinegar and cornflour/cornstarch and continue whisking until stiff. Gradually whisk in the remaining sugar, a teaspoonful at a time, until the mixture is very stiff and glossy. Using a large spoon, arrange the meringue in a circle on the greaseproof paper or baking parchment.

Bake in the preheated oven for 1 hour until crisp and dry. Turn the oven off and leave the meringue in the oven to cool completely. Remove the meringue from the baking sheet and peel away the paper. Mix together the yogurt and honey. Place the pavlova on a serving plate and spoon the yogurt into the centre.

Sprinkle with the strawberries, raspberries, blueberries and kiwis. Dust with the icing/confectioners' sugar and serve.

Difficulty Rating: 3 points

Autumn Fruit Layer

Serves 4

Ingredients

450 g/1 lb Bramley/tart cooking apples
225 g/8 oz/2 cups blackberries
50 g/2 oz/¼ cup soft brown sugar
juice of 1 lemon
50 g/2 oz/¼ cup low-fat spread
200 g/7 oz1¾ cups breadcrumbs
225 g/8 oz/2 cups chopped honey-coated nut mix
redcurrants and fresh mint leaves, to decorate
half/reduced-fat whipped cream or reduced-fat ice cream, to serve

Peel, core and slice the cooking apples and place in a saucepan with the blackberries, sugar and lemon juice.

Cover the fruit mixture and simmer, stirring occasionally for about 15 minutes, or until the apples and blackberries have formed into a thick purée. Remove the pan from the heat and leave to cool.

Melt the low–fat spread in a frying pan and cook the breadcrumbs for 5–10 minutes, stirring occasionally until golden and crisp. Remove the pan from the heat and stir in the nuts. Leave to cool. Alternately layer the fruit purée and breadcrumbs into four tall glasses.

Store the desserts in the refrigerator to chill and remove when ready to serve.

Decorate with redcurrants and mint leaves and serve with half–fat whipped cream or a reduced–fat vanilla or raspberry ice cream.

Difficulty Rating: 2 points

Chocolate Brandy Dream

Serves 4

Ingredients

175 g/6 oz low-fat chocolate, broken into pieces

300 ml/½ pint/1 cup whipping cream

2 tbsp brandy

1 tbsp coffee extract

1 medium/large egg white

To decorate:

fresh raspberries

fresh blueberries

fresh mint leaves

cocoa powder (unsweetened)

Place the pieces of chocolate into a heatproof bowl placed over a saucepan of gently simmering water and leave to slowly melt, stirring occasionally. Carefully remove the pan and the bowl from the heat and leave cool.

Pour the cream into a small bowl, whip until soft peaks form, then reserve.

Gently stir the brandy and coffee extract into the chocolate. Mix together gently until blended, then fold in the whipped cream with a metal spoon or rubber spatula.

Briskly whisk the egg white in a small bowl until stiff, then fold into the chocolate mixture with a metal spoon or rubber spatula.

Mix the chocolate mixture gently, taking care not to remove the air already whisked into the egg white.

Spoon into four tall glasses and chill for at least 2 hours. Decorate with raspberries, blueberries and mint leaves. Dust with cocoa powder and serve.

Difficulty Rating: 3 points

Sweet-stewed Dried Fruits

Serves 4

Ingredients

500 g/1 lb 2 oz packet mixed dried fruit salad
450 ml/³⁄₄ pint/1³⁄₄ cups apple juice
2 tbsp clear honey
2 tbsp brandy
1 lemon
1 orange

To decorate:
half-fat crème fraîche/sour cream
fine strips of pared orange rind

Place the fruits, apple juice, honey and brandy into a small saucepan.

Using a small, sharp knife or a zester, carefully remove the zest from the lemon and orange and place in the pan.

Squeeze the juice from the lemon and orange and add to the pan. Bring the fruit mixture to the boil and simmer for about 1 minute. Remove the pan from the heat and leave the mixture to cool completely.

Transfer the mixture to a large bowl, cover with plastic wrap and chill in the refrigerator overnight to allow the flavours to blend.

Spoon the stewed fruit into four shallow dessert dishes. Decorate with a large spoonful of half-fat crème fraîche/sour cream and a few strips of the pared orange rind and serve.

Difficulty Rating: 2 points

Fruity Roulade

Serves 4

Ingredients

3 medium/large eggs
75 g/3 oz/¹⁄₃ cup caster/superfine sugar, plus 1–2 tbsp, for sprinkling
75 g/3 oz/²⁄₃ cup sifted plain/all-purpose flour

For the filling:
125 g/4 oz/¹⁄₂ cup Quark
125 g/4 oz/¹⁄₂ cup low-fat Greek yogurt
2 tbsp caster/superfine sugar
1 tbsp orange liqueur (optional)
grated zest of 1 orange
125 g/4 oz/1 cup fresh strawberries, hulled, cut into quarters

To decorate:
fresh strawberries
sifted icing/confectioners' sugar

Preheat the oven to 220°C/425°F/Gas Mark 7. Lightly oil and line a 33 x 23 cm/13 x 9 inch Swiss roll tin/jelly-roll pan with greaseproof/wax paper or baking parchment. Using an electric whisk, whisk the eggs and the 75 g/3 oz/¹⁄₃ cup caster/superfine sugar until the mixture has doubled in volume and leaves a trail across the top. Fold in the flour with a metal spoon or rubber spatula. Pour into the prepared tin and bake in the preheated oven for 10–12 minutes until well risen and golden.

Place a sheet of greaseproof/wax paper or baking parchment out on a flat work surface and sprinkle evenly with caster sugar. Turn the cooked sponge out onto the paper, discard the paper, trim the sponge and roll up, encasing the paper inside. Reserve until cool.

To make the filling, mix together the Quark, yogurt, caster sugar, liqueur, if using, and orange zest. Unroll the roulade and spread the mixture over the sponge. Scatter over the strawberries and roll up. Decorate the roulade with the strawberries. Dust with the icing/confectioners' sugar and serve.

Difficulty Rating: 3 points

Fruit Salad

Serves 4

Ingredients

125 g/4½ oz/⅔ cup caster/superfine sugar

3 oranges

700 g/1½ lb lychees, peeled and stoned

1 small mango

1 small pineapple

1 papaya

4 pieces stem preserved ginger in syrup

4 tbsp stem preserved ginger syrup

125 g/4½ oz/¾ cup Cape gooseberries/ground cherries

125 g/4½ oz/1 cup fresh hulled strawberries

½ tsp almond extract

To decorate:

fresh mint leaves; lime zest

Place the sugar and 300 ml/½ pint/1¼ cups water in a small pan and heat, stirring gently, until the sugar has dissolved. Bring to the boil and simmer for 2 minutes. Once a syrup has formed, remove from the heat and leave to cool.

Using a sharp knife, cut away the skin from the oranges, then slice thickly. Cut each slice in half and place in a serving dish with the syrup and lychees. Peel the mango, then cut into thick slices around each side of the stone. Discard the stone, cut the slices into bite-sized pieces and add to the syrup. Using a sharp knife again, carefully cut away the skin from the pineapple. Remove the central core using the knife or an apple corer, then cut the pineapple into segments and add to the syrup.

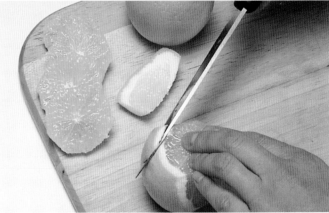

Peel the papaya, then cut in half and remove the seeds. Cut the flesh into chunks, slice the ginger into matchsticks and add with the ginger syrup to the fruit in the syrup. Prepare the Cape gooseberries/ground cherries by removing the thin, papery skins and rinsing lightly. Halve the strawberries, add to the fruit with the almond extract and chill for 30 minutes. Scatter with fresh mint leaves and lime zest to decorate and serve.

Difficulty Rating: 3 points

Orange Freeze

Serves 4

Ingredients

4 large oranges
about 300 ml/¹/₂ pint/1¹/₄ cups vanilla ice cream
225 g/8 oz/2 cups raspberries
75 g/3 oz/²/₃ cups sifted icing/confectioners' sugar
redcurrant sprigs, to decorate

Set the freezer to rapid freeze. Using a sharp knife, carefully cut the top off each orange. Scoop out the flesh from the orange, discarding any pips and thick pith. Place the shells and lids in the freezer and chop any remaining orange flesh.

Whisk together the orange juice, orange flesh and vanilla ice cream until well blended. Cover and freeze for about 2 hours, occasionally breaking up the ice crystals with a fork or a whisk. Stir the mixture from around the edge of the container into the centre, then level and return to the freezer. Do this two or three times then leave until almost frozen solid.

Place a large scoop of the ice cream mixture into the frozen shells. Add another scoop on top, so that there is plenty outside of the orange shell, and return to the freezer for 1 hour. Arrange the lids on top and freeze for a further 2 hours, until the filled orange shell is completely frozen solid.

Using a nylon sieve, press the raspberries into a bowl using the back of a wooden spoon and mix together with the icing/confectioners' sugar. Spoon the raspberry coulis on to four serving plates and place an orange at the centre of each. Dust with icing/confectioners' sugar, and serve decorated with the redcurrants. Remember to return the freezer to its normal setting.

Difficulty Rating: 4 points

Chocolate Mousse

Serves 6

Ingredients

175 g/6 oz milk or dark/semisweet chocolate
535 g carton/1 lb can ready-made custard
450 ml/³/₄ pint/2 cups double/heavy cream
12 Cape gooseberries/ground cherries, to decorate
sweet biscuits/cookies, to serve

Break the chocolate into segments and place in a bowl set over a saucepan of simmering water. Leave until melted, stirring occasionally. Remove the bowl in the pan from the heat and leave the melted chocolate to cool slightly.

Place the custard in a bowl and fold the melted chocolate into it using a metal spoon or rubber spatula. Stir well until completely combined.

Pour the cream into a small bowl and whip until the cream forms soft peaks. Using a metal spoon or rubber spatula, fold most of the whipped cream into the chocolate mixture.

Spoon into six tall glasses and carefully top with the remaining cream. Leave the desserts to chill in the refrigerator for at least 1 hour, or preferably overnight.

Peel back the skins from the gooseberries to form petal shapes and use to decorate the chocolate desserts. Serve with sweet biscuits/cookies.

Difficulty Rating: 2 points

Fat-free Sponge

Serves 8

Ingredients

175 g/6 oz/³/₄ cup caster/superfine sugar, plus extra for dusting
125 g/4 oz/1 cup self-raising flour, plus extra for dusting
3 medium/large eggs

To decorate:
150 ml/¹/₄ pint/²/₃ cup low-fat whipping cream, or low-fat crème fraîche or yogurt
2 tbsp lemon curd
125 g/4 oz/1 cup blueberries
zest of 1 lemon, cut into long thin strips

Preheat the oven to 190°C/375°F/Gas Mark 5. Grease two nonstick 18 cm/7 inch sandwich tins/layer-pans, line with baking parchment, then dust with a mixture of flour and caster/superfine sugar.

Put the eggs and sugar in a large bowl and stand this over a pan of hot water. Whisk the eggs and sugar until doubled in volume and the mixture is thick enough to leave a trail on the surface of the batter when the whisk is lifted away.

Remove the bowl from the heat and continue whisking for a further 5 minutes until the mixture is cool. Sift half the flour over the mixture and fold in very lightly, using a large metal spoon. Sift in the remaining flour and fold in the same way.

Pour the mixture into the prepared tins and tilt them to spread the mixture evenly. Bake for 15–20 minutes until risen and firm and the cakes are beginning to shrink away from the sides of the tins. Leave to stand for 2 minutes, then turn out to cool on a wire rack.

To decorate, whip the cream, if using, and spread half the cream (or crème fraîche or yogurt) over one cake. Swirl 1 tablespoon lemon curd into the cream, crème fraîche or yogurt and scatter over half the blueberries. Place the other cake on top and swirl over the remaining cream/yogurt. Swirl over 1 tablespoon lemon curd and sprinkle with the remaining berries. Scatter the strips of lemon zest over the top.

Difficulty Rating: 3 points

Special, Exotic & Creamy Concoctions

From classics such as Sachertorte and Supreme Chocolate Gateau to new, exciting ideas such as Rose-water Doughballs with Yogurt Sauce and Italian Polenta Cake with Mascarpone Cream, this chapter is filled with dessert ideas for fancier occasions. A Bomba Siciliana or Chocolate Raspberry Mille Feuille will help make your dinner party a hit, while the Hazelnut, Chocolate & Chestnut Meringue Torte or Chocolate Roulade will make you a certain favourite if it is your turn to provide the dessert at a family get-together. The large number of recipes, including classic cakes and gateaux as well as mousses, ice creams and brûlées, means you certainly don't have far to look to find a delicious recipe that will impress your family and friends.

Rose-water Doughballs with Yogurt Sauce

Makes 30

Ingredients

300 g/11 oz/2³⁄₄ cups self-raising flour, sifted
50 g/2 oz/¹⁄₂ cup ground almonds
75 g/3 oz/6 tbsp butter, cubed
75 ml/3 fl oz/5 tbsp natural/plain yogurt
2 tsp rose water
grated zest of 1 orange
600 ml/1 pint/2¹⁄₂ cups vegetable oil
65 g/2¹⁄₂ oz/¹⁄₂ cup caster/superfine sugar
lime zest, to decorate

For the yogurt sauce:
200 ml/7 fl oz/³⁄₄ cup natural/plain yogurt
2 tsp rose water
grated zest of 1 lime
1 tbsp sifted icing/confectioners' sugar

To make the yogurt sauce, blend the yogurt with the rose water, lime zest and sugar in a small bowl. Pour into a serving jug/pitcher, cover with plastic wrap and refrigerate until ready to serve.

Place the flour and ground almonds in a large bowl and, using your fingertips, rub in the butter until the mixture resembles fine breadcrumbs.

Add the yogurt, rose water and orange zest to the crumbed mixture, pour in 50 ml/2 fl oz/¹⁄₄ cup warm water and mix with a knife to form a soft pliable dough. Turn on to a lightly floured board and knead for 2 minutes or until smooth, then divide the dough into 30 small balls.

Heat the vegetable oil in a large wok or deep-fat fryer to 190˚C/375˚F, or until a bread cube dropped into the oil sizzles and turns golden brown. Working in batches of a few at a time, deep-fry the dough balls for 5–6 minutes until golden brown. Using a slotted spoon, remove the balls from the oil and drain on paper towels.

Pour the caster/superfine sugar on a plate and roll all the dough balls in the sugar until well coated. Decorate with a little lime zest and serve immediately with the yogurt sauce.

Difficulty Rating: 3 points

Coconut Rice Served with Stewed Ginger Fruits

Serves 6–8

Ingredients

1 vanilla pod/bean

450 ml/³/₄ pint/2 cups coconut milk

1.1 litres/2 pints/1¹/₄ quarts
   semi-skimmed/low-fat milk

600 ml/1 pint/2¹/₂ cups double/heavy cream

100 g/4 oz/¹/₂ cup caster/superfine sugar

2 star anise

8 tbsp toasted desiccated/shredded coconut

250 g/9 oz/1¹/₂ cups short-grain pudding rice

a knob butter, melted

2 mandarin oranges, peeled, pith removed

1 carambola or star fruit, sliced

50 g/2 oz/¹/₃ cup finely diced stem preserved ginger

300 ml/¹/₂ pint/1¹/₄ cups sweet white wine

caster/superfine sugar, to taste

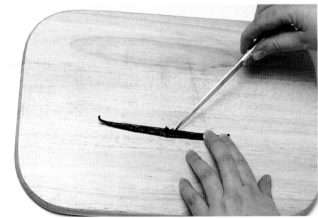

Preheat the oven to 160°C/325°F/Gas Mark 3. With a sharp knife split the vanilla pod/bean in half, scrape out the seeds. Place the pod and seeds in a large, heavy-based casserole dish. Pour in the coconut milk, the semi-skimmed/low-fat milk and the double/heavy cream. Stir in the sugar, star anise and 4 tablespoons of the toasted coconut. Bring to the boil. Simmer for 10 minutes, stirring occasionally. Remove the vanilla pod and star anise.

Wash the rice and add to the milk. Simmer gently for 25–30 minutes until the rice is tender, stirring frequently. Stir in the melted butter. Divide the mandarins into segments. Place in a saucepan with the sliced carambola or star fruit and stem preserved ginger. Pour in the white wine and 300 ml/¹/₂ pint/1¹/₄ cups water. Bring to the boil. Reduce the heat and simmer for 20 minutes, or until the liquid has reduced and the fruits softened. Add sugar to taste. Serve the rice, topped with the stewed fruits and the remaining toasted coconut.

Difficulty Rating: 3 points

Stir-fried Bananas & Peaches with Rum Butterscotch Sauce

Serves 4

Ingredients

2 medium-firm bananas, peeled, cut into 2.5 cm/1 inch
  diagonal slices
1 tbsp caster/superfine sugar
2 tsp lime juice
4 firm, ripe peaches or nectarines
1 tbsp sunflower/corn oil

For the sauce:
50 g/2 oz/4 tbsp unsalted butter
50 g/2 oz/$\frac{1}{4}$ cup soft light brown sugar
125 g/4$\frac{1}{2}$ oz/$\frac{2}{3}$ cup demerara/light brown sugar
300 ml/$\frac{1}{2}$ pint/1$\frac{1}{4}$ cups double/heavy cream
2 tbsp dark rum

Place the bananas in a bowl, sprinkle with the caster/superfine sugar and lime juice and stir until lightly coated. Reserve.

Place the peaches or nectarines in a large bowl and pour over boiling water to cover. Leave for 30 seconds, then plunge them into cold water and peel off their skins. Cut each one into eight thick slices, discarding the stone.

Heat a wok, add the oil and swirl it round the wok to coat the sides. Add the fruit and cook for 3–4 minutes, shaking the wok and gently turning the fruit until lightly browned. Spoon the fruit into a warmed serving bowl and clean the wok with paper towels.

Add the butter and sugars to the wok and stir continuously over a very low heat until the sugar has dissolved. Remove from the heat and leave to cool for 2–3 minutes.

Stir the cream and rum into the sugar syrup and return to the heat. Bring to the boil and simmer for 2 minutes, stirring continuously until smooth. Leave for 2–3 minutes to cool slightly, then serve warm with the stir-fried peaches and bananas.

Difficulty Rating: 2 points

Spicy White Chocolate Mousse

Serves 4–6

Ingredients

6 cardamom pods
125 ml/4 fl oz/½ cup milk
3 bay leaves
200 g/7 oz white chocolate
300 ml/½ pint/1¼ cups double/heavy cream
3 medium/large egg whites
1–2 tsp cocoa powder (unsweetened), sifted, for dusting

Tap the cardamom pods lightly so they split. Remove the seeds, then crush lightly in a pestle and mortar. Pour the milk into a small saucepan and add the crushed seeds and the bay leaves. Bring to the boil gently over a medium heat. Remove from the heat, cover and leave in a warm place for at least 30 minutes to infuse.

Break the chocolate into small pieces and place in a heatproof bowl set over a saucepan of gently simmering water. Ensure the water is not touching the base of the bowl. When the chocolate has melted, remove the bowl from the heat and stir until smooth.

Whip the cream until it has slightly thickened and holds its shape but does not form peaks. Reserve.

Whisk the egg whites in a clean, grease-free bowl until stiff and standing in soft peaks.

Strain the milk through a sieve into the cooled, melted chocolate and beat until smooth. Spoon the chocolate mixture into the egg whites, then, using a large metal spoon, fold gently. Add the whipped cream and fold in gently.

Spoon into a large serving dish or individual small cups. Chill in the refrigerator for 3–4 hours. Just before serving, dust with a little sifted cocoa powder.

Difficulty Rating: 3 points

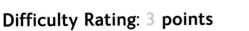

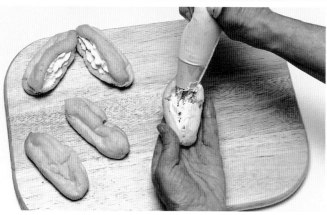

White Chocolate Eclairs

Serves 4–6

Ingredients

50 g/2 oz/4 tbsp unsalted butter
65 g/2¹/₂ oz/¹/₂ cup plain/all-purpose flour, sifted
2 medium/large eggs, lightly beaten
6 ripe passion fruit
300 ml/¹/₂ pint/1¹/₄ cups double/heavy cream
3 tbsp kirsch
1 tbsp icing/confectioners' sugar
125 g/4 oz white chocolate, broken into pieces

Preheat the oven to 190°C/375°F/Gas Mark 5, 10 minutes before baking. Lightly oil a baking sheet. Place the butter and 150 ml/¹/₄ pint/²/₃ cup water in a saucepan and heat until the butter has melted, then bring to the boil. Remove the saucepan from the heat and immediately add the flour all at once, beating with a wooden spoon until the mixture forms a ball in the centre of the saucepan. Leave to cool for 3 minutes. Add the eggs a little at a time, beating well after each addition, until the paste is smooth, shiny and of a piping consistency. Spoon the mixture into a decorating bag fitted with a plain tip. Sprinkle the oiled baking sheet with water. Pipe the mixture onto the baking sheet in 7.5 cm/3 inch lengths, using a knife to cut each pastry length neatly. Bake in the preheated oven for 18–20 minutes until well risen and golden. Make a slit along the side of each eclair to let the steam escape. Return the eclairs to the oven for a further 2 minutes to dry out. Transfer to a wire rack and leave to cool.

Halve the passion fruit and, using a small spoon, scoop the pulp of four of the fruits into a bowl. Add the cream, kirsch and icing/confectioners' sugar and whip until the cream holds its shape. Carefully spoon or pipe into the eclairs.

Melt the chocolate in a small heatproof bowl set over a saucepan of simmering water and stir until smooth. Leave the chocolate to cool slightly, then spread over the tops of the eclairs. Scoop the seeds and pulp out of the remaining passion fruit. Sieve. Use the juice to drizzle around the eclairs when serving.

Difficulty Rating: 3 points

Chocolate Rice Pudding Brûlée

Serves 6

Ingredients

2 tbsp cocoa powder (unsweetened)

75 g/3 oz/$\frac{1}{3}$ cup short-grain rice

600 ml/1 pint/2$\frac{1}{2}$ cups milk

1 bay leaf

grated zest of 1 orange

50 g/2 oz white chocolate, roughly chopped

1 tbsp golden caster/unrefined superfine sugar

4 medium/large egg yolks

250 ml/8 fl oz/1 cup double/heavy cream

$\frac{1}{2}$ tsp vanilla extract

4 tbsp demerara/turbinado sugar

Preheat the oven to 150˚C/300˚F/Gas Mark 2, 10 minutes before baking. Preheat the grill/broiler on high when ready to use. Gradually blend the cocoa powder with 3 tablespoons boiling water to form a soft, smooth paste. Place the rice and milk, bay leaf, orange zest and the cocoa powder paste in a saucepan. Bring to the boil, stirring constantly. Reduce the heat and simmer for 20 minutes, or until the rice is tender. Remove from the heat and discard the bay leaf, then add the white chocolate and stir until melted.

Whisk together the caster/superfine sugar and egg yolks until thick, then stir in the cream. Stir in the rice mixture together with the vanilla extract. Pour into a buttered shallow dish. Stand the dish in a baking tin/pan with sufficient hot water to come halfway up the sides of the dish. Cook in the preheated oven for 1$\frac{1}{2}$ hours, or until set. Stir occasionally during cooking, either removing the skin from the top or stirring the skin into the pudding. Remove from the tin and leave until cool.

Sprinkle the demerara/turbinado sugar over the surface of the pudding. Place under the preheated grill and cook until the sugar melts and caramelizes, turning the dish occasionally. Serve immediately or chill in the refrigerator for 1 hour before serving.

Difficulty Rating: 3 points

Chocolaty Puffs

Makes 12 large puffs

Ingredients

For the choux pastry:
150 g/5 oz/1¼ cups plain/all-purpose flour
2 tbsp cocoa powder (unsweetened)
½ tsp salt
1 tbsp sugar
125 g/4 oz/½ cup (1 stick) butter, cut into pieces
5 large/extra-large eggs

For the chocolate cream filling:
225 g/8 oz dark/semisweet chocolate, chopped
600 ml/1 pint/2 cups double/heavy cream
1 tbsp caster/superfine sugar (optional)
2 tbsp crème de cacao (optional)

For the chocolate sauce:
225 g/8 oz dark/semisweet chocolate
300 ml/½ pint/1 cup whipping/heavy cream
50 g/2 oz/4 tbsp butter, diced
1–2 tbsp golden/light corn syrup
1 tsp vanilla extract

Preheat the oven to 220°C/425°F/Gas Mark 7, 15 minutes before baking. Lightly oil a large baking sheet. To make the choux pastry, sift the flour and cocoa powder together. Place 250 ml/8 fl oz/1 cup water, the salt, sugar and butter in a saucepan and bring to the boil. Remove from the heat and add the flour mixture all at once, beating vigorously with a wooden spoon until the mixture forms a ball in the centre of the saucepan. Return to the heat and cook for 1 minute stirring, then cool slightly.

Using an electric mixer, beat in 4 of the eggs, 1 at a time, beating well after each addition. Beat the last egg and add a little at a time until the dough is thick and shiny and just falls from a spoon when tapped lightly on the side of the saucepan.

Pipe or spoon 12 large puffs onto the prepared baking sheet, leaving space between them. Cook in the preheated oven for 30–35 minutes until puffy and golden.

Remove from the oven, slice off the top third of each bun and return to the oven for 5 minutes to dry out. Remove and leave to cool.

For the filling, heat the chocolate with 125 ml/4 fl oz/½ cup of the double/heavy cream and 1 tablespoon of caster/superfine sugar, if using, stirring until smooth, then leave to cool. Whip the remaining cream until soft peaks form and stir in the crème de cacao, if using. Quickly fold the cream into the chocolate, then spoon or pipe into the choux buns and place the lids on top.

Place all the ingredients for the sauce in a small saucepan and heat gently, stirring until smooth. Remove from the heat and leave to cool, stirring occasionally until thickened. Pour over the puffs and serve immediately.

Difficulty Rating: 4 points

Crème Brûlée with Sugared Raspberries

Serves 6

Ingredients

600 ml/1 pint/2½ cups fresh whipping cream
4 egg yolks
75 g/3 oz/⅓ cup caster/superfine sugar
½ tsp vanilla extract
25 g/1 oz/2 tbsp demerara/turbinado sugar
175 g/6 oz/1 heaping cup fresh raspberries

Preheat the oven to 150°C/300°F/Gas Mark 2. Pour the cream into a bowl and place over a saucepan of gently simmering water. Heat gently but do not allow to boil.

Meanwhile, whisk together the egg yolks, 50 g/2 oz/4 tablespoons of the caster/superfine sugar and the vanilla extract. When the cream is warm, pour it over the egg mixture, whisking briskly until it is completely mixed. Pour into six individual ramekin dishes and place in a roasting tin/pan. Fill the tin with enough water to come halfway up the sides of the dishes. Bake in the preheated oven for about 1 hour until the puddings are set. (To test if set, carefully insert a round-bladed knife into the centre. If the knife comes out clean, they are set.) Remove the puddings from the roasting tin and leave to cool. Chill in the refrigerator, preferably overnight.

Sprinkle the demerara/turbinado sugar over the top of each dish and place the puddings under a preheated hot grill/broiler. When the sugar has caramelized and turned deep brown, remove from the heat and cool. Chill the puddings in the refrigerator for 2–3 hours before serving.

Toss the raspberries in the remaining caster sugar and sprinkle over the top of each dish. Serve with a little extra cream, if liked.

Difficulty Rating: 4 points

Chocolate Brûlée

Serves 6

Ingredients

175 g/6 oz/1½ cups fresh raspberries
125 g/4 oz/½ cup caster/superfine sugar
5 medium/large egg yolks
600 ml/1 pint/2 cups double/heavy cream
1 tsp vanilla extract
175 g/6 oz white chocolate, chopped
6 tbsp demerara/turbinado sugar

Hull and clean the raspberries. Rinse lightly, then leave to dry on paper towels. Once dry, divide the raspberries evenly between 6 x 150 ml/¼ pint/⅔ cup ramekins or individual dishes.

Whisk the caster/superfine sugar and egg yolks in a large bowl until very thick. Pour the cream into a heavy-based saucepan, place over a medium–high heat and bring to the boil. Remove from the heat and gradually whisk into the egg mixture, then whisk in the vanilla extract.

Place the bowl over a saucepan of simmering water and cook for about 15–20 minutes, stirring frequently, or until thick and the custard coats the back of a wooden spoon.

Remove the bowl from the heat, add the chopped white chocolate and stir until melted and well blended. Pour over the raspberries in the ramekins and leave to cool. Cover with plastic wrap and chill in the refrigerator for 6 hours, or until firm.

Preheat the grill/broiler. Remove the ramekins from the refrigerator and sprinkle 1 tablespoon of the demerara/turbinado sugar over each, ensuring that the custard is completely covered.

Cook under the preheated grill for 5–6 minutes until the sugar has melted and begun to caramelize. Remove from the grill, leave to cool slightly, then chill again in the refrigerator for at least 1 hour. Serve immediately.

Difficulty Rating: 3 points

Chocolate Raspberry Mille Feuille

Serves 6

Ingredients

450 g/1 lb puff pastry dough, thawed if frozen
1 quantity raspberry chocolate ganache (*see* page 80), chilled
700 g/1½ lb/5¾ cups fresh raspberries, plus extra to decorate
icing/confectioners' sugar, for dusting

For the raspberry sauce:
225 g/8 oz/2 scant cups fresh raspberries
2 tbsp seedless raspberry jam/jelly
1–2 tbsp caster/superfine sugar, or to taste
2 tbsp lemon juice or framboise liqueur

Preheat the oven to 200°C/400°F/Gas Mark 6, 15 minutes before baking. Lightly oil a large baking sheet and sprinkle with a little water. Roll out the pastry dough on a lightly floured surface to a rectangle about 43 x 28 cm/17 x 11 inches. Cut into three long strips. Mark each strip crossways at 6.5 cm/2½ inch intervals using a sharp knife; this will make cutting the baked pastry easier and neater. Carefully transfer to the baking sheet, keeping the edges as straight as possible. Bake in the preheated oven for 20 minutes, or until well risen and golden brown. Place on a wire rack and leave to cool. Carefully transfer each rectangle to a work surface and, using a sharp knife, trim the long edges straight. Cut along the knife marks to make 18 rectangles.

Place all the ingredients for the raspberry sauce in a food processor and blend until smooth. If the purée is too thick, add a little water. Taste and adjust the sweetness if necessary. Strain into a bowl, cover and chill in the refrigerator.

Place one pastry rectangle on the work surface flat-side down, spread with a little chocolate ganache and sprinkle with a few fresh raspberries. Spread a second rectangle with a little ganache, place over the first, pressing gently, then sprinkle with a few raspberries. Place a third rectangle on top, flat-side up, and spread with a little chocolate ganache.

Arrange some raspberries on top and dust lightly with a little icing/confectioners' sugar. Repeat with the remaining pastry rectangles, chocolate ganache and fresh raspberries. Chill in the refrigerator until required and serve with the raspberry sauce and any remaining fresh raspberries.

Difficulty Rating: 4 points

Chocolate Profiteroles

Serves 4

Ingredients

For the pastry:
50 g/2 oz/4 tbsp butter
65 g/2½ oz/½ cup sifted plain/all-purpose flour
2 medium/large eggs, lightly beaten

For the custard:
300 ml/½ pint/1¼ cups milk
pinch freshly grated nutmeg
3 egg yolks
50 g/2 oz/¼ cup caster/superfine sugar
2 tbsp sifted plain/all-purpose flour
2 tbsp sifted cornflour/cornstarch

For the sauce:
175 g/6 oz/1 scant cup soft brown sugar
150 ml/¼ pint/⅔ cup boiling water
1 tsp instant coffee
1 tbsp cocoa powder (unsweetened)
1 tbsp brandy
75 g/3 oz/6 tbsp butter
1 tbsp golden/light corn syrup

Preheat the oven to 220°C/425°F/Gas Mark 7, 15 minutes before baking. Lightly oil two baking sheets. For the pastry, place 150 ml/¼ pint/⅔ cup water and the butter in a heavy-based saucepan and bring to the boil. Remove from the heat and beat in the flour. Return to the heat and cook for 1 minute, or until the mixture forms a ball in the centre of the saucepan. Remove from the heat and leave to cool slightly, then gradually beat in the eggs a little at a time, beating well after each addition. Once all the eggs have been added, beat until the paste is smooth and glossy.

Pipe or spoon the dough in 20 small balls onto the baking sheets, allowing plenty of room for expansion. Bake in the preheated oven for 25 minutes, or until well risen and golden brown. Reduce the oven temperature to 180°C/350°F/Gas Mark 4. Make a hole in each ball and continue to bake for a further 5 minutes. Remove from the oven and leave to cool.

For the custard, place the milk and nutmeg in a heavy-based saucepan and bring to the boil. In another saucepan, whisk together the egg yolks, sugar and flours, then beat in the hot milk. Bring to the boil and simmer, whisking constantly, for 2 minutes. Cover and leave to cool. Spoon the custard into the profiteroles and arrange on a serving dish. Place all the sauce ingredients in a small saucepan and bring to the boil, then simmer for 10 minutes. Cool slightly before serving with the profiteroles.

Difficulty Rating: 4 points

Rich Chocolate & Orange Mousse

Serves 8

Ingredients

12 sponge finger biscuits/ladyfingers

225 g/8 oz dark/semisweet chocolate, broken into pieces

225 g/8 oz/1 cup (2 sticks) unsalted butter

2 tbsp orange flower water

40 g/1½ oz/⅓ cup sifted cocoa powder (unsweetened)

100 g/4 oz/1 cup sifted icing/confectioners' sugar

5 medium/large eggs, separated

50 g/2 oz/¼ cup sugar

1 orange, thinly sliced

300 ml/½ pint/1¼ cups double/heavy cream

Oil and line a 900 g/2 lb loaf tin/pan with plastic wrap; take care to keep it as wrinkle free as possible. Arrange the sponge fingers/ladyfingers around the edge of the loaf tin/pan, trimming to fit if necessary.

Place the chocolate, butter and orange flower water in a heavy-based saucepan and heat gently, stirring occasionally, until the chocolate has melted and is smooth. Remove the saucepan from the heat, add the cocoa and 50 g/2 oz/½ cup of the icing/confectioners' sugar. Stir until smooth, then beat in the egg yolks.

In a clean, grease-free bowl, whisk the egg whites until stiff but not dry. Sift in the remaining icing/confectioners' sugar and whisk until stiff and glossy. Fold the egg white mixture into the chocolate mixture and, using a metal spoon or rubber spatula, stir until well blended.

Spoon the mousse mixture into the prepared loaf tin/pan and level the surface. Cover and chill in the refrigerator until set.

Meanwhile, place the sugar with 150 ml/¼ pint/⅔ cup water in a heavy-based saucepan and heat until the sugar has dissolved. Bring to the boil and boil for 5 minutes. Add the orange slices and simmer for about 2–4 minutes, until the slices become opaque. Drain on paper towels and reserve.

Trim the top of the sponge fingers/ladyfingers to the same level as the mousse. Invert onto a plate and remove the tin/pan and plastic wrap.

Whip the cream until soft peaks form and spoon into a decorating bag fitted with a star-shaped tip. Pipe swirls on top of the mousse and decorate with the orange slices. Chill in the refrigerator before serving.

Difficulty Rating: 4 points

Chocolate & Rum Truffles

Makes 44

Ingredients

For the chocolate truffles:
225 g/8 oz plain/semisweet chocolate
25 g/1 oz/2 tbsp butter, softened
2 medium/large egg yolks
2 tsp brandy or kirsch
2 tsp double/heavy cream
24 maraschino cherries, drained
2 tbsp sifted cocoa powder (unsweetened)

For the rum truffles:
125 g/4 oz dark/semisweet chocolate
125 ml/4 fl oz/¹/₂ cup double/heavy cream
2 tbsp rum
50 g/2 oz/¹/₂ cup ground almonds
2 tbsp sifted icing/confectioners' sugar

For the chocolate truffles, break the chocolate into pieces and place in a heatproof bowl set over a saucepan of gently simmering water. Leave for 20 minutes, or until the chocolate has melted. Stir until the chocolate is smooth and remove from the heat. Leave to stand for about 6 minutes.

Beat the butter, the egg yolks, the brandy or kirsch and double/heavy cream together until smooth. Stir the melted chocolate into the butter and egg yolk mixture and stir until thick. Cover and leave to cool for about 30 minutes. Chill in the refrigerator for 1¹/₂ hours, or until firm.

Divide the truffle mixture into 24 pieces and mould around the drained cherries. Roll in the cocoa powder until evenly coated. Place the truffles in petit four paper cases and chill in the refrigerator for 2 hours before serving.

To make the rum truffles, break the chocolate into small pieces and place in a heavy-based saucepan with the cream and rum. Heat gently until the chocolate has melted, then stir until smooth. Stir in the ground almonds and pour into a small bowl and chill in the refrigerator for at least 6 hours, or until the mixture is thick.

Remove the truffle from the refrigerator and shape small spoonfuls, about the size of a cherry, into balls. Roll in the sifted icing/confectioners' sugar and place in petit four paper cases. Store the truffles in the refrigerator until ready to serve.

Difficulty Rating: 3 points

Apricot & Almond Layer Cake

Cuts into 8–10 slices

Ingredients

150 g/5 oz/²⁄₃ cup (1¼ sticks) unsalted butter, softened

125 g/4 oz/¹⁄₃ cup caster/superfine sugar

5 medium/large eggs, separated

150 g/5 oz dark/semisweet chocolate, melted and cooled

150 g/5 oz/1 heaping cup sifted self-raising flour

50 g/2 oz/¹⁄₂ cup ground almonds

75 g/3 oz/³⁄₄ cup sifted icing/confectioners' sugar

300 g/11 oz/1 cup apricot jam/jelly

1 tbsp amaretto liqueur

125 g/4 oz/¹⁄₂ cup (1 stick) unsalted butter, melted

125 g/4 oz dark/semisweet chocolate, melted

Preheat the oven to 180°C/350°F/Gas Mark 4, 10 minutes before baking. Lightly oil and line two 23 cm/9 inch round cake tins/pans. Cream the butter and sugar together until light and fluffy, then beat in the egg yolks, one at a time, beating well after each addition. Stir in the cooled chocolate with 1 tablespoon cooled boiled water, then fold in the flour and ground almonds.

Whisk the egg whites until stiff, then gradually whisk in the icing/confectioners' sugar, beating well after each addition. Whisk until the egg whites are stiff and glossy, then fold the egg whites into the chocolate mixture in two batches.

Divide the mixture evenly between the prepared tins and bake in the preheated oven for 30–40 minutes until firm. Leave for 5 minutes before turning out onto wire racks. Leave to cool completely.

Split the cakes in half. Gently heat the jam/jelly, pass through a sieve and stir in the amaretto liqueur. Place one cake layer onto a serving plate. Spread with a little of the jam, then sandwich with the next layer. Repeat with all the layers and use any remaining jam to brush over the entire cake. Leave until the jam sets.

Meanwhile, beat the butter and chocolate together until smooth, then cool at room temperature until thick enough to spread. Cover the top and sides of the cake with the chocolate icing and leave to set before slicing and serving.

Difficulty Rating: 4 points

Black & White Torte

Cuts into 8–10 slices

Ingredients

4 medium/large eggs
150 g/5 oz/³/₄ cup caster/superfine sugar
50 g/2 oz/¹/₃ cup cornflour/cornstarch
50 g/2 oz/¹/₃ cup plain/all-purpose flour
50 g/2 oz/¹/₃ cup self-raising flour
900 ml/1¹/₂ pints/3³/₄ cups double/heavy cream
150 g/5 oz dark/semisweet chocolate, chopped
300 g/11 oz white chocolate, chopped
6 tbsp Grand Marnier, or other orange liqueur
cocoa powder (unsweetened), for dusting

Preheat the oven to 180°C/350°F/Gas Mark 4, 10 minutes before baking. Lightly oil and line a 23 cm/9 inch round cake tin/pan. Beat the eggs and sugar in a large bowl until thick and creamy. Sift together the cornflour/cornstarch, plain/all-purpose flour and self-raising flour three times, then lightly fold into the egg mixture. Spoon the mixture into the prepared tin and bake in the preheated oven for 35–40 minutes, until firm. Turn the cake out onto a wire rack and leave to cool.

Place 300 ml/¹/₂ pint/1¹/₄ cups of the double/heavy cream in a saucepan and bring to the boil. Remove from the heat and add the dark/bittersweet chocolate and a tablespoon of the liqueur. Stir until smooth. Repeat using the remaining cream, white chocolate and 2 tablespoons of the liqueur. Refrigerate for 2 hours, then whisk each mixture until thick and creamy.

Place the dark chocolate mixture in a decorating bag fitted with a plain tip and place half the white chocolate mixture in a separate decorating bag fitted with a plain tip. Reserve the remaining white chocolate mixture. Split the cold cake horizontally into two layers. Brush or drizzle the remaining 3 tablespoons of liqueur over the cakes. Put one layer onto a serving plate. Pipe alternating rings of white and dark chocolate mixture to cover the first layer of cake. Use the reserved white chocolate mixture to cover the top and sides of the cake. Dust with cocoa powder, cut into slices and serve. Store in the refrigerator.

Difficulty Rating: 4 points

Mocha Truffle Cake

Cuts into 8–10 slices

Ingredients

3 medium/large eggs

125 g/4 oz/$^2/_3$ cup caster/superfine sugar

40 g/1$^1/_2$ oz/$^1/_3$ cup cornflour/cornstarch

40 g/1$^1/_2$ oz/$^1/_3$ cup self-raising flour

2 tbsp cocoa powder (unsweetened)

2 tbsp milk

2 tbsp coffee liqueur

100 g/3$^1/_2$ oz white chocolate, melted and cooled

200 g/7 oz dark/semisweet chocolate, melted and cooled

600 ml/1 pint/2$^1/_2$ cups double/heavy cream

200 g/7 oz milk chocolate

100 g/3$^1/_2$ oz/7 tbsp unsalted butter

Preheat the oven to 180°C/350°F/Gas Mark 4, 10 minutes before baking. Lightly oil and line a deep 23 cm/9 inch round cake tin/pan. Beat the eggs and sugar in a bowl until thick and creamy.

Sift together the cornflour/cornstarch, self-raising flour and cocoa powder and fold lightly into the egg mixture. Spoon into the prepared tin and bake in the preheated oven for 30 minutes, or until firm. Turn out onto a wire rack and leave until cold. Split the cold cake horizontally into two layers. Mix together the milk and coffee liqueur and brush onto the cake layers.

Stir the cooled white chocolate into one bowl and the cooled dark/semisweet chocolate into another one. Whip the cream until soft peaks form, then divide between the two bowls and stir. Place one layer of cake in a 23 cm/9 inch springform tin. Spread with half the white chocolate cream. Top with the dark chocolate cream, then the remaining white chocolate cream. Finally, place the remaining cake layer on top. Chill in the refrigerator for 4 hours, or overnight, until set. When ready to serve, melt the milk chocolate and butter in a heatproof bowl set over simmering water and stir until smooth. Remove from the heat and leave until thick enough to spread, then use to cover the top and sides of the cake. Leave to set at room temperature, then chill in the refrigerator. Cut the cake into slices and serve.

Difficulty Rating: 4 points

Double Marble Cake

Cuts into 8–10 slices

Ingredients

75 g/3 oz white chocolate

75 g/3 oz dark/semisweet chocolate

175 g/6 oz/1 scant cup caster/superfine sugar

175 g/6 oz/³⁄₄ cup (1¹⁄₂ sticks) butter

4 medium/large eggs, separated

125 g/4 oz/1 cup sifted plain/all-purpose flour

75 g/3 oz/³⁄₄ cup ground almonds

For the topping:

100 ml/3¹⁄₂ fl oz/¹⁄₃ cup double/heavy cream

200 g/7 oz/³⁄₄ cup plus 2 tbsp (1³⁄₄ sticks) unsalted butter

100 g/3¹⁄₂ oz dark/semisweet chocolate, chopped

100 g/3¹⁄₂ oz white chocolate, chopped

Preheat the oven to 180°C/350°F/Gas Mark 4, 10 minutes before baking. Lightly oil and line the base of a 20.5 cm/8 inch cake tin/pan. Break the white and dark/semisweet chocolate into small pieces, then place in two separate bowls placed over two pans of simmering water. Heat the chocolate until melted and smooth.

In a large bowl, cream the sugar and butter together until light and fluffy. Beat in the egg yolks, one at a time, adding a spoonful of flour after each one. Stir in the ground almonds. In another bowl, whisk the egg whites. Gently fold in the whites and the remaining flour alternately into the almond mixture until they have all been incorporated. Divide the mixture between two bowls. Gently stir the white chocolate into one bowl and the dark chocolate into the other. Place alternating spoonfuls of the mixtures in the cake tin. Using a skewer, swirl together to get a marbled effect. Tap the tin on the work surface to level. Bake in the oven for 40 minutes, or until cooked through, then leave to cool for 5 minutes in the tin before turning out onto a wire rack to cool completely.

For the topping, melt half of the cream and butter with the dark chocolate and the other half with the white chocolate and stir both until smooth. Cool, then whisk until thick and swirl both colours over the top of the cake to create a marbled effect.

Difficulty Rating: 3 points

Chocolate Buttermilk Cake

Cuts into 8–10 slices

Ingredients

175 g/6 oz/³/₄ cup (1¹/₂ sticks) butter

1 tsp vanilla extract

350 g/12 oz/1³/₄ cups caster/superfine sugar

4 medium/large eggs, separated

100 g/3¹/₂ oz/³/₄ cup self-raising flour

40 g/1¹/₂ oz/¹/₂ cup cocoa powder (unsweetened)

175 ml/6 fl oz/scant ³/₄ cup buttermilk

200 g/7 oz dark/semisweet chocolate

100 g/3¹/₂ oz/7 tbsp butter

300 ml/¹/₂ pint/1¹/₄ cups double/heavy cream

Preheat the oven to 180°C/350°F/Gas Mark 4, 10 minutes before baking. Lightly oil and line a deep 23 cm/9 inch round cake tin/pan. Cream together the butter, vanilla extract and sugar until light and fluffy, then beat in the egg yolks, one at a time.

Sift together the flour and cocoa powder and fold into the egg mixture together with the buttermilk. Whisk the egg whites until soft peaks form and fold carefully into the chocolate mixture in two batches. Spoon the mixture into the prepared tin and bake in the preheated oven for 1 hour, or until firm. Cool slightly, then turn out onto a wire rack and leave until completely cold.

Place the chocolate and butter together in a heatproof bowl set over a saucepan of simmering water and heat until melted. Stir until smooth, then leave at room temperature until the chocolate is thick enough to spread.

Split the cake horizontally in half. Use some of the chocolate mixture to sandwich the two halves together. Spread and decorate the top of the cake with the remaining chocolate mixture. Finally, whip the cream until soft peaks form and use to spread around the sides of the cake. Chill in the refrigerator until required. Serve cut into slices. Store in the refrigerator.

Difficulty Rating: 3 points

Peach & White Chocolate Gateau

Cuts into 8–10 slices

Ingredients

175 g/6 oz/³/₄ cup (1¹/₂ sticks) unsalted butter, softened

2 tsp grated orange zest

175 g/6 oz/1 scant cup caster/superfine sugar

3 medium/large eggs

100 g/3¹/₂ oz white chocolate, melted and cooled

225 g/8 oz/1³/₄ sifted cups self-raising flour

300 ml/¹/₂ pint/1¹/₄ cups double/heavy cream

40 g/1¹/₂ oz/scant ¹/₂ cup icing/confectioners' sugar

125 g/4 oz/1 cup hazelnuts, toasted and chopped

For the peach filling:

2 ripe peaches, peeled and chopped

2 tbsp peach or orange liqueur

300 ml/¹/₂ pint/1¹/₄ cups double/heavy cream

40 g/1¹/₂ oz/scant ¹/₂ cup icing/confectioners' sugar

Preheat the oven to 170°C/325°F/Gas Mark 3, 10 minutes before baking. Lightly oil and line a deep 23 cm/9 inch round cake tin/pan. Cream the butter, orange zest and sugar together until light and fluffy. Add the eggs, one at a time, beating well after each addition, then beat in the cooled white chocolate. Add the flour and 175 ml/6 fl oz water in two batches. Spoon into the prepared tin and bake in the preheated oven for 1¹/₂ hours, or until firm. Leave to stand for at least 5 minutes before turning out onto a wire rack to cool completely.

To make the filling, place the peaches in a bowl and pour over the liqueur. Leave to stand for 30 minutes. Whip the cream with the icing/confectioners' sugar until soft peaks form, then fold in the peach mixture.

Split the cold cake into three layers, place one layer on a serving plate and spread with half the peach filling. Top with a second sponge layer and spread with the remaining peach filling. Top with the remaining cake.

Whip the cream and icing sugar together until soft peaks form. Spread over the top and sides of the cake, piping some onto the top if liked. Press the hazelnuts into the side of the cake and if liked sprinkle a few on top. Chill in the refrigerator until required. Serve cut into slices. Store the cake in the refrigerator.

Difficulty Rating: 4 points

Dark Chocolate Layered Torte

Cuts into 10–12 slices

Ingredients

175 g/6 oz/³/₄ cup (1¹/₂ sticks) butter

1 tbsp instant coffee granules

150 g/5 oz dark/semisweet chocolate

350 g/12 oz/1¹/₄ cups caster/superfine sugar

150 g/5 oz/1 heaping cup self-raising flour

125 g/4 oz/1 cup plain/all-purpose flour

2 tbsp cocoa powder (unsweetened)

2 medium/large eggs

1 tsp vanilla extract

215 g/7¹/₂ oz dark/semisweet chocolate, melted

125 g/4 oz/¹/₂ cup (1 stick) butter, melted

40 g/1¹/₂ oz/scant ¹/₂ cup sifted icing/confectioners' sugar

2 tsp raspberry jam/jelly

2¹/₂ tbsp chocolate liqueur

100 g/3¹/₂ oz/1 cup toasted flaked/slivered almonds

Preheat the oven to 150°C/300°F/Gas Mark 2, 10 minutes before baking. Lightly oil and line a 23 cm/9 inch square cake tin/pan. Melt the butter in a saucepan, remove from the heat and stir in the coffee granules and 250 ml/8 fl oz/1 cup hot water. Add the dark/semisweet chocolate and sugar and stir until smooth, then pour into a bowl. In another bowl, sift together the flours and cocoa powder. Using an electric whisk, whisk the sifted mixture into the chocolate mixture until smooth. Beat in the eggs and vanilla extract. Pour into the prepared tin and bake in the preheated oven for 1¹/₄ hours, or until firm. Leave for at least 5 minutes before turning out onto a wire rack to cool.

Meanwhile, mix together all but 1 tablespoon of the melted dark chocolate with the butter and icing/confectioners' sugar and beat until smooth. Leave to cool, then beat again. Reserve 4–5 tablespoons of the chocolate filling. Cut the cooled cake in half to make two rectangles, then split each rectangle in three horizontally. Place one cake layer on a serving plate and spread thinly with the jam/jelly, then a thin layer of dark chocolate filling. Top with a second cake layer and sprinkle with a little liqueur, then spread thinly with filling. Repeat with the remaining cake layers, liqueur and filling. Chill in the refrigerator for 2–3 hours until firm. Cover the cake with the reserved chocolate filling and press the flaked/slivered almonds into the sides of the cake. Place the remaining melted chocolate in a nonstick baking parchment decorating bag. Snip a small hole in the tip and pipe thin lines 2 cm/³/₄ inch apart crossways over the cake. Drag a cocktail stick/toothpick lengthways through the icing in alternating directions to create a feathered effect on the top. Serve.

Difficulty Rating: 4 points

Chocolate Mousse Sponge

Cuts into 8–10 slices

Ingredients

3 medium/large eggs

75 g/3 oz/¹/₃ cup caster/superfine sugar

1 tsp vanilla extract

50 g/2 oz/¹/₃ cup sifted self-raising flour

25 g/1 oz/¹/₄ cup ground almonds

50 g/2 oz dark/semisweet chocolate, grated

icing/confectioners' sugar, for dusting

sliced fresh strawberries, to decorate

For the mousse:

2 sheets gelatine

50 ml/2 fl oz/¹/₄ cup double/heavy cream

100 g/3¹/₂ oz dark/semisweet chocolate, chopped

1 tsp vanilla extract

4 medium egg whites

125 g/4 oz/²/₃ cup caster/superfine sugar

Preheat the oven to 180°C/350°F/Gas Mark 4, 10 minutes before baking. Lightly oil and line a 23 cm/9 inch round cake tin/pan and lightly oil the sides of a 23 cm/9 inch springform tin. Whisk the eggs, caster/superfine sugar and vanilla extract until thick and creamy. Fold in the flour, ground almonds and dark chocolate. Spoon the mixture into the prepared round cake tin and bake in the preheated oven for 25 minutes, or until firm. Turn out onto a wire rack to cool.

For the mousse, soak the gelatine in 50 ml/2 fl oz/¹/₄ cup of cold water for 5 minutes until softened. Meanwhile, heat the double/heavy cream in a small saucepan. When almost boiling, remove from the heat and stir in the chocolate and vanilla extract. Stir until the chocolate melts. Squeeze the excess water out of the gelatine and add to the chocolate mixture. Stir until dissolved, then pour into a large bowl.

Whisk the egg whites until stiff, then gradually add the caster sugar, whisking well between each addition. Fold the egg white mixture into the chocolate mixture in two batches.

Split the cake into two layers. Place one layer in the bottom of the springform tin. Pour in the chocolate mousse mixture, then top with the second layer of cake. Chill in the refrigerator for 4 hours, or until the mousse has set. Loosen the sides and remove the cake from the tin. Dust with icing/confectioners' sugar and decorate the top with a few freshly sliced strawberries. Serve cut into slices.

Difficulty Rating: 3 points

Chocolate Chiffon Cake

Cuts into 10–12 slices

Ingredients

50 g/2 oz /¹/₂ cup cocoa powder (unsweetened)

300 g/11 oz/2¹/₃ cups self-raising flour

550 g/1¹/₄ lb/2³/₄ cups caster/superfine sugar

7 medium/large eggs, separated

125 ml/4 fl oz/¹/₂ cup vegetable oil

1 tsp vanilla extract

75 g/3 oz/³/₄ cup walnuts

200 g/7 oz dark/semisweet chocolate, melted

For the icing:

175 g/6 oz/³/₄ cup (1¹/₂ sticks) butter

275 g/10 oz/1¹/₃ cups sifted icing/confectioners' sugar

2 tbsp sifted cocoa powder (unsweetened)

2 tbsp brandy

Preheat the oven to 170°C/325°F/Gas Mark 3, 10 minutes before baking. Lightly oil and line a 23 cm/9 inch round cake tin/pan. Lightly oil a baking sheet. Blend the cocoa powder with 175 ml/6 fl oz/scant ³/₄ cups boiling water and leave to cool. Place the flour and 350 g/12 oz/1³/₄ cups of the caster/superfine sugar in a large bowl and add the cocoa mixture, egg yolks, oil and vanilla extract. Whisk until smooth and lighter in colour.

Whisk the egg whites in a clean, grease-free bowl until soft peaks form, then fold into the cocoa mixture. Pour into the prepared tin and bake in the preheated oven for 1 hour, or until firm. Leave for 5 minutes before turning out onto a wire rack to cool.

To make the icing, cream together 125 g/4 oz/¹/₂ cup (1 stick) of the butter with the icing/confectioners' sugar, cocoa powder and brandy until smooth, then reserve. Melt the remaining butter and blend with three quarters of the melted dark chocolate. Stir until smooth and then leave until thickened.

Place the remaining caster sugar into a heavy-based saucepan over a low heat and heat until the sugar has melted and is a deep golden brown. Add the walnuts and the remaining melted chocolate to the melted sugar and pour onto the prepared baking sheet. Leave until cold and brittle, then chop finely. Reserve.

Split the cake into three layers. Place one layer onto a serving plate and spread with half of the brandy butter icing. Top with a second layer and spread with the remaining brandy butter icing. Arrange the third cake layer on top. Cover the cake with the thickened chocolate glaze. Sprinkle with the walnut praline and serve.

Difficulty Rating: 5 points

Grated Chocolate Roulade

Cuts into 8 slices

Ingredients

4 medium/large eggs, separated
125 g/4 oz/²/₃ cup caster/superfine sugar
60 g/2¹/₂ oz dark/semisweet chocolate, grated
75 g/3 oz/²/₃ cup self-raising flour, sifted
2 tbsp caster/superfine sugar, plus extra for sprinkling
150 ml/¹/₄ pint/²/₃ cup double/heavy cream
2 tsp icing/confectioners' sugar
1 tsp vanilla extract
chocolate curls, to decorate

Preheat the oven to 180°C/350°F/Gas Mark 4, 10 minutes before baking. Lightly oil and line a 20.5 x 30.5 cm/8 x 12 inch Swiss roll tin/jelly roll pan. Beat the egg yolks and sugar with an electric mixer for 5 minutes, or until thick, then stir in 2 tablespoons hot water and the grated chocolate. Finally, fold in the sifted flour.

Whisk the egg whites until stiff, then fold 1–2 tablespoons of egg white into the chocolate mixture. Mix lightly, then gently fold in the remaining egg white. Pour into the prepared tin and bake in the preheated oven for about 12 minutes, or until firm.

Place a large sheet of nonstick baking parchment onto a work surface and sprinkle liberally with caster/superfine sugar. Turn the cake onto the baking parchment, discard the lining paper and trim away the crisp edges. Roll up as for a Swiss/jelly roll cake, leave for 2 minutes, then unroll and leave to cool.

Beat the double/heavy cream with the icing/confectioners' sugar and vanilla extract until thick. Reserve a little for decoration, then spread the remaining cream over the cake, leaving a 2.5 cm/1 inch border all round. Using the baking parchment, roll up from a short end. Carefully transfer the roulade to a large serving plate and use the reserved cream to decorate the top. Add the chocolate curls just before serving, then cut into slices and serve. Store in the refrigerator.

Difficulty Rating: 4 points

Rich Devil's Food Cake

Cuts into 12–16 slices

Ingredients

450 g/1 lb/3¹/₂ cups plain/all-purpose flour
1 tbsp bicarbonate of soda/baking soda
¹/₂ tsp salt
75 g/3 oz/1 scant cup cocoa powder (unsweetened)
300 ml/¹/₂ pint/1¹/₄ cups milk
150 g/5 oz/²/₃ cup (1¹/₄ sticks) butter, softened
400 g/14 oz/2 cups soft dark brown sugar
2 tsp vanilla extract
4 large/extra-large eggs

For the chocolate fudge icing:
275 g/10 oz/1¹/₃ cups caster/superfine sugar
¹/₂ tsp salt
125 g/4 oz dark/semisweet chocolate, chopped
250 ml/8 fl oz/1 cup milk
2 tbsp golden/light corn syrup
125 g/4 oz/¹/₂ cup (1 stick) butter, diced
2 tsp vanilla extract

Preheat the oven to 180°C/350°F/Gas Mark 4. Lightly oil and line the bases of three 23 cm/9 inch cake tins/pans with greaseproof/wax paper or baking parchment. Sift the flour, bicarbonate of soda/baking soda and salt into a bowl. Sift the cocoa powder in another bowl and whisk in the milk to form a paste. Beat the butter, sugar and vanilla extract. Then beat in the eggs. Stir in the flour and cocoa mixtures in batches. Split the mixture between the tins. Bake for 25–35 minutes. Remove, cool and turn out onto a wire rack.

For the icing, put the sugar, salt and chocolate into a saucepan and blend in the milk. Add the golden/light corn syrup and butter. Bring to the boil, stirring to dissolve the sugar. Boil for 1 minute, stirring constantly. Remove from the heat, stir in the vanilla extract and cool. Then whisk until thickened and lighter in colour. Sandwich the three cake layers together with a third of the icing, placing the third cake layer with the flat side up. Transfer the cake to a serving plate and spread the remaining icing over the top and sides. Swirl the top to create a decorative effect and serve.

Difficulty Rating: 3 points

White Chocolate & Passion Fruit Cake

Cuts into 8–10 slices

Ingredients

125 g/4 oz white chocolate

125 g/4 oz/¹/₂ cup (1 stick) butter

225 g/8 oz/1 heaping cup caster/superfine sugar

2 medium/large eggs

125 ml/4 fl oz/¹/₂ cup sour cream

200 g/7 oz/1¹/₂ cups sifted plain/all-purpose flour

75 g/3 oz/scant ²/₃ cup sifted self-raising flour

125 g/4 oz white chocolate, coarsely grated, to decorate

For the syrup and icing:

200 g/7 oz/1 cup caster/superfine sugar

4 tbsp passion fruit juice (about 8–10 passion fruit, sieved)

1¹/₂ tbsp passion fruit seeds

250 g/9 oz/1 cup plus 2 tbsp (2¹/₄ sticks) unsalted butter

Preheat the oven to 180°C/350°F/Gas Mark 4, 10 minutes before baking. Lightly oil and line two 20.5 cm/8 inch cake tins/pans. Melt the white chocolate in a heatproof bowl set over a saucepan of simmering water. Stir in 125 ml/4 fl oz/¹/₂ cup warm water and stir, then leave to cool.

Whisk the butter and sugar together until light and fluffy, add the eggs, one at a time, beating well after each addition. Beat in the chocolate mixture, sour cream and sifted flours. Divide the mixture into eight portions. Spread one portion into each of the prepared tins. Bake in the preheated oven for 10 minutes, or until firm, then turn out onto wire racks. Repeat with the remaining mixture to make eight cake layers.

To make a thin syrup, place 125 ml/4 fl oz/¹/₂ cup water with 50 g/2 oz/¹/₄ cup of the sugar in a saucepan. Heat gently, stirring, until the sugar has dissolved. Bring to the boil, simmer for 2 minutes. Remove from the heat and cool, then add 2 tablespoons of the passion fruit juice. Reserve.

To make the icing, blend the remaining sugar with 50 ml/2 fl oz/ ¹/₄ cup water in a small saucepan and stir constantly over a low

heat, without boiling, until the sugar has dissolved. Remove from the heat and cool. Stir in the remaining passion fruit juice and the seeds. Cool, then strain. Using an electric whisk, beat the butter in a bowl until very pale. Gradually beat in the thick syrup. Place one layer of cake on a serving plate. Brush with the thin syrup and spread with a thin layer of icing. Repeat with the remaining cake, syrup and icing. Cover the cake with the remaining icing. Press the grated chocolate into the top and sides to decorate.

Difficulty Rating: 5 points

Sachertorte

Cuts into 10–12 slices

Ingredients

150 g/5 oz dark/semisweet chocolate
150 g/5 oz/²⁄₃ cup (1¹⁄₄ sticks) unsalted butter, softened
125 g/4 oz/²⁄₃ cup, plus 2 tbsp caster/superfine sugar
3 medium/large eggs, separated
150 g/5 oz/1 heaping cup sifted plain/all-purpose flour

To decorate:
225 g/8 oz/³⁄₄ cup apricot jam/jelly
125 g/4 oz dark/semisweet chocolate, chopped
125 g/4 oz/¹⁄₂ cup (1 stick) unsalted butter
25 g/1 oz milk chocolate

Preheat the oven to 180˚C/ 350˚F/Gas Mark 4. Lightly oil and line a deep 23 cm/9 inch cake tin/pan. Melt the chocolate for the cake in a heatproof bowl set over simmering water. Stir in 1 tablespoon water and leave to cool. Beat the butter and 125 g/4 oz/²⁄₃ cup of the sugar together until light and fluffy. Beat in the egg yolks, one at a time. Stir in the melted chocolate. then the flour.

In a clean, grease–free bowl, whisk the egg whites until stiff peaks form, then whisk in the remaining sugar. Fold into the chocolate mixture and spoon into the prepared tin. Bake in the preheated oven for 30 minutes until firm. Leave for 5 minutes, then turn out onto a wire rack to cool. Leave the cake upside down.

To decorate, split the cake in two and place one half on a serving plate. Heat the jam/jelly and rub through a fine sieve. Brush half the jam onto the first cake half, then cover with the remaining cake layer and brush with the remaining jam. Leave at room temperature for 1 hour, or until the jam has set. Place the dark/ semisweet chocolate with the butter into a heatproof bowl set over a saucepan of simmering water and heat until melted. Stir occasionally until smooth, then leave until thickened. Use to cover the cake. Melt the milk chocolate in a heatproof bowl set over simmering water. Place in a small greaseproof decorating bag and snip a small hole at the tip. Pipe 'Sacher' with a large 'S' on the top. Leave to set at room temperature.

Difficulty Rating: 4 points

Chocolate Roulade

Cuts into 8 slices

Ingredients

200 g/7 oz dark/semisweet chocolate

7 medium/large eggs, separated

200 g/7 oz/1 cup caster/superfine sugar

4 tbsp icing/confectioners' sugar, for dusting

300 ml/¹/₂ pint/1¹/₄ cups double/heavy cream

3 tbsp Cointreau or Grand Marnier

To decorate:

fresh raspberries

fresh mint sprigs

Preheat the oven to 180°C/350°F/Gas Mark 4, 10 minutes before baking. Lightly oil and line a 33 x 23 cm/13 x 9 inch Swiss roll tin/jelly roll pan with nonstick baking parchment. Break the chocolate into small pieces into a heatproof bowl set over a saucepan of simmering water. Leave until almost melted, stirring occasionally. Remove from the heat and leave to stand for 5 minutes. Whisk the egg yolks with the sugar until pale and creamy and the whisk leaves a trail in the mixture when lifted, then carefully fold in the melted chocolate.

In a clean, grease-free bowl, whisk the egg whites until stiff, then fold 1 large spoonful into the chocolate mixture. Mix lightly, then gently fold in the remaining egg whites. Pour the mixture into the prepared tin and level the surface. Bake in the preheated oven for 20–25 minutes until firm. Remove the cake from the oven, leave in the tin and cover with a wire rack and a damp dishtowel. Leave for 8 hours, or preferably overnight.

Dust a large sheet of nonstick baking parchment generously with 2 tablespoons of the icing/confectioners' sugar. Unwrap the cake and turn out onto the paper. Remove the lining paper. Whip the cream with the liqueur until soft peaks form. Spread over the cake, leaving a 2.5 cm/1 inch border all round. Using the paper to help, roll the cake up from a short end. Transfer to a serving plate, seam-side down, and dust with the remaining icing sugar. Decorate with fresh raspberries and mint. Serve.

Difficulty Rating: 4 points

Supreme Chocolate Gateau

Cuts into 10–12 slices

Ingredients

175 g/6 oz/1¹/₃ cups sifted self-raising flour
1¹/₂ tsp sifted baking powder
3 tbsp sifted cocoa powder (unsweetened)
175 g/6 oz/³/₄ cup (1¹/₂ sticks) margarine or butter, softened
175 g/6 oz/1 scant cup caster/superfine sugar
3 large/extra-large eggs

To decorate:
350 g/12 oz dark/semisweet chocolate
1 gelatine leaf
200 ml/7 fl oz/³/₄ cup double/heavy cream
75 g/3 oz/6 tbsp butter
cocoa powder (unsweetened), for dusting

Preheat the oven to 180°C/350°F/Gas Mark 4. Lightly oil and line three 20.5 cm/8 inch round cake tins/pans. Place all the cake ingredients into a bowl and whisk together until thick; add a little warm water if very thick. Divide the mixture between the prepared tins. Bake in the preheated oven for 35–40 minutes until a skewer inserted in the centre comes out clean. Cool on wire racks.

Gently heat 2 tablespoons hot water with 50 g/2 oz of the chocolate and stir until combined. Remove from the heat and leave for 5 minutes. Place the gelatine into a shallow dish and add 2 tablespoons cold water. Leave for 5 minutes, then squeeze out any excess water and add to the chocolate and water mixture. Stir until dissolved. Whip the double/heavy cream until just thickened. Add the chocolate mixture and continue whisking until soft peaks form. Leave until starting to set. Place one of the cakes onto a serving plate and spread with half the cream mixture. Top with a second cake and the remaining cream, cover with the third cake and chill in the refrigerator until the cream has set.

Melt 175 g/6 oz of the chocolate with the butter and stir until smooth; leave until thickened. Melt the remaining chocolate. Cut twelve 10 cm/4 inch squares of kitchen foil. Spread the chocolate evenly over the squares to within 2.5 cm/1 inch of

the edges. Refrigerate for 3–4 minutes until just set but not brittle. Gather up the corners and crimp together. Return to the refrigerator until firm.

Spread the chocolate and butter mixture over the top and sides of the cake. Remove the foil from the giant curls and use to decorate the top of the cake. Dust with cocoa powder and serve cut into wedges.

Difficulty Rating: 3 points

Chocolate Hazelnut Meringue Gateau

Cuts into 8–10 slices

Ingredients

5 medium/large egg whites

275 g/10 oz/1⅓ cups caster/superfine sugar

125 g/4 oz/1 cup hazelnuts, toasted and finely chopped

175 g/6 oz dark/semisweet chocolate

100 g/3½ oz/7 tbsp butter

3 medium/large eggs, separated, plus 1 medium egg white

25 g/1 oz/¼ cup icing/confectioners' sugar

125 ml/4 fl oz/½ cup double/heavy cream

hazelnuts, toasted and chopped, to decorate

Preheat the oven to 150°C/300°F/Gas Mark 2, 5 minutes before baking. Cut three pieces of nonstick baking parchment into 30.5 x 12.5 cm/12 x 5 inch rectangles and then place onto two or three baking sheets.

Whisk the egg whites until stiff, add half the sugar and whisk until the mixture is stiff, smooth and glossy. Whisk in the remaining sugar, 1 tablespoon at a time, beating well between each addition. When all the sugar has been added, whisk for 1 minute. Stir in the hazelnuts.

Spoon the meringue inside the marked rectangles, spreading in a continuous backwards and forwards movement. Bake in the preheated oven for 1¼ hours, remove and leave until cold. Trim the meringues until they measure 25.5 x 10 cm/10 x 4 inches. Reserve all the trimmings.

Melt the chocolate and the butter in a heatproof bowl set over a saucepan of gently simmering water and stir until smooth. Remove from the heat and beat in the egg yolks. Whisk the egg white until stiff, then whisk in the icing/confectioners' sugar a little at a time. Fold the egg whites into the chocolate mixture and chill in the refrigerator for 20–30 minutes until thick enough to spread. Whip the double/heavy cream until soft peaks form. Reserve.

Place one of the meringue layers onto a serving plate. Spread with about half of the mousse mixture, then top with a second meringue layer. Spread the remaining mousse mixture over the top with the third meringue. Spread the cream over the top and sprinkle with the chopped hazelnuts. Chill in the refrigerator for at least 4 hours and up to 24 hours. Serve cut into slices.

Difficulty Rating: 3 points

Black Forest Gateau

Cuts into 10–12 slices

Ingredients

250 g/9 oz/1 cup plus 2 tbsp (2¼ sticks) butter

1 tbsp instant coffee granules

200 g/7 oz dark/semisweet chocolate, chopped or broken

400 g/14 oz/2 cups caster/superfine sugar

225 g/8 oz/1¾ cups self-raising flour

150 g/5 oz/1 heaping cup plain/all-purpose flour

50 g/2 oz/⅔ cup cocoa powder (unsweetened)

2 medium/large eggs

2 tsp vanilla extract

2 x 400 g/14 oz cans stoned cherries in juice

2 tsp arrowroot

600 ml/1 pint/2½ cups double/heavy cream

50 ml/2 fl oz/¼ cup kirsch

Preheat the oven to 150°C/300°F/Gas Mark 2, 5 minutes before baking. Lightly oil and line a deep 23 cm/9 inch cake tin/pan.

Melt the butter in a large saucepan. Blend the coffee with 350 ml/12 fl oz/1½ cups hot water, add to the butter with the chocolate and sugar and heat gently, stirring until smooth. Pour into a large bowl and leave until just warm.

Sift together the flours and cocoa powder. Using an electric mixer, whisk the warm chocolate mixture on a low speed, then gradually whisk in the dry ingredients. Whisk in the eggs, one at a time, then the vanilla extract. Pour the mixture into the prepared tin and bake in the preheated oven for 1¾ hours, or until firm and a skewer inserted into the centre comes out clean. Leave in the tin for 5 minutes to cool slightly before turning out onto a wire rack.

Place the cherries and their juice in a small saucepan and heat gently. Blend the arrowroot with 2 teaspoons water until smooth, then stir into the cherries. Cook, stirring, until the liquid thickens. Simmer very gently for 2 minutes, then leave until cold.

Whip the double/heavy cream until thick. Trim the top of the cake if necessary, then split the cake into three layers. Brush the base of the cake with half the kirsch. Top with a layer of cream and one third of the cherries. Repeat the layering, then place the third layer on top. Reserve a little cream for decorating and use the remainder to cover the top and sides of the cake. Pipe a decorative edge around the cake, then arrange the remaining cherries in the centre and serve.

Difficulty Rating: 4 points

Whole Orange & Chocolate Cake with Marmalade Cream

Cuts into 6–8 slices

Ingredients

1 small orange, scrubbed

2 medium/large eggs, separated, plus 1 whole egg

150 g/5 oz/³/₄ cup caster/superfine sugar

125 g/4 oz/1¹/₃ cups ground almonds

75 g/3 oz dark/semisweet chocolate, melted

100 ml/3¹/₂ fl oz/¹/₃ cup double/heavy cream

200 g/7 oz/1 scant cup full fat soft cheese

25 g/1 oz/¹/₄ cup icing/confectioners' sugar

2 tbsp orange marmalade

orange zest, to decorate

Preheat the oven to 180°C/350°F/Gas Mark 4, 10 minutes before baking. Lightly oil and line the base of a 900 g/2 lb loaf tin/pan. Place the orange in a small saucepan, cover with cold water and bring to the boil. Simmer for 1 hour until completely soft. Drain and leave to cool.

Place 2 egg yolks, 1 whole egg and the caster/superfine sugar in a heatproof bowl set over a saucepan of simmering water and whisk until doubled in bulk. Remove from the heat and continue to whisk for 5 minutes until cooled.

Cut the whole orange in half and discard the seeds, then place into a food processor or blender and blend to a purée. Carefully fold the purée into the egg yolk mixture with the ground almonds and melted chocolate.

Whisk the egg whites until stiff peaks form. Fold a large spoonful of the egg whites into the chocolate mixture, then gently fold the remaining egg whites into the mixture. Pour into the prepared tin and bake in the preheated oven for 50 minutes, or until firm and a skewer inserted into the centre comes out clean. Cool in the tin before turning out of the tin and carefully discarding the lining paper.

Meanwhile, whip the double/heavy cream until just thickened. In another bowl, blend the soft cheese with the icing/confectioners' sugar and marmalade until smooth, then fold in the double cream. Chill the marmalade cream in the refrigerator until required. Decorate with orange zest and serve the cake cut into slices with the marmalade cream.

Difficulty Rating: 4 points

White Chocolate Cheesecake

Cuts into 16 slices

Ingredients

For the base:
150 g/5 oz/1²/₃ cups digestive biscuits/Graham crackers
50 g/2 oz/¹/₂ cup whole almonds, lightly toasted
50 g/2 oz/4 tbsp butter, melted
¹/₂ tsp almond extract

For the filling:
350 g/12 oz good-quality white chocolate, chopped
125 ml/4 fl oz/¹/₂ cup double/heavy cream
700 g/1¹/₂ lb/3 cups cream cheese, softened
50 g/2 oz/¹/₄ cup caster/superfine sugar
4 large/extra-large eggs
2 tbsp amaretto or almond-flavoured liqueur

For the topping:
450 ml/³/₄ pint/2 cups sour cream
50 g/2 oz/¹/₄ cup caster/superfine sugar
¹/₂ tsp almond or vanilla extract
white chocolate curls

Preheat the oven to 180°C/350°F/Gas Mark 4, 10 minutes before baking. Lightly oil a 23 x 7.5 cm/9 x 3 inch springform tin/pan. Crush the biscuits/crackers and almonds in a food processor to form fine crumbs. Pour in the butter and almond extract and blend. Pour the crumbs into the prepared tin. Using the back of a spoon, press onto the bottom and up the sides to within 1 cm/¹/₂ inch of the top of the tin edge. Bake in the preheated oven for 5 minutes to set. Remove and transfer to a wire rack. Reduce the oven temperature to 150°C/300°F/Gas Mark 2.

Heat the white chocolate and cream in a saucepan over a low heat, stirring constantly, until melted. Remove and cool.

Beat the cream cheese and sugar until smooth. Add the eggs, one at a time, beating well after each addition. Slowly beat in the cooled white chocolate cream and the amaretto.

Pour into the baked crust. Place on a baking sheet and bake for 45–55 minutes until the edge of the cake is firm but the centre slightly soft. Reduce the temperature of the oven if the top begins to brown. Remove to a wire rack and increase the temperature to 200°C/400°F/Gas Mark 6.

To make the topping, beat the sour cream, sugar and almond or vanilla extract until smooth. Pour gently over the cheesecake, tilting the pan to distribute the topping evenly. Alternatively, spread with a metal palette knife. Bake for another 5 minutes to set. Turn off the oven and leave the door halfway open for about 1 hour. Transfer to a wire rack and run a sharp knife around the edge of the crust to separate from the tin. Cool and refrigerate until chilled. Remove from the tin, decorate with white chocolate curls and serve.

Difficulty Rating: 3 points

Cranberry & White Chocolate Cake

Serves 4

Ingredients

225 g/8 oz/1 cup (2 sticks) butter, softened

250 g/9 oz/1 scant cup full fat soft cheese

150 g/5 oz/³/₄ cup soft light brown sugar

200 g/7 oz/1 cup caster/superfine sugar

grated zest of ¹/₂ orange

1 tsp vanilla extract

4 medium/large eggs

375 g/13 oz/3 cups plain/all-purpose flour

2 tsp baking powder

200 g/7 oz/2 cups cranberries, thawed if frozen

225 g/8 oz white chocolate, coarsely chopped

2 tbsp orange juice

Preheat the oven to 180°C/350°F/Gas Mark 4, 10 minutes before baking. Lightly oil and flour a 23 cm/9 inch kugelhopf tin/pan or ring tin. Using an electric mixer, cream the butter and cheese with the sugars until light and fluffy. Add the grated orange zest and vanilla extract and beat until smooth, then beat in the eggs, one at a time.

Sift the flour and baking powder together and stir into the creamed mixture, beating well after each addition. Fold in the cranberries and 175 g/6 oz of the white chocolate. Spoon into the prepared tin and bake in the preheated oven for 1 hour, or until firm and a skewer inserted into the centre comes out clean. Cool in the tin before turning out onto a wire rack.

Melt the remaining white chocolate, stir until smooth, then stir in the orange juice and leave to cool until thickened. Transfer the cake to a serving plate and spoon over the white chocolate and orange glaze. Leave to set.

Difficulty Rating: 3 points

Almond Angel Cake with Amaretto Cream

Cuts into 10–12 slices

Ingredients

175 g/6 oz/1³/₄ cups, plus 2–3 tbsp icing/confectioners' sugar

150 g/5 oz/1 heaping cup plain/all-purpose flour

350 ml/12 fl oz egg whites (about 10 large/extra-large egg whites)

1¹/₂ tsp cream of tartar

¹/₂ tsp vanilla extract

1 tsp almond extract

¹/₄ tsp salt

200 g/7 oz/1 cup caster/superfine sugar

175 ml/6 fl oz/scant ³/₄ cup double/heavy cream

2 tbsp amaretto liqueur

fresh raspberries, to decorate

Preheat the oven to 180°C/350°F/Gas Mark 4. Sift together the 175 g/6 oz icing/confectioners' sugar and flour. Stir to blend, then sift again and reserve. Beat the egg whites, cream of tartar, vanilla extract, ¹/₂ teaspoon of the almond extract and salt until soft peaks form. Gradually add the caster/superfine sugar, 2 tablespoons at a time, beating well after each addition, until stiff peaks form.

Sift about one third of the flour mixture over the egg white mixture and gently fold into the egg white mixture. Repeat, folding the flour mixture into the egg white mixture in two more batches. Spoon gently into an angel-food cake tin/pan or 25.5 cm/10 inch tube tin. Bake in the preheated oven until risen and golden on top. Immediately invert the cake tin and cool completely in the tin. When cool, carefully run a sharp knife around the edge of the tin and the centre ring to loosen the cake from the edge. Using the fingertips, ease the cake from the tin and invert onto a cake plate. Thickly dust the cake with the extra icing sugar.

Whip the cream with the remaining almond extract, amaretto liqueur and a little more icing sugar until soft peaks form. Fill a decorating bag fitted with a star tip with half the cream and pipe around the bottom edge of the cake. Decorate with the fresh raspberries and serve with the remaining cream.

Difficulty Rating: 5 points

White Chocolate & Raspberry Mousse Gateau

Cuts into 8 slices

Ingredients

4 medium/large eggs

125 g/4 oz/²/₃ cup caster/superfine sugar

75 g/3 oz/scant ²/₃ cup sifted plain/all-purpose flour

25 g/1 oz/scant ¹/₄ cup sifted cornflour/cornstarch

3 gelatine leaves

450 g/1 lb/3²/₃ cups raspberries, thawed if frozen

400 g/14 oz white chocolate

200 g/7 oz/1 scant cup plain fromage frais/Quark or Greek yogurt

2 medium/large egg whites

2 tbsp caster/superfine sugar

4 tbsp raspberry or orange liqueur

200 ml/7 fl oz/³/₄ cup double/heavy cream

fresh raspberries, halved, to decorate

Preheat the oven to 190°C/375°F/Gas Mark 5. Oil and line two 23 cm/9 inch cake tins/pans. Whisk the eggs and sugar until thick and creamy and the whisk leaves a trail in the mixture. Fold in the flour and cornflour/cornstarch, then divide between the prepared tins. Bake in the preheated oven for 12–15 minutes until risen and firm. Cool in the tins, then turn out onto wire racks.

Place the gelatine with 4 tablespoons cold water in a dish and leave to soften for 5 minutes. Purée half the raspberries, press through a sieve, then heat until nearly boiling. Squeeze out excess water from the gelatine, add to the purée and stir until dissolved. Reserve.

Melt 175 g/6 oz of the chocolate in a bowl set over a saucepan of simmering water. Leave to cool, then stir in the fromage frais and the purée. Whisk the egg whites until stiff and whisk in the sugar. Fold into the raspberry mixture with the rest of the berries. Line the sides of a 23 cm/9 inch springform tin with nonstick baking parchment. Place one layer of sponge in the base and sprinkle with half the liqueur. Pour in the raspberry mixture and top with the second sponge. Brush with the

remaining liqueur. Press down and chill in the refrigerator for 4 hours. Unmould onto a plate. Cut a strip of double thickness nonstick baking parchment to fit around the cake and stand 1 cm/¹/₂ inch higher. Melt the remaining white chocolate and spread thickly onto the parchment. Leave until just setting. Wrap around the cake and freeze for 15 minutes. Peel away the parchment. Whip the cream until thick and spread over the top. Decorate with raspberries.

Difficulty Rating: 5 points

Chocolate Orange Fudge Cake

Cuts into 8–10 slices

Ingredients

65 g/2¹/₂ oz/³/₄ cup cocoa powder (unsweetened)

grated zest of 1 orange

350 g/12 oz/2³/₄ cups self-raising flour

2 tsp baking powder

1 tsp bicarbonate of soda/baking soda

¹/₂ tsp salt

225 g/8 oz/1 heaping cup soft light brown sugar

175 g/6 oz/³/₄ cup (1¹/₂ sticks) butter, softened

3 medium/large eggs

1 tsp vanilla extract

250 ml/8 fl oz/1 cup sour cream

6 tbsp butter

6 tbsp milk

thinly pared rind of 1 orange

6 tbsp cocoa powder (unsweetened)

250 g/9 oz/2¹/₂ cups sifted icing/confectioners' sugar

Preheat the oven to 180˚C/350˚F/Gas Mark 4, 10 minutes before baking. Lightly oil and line two 23 cm/9 inch round cake tins/pans with nonstick baking parchment. Blend the cocoa powder and 50 ml/2 fl oz/¹/₄ cup boiling water until smooth. Stir in the orange zest and reserve. Sift together the flour, baking powder, bicarbonate of soda/baking soda and salt, then reserve. Cream together the sugar and softened butter and beat in the eggs, one at a time, then the cocoa mixture and vanilla extract. Finally, stir in the flour mixture and the sour cream in alternate spoonfuls.

Divide the mixture between the prepared tins and bake in the preheated oven for 35 minutes, or until the edges of the cake pull away from the tin and the tops spring back when lightly pressed. Cool in the tins for 10 minutes, then turn out onto wire racks until cold.

Gently heat together the butter and milk with the pared orange rind. Simmer for 10 minutes, stirring occasionally. Remove from the heat and discard the orange rind. Pour the warm orange and milk mixture into a large bowl and stir in the cocoa powder.

Gradually beat in the sifted icing/confectioners' sugar and beat until the icing is smooth and spreadable. Place one cake onto a large serving plate. Top with about one quarter of the icing, place the second cake on top, then cover the cake completely with the remaining icing. Serve.

Difficulty Rating: 3 points

Luxury Carrot Cake

Cuts into 12 slices

Ingredients

275 g/10 oz/2 heaping cups plain/all-purpose flour

2 tsp baking powder

1 tsp bicarbonate of soda/baking soda

1 tsp salt

2 tsp ground cinnamon

1 tsp ground ginger

200 g/7 oz/1 cup soft dark brown sugar

100 g/3½ oz/½ cup caster/superfine sugar

4 large/extra-large eggs, beaten

250 ml/8 fl oz/1 cup sunflower/corn oil

1 tbsp vanilla extract

4 carrots, peeled and shredded (about 450 g/1 lb)

400 g/14 oz can crushed pineapple, well drained

125 g/4 oz/1¼ cups toasted and chopped pecans or walnuts

For the frosting:

175 g/6 oz/¾ cup cream cheese, softened

50 g/2 oz/4 tbsp butter, softened

1 tsp vanilla extract

225 g/8 oz/2¼ cups sifted icing/confectioners' sugar

1–2 tbsp milk

Preheat the oven to 180°C/350°F/Gas Mark 4, 10 minutes before baking. Lightly oil a 33 x 23 cm/13 x 9 inch baking tin/pan. Line the base with nonstick baking parchment, oil and dust with flour.

Sift the first six ingredients into a large bowl and stir in the sugars to blend. Make a well in the centre.

Beat the eggs, oil and vanilla extract together and pour into the well. Using an electric whisk, gradually beat, drawing in the flour mixture from the side until a smooth batter forms. Stir in the carrots, crushed pineapple and chopped nuts until blended. Pour into the prepared tin and level the surface evenly. Bake in the preheated oven for 50 minutes, or until firm and a skewer inserted into the centre comes out clean. Remove from the oven and leave to cool before removing from the tin and discarding the lining paper.

For the frosting, beat the cream cheese, butter and vanilla extract together until smooth, then gradually beat in the icing/confectioners' sugar until the frosting is smooth. Add a little milk if necessary. Spread the frosting over the top. Refrigerate for about 1 hour to set the frosting, then cut into squares and serve.

Difficulty Rating: 2 points

Fresh Strawberry Sponge Cake

8–10 servings

Ingredients

175 g/6 oz/³⁄₄ cup (1¹⁄₂ sticks) unsalted butter, softened

175 g/6 oz/³⁄₄ cup caster/superfine sugar

1 tsp vanilla extract

3 large/extra large eggs, beaten

175 g/6 oz/1¹⁄₂ cups self-raising flour

150 ml/¹⁄₄ pint/²⁄₃ cup double/heavy cream

2 tbsp sifted icing/confectioners' sugar

225 g/8 oz/1¹⁄₂ cups fresh strawberries, hulled and chopped

few extra strawberries, to decorate

Preheat the oven to 190°C/ 375°F/Gas Mark 5 10 minutes before baking. Lightly oil and line the bases of 2 x 20.5 cm/8 inch round cake tins/pans with greaseproof/wax or baking paper.

Using an electric whisk, beat the butter, sugar and vanilla extract until pale and fluffy. Gradually beat in the eggs a little at a time, beating well between each addition.

Sift half the flour over the mixture and using a metal spoon or rubber spatula gently fold into the mixture. Sift over the remaining flour and fold in until just blended.

Divide the mixture between the prepared tins, spreading evenly. Gently smooth the surfaces with the back of a spoon. Bake in the centre of the preheated oven for 20–25 minutes until well risen and golden.

Remove and leave to cool before turning out onto a wire rack. Whip the cream with 1 tablespoon of the icing/confectioners' sugar until it forms soft peaks. Fold in the chopped strawberries.

Spread one cake layer evenly with the mixture and top with the second cake layer, rounded side up. Thickly dust the cake with the remaining icing sugar and decorate with the reserved strawberries. Carefully slide on to a serving plate and serve.

Difficulty Rating: 2 points

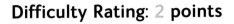

Italian Polenta Cake with Mascarpone Cream

Cuts into 6–8 slices

Ingredients

100 g/3¹/₂ oz/³/₄ cup plain/all-purpose flour

40 g/1¹/₂ oz/¹/₄ cup polenta or yellow cornmeal

1 tsp baking powder

¹/₄ tsp salt

grated zest of 1 lemon

2 large/extra-large eggs

150 g/5 oz/³/₄ cup caster/superfine sugar

5 tbsp milk

¹/₂ tsp almond extract

2 tbsp raisins or sultanas/golden raisins

75 g/3 oz/6 tbsp unsalted butter, softened

2 medium dessert pears, peeled, cored and thinly sliced

2 tbsp apricot jam/jelly

175 g/6 oz/³/₄ cup mascarpone cheese

1–2 tsp sugar

50 ml/2 fl oz/¹/₄ cup double/heavy cream

2 tbsp amaretto liqueur or rum

2–3 tbsp toasted flaked/slivered almonds

icing/confectioners' sugar, to dust

Preheat the oven to 190°C/375°F/Gas Mark 5, 10 minutes before baking. Butter a 23 cm/9 inch springform tin/pan. Dust lightly with flour. Stir the flour, polenta or cornmeal, baking powder, salt and lemon zest together.

Beat the eggs and half the sugar until light and fluffy. Slowly beat in the milk and almond extract. Stir in the raisins or sultanas/golden raisins, then beat in the flour mixture and 50 g/2 oz/¹/₄ cup of the butter. Spoon into the prepared tin and level the top evenly. Arrange the pear slices on top in overlapping concentric circles.

Melt the remaining butter and brush over the pear slices. Sprinkle with the rest of the sugar. Bake in the preheated oven for about 40 minutes until puffed and golden and the edges of the pears are lightly caramelized. Transfer to a wire rack. Reserve to cool in the tin for 15 minutes. Remove the cake from the tin.

Heat the apricot jam/jelly with 1 tablespoon water and brush over the top of the cake to glaze. Beat the mascarpone cheese with the sugar to taste, the cream and amaretto or rum until smooth and forming a soft dropping consistency. When the cake is cool, sprinkle over the almonds and dust generously with the icing/confectioners' sugar. Serve the cake with the liqueur-flavoured mascarpone cream on the side.

Difficulty Rating: 3 points

Christmas Cranberry Chocolate Roulade

Cuts into 12–14 slices

Ingredients

For the chocolate ganache frosting:
300 ml/¹/₂ pint/1¹/₄ cups double/heavy cream
350 g/12 oz dark/semisweet chocolate, chopped
2 tbsp brandy (optional)

For the roulade:
5 large/extra-large eggs, separated
3 tbsp cocoa powder (unsweetened), sifted, plus extra for dusting
125 g/4 oz/1¹/₄ cups sifted icing/confectioners' sugar, plus extra
   for dusting
¹/₄ tsp cream of tartar

For the filling:
175 g/6 oz/²/₃ cup cranberry sauce
1–2 tbsp brandy (optional)
450 ml/³/₄ pint/1³/₄ cups double/heavy cream, whipped to
   soft peaks

To decorate:
caramelized orange strips
dried cranberries

Preheat the oven to 200˚C/400˚F/Gas Mark 6. Bring the cream to the boil over a medium heat. Remove from the heat and add all of the chocolate, stirring until melted. Stir in the brandy, if using, and strain into a medium bowl. Cool, then refrigerate for 6–8 hours.

Lightly oil and line a 39 x 26 cm/15¹/₂ x 10¹/₂ inch Swiss roll tin/jelly roll pan with nonstick baking parchment. Using an electric whisk, beat the egg yolks until thick and creamy. Slowly beat in the cocoa powder and half the icing/confectioners' sugar and reserve. Whisk the egg whites and cream of tartar into soft peaks. Gradually whisk in the remaining sugar until the mixture is stiff and glossy. Gently fold the yolk mixture into the egg whites with a metal spoon or rubber spatula. Spread evenly into the prepared tin. Bake in the preheated oven for 15 minutes.

Remove and invert onto a large sheet of greaseproof/wax paper, dusted with cocoa powder. Cut off the crisp edges of the cake, then roll up. Leave on a wire rack until cold.

For the filling, heat the cranberry sauce with the brandy, if using, until warm and spreadable. Unroll the cooled cake and spread with the cranberry sauce. Leave to cool and set. Carefully spoon the whipped cream over the surface and spread to within 2.5 cm/1 inch of the edges. Re-roll the cake. Transfer to a cake plate or tray.

Allow the chocolate ganache to soften at room temperature, then beat until soft and of a spreadable consistency. Spread over the roulade and, using a fork, mark the roulade with ridges to resemble tree bark. Dust with icing sugar. Decorate with the caramelized orange strips and dried cranberries and serve.

Difficulty Rating: 5 points

Christmas Cake

Serves 12–14

Ingredients

900 g/2 lb/5 cups mixed dried fruit

75 g/3 oz/¹⁄₃ cup glacé/candied cherries, rinsed and halved

3 tbsp brandy or orange juice

finely grated zest and juice of 1 lemon

225 g/8 oz/1 cup packed soft dark muscovado/brown sugar

225 g/8 oz/1 cup (2 sticks butter), at room temperature

4 medium/large eggs, beaten

225 g/8 oz/1³⁄₄ cups plain/all-purpose flour

1 tbsp black treacle/molasses

1 tbsp mixed spice

To decorate:

2–4 tbsp brandy (optional)

4 tbsp sieved apricot jam/jelly

700 g/1¹⁄₂ lb almond paste

1 kg/2 lb 3 oz ready-to-roll sugarpaste

icing/confectioners' sugar, for dusting

bought decorations and ribbon

Place the mixed dried fruit and cherries in a bowl and sprinkle over the brandy or orange juice and the lemon zest and juice. Stir and leave to soak for 2–4 hours. Preheat the oven to 150°C/300°F/Gas Mark 2. Grease and double line the base and sides of a 20.5 cm/8 inch round deep cake tin. Beat the sugar and butter together until soft and fluffy. Beat the eggs in gradually, adding 1 teaspoon flour with each addition. Stir in the treacle/molasses, then sift in the rest of the flour and the spice. Add the soaked fruit and stir until the mixture is smooth. Spoon into the prepared tin and level the top. Bake for 1 hour, then reduce the temperature to 140°C/275°F/Gas Mark 1 and bake for a further 2–2¹⁄₂ hours until a skewer inserted into the centre comes out clean. Leave the cake to cool in the tin, then, when completely cold, remove from the tin, wrap in greaseproof/wax paper and then in foil and store in a cool place for 1–3 months.

To decorate, brush the cake all over with brandy, if using. Heat the jam and brush over the top and sides. Roll out one third of the almond paste and cut into a disc the size of the top of the cake using the empty tin as a guide. Place the disc on top.

Roll the remaining paste into a strip long enough to cover the sides of the cake and press on. Leave the almond paste to dry out for two days in a cool place. On a surface dusted with icing/confectioners' sugar, roll out the sugarpaste to a circle large enough to cover the top and sides of the cake. Brush 1 tablespoon brandy, or cold boiled water, over the almond paste and place the sugarpaste on top. Smooth down and trim. Make a border from tiny balls of sugarpaste and decorate.

Difficulty Rating: 5 points

French Chocolate Pecan Torte

Cuts into 16 slices

Ingredients

200 g/7 oz dark/semisweet chocolate, chopped

150 g/5 oz/²/₃ cup (1¹/₄ sticks) butter, diced

4 large/extra-large eggs

100 g/3¹/₂ oz/¹/₂ cup caster/superfine sugar

2 tsp vanilla extract

125 g/4 oz/1¹/₄ cups finely ground pecans

2 tsp ground cinnamon

24 lightly toasted pecan halves, to decorate

For the chocolate glaze:

125 g/4 oz dark/semisweet chocolate, chopped

65 g/2¹/₂ oz/5 tbsp butter, diced

2 tbsp clear honey

¹/₄ tsp ground cinnamon

Preheat the oven to 180°C/350°F/Gas Mark 4, 10 minutes before baking. Lightly butter and line a 20.5 x 5 cm/8 x 2 inch springform tin/pan with nonstick baking parchment. Wrap the tin in a large sheet of kitchen foil to prevent water seeping in.

Melt the chocolate and butter in a saucepan over a low heat and stir until smooth. Remove from the heat and cool.

Using an electric whisk, beat the eggs, sugar and vanilla extract until light and foamy. Gradually beat in the melted chocolate, ground nuts and cinnamon, then pour into the prepared tin.

Set the foil-wrapped tin in a large roasting tin and pour in enough boiling water to come 2 cm/³/₄ inch up the sides of the tin. Bake in the preheated oven until the edge is set, but the centre is still soft when the tin is gently shaken. Remove from the oven and place on a wire rack to cool.

For the glaze, melt all the ingredients over a low heat until melted and smooth, then remove from the heat. Dip each pecan halfway into the glaze and set on a sheet of nonstick baking parchment until set. Allow the remaining glaze to thicken slightly.

Remove the cake from the tin and invert. Pour the glaze over the cake, smoothing the top and spreading the glaze around the sides. Arrange the glazed pecans around the edge of the torte. Leave to set and serve.

Difficulty Rating: 4 points

Cassatta

Serves 6–8

Ingredients

300 g/11 oz dark/semisweet chocolate, broken into pieces
200 g/7 oz/1 cup fresh chilled custard
150 ml/¼ pint/²⁄₃ cup whipping cream
275 g/10 oz/2½ cups good-quality pistachio ice cream
25 g/1 oz/¼ cup shelled pistachios, toasted
50 g/2 oz/¹⁄₃ cup candied peel, finely chopped
25 g/1 oz/1 tbsp finely chopped glacé/candied cherries
275 g/10 oz/2½ cups good-quality strawberry ice cream

Line a 450 g/1 lb loaf tin/pan with plastic wrap. Place in the freezer. Melt 100 g/3½ oz of the chocolate into a heatproof bowl set over a saucepan of simmering water, stir until smooth, then cool. Place the custard into a bowl. Stir in the cream and the chocolate and stir until mixed. Spoon into a shallow, lidded freezer box and transfer to the freezer. Every 2 hours remove from the freezer and using an electric whisk, whisk thoroughly. Repeat 3 times, then leave until frozen solid.

Remove the chocolate ice cream from the freezer and allow to soften. Remove the loaf tin from the freezer and press the chocolate ice cream into the bottom of the tin, press down well and allow it to come up the sides of the tin. Return to the freezer and leave until solid.

Soften the pistachio ice cream, then beat in the pistachios, candied peel and cherries. Spoon into the tin, pressing down well and levelling the top. Return to the freezer until hard. Soften the strawberry ice cream and spread on to the pistachio ice cream. Smooth the top. Return to the freezer for at least 1 hour, or until completely solid.

Meanwhile, melt the remaining chocolate, stir until smooth and cool slightly. Remove the loaf tin from the freezer. Dip into hot water and turn out onto a serving dish. Using a teaspoon, drizzle the chocolate over the ice cream in a haphazard pattern. Return the cassatta to the freezer, until the chocolate has set. Dip a knife in hot water and use to slice the cassatta. Serve immediately.

Difficulty Rating: 4 points

Summer Fruit Semifreddo

Serves 6–8

Ingredients

225 g/8 oz/2 cups raspberries
125 g/4½ oz/1 cup blueberries
125 g/4½ oz/1 cup redcurrants
50 g/2 oz/½ cup icing/confectioners' sugar
juice of 1 lemon
1 vanilla pod/bean, split
50 g/2 oz/¼ cup sugar
4 large/extra-large eggs, separated
600 ml/1 pint/2½ cups double/heavy cream
pinch salt
fresh redcurrants, to decorate

Wash and remove stalks from the fruits, as necessary, then put them into a food processor or blender with the icing/confectioners' sugar and lemon juice. Blend to a purée. pour into a jug/pitcher and chill in the refrigerator until needed.

Remove the seeds from the vanilla pod/bean by opening the pod and scraping with the back of a knife. Add the seeds to the sugar and whisk with the egg yolks until pale and thick.

In another bowl, whip the cream until soft peaks form. Do not overwhip. In a third bowl, whisk the egg whites with the salt until stiff peaks form. Using a large metal spoon (to avoid knocking any air from the mixture) fold together the fruit purée, egg yolk mixture, the cream and egg whites. Transfer the mixture to a round, shallow, lidded freezer box and put into the freezer until almost frozen. If the mixture freezes solid, thaw in the refrigerator until semi-frozen. Turn out the semi-frozen mixture, cut into wedges and serve decorated with a few fresh redcurrants. If the mixture thaws completely, eat immediately and do not re-freeze.

Difficulty Rating: 3 points

Lemony Coconut Cake

Cuts into 10–12 slices

Ingredients

275 g/9½ oz/2½ cups plain/all-purpose flour

2 tbsp cornflour/cornstarch

1 tbsp baking powder

1 tsp salt

150 g/5 oz/½ cup white vegetable fat/shortening or soft
  margarine

275 g/10 oz/1¼ cups caster/superfine sugar

grated zest of 2 lemons

1 tsp vanilla extract

3 large/extra-large eggs

150 ml/¼ pint/⅔ cup milk

4 tbsp Malibu or rum

450 g/1 lb jar lemon curd

lime zest, to decorate

For the frosting:

275 g/10 oz/1¼ cups caster/superfine sugar

1 tbsp glucose

¼ tsp salt

1 tsp vanilla extract

3 large/extra-large egg whites

75 g/3 oz/½ cup desiccated/shredded coconut

Preheat the oven to 180°C/350°F/Gas Mark 4, 10 minutes
before baking. Lightly oil and flour two 20.5 cm/8 inch nonstick
cake tins/pans.

Sift the flour, cornflour/cornstarch, baking powder and salt into
a large bowl and add the white vegetable fat/shortening or
margarine, sugar, lemon zest, vanilla extract, eggs and milk. With
an electric whisk on a low speed, beat until blended, adding a
little extra milk if the mixture is very stiff. Increase the speed to
medium and beat for about 2 minutes.

Divide the mixture between the prepared tins and level the tops
evenly. Bake in the preheated oven for 20–25 minutes until the
cakes feel firm and are cooked. Remove from the oven and cool
before removing from the tins.

Put all the ingredients for the frosting, except the coconut, into
a heatproof bowl placed over a saucepan of simmering water.
(Do not allow the base of the bowl to touch the water.) Pour in
125 ml/4 fl oz/½ cup water, then, using an electric whisk, blend
the frosting ingredients on a low speed. Increase the speed to
high and beat for 7 minutes until the whites are stiff and glossy.
Remove the bowl from the heat and continue beating until
cool. Cover with plastic wrap.

Using a serrated knife, split the cake layers horizontally in half
and sprinkle each cut surface with the Malibu or rum. Sandwich
the cakes together with the lemon curd and press lightly.
Spread the top and sides generously with the frosting, swirling
and peaking the top.

Sprinkle the coconut over the top of the cake and gently press
onto the sides to cover. Decorate the coconut cake with the
lime zest and serve.

Difficulty Rating: 4 points

Coffee & Walnut Gateau with Brandied Prunes

Cuts into 10–12 slices

Ingredients

For the prunes:
225 g/8 oz/1¼ cups ready-to-eat pitted dried prunes
150 ml/¼ pint/²⁄₃ cup cold tea
3 tbsp brandy

For the cake:
450 g/1 lb/4½ cups walnut pieces
50 g/2 oz/⅓ cup self-raising flour
½ tsp baking powder
1 tsp instant coffee powder (not granules)
5 large/extra-large eggs, separated
¼ tsp cream of tartar
150 g/5 oz/¾ cup caster/superfine sugar
2 tbsp sunflower/corn oil
8 walnut halves, to decorate

For the filling:
600 ml/1 pint/2½ cups double/heavy cream
4 tbsp sifted icing/confectioners' sugar, sifted
2 tbsp coffee-flavoured liqueur

Preheat the oven to 180°C/350°F/Gas Mark 4, 10 minutes before baking. Put the prunes in a small bowl with the tea and brandy and leave to stand for 3–4 hours or overnight. Oil and line the bases of two 23 cm/9 inch cake tins/pans. Chop the walnut pieces in a food processor. Reserve a quarter of the nuts. Add the flour, baking powder and coffee and blend until finely ground.

Whisk the egg whites with the cream of tartar until soft peaks form. Sprinkle in one third of the sugar, 2 tablespoons at a time, until stiff peaks form. In another bowl, beat the egg yolks, oil and the remaining sugar until thick. Using a metal spoon or rubber spatula, alternately fold in the nut mixture and egg whites until just blended. Divide the mixture evenly between the prepared tins, levelling the tops.

Bake in the preheated oven for 30–35 minutes until the tops of the cakes spring back when lightly pressed with a clean finger. Remove from the oven and cool. Remove from the tins and discard the lining paper.

Drain the prunes, reserving the soaking liquid. Dry on paper towels, then chop and reserve. Whip the cream with the icing/confectioners' sugar and liqueur until soft peaks form. Spoon one eighth of the cream into a decorating bag fitted with a star tip.

Cut the cake layers in half horizontally. Sprinkle each cut side with 1 tablespoon of the reserved prune–soaking liquid. Sandwich the cakes together with half of the cream and all of the chopped prunes. Spread the remaining cream around the sides of the cake and press in the reserved chopped walnuts. Pipe rosettes around the edge of the cake. Decorate with walnut halves and serve.

Difficulty Rating: 4 points

Wild Strawberry & Rose Petal Jam Cake

Cuts into 8 servings

Ingredients

275 g/10 oz/2 heaping cups plain/all-purpose flour

1 tsp baking powder

¼ tsp salt

150 g/5 oz/⅔ cup (1¼ sticks) unsalted butter, softened

200 g/7 oz/1 cup caster/superfine sugar

2 large/extra-large eggs, beaten

2 tbsp rosewater

125 ml/4 fl oz/½ cup milk

125 g/4 oz/⅓ cup slightly warmed rose petal or
　strawberry jam/jelly,

125 g/4 oz/1 scant cup wild strawberries, hulled, or baby
　strawberries, chopped

frosted rose petals, to decorate

For the rose cream filling:

200 ml/7 fl oz/¾ cup double/heavy cream

25 ml/1 fl oz/2 tbsp plain Greek yogurt

2 tbsp rosewater

1–2 tbsp icing/confectioners' sugar

Preheat the oven to 180°C/350°F/Gas Mark 4, 10 minutes before baking. Lightly oil and flour a 20.5 cm/8 inch nonstick cake tin/pan. Sift the flour, baking powder and salt into a bowl and reserve.

Beat the butter and sugar until light and fluffy. Beat in the eggs, a little at a time, then stir in the rosewater. Gently fold in the flour mixture and milk with a metal spoon or rubber spatula and mix lightly together. Spoon the cake mixture into the prepared tin, spreading evenly and smoothing the top. Bake in the preheated oven for 25–30 minutes until well risen and golden and the centre springs back when pressed with a clean finger. Remove and cool, then remove from the tin.

For the filling, whip the cream, yogurt, 1 tablespoon of rosewater and 1 tablespoon of icing/confectioners' sugar until soft peaks form. Split the cake horizontally in half and sprinkle with the remaining rosewater.

Spread the warmed jam/jelly on the base of the cake. Top with half the whipped cream mixture, then sprinkle with half the strawberries. Place the remaining cake half on top. Spread with the remaining cream and swirl if desired. Decorate with the rose frosted petals. Dust the cake lightly with a little icing sugar and serve.

Difficulty Rating: 4 points

Celebration Fruit Cake

Cuts into 16 slices

Ingredients

125 g/4 oz/^{1}/$_2$ cup (1 stick) butter or margarine

125 g/4 oz/^{2}/$_3$ cup soft dark brown sugar

400 g/13 oz canned crushed pineapple

150 g/5 oz/1 cup raisins

150 g/5 oz/1 cup sultanas/golden raisins

125 g/4 oz/^{3}/$_4$ cup finely chopped crystallized/candied ginger

125 g/4 oz/^{2}/$_3$ cup finely chopped glacé/candied cherries

125 g/4 oz/^{3}/$_4$ cup mixed/candied cut peel

225 g/8 oz/1^3/$_4$ cups self-raising flour

1 tsp bicarbonate of soda/baking soda

2 tsp mixed/pumpkin pie spice

1 tsp ground cinnamon

^{1}/$_2$ tsp salt

2 large/extra-large eggs, beaten

For the topping:

100 g/3^1/$_2$ oz/1 cup pecan or walnut halves, lightly toasted

125 g/4 oz/^{3}/$_4$ cup red, green and yellow glacé/candied cherries

100 g/3^1/$_2$ oz/^{2}/$_3$ cup small pitted prunes or dates

2 tbsp clear honey

Preheat the oven to 170°C/325°F/Gas Mark 3, 10 minutes before baking. Heat the butter and sugar in a saucepan until the sugar has dissolved, stirring frequently. Add the pineapple and juice, dried fruits and peel. Bring to the boil, simmer for 3 minutes, stirring occasionally, then remove from the heat to cool completely.

Lightly oil and line the base of a 20.5 x 7.5 cm/8 x 3 inch loose-bottomed cake tin/pan with nonstick baking parchment.

Sift the flour, bicarbonate of soda/baking soda, spices and salt into a bowl. Add the boiled fruit mixture to the flour with the eggs and mix. Spoon into the prepared tin and level the top. Bake in the preheated oven for 1^1/$_4$ hours, or until a skewer inserted into the centre comes out clean. (If the cake is browning too quickly, cover loosely with kitchen foil and reduce the oven temperature.) Remove and cool completely before removing from the tin and discarding the lining paper.

Arrange the nuts, cherries and prunes or dates in an attractive pattern on top of the cake. Heat the honey and brush over the topping to glaze. Alternatively, toss the nuts and fruits in the warm honey and spread evenly over the top of the cake. Cool completely and store in a cake tin for a day or two before serving to allow the flavours to develop.

Difficulty Rating: 3 points

Toffee Walnut Swiss Roll

Cuts into 10–12 slices

Ingredients

4 large/extra-large eggs, separated
$^1/_2$ tsp cream of tartar
125 g/4 oz/1$^1/_4$ cups icing/confectioners' sugar, plus extra for
    dusting
$^1/_2$ tsp vanilla extract
125 g/4 oz/1 cup self-raising flour

For the toffee walnut filling:

2 tbsp plain/all-purpose flour
150 ml/$^1/_4$ pint/$^2/_3$ cup milk
5 tbsp golden/light corn syrup or maple syrup
2 large/extra-large egg yolks, beaten
100 g/3$^1/_2$ oz/1 cup toasted and chopped walnuts or pecans,
300 ml/$^1/_2$ pint/1$^1/_4$ cups double/heavy cream, whipped

Preheat the oven to 190°C/375°F/Gas Mark 5, 10 minutes before baking. Lightly oil and line a Swiss roll tin/jelly roll pan with nonstick baking parchment. Beat the egg whites and cream of tartar until softly peaking. Gradually beat in 50 g/2 oz/$^1/_2$ cup of the icing/confectioners' sugar until stiff peaks form.

In another bowl, beat the egg yolks with the remaining icing sugar until thick. Beat in the vanilla extract. Gently fold in the flour and egg whites alternately, using a metal spoon or rubber spatula. Do not overmix. Spoon the batter into the prepared tin and spread evenly. Bake in the preheated oven for 12 minutes, or until well risen and golden and the cake springs back when pressed with a clean finger.

Lay a clean dishtowel on a work surface and lay a piece of baking parchment about 33 cm/13 inches long on the towel. Dust with icing sugar. As soon as the cake is cooked, turn out onto the paper. Peel off the lining paper and cut off the crisp edges of the cake. Starting at one narrow end, roll the cake with the paper and towel. Transfer to a wire rack and cool completely.

For the filling, put the flour, milk and syrup into a small saucepan and place over a gentle heat. Bring to the boil, whisking until thick and smooth. Remove from the heat and

slowly beat into the beaten egg yolks. Pour the mixture back into the saucepan and cook over a low heat until it thickens and coats the back of a spoon. Strain the mixture into a bowl and stir in the chopped walnuts or pecans. Cool, stirring occasionally, then fold in about half of the whipped cream. Unroll the cooled cake and spread the filling over the cake. Re-roll and decorate with the remaining cream. Sprinkle with icing sugar and serve.

Difficulty Rating: 4 points

Raspberry & Hazelnut Meringue Cake

Cuts into 8 slices

Ingredients

For the meringue:
4 large/extra-large egg whites
¼ tsp cream of tartar
225 g/8 oz/1 heaping cup caster/superfine sugar
75 g/3 oz/¾ cup skinned, toasted and finely ground hazelnuts

For the filling:
300 ml/½ pint/1¼ cups double/heavy cream
1 tbsp icing/confectioners' sugar
1–2 tbsp raspberry-flavoured liqueur (optional)
350 g/12 oz/3 scant cups fresh raspberries

Preheat the oven to 140°C/275°F/Gas Mark 1. Line two baking sheets with nonstick baking parchment and draw a 20.5 cm/ 8 inch circle on each. Whisk the egg whites and cream of tartar until soft peaks form, then gradually beat in the sugar, 2 tablespoons at a time. Beat well after each addition, beating until the whites are stiff and glossy. Using a metal spoon or rubber spatula, gently fold in the ground hazelnuts.

Divide the mixture evenly between the two circles and spread neatly. Swirl one of the circles to make a decorative top layer. Bake in the preheated oven for about 1½ hours until crisp and dry. Turn off the oven and leave the meringues to cool for 1 hour. Transfer to a wire rack to cool completely. Carefully peel off the papers.

For the filling, whip the cream, icing/confectioners' sugar and liqueur, if using, together until soft peaks form. Place the flat round on a serving plate. Spread over most of the cream, reserving some for decorating, and arrange the raspberries in concentric circles over the cream. Place the swirly meringue on top of the cream and raspberries, pressing down gently. Pipe the remaining cream onto the meringue and decorate with a few raspberries and serve.

Difficulty Rating: 2 points

Chocolate & Almond Daquoise with Summer Berries

Cuts into 8 servings

Ingredients

For the almond meringues:
6 large/extra-large egg whites
¼ tsp cream of tartar
275 g/10 oz/1⅓ cups caster/superfine sugar
½ tsp almond extract
50 g/2 oz/½ cup blanched or flaked/slivered almonds,
   lightly toasted and finely ground

For the chocolate buttercream:
75 g/3 oz/6 tbsp butter, softened
450 g/1 lb/4½ cups sifted icing/confectioners' sugar
50 g/2 oz/½ cup sifted cocoa powder (unsweetened)
3–4 tbsp milk or single/light cream
550 g/1¼ lb/4½ cups mixed summer berries,
   such as raspberries, strawberries and blackberries

To decorate:
toasted flaked/slivered almonds
icing/confectioners' sugar

Preheat the oven to 140°C/275°F/Gas Mark 1, 10 minutes before baking. Line three baking sheets with nonstick baking parchment and draw a 20.5 cm/8 inch round on each one.

Whisk the egg whites and cream of tartar until soft peaks form. Gradually beat in the sugar, 2 tablespoons at a time, beating well after each addition, until the whites are stiff and glossy. Beat in the almond extract, then, using a metal spoon or rubber spatula, gently fold in the ground almonds. Divide the mixture evenly between the three circles of baking parchment, spreading neatly into the rounds and levelling the tops evenly. Bake in the preheated oven for about 1¼ hours until crisp, rotating the baking sheets halfway through cooking. Turn off the oven, leave to cool for about 1 hour, then remove and cool completely before discarding the lining paper.

Beat the butter, icing/confectioners' sugar and cocoa until smooth and creamy, adding the milk or cream to form a soft consistency.

Reserve a quarter of the berries to decorate. Spread one meringue with a third of the buttercream and top with a third of the remaining berries. Repeat with the other meringues, buttercream and berries. Scatter with the toasted flaked/slivered almonds and the reserved berries and sprinkle with icing sugar and serve.

Difficulty Rating: 3 points

Orange Fruit Cake

Cuts into 10–12 slices

Ingredients

225 g/8 oz/1¾ cups self-raising flour

2 tsp baking powder

225 g/8 oz/1 heaping cup caster/superfine sugar

225 g/8 oz/1 cup (2 sticks) butter, softened

4 large/extra-large eggs

grated zest of 1 orange

2 tbsp orange juice

2–3 tbsp Cointreau

125 g/4 oz/1 cup chopped nuts

Cape gooseberries/ground cherries, blueberries, raspberries and
    mint sprigs, to decorate

icing/confectioners' sugar, to dust (optional)

For the filling:

450 ml/¾ pint/1¾ cups double/heavy cream

50 ml/2 fl oz/¼ cup plain Greek yogurt

½ tsp vanilla extract

2–3 tbsp Cointreau

1 tbsp icing/confectioners' sugar

450 g/1 lb orange fruits, such as mango, peach, nectarine,
    papaya and yellow plums

Preheat the oven to 180°C/350°F/Gas Mark 4, 10 minutes before baking. Lightly oil and line the base of a 25.5 cm/10 inch deep cake tin/pan or springform tin with nonstick baking parchment.

Sift the flour and baking powder into a large bowl and stir in the sugar. Make a well in the centre and add the butter, eggs, grated zest and orange juice. Beat until blended and a smooth batter is formed. Turn into the prepared tin and level the top.

Bake in the preheated oven for 35–45 minutes until golden and the sides begin to shrink from the edge of the tin. Cool before removing from the tin and discard the lining paper.

Using a serrated knife, slice off the top third of the cake, cutting horizontally. Sprinkle the cut sides with the Cointreau.

For the filling, whip the cream and yogurt with the vanilla extract, Cointreau and icing/confectioners' sugar until soft peaks form. Chop the orange fruit and fold into the cream. Spread some of this mixture onto the bottom cake layer. Transfer to a serving plate. Cover with the top layer of sponge and spread the remaining cream mixture over the top and sides. Press the chopped nuts into the sides of the cake and decorate the top with the berries. If liked, dust the top with icing sugar before serving.

Difficulty Rating: 4 points

Chocolate Mousse Cake

Cuts into 8–10 servings

Ingredients

450 g/1 lb dark/semisweet chocolate, chopped
125 g/4 oz/¹/₂ cup (1 stick) butter, softened
3 tbsp brandy
9 large/extra-large eggs, separated
150 g/5 oz/³/₄ cup caster/superfine sugar

For the chocolate glaze:
250 ml/8 fl oz/1 cup double/heavy cream
225 g/8 oz dark/semisweet chocolate, chopped
2 tbsp brandy
1 tbsp single/light cream and white chocolate curls, to decorate

Preheat the oven to 180 C/350 F/Gas Mark 4, 10 minutes before baking. Lightly oil and line the bases of two 20.5 cm/ 8 inch springform tins/pans with baking parchment. Melt the chocolate and butter in a bowl set over a saucepan of simmering water. Stir until smooth. Remove from the heat and stir in the brandy.

Whisk the egg yolks and the sugar, reserving 2 tablespoons of the sugar, until thick and creamy. Slowly beat in the chocolate mixture until smooth and well blended.

Whisk the egg whites until soft peaks form, then sprinkle over the remaining sugar and continue whisking until stiff but not dry. Fold a large spoonful of the egg whites into the chocolate mixture. Gently fold in the remaining egg whites. Divide about two thirds of the mixture evenly between the prepared tins, tapping to distribute the mixture evenly. Reserve the remaining one third of the chocolate mousse mixture for the filling. Bake in the preheated oven for about 20 minutes until the cakes are well risen and set. Remove and cool for at least 1 hour.

Loosen the edges of the cake layers with a knife. Using the fingertips, lightly press the crusty edges down. Pour the rest of the mousse over one layer, spreading until even. Carefully unclip the side, remove the other cake from the tin and gently invert onto the mousse, bottom side up to make a flat top layer. Discard lining paper and chill for 4–6 hours until set.

To make the glaze, melt the cream and chocolate with the brandy in a heavy-based saucepan and stir until smooth. Cool until thickened. Unclip the side of the mousse cake and place on a wire rack. Pour over half the glaze and spread to cover. Leave to set, then decorate with chocolate curls. To serve, heat the remaining glaze and pour round each slice, and dot with cream.

Difficulty Rating: 4 points

Chocolate Box Cake

Cuts into 16 slices

Ingredients

175 g/6 oz/1⅓ cups self-raising flour

1 tsp baking powder

175 g/6 oz/1 scant cup caster/superfine sugar

175 g/6 oz/¾ cup (1½ sticks) butter, softened

3 large/extra-large eggs

25 g/1 oz/¼ cup cocoa powder (unsweetened)

150 g/5 oz/½ cup apricot preserve

cocoa powder (unsweetened), to dust

For the chocolate box:

275 g/10 oz dark/semisweet chocolate

For the chocolate whipped cream topping:

450 ml/¾ pint/1¾ cups double/heavy cream

275 g/10 oz dark/semisweet chocolate, melted

2 tbsp brandy

1 tsp cocoa powder (unsweetened), to decorate

Preheat the oven to 180°C/350°F/Gas Mark 4, 10 minutes before baking. Lightly oil and flour a 20.5 cm/8 inch square cake tin/pan. Sift the flour and baking powder into a large bowl and stir in the sugar. Using an electric whisk, beat in the butter and eggs.

Blend the cocoa powder with 1 tablespoon water, then beat into the creamed mixture. Turn into the prepared tin and bake in the preheated oven for about 25 minutes until well risen and cooked. Remove and cool before removing the cake from the tin.

To make the chocolate box, break the chocolate into small pieces, place in a heatproof bowl over a saucepan of gently simmering water and leave until soft. Stir occasionally until melted and smooth. Line a Swiss roll tin/jelly roll pan with nonstick baking parchment, then pour in the chocolate, tilting the tin to level. Leave to set. Once set, turn out onto a chopping board and carefully strip off the paper. Cut into four strips, the same length as the cooked sponge, using a large sharp knife that has been dipped into hot water. Gently heat the apricot preserve and sieve to remove lumps. Brush over the top and sides of the cake.

Carefully place the chocolate strips around the cake sides and press lightly. Leave to set for at least 10 minutes.

For the topping, whip the cream to soft peaks and quickly fold into the melted chocolate with the brandy. Spoon the chocolate whipped cream into a decorating bag fitted with a star tip and pipe a decorative design of rosettes or shells over the surface. Dust with cocoa powder and serve.

Difficulty Rating: 4 points

Vanilla & Lemon Panna Cotta with Raspberry Sauce

Serves 6

Ingredients

900 ml/1½ pints/3½ cups double/heavy cream
1 vanilla pod/bean, split
100 g/3½ oz/½ cup sugar
zest of 1 lemon
3 sheets gelatine
5 tbsp milk
450 g/1 lb/3 cups raspberries
3–4 tbsp icing/confectioners' sugar, to taste
1 tbsp lemon juice
extra lemon zest, to decorate

Put the cream, vanilla pod/bean and sugar into a saucepan. Bring to the boil, then simmer for 10 minutes until slightly reduced, stirring to prevent scalding. Remove from the heat, stir in the lemon zest and remove the vanilla pod.

Soak the gelatine in the milk for 5 minutes, or until softened. Squeeze out any excess milk and add to the hot cream. Stir well until dissolved.

Pour the cream mixture into six ramekins or mini pudding moulds and leave in the refrigerator for 4 hours, or until set.

Meanwhile, put 175 g/6 oz/1½ cups of the raspberries in a food processor with the icing/confectioners' sugar and lemon juice. Blend to a purée, then pass the mixture through a sieve. Stir in the remaining raspberries with a metal spoon or rubber spatula and chill in the refrigerator until ready to serve.

To serve, dip each of the moulds into hot water for a few seconds, then turn out on to individual serving plates. Spoon some of the raspberry sauce over and around the panna cotta, decorate with extra lemon zest and serve.

Difficulty Rating: 3 points

Ricotta Cheesecake with Strawberry Coulis

Serves 6–8

Ingredients

8 digestive biscuits/Graham crackers

100 g/3$\frac{1}{2}$ oz/$\frac{2}{3}$ cup mixed/candied peel, chopped

65 g/2$\frac{1}{2}$ oz/5 tbsp butter, melted

150 ml/$\frac{1}{4}$ pint/$\frac{2}{3}$ cup crème fraîche/sour cream

375 g/13 oz/1 cup ricotta cheese

100 g/3$\frac{1}{2}$ oz/$\frac{1}{2}$ cup caster/superfine sugar

1 vanilla pod/bean, seeds only

2 large/extra-large eggs

225 g/8 oz/1$\frac{1}{2}$ cups hulled fresh strawberries

2–4 tbsp caster/superfine sugar, to taste

zest and juice of 1 orange

Preheat the oven to 170°C/325°F/Gas Mark 3. Line a 20.5 cm/ 8 inch springform tin/pan with baking parchment. Put the biscuits/crackers in a food processor together with the peel. Blend until the biscuits are crushed and the peel is chopped. Add 50 g/ 2 oz/$\frac{1}{2}$ cup of the melted butter and process until mixed. Tip into the prepared tin and spread firmly and evenly over the bottom.

Blend together the crème fraîche/sour cream, ricotta cheese, sugar, vanilla seeds and eggs in a food processor. With the motor running, add the remaining melted butter and blend for a few seconds. Pour the mixture onto the base. Transfer to the preheated oven and cook for about 1 hour until set and risen round the edges, but slightly wobbly in the centre. Switch off the oven and allow to cool there. Chill in the refrigerator for at least 8 hours, or preferably overnight.

Wash and drain the strawberries. Put into the food processor along with 2 tablespoons of the sugar, the orange zest and juice. Blend until smooth. Add any remaining sugar, to taste. Pass through a sieve to remove seeds and chill in the refrigerator until needed. Cut the cheesecake into wedges, spoon over some of the strawberry coulis and serve.

Difficulty Rating: 2 points

Hazelnut, Chocolate & Chestnut Meringue Torte

Serves 8–10

Ingredients

For the chocolate meringue:
1 medium/large egg white
50 g/2 oz/¼ cup caster/superfine sugar
2 tbsp cocoa powder (unsweetened)

For the hazelnut meringue:
75 g/3 oz/¾ cup hazelnuts, toasted
2 medium/large egg whites
125 g/4 oz/⅔ cup caster/superfine sugar

For the filling:
300 ml/½ pint/1¼ cups double/heavy cream
250 g/9 oz can sweetened chestnut purée
50 g/2 oz dark/semisweet chocolate, melted
25 g/1 oz dark/semisweet chocolate, grated

Preheat the oven to 130°C/250°F/Gas Mark ½. Line three baking sheets with nonstick baking parchment and draw a 20.5 cm/ 8 inch circle on each. Beat 1 egg white until stiff peaks form. Add 25 g/1 oz/⅛ cup of the sugar and beat until shiny. Mix the cocoa powder with the remaining 25 g/1 oz/⅛ cup of sugar, adding 1 tablespoon at a time, beating well after each addition, until all the sugar is added and the mixture is stiff and glossy. Spread on to one of the baking sheets within the circle drawn on the underside.

Put the hazelnuts in a food processor and blend until chopped. In a clean bowl, beat the 2 egg whites until stiff. Add 50 g/ 2 oz/¼ cup of the sugar and beat. Add the remaining sugar about 1 tablespoon at a time, beating after each addition, until all the sugar is added and the mixture is stiff and glossy.

Reserve 2 tablespoons of the nuts, then fold in the remainder and divide between the two remaining baking sheets. Sprinkle one of the hazelnut meringues with the reserved hazelnuts and transfer all the baking sheets to the oven. Bake in the preheated oven for 1½ hours. Turn the oven off and leave in the oven until cold.

Whip the cream until thick. Beat the chestnut purée in another bowl until soft. Add a spoonful of the cream and fold together before adding the remaining cream and melted chocolate and folding together. Place the plain hazelnut meringue on a serving plate. Top with half the cream and chestnut mixture. Add the chocolate meringue and top with the remaining cream. Add the final meringue. Sprinkle over the grated chocolate and serve.

Difficulty Rating: 3 points

Bomba Siciliana

Serves 6–8

Ingredients

100 g/3¹/₂ oz dark/semisweet chocolate, in pieces

200 g/7 oz/1 cup fresh chilled custard

150 ml/¹/₄ pint/²/₃ cup whipping cream

2 tbsp finely chopped mixed/candied peel

2 tbsp sultanas/golden raisins

2 tbsp chopped glacé/candied cherries,

3 tbsp rum

225 g/8 oz/2 cups vanilla ice cream

200 ml/7 fl oz/³/₄ cup double/heavy cream

3 tbsp caster/superfine sugar

Melt the chocolate in a bowl set over a saucepan of simmering water until smooth, then leave to cool. Whisk together the custard with the whipping cream and slightly cooled chocolate. Spoon the mixture into a shallow, lidded freezer box and freeze. Every 2 hours, remove from the freezer and whisk using an electric or balloon whisk. Repeat three times, then leave until frozen solid. Soak the mixed/candied peel, sultanas/golden raisins and glacé/candied cherries in the rum and reserve.

Chill a bombe or 1 litre/1³/₄ pint/4 cup dessert mould in the freezer for 30 minutes. Remove the chocolate ice cream from the freezer to soften, then spoon the ice cream into the mould and press down well, smoothing around the edges and leaving a hollow in the centre. Return the ice cream to the freezer until frozen hard.

Remove the vanilla ice cream from the freezer to soften. Spoon it into the hollow, making sure to leave another hollow for the cream. Return to the freezer again and freeze until hard. Whip the cream and sugar until it is just holding its shape, then fold in the soaked fruit. Remove the mould from the freezer and spoon in the cream mixture. Return to the freezer for at least another hour.

When ready to serve, remove the mould from the freezer and dip into hot water for a few seconds, then turn on to a large serving plate. Dip a knife into hot water and cut into wedges to serve.

Difficulty Rating: 4 points

Marzipan Cake

Serves 12–14

Ingredients

450 g/1 lb/4 cups blanched almonds

300 g/11 oz/2¾ cups icing/confectioner's sugar, plus extra for dusting and rolling

4 egg whites

125 g/4½ oz/1 small Madeira or plain sponge cake

2 tbsp Marsala wine

225 g/8 oz/1 cup ricotta cheese

50 g/2 oz/¼ cup caster/superfine sugar

grated zest of 1 lemon

50 g/2 oz/⅓ cup finely chopped mixed/candied peel

25 g/1 oz/1 tbsp chopped glacé/candied cherries,

425 g/15 oz can peach halves, drained

200 ml/7 fl oz/¾ cup double/ heavy cream

Grind the blanched almonds in a food processor until fairly fine. Mix with 200 g/7 oz/⅔ cup of the icing/confectioners' sugar. Beat the egg whites until stiff then fold into the almond mixture to form a stiffish dough. Rest for 30 minutes.

Dust a work surface with some of the remaining icing sugar so that the marzipan does not stick. Roll out two thirds of the marzipan to a thickness of about 5 mm/¼ inches. Use to line a 25 x 20 cm/10 x 8 inch baking dish. Trim the edges; put the trimmings with the remainder of the marzipan.

Cut the Madeira cake into thin slices and make a layer of sponge to cover the bottom of the marzipan. Sprinkle with the Marsala wine. Beat the ricotta with the sugar and add the lemon zest, mixed/candied peel and glacé/candied cherries. Spread over the sponge. Slice the peaches and put them on top of the ricotta. Whip the cream and spread it over the peaches. Roll out the remaining marzipan and lay it over the cream to seal the whole cake, pressing down gently to remove any air. Press the edges of the marzipan together. Chill in the refrigerator for 2 hours. Turn the cake out on to a serving plate. Dust with icing sugar. Slice thickly and serve immediately.

Difficulty Rating: 4 points

Chestnut Cake

Serves 8–10

Ingredients

175 g/6 oz/¾ cup (1½ sticks) butter, softened

175 g/6 oz/¾ cup caster/superfine sugar

250 g/9 oz can sweetened chestnut purée

3 eggs, lightly beaten

175 g/6 oz/1½ cups plain/all-purpose flour

1 tsp baking powder

pinch ground cloves

1 tsp fennel seeds, crushed

75 g/3 oz/½ cup raisins

50 g/2 oz/½ cup toasted pine nuts

100 g/4 oz/1 cup icing/confectioners' sugar

5 tbsp lemon juice

pared strips of lemon rind, to decorate

Preheat the oven to 150°C/300°F/Gas Mark 2. Oil and line a 23 cm/9 inch springform tin/pan. Beat together the butter and sugar until light and fluffy. Add the chestnut purée and beat. Gradually add the eggs, beating after each addition. Sift in the flour with the baking powder and cloves. Add the fennel seeds and beat. The mixture should drop easily from a wooden spoon when tapped against the side of the bowl. If not, add a little milk.

Beat in the raisins and pine nuts. Spoon the mixture into the prepared tin/pan and level the top. Put in the centre of the preheated oven and bake for 55–60 minutes until a skewer inserted in the centre of the cake comes out clean. Remove from the oven and leave in the tin.

Meanwhile, mix together the icing/confectioners' sugar and lemon juice in a small saucepan until smooth. Heat gently until hot, but not boiling. Using a cocktail stick/toothpick or skewer, poke holes into the cake all over. Pour the hot syrup evenly over the cake and leave to soak into the cake. Decorate with pared strips of lemon rind and serve.

Difficulty Rating: 2 points

Sauternes & Olive Oil Cake

Cuts into 8–10 slices

Ingredients

125 g/4 oz/1 cup plain/all-purpose flour, plus extra for dusting
4 medium/large eggs
125 g/4 oz/²⁄₃ cup caster/superfine sugar
grated zest of ¹⁄₂ lemon
grated zest of ¹⁄₂ orange
2 tbsp Sauternes or other sweet dessert wine
3 tbsp very best-quality extra virgin olive oil
4 ripe peaches
1–2 tsp soft brown sugar, or to taste
1 tbsp lemon juice
icing/confectioners' sugar, for dusting

Preheat the oven to 140°C/275°F/Gas Mark 1. Oil and line a 25.5 cm/10 inch springform tin/pan. Sift the flour onto a large sheet of greaseproof/wax paper. Reserve.

Using a freestanding electric mixer, if possible, whisk the eggs and sugar together until pale and stiff. Add the lemon and orange zest. Turn the speed to low and pour the flour from the paper in a slow, steady stream onto the eggs and sugar mixture. Immediately add the wine and olive oil and switch the machine off, as the olive oil should not be incorporated completely.

Using a rubber spatula, fold the mixture very gently three or four times, so that the ingredients are just incorporated. Pour the mixture immediately into the prepared tin and bake in the oven for 20–25 minutes without opening the door for at least 15 minutes. Test if cooked by pressing the top lightly with a clean finger – if it springs back, remove from the oven. If not, bake for a little longer. Leave the cake to cool in the tin on a wire rack. Remove the cake from the tin when cool enough to handle.

Meanwhile, skin the peaches and cut into segments. Toss with the brown sugar and lemon juice and reserve. When the cake is cold, dust generously with icing/confectioners' sugar, cut into wedges and serve with the peaches.

Difficulty Rating: 4 points

Tiramisu

Serves 4

Ingredients

225 g/8 oz/1 cup mascarpone cheese

25 g/1 oz/¼ cup sifted icing/confectioners' sugar

150 ml/¼ pint/⅔ cup strong brewed coffee, chilled

300 ml/½ pint/1¼ cups double/heavy cream

3 tbsp coffee liqueur

125 g/4½ oz Savoiardi or sponge fingers/ladyfingers

50 g/2 oz dark/semisweet chocolate, grated or made
   into small curls

cocoa powder (unsweetened), for dusting

assorted summer berries, to serve

Lightly oil and line a 900 g/2 lb loaf tin with a piece of plastic wrap. Put the mascarpone cheese and icing/confectioners' sugar into a large bowl and, using a rubber spatula, beat until smooth. Stir in 2 tablespoons chilled coffee and mix thoroughly.

Whip the cream with 1 tablespoon of the coffee liqueur until just thickened. Stir a spoonful of the whipped cream into the mascarpone mixture, then fold in the rest. Spoon half of the mascarpone mixture into the prepared loaf tin and level the top.

Put the remaining coffee and coffee liqueur into a shallow dish just bigger than the sponge fingers/ladyfingers. Using half of them, dip one side of each sponge finger into the coffee mixture, then arrange on top of the mascarpone mixture in a single layer. Spoon the rest of the mascarpone mixture over the sponge fingers and level the top. Dip the remaining sponge fingers in the coffee mixture and arrange on top of the mascarpone mixture. Drizzle with any remaining coffee mixture. Cover with plastic wrap and chill in the refrigerator for 4 hours.

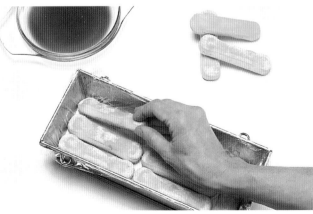

Carefully turn the tiramisu out on to a large serving plate. Sprinkle with the grated chocolate or chocolate curls. Dust with cocoa powder, cut into slices and serve with a few summer berries.

Difficulty Rating: 3 points

Cannoli with Ricotta Cheese

Makes 24

Ingredients

For the pastry:
25 g/1 oz/2 tbsp butter
25 g/1 oz/2 tbsp caster/superfine sugar
3 tbsp dry white wine
pinch salt
150 g/5 oz/1¼ cups plain/all-purpose flour
1 medium/large egg, lightly beaten
vegetable oil, for deep-frying

For the filling:
450 g/1 lb/2 cups ricotta cheese
125 g/4 oz/½ cup caster/superfine sugar
2 tbsp orange water
1 tsp vanilla extract
50 g/2 oz/2 tbsp chopped glacé/candied cherries
50 g/2 oz/2 tbsp chopped angelica
125 g/4 oz/⅔ cup chopped candied peel
75 g/3 oz dark/semisweet chocolate, finely chopped
icing/confectioners' sugar, for dusting

Beat together the butter and 25 g/1 oz of the sugar until light and fluffy. Add the white wine and salt and mix together well. Fold in the flour and knead to form a soft dough. Reserve for 2 hours.

Lightly flour a work surface and roll the dough out to a thickness of about ½ cm/¼ inch. Cut into 12.5 cm/5 inch squares. Wrap the pastry around the cannoli or cream horn moulds using the beaten egg to seal. Make 3–4 at a time.

Heat the vegetable oil to 180°C/350°F in a deep–fat fryer and fry the cannoli for 1–2 minutes until puffed and golden. Drain well on paper towels and leave to cool. Remove the moulds when the cannoli are cool enough to handle. Repeat until all the cannoli are cooked.

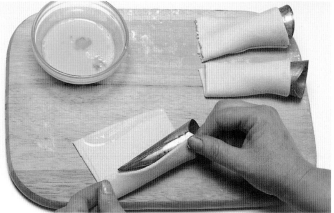

Beat the ricotta cheese with 125 g/4 oz/½ cup of caster/superfine sugar, orange water and vanilla extract until creamy. Add the cherries, angelica, candied peel and chopped chocolate. Fill each cannoli using a decorating bag with a large plain tip or a small spoon. Dust with icing/confectioner' sugar and serve cool, but not cold.

Difficulty Rating: 4 points

Raspberry Soufflé

Serves 4

Ingredients

125 g/4 oz/1 cup redcurrants
50 g/2 oz/¼ cup caster/superfine sugar
1 sachet (3 tsp) powdered gelatine
3 medium eggs, separated
300 g/½ pint/1 cup half-fat Greek yogurt
450 g/1 lb/4 cups raspberries, thawed if frozen

To decorate:
fresh mint sprigs
extra fruits

Wrap a band of double thickness greaseproof/wax paper around four ramekin dishes, making sure that 5 cm/2 inches of the paper stays above the top of each dish. Secure the paper to the dish with an elastic band or Sellotape/Scotch tape.

Place the redcurrants and 1 tablespoon of the sugar in a small saucepan. Cook for 5 minutes until softened. Remove from the heat, sieve and reserve.

Place 3 tablespoons water in a small bowl and sprinkle over the gelatine. Leave to stand for 5 minutes until spongy. Place the bowl over a pan of simmering water and leave until dissolved. Remove and leave to cool.

Beat together the remaining sugar and egg yolks until pale thick and creamy, then fold in the yogurt with a metal spoon or rubber spatula until well blended.

Sieve the raspberries and fold into the yogurt mixture with the gelatine. Whisk the egg whites until stiff and fold into the yogurt mixture. Pour into the prepared dishes and chill in the refrigerator for 2 hours until firm.

Remove the paper from the dishes and spread the redcurrant purée over the top of the soufflés. Decorate with fresh mint sprigs and extra fruits and serve.

Difficulty Rating: 4 points

Sweet Bites for After Dinner

Easily adaptable for any occasion, the varied dessert options in this section, from sophisticated selections such as Blackcurrant & Lemon Muffins or Black Forest Cupcakes, to tasty delights for kids such as Traffic Lights or Fondant Fancies, are sure to provide the simple dessert solution you're looking for. Why not try making Miracle Bars or Raspberry Butterfly Cupcakes? These little dessert bites are sure to delight any sweet tooth.

Cantuccini

Makes 24 biscuits

Ingredients

250 g/9 oz/2 cups plain/all-purpose flour

250 g/9 oz/2¼ cups caster/superfine sugar

½ tsp baking powder

½ tsp vanilla extract

2 medium/large eggs

1 medium/large egg yolk

100 g/3½ oz/¾ cup toasted and roughly chopped mixed
almonds and hazelnuts

1 tsp whole aniseed

1 medium/large egg yolk mixed with 1 tbsp water, to glaze

Vin Santo dessert wine or coffee, to serve

Preheat the oven to 180°C/350°F/Gas Mark 4. Line a large
baking sheet with nonstick baking parchment. Place the flour,
caster/superfine sugar, baking powder, vanilla extract, the whole
eggs and one of the egg yolks into a food processor and blend
until the mixture forms a ball, scraping down the sides once or
twice. Turn the mixture out onto a lightly floured surface and
knead in the chopped nuts and aniseed.

Divide the paste into three pieces and roll into logs about
4 cm/1½ inches wide. Place the logs onto the baking sheet at
least 5 cm/2 inches apart. Brush lightly with the other egg yolk
beaten with 1 tablespoon water and bake in the preheated
oven for 30–35 minutes.

Remove from the oven and reduce the oven temperature to
150°C/300°F/Gas Mark 2. Cut the logs diagonally into 2.5 cm/
1 inch slices and lay cut-side down on the baking sheet. Return
to the oven for a further 30–40 minutes until dry and firm. Cool
on a wire rack and store in an airtight container. Serve with Vin
Santo or coffee.

Difficulty Rating: 2 points

Almond & Pistachio Biscotti

Makes 12 biscuits

Ingredients

125 g/4 oz/1⅓ cups ground almonds
50 g/2 oz/⅓ cup shelled pistachios
50 g/2 oz/⅓ cup blanched almonds
2 medium/large eggs
1 egg yolk
125 g/4 oz/1¼ cups icing/confectioners' sugar
225 g/8 oz/1¾ cups plain/all-purpose flour
1 tsp baking powder
pinch salt
zest of ½ lemon

Preheat the oven to 180°C/350°F/Gas Mark 4, 10 minutes before baking. Line a large baking sheet with nonstick baking parchment. Toast the ground almonds and whole nuts lightly and reserve until cool.

Beat together the eggs, egg yolk and icing/confectioners' sugar until thick, then beat in the flour, baking powder and salt. Add the lemon zest, ground almonds and whole nuts and mix to form a slightly sticky dough.

Turn the dough onto a lightly floured surface and, using lightly floured hands, form into a log measuring approximately 30 cm/12 inches long. Place down the centre of the prepared baking sheet and transfer to the preheated oven. Bake for 20 minutes.

Remove from the oven and increase the oven temperature to 200°C/400°F/Gas Mark 6. Cut the log diagonally into 2.5 cm/ 1 inch slices. Return to the baking sheet, cut-side down, and bake for a further 10–15 minutes until golden, turning once. Leave to cool on a wire rack and store in an airtight container.

Difficulty Rating: 2 points

Lamington Cupcakes

Makes 12

Ingredients

125 g/4 oz/1 cup self-raising flour
125 g/4 oz/$^1/_2$ cup (1 stick) butter, softened
125 g/4 oz/$^1/_2$ cup golden caster/superfine sugar
2 medium/large eggs, beaten
1 tsp vanilla extract

To decorate:
350 g/12 oz/1$^1/_3$ cups caster/superfine sugar
1 tbsp cocoa powder (unsweetened)
65 g/2$^1/_2$ oz/$^3/_4$ cup desiccated/shredded coconut
ready-made chocolate decorations

Preheat the oven to 180°C/350°F/Gas Mark 4. Line a 12-hole muffin tray with deep paper cases.

Sift the flour into a bowl and add the butter, sugar, eggs and vanilla extract. Beat for about 2 minutes until smooth, then spoon into the paper cases.

Bake in the centre of the oven for about 18 minutes until well risen and springy in the centre. Transfer to a wire rack to cool.

To make the icing, place the caster/superfine sugar, cocoa powder and 125 ml/4 fl oz/$^1/_2$ cup water in a large heavy-based pan. Heat over a low heat until every grain of sugar has dissolved. Bring to the boil and then simmer for about 6 minutes, without stirring, until thickened into syrup. Pour into a bowl and use the syrup while it is still hot, as it will set as it cools.

Place the coconut into a large bowl. Dip the top of each cupcake into the hot chocolate syrup to coat the top, then dip in coconut, decorate with chocolate decorations and place on a tray to dry. Keep for 2–3 days in an airtight container.

Difficulty Rating: 3 points

Raspberry Butterfly Cupcakes

Makes 12–14

Ingredients

125 g/4 oz/¹/₂ cup caster/superfine sugar
125 g/4 oz/¹/₂ cup soft tub margarine
2 medium/large eggs
125 g/4 oz/1 cup self-raising flour
¹/₂ tsp baking powder
¹/₂ tsp vanilla extract

To decorate:
4 tbsp seedless raspberry jam
12–14 fresh raspberries
icing/confectioners' sugar, to dust

Preheat the oven to 190°C/375°F/Gas Mark 5. Line one or two bun trays with 12–14 paper cases, depending on the depth of the holes.

Place all the cupcake ingredients in a large bowl and beat with an electric mixer for about 2 minutes until smooth. Fill the paper cases halfway up with the mixture.

Bake for about 15 minutes until firm, risen and golden. Remove to a wire rack to cool. When cold, cut a small circle out of the top of each cupcake and then cut the circle in half to form wings.

Fill each cupcake with a teaspoon of raspberry jam. Replace the wings at an angle and top each with a fresh raspberry. Dust lightly with icing/confectioners' sugar and serve immediately.

Difficulty Rating: 2 points

Fruited Brioche Buns

Makes 12

Ingredients

225 g/8 oz/1¾ cups strong white/bread flour
pinch salt
1 tbsp caster/superfine sugar
7 g/¼ oz sachet easy-blend dried yeast
2 large/extra-large eggs, beaten
50 g/2 oz/4 tbsp butter, melted
beaten egg, for glazing

For the filling:
40 g/1½ oz/⅓ cup chopped blanched almonds
50 g/2 oz/⅓ cup luxury mixed dried fruit
1 tsp soft light brown sugar
2 tsp orange liqueur or brandy

Preheat the oven to 220°C/425°F/Gas Mark 7, 15 minutes before baking. Sift the flour and salt into a bowl. Stir in the sugar and yeast. Make a well in the centre. Add the eggs, butter and 2 tablespoons warm water and mix to a soft dough. Knead the dough on a lightly floured surface for 5 minutes until smooth and elastic. Put in an oiled bowl, cover with plastic wrap and leave to rise in a warm place for 1 hour, or until it has doubled in size.

Mix the ingredients for the filling together, cover the bowl and leave to soak while the dough is rising. Re-knead the dough for a minute or two, then divide into 12 pieces. Taking one at a time, flatten three quarters of each piece into a 6.5 cm/2½ inch round. Spoon a little filling in the centre, then pinch the edges together to enclose. Put seam-side down into a well-greased fluted 12-hole muffin tin/pan. Shape the smaller piece of dough into a round and place on top of the larger one.

Push a finger or floured wooden spoon handle through the middle of the top one and into the bottom one to join them together. Repeat with the remaining balls of dough. Cover the brioches with oiled plastic wrap and leave for about 20 minutes, or until risen. Brush the brioches with beaten egg and bake for 10–12 minutes until golden. Cool on a wire rack and serve.

Difficulty Rating: 4 points

Black Forest Cupcakes

Makes 12

Ingredients

1 tbsp cocoa powder (unsweetened)
175 g/6 oz/1½ cups self-raising flour
1 tsp baking powder
125 g/4 oz/½ cup soft tub margarine
175 g/6 oz/1 cup soft dark brown sugar
2 medium/large eggs
3 tbsp milk

To decorate:
125 g/4 oz dark/semisweet chocolate
4 tbsp warmed seedless raspberry jam
150 ml/¼ pint/⅔ cup double/heavy cream
1 tbsp kirsch (optional)
12 natural-coloured glacé/candied cherries

Preheat the oven to 180°C/350°F/Gas Mark 4. Line a 12-hole muffin tray with large paper cases. Blend the cocoa powder with 2 tablespoons boiling water and leave to cool.

Sift the flour and baking powder into a bowl and add the margarine, sugar, eggs, milk and the cocoa mixture. Whisk together for about 2 minutes until smooth, then spoon into the paper cases.

Bake for 15–20 minutes until springy to the touch. Cool in the tray for 5 minutes, then turn out onto a wire rack to cool.

To decorate the cupcakes, melt the chocolate and spread it out to cool on a clean plastic board. When it is almost set, pull a sharp knife through the chocolate to make curls. Refrigerate these until needed. Brush the top of each cupcake with a little raspberry jam. Whip the cream until it forms soft peaks, then fold in the kirsch, if using. Pipe or swirl the cream on top of each cupcake. Top with chocolate curls and glacé/candied cherries. Eat fresh or keep for 1 day in the refrigerator.

Difficulty Rating: 2 points

Strawberry Swirl Cupcakes

Makes 12

Ingredients

125 g/4 oz/¹/₂ cup caster/superfine sugar
125 g/4 oz/¹/₂ cup soft tub margarine
2 medium/large eggs
125 g/4 oz/1 cup self-raising flour
¹/₂ tsp baking powder
2 tbsp sieved strawberry jam

To decorate:

50 g/2 oz/4 tbsp unsalted butter at room temperature
300 g/11 oz/1¹/₃ sifted cups icing/confectioners' sugar
125 g/4 oz/¹/₂ cup full-fat cream cheese
1 tbsp sieved strawberry jam
pink food colouring

Preheat the oven to 190°C/375°F/Gas Mark 5. Line a muffin tray with 12 deep paper cases.

Place all the cupcake ingredients except the jam in a large bowl and beat with an electric mixer for about 2 minutes until smooth. Fill the paper cases halfway up with the mixture.

Add ¹/₂ teaspoon jam to each case and swirl it into the mixture. Bake for about 15 minutes until firm, risen and golden. Remove to a wire rack to cool.

To prepare the frosting, beat the butter until soft, then gradually add the icing/confectioners' sugar until the mixture is light. Add the cream cheese and whisk until light and fluffy. Divide the mixture in half and beat the strawberry jam and pink food colouring into one half. Fit a decorating bag with a wide star tip and spoon strawberry cream on one side of the bag and the plain cream on the other. Pipe swirls on top of the cupcakes. Keep for three days in an airtight container in a cool place.

Difficulty Rating: 2 points

Spiced Apple Doughnuts

Makes 8

Ingredients

225 g/8 oz/2 cups strong white/bread flour

$^1/_2$ tsp salt

1$^1/_2$ tsp ground cinnamon

1 tsp easy-blend dried yeast

75 ml/3 fl oz/6 tbsp warm milk

25 g/1 oz/2 tbsp butter, melted

1 medium/large egg, beaten

oil, for deep-frying

4 tbsp caster/superfine sugar, for coating

For the filling:

2 small eating apples, peeled, cored and chopped

2 tsp soft light brown sugar

2 tsp lemon juice

Sift the flour, salt and 1 teaspoon of the cinnamon into a large bowl. Stir in the yeast and make a well in the centre. Add the milk, butter and egg and mix to a soft dough. Knead on a lightly floured surface for 10 minutes until smooth and elastic.

Divide the dough into 8 pieces and shape each into a ball. Put on a floured baking sheet, cover with oiled plastic wrap and leave in a warm place for 1 hour, or until doubled in size.

To make the filling, put the apples in a saucepan with the sugar, lemon juice and 3 tablespoons water. Cover and simmer for about 10 minutes, then uncover and cook until fairly dry, stirring occasionally. Mash or blend in a food processor to a purée.

Pour enough oil into a deep-fat frying pan to come one-third of the way up the pan. Heat the oil to 180°C/350°F, then deep-fry the doughnuts for 1$^1/_2$–2 minutes on each side, until well browned.

Drain the doughnuts on paper towels, then roll in the caster/superfine sugar mixed with the remaining $^1/_2$ teaspoon ground cinnamon. Push a thick skewer into the centre to make a hole, then pipe in the apple filling. Serve warm or cold.

Difficulty Rating: 3 points

Coconut Macaroons

Makes 18

Ingredients

rice paper

2 medium/large egg whites

125 g/4 oz/1 cup icing/confectioners' sugar

125 g/4 oz/1⅓ cups desiccated/shredded coconut

125 g/4 oz/1⅓ cups ground almonds

finely grated zest of ½ lemon or lime

Difficulty Rating: 1 point

Preheat the oven to 180°C/350°F/Gas Mark 4. Line two baking sheets with rice paper.

Whisk the egg whites in a clean, dry bowl until soft peaks form. Using a large metal spoon, fold in the icing/confectioners' sugar. Fold in the coconut, almonds and lemon or lime zest until a sticky dough forms.

Heap dessertspoonfuls of the mixture onto the rice paper on the baking sheets. Bake for 10 minutes, then reduce the oven temperature to 150°C/300°F/Gas Mark 2.

Bake for a further 5–8 minutes until firm and golden, then remove to a wire rack to cool, breaking off any excess rice paper.

Chewy Choc & Nut Cookies

Makes 18

Ingredients

4 egg whites

350 g/12 oz/3 cups icing/confectioners' sugar

75 g/3 oz/³/₄ cup cocoa powder (unsweetened)

2 tbsp plain/all-purpose flour

1 tsp instant coffee powder

125 g/4 oz/1 cup finely chopped walnuts

Preheat the oven to 180°C/350°F/Gas Mark 4, 10 minutes before baking. Lightly grease several baking sheets. Line with a sheet of nonstick baking parchment.

Place the egg whites in a large, grease-free bowl. Whisk with an electric mixer until very frothy.

Add the sugar, cocoa powder, flour and coffee powder. Whisk again until the ingredients are blended thoroughly. Add 1 tablespoon water and continue to whisk on the highest speed until the mixture is very thick. Fold in the chopped walnuts.

Place tablespoons of the mixture onto the prepared baking sheets, leaving plenty of space between to allow them to expand during cooking. Bake in the preheated oven for 12–15 minutes until the tops are firm, golden and quite cracked. Leave to cool for 30 seconds, then, using a spatula, transfer to a wire rack and leave to cool. Store in an airtight container.

Difficulty Rating: 2 points

Double Cherry Cupcakes

Makes 12

Ingredients

50 g/2 oz/^{1}/$_2$ cup washed, dried and chopped
glacé/candied cherries
125 g/4 oz/1 cup self-raising flour
25 g/1 oz/^{1}/$_2$ cup dried morello/sour cherries
125 g/4 oz/^{1}/$_2$ cup soft margarine
125 g/4 oz/^{1}/$_2$ cup caster/superfine sugar
2 medium/large eggs
^{1}/$_2$ tsp almond extract

To decorate:
125 g/4 oz/1^1/$_4$ cup fondant icing/confectioners' sugar
pale pink liquid food colouring
40 g/1^1/$_2$ oz/2 tbsp glacé/candied cherries

Preheat the oven to 190°C/375°F/Gas Mark 5. Line a 12-hole muffin tray with deep paper cases.

Dust the chopped glacé/candied cherries lightly in a tablespoon of the flour, then mix with the morello cherries and reserve. Sift the rest of the flour into a bowl, then add the margarine, sugar, eggs and almond extract. Beat for about 2 minutes until smooth, then fold in the cherries.

Spoon the batter into the paper cases and bake for 15–20 minutes until well risen and springy in the centre. Turn out to cool on a wire rack.

To decorate the cupcakes, trim the tops level. Mix the icing/confectioners' sugar with 2–3 teaspoons warm water and a few drops of pink food colouring to make a thick consistency. Spoon the icing over each cupcake filling right up to the edge. Chop the cherries finely and sprinkle over the icing.

Leave to set for 30 minutes. Keep for three days in an airtight container.

Difficulty Rating: 2 points

Rocky Road Cupcakes

Makes 14–18

Ingredients

125 g/4 oz/1 cup self-raising flour
25 g/1 oz/^{1}/$_4$ cup cocoa powder (unsweetened)
125 g/4 oz/^{2}/$_3$ cup soft dark brown sugar
125 g/4 oz/^{1}/$_2$ cup soft margarine
2 medium/large eggs, beaten
2 tbsp milk

To decorate:
75 g/3 oz dark/semisweet chocolate, broken into pieces
40 g/1^1/$_2$ oz/3 tbsp butter
75 g/3 oz/1^2/$_3$ cups mini marshmallows
40 g/1^1/$_2$ oz/^{1}/$_4$ cup chopped mixed nuts

Preheat the oven to 180°C/350°F/Gas Mark 4. Line bun trays/shallow muffin pans with 14–18 paper cases or silicone cupcake moulds, depending on the depth of the holes.

Sift the flour and cocoa powder into a large bowl. Add the sugar, margarine, eggs and milk and whisk with an electric beater for about 2 minutes until smooth.

Divide the mixture evenly between the paper cases and bake for about 20 minutes until a skewer inserted into the middle comes out clean. Remove the tray from the oven but leave the oven on.

To make the topping, gently melt the chocolate and butter together in a small pan over a low heat. Place the melted chocolate mixture in a decorating bag made of greaseproof/wax paper and snip away the end. Pipe a little of the mixture on top of each cupcake, then scatter the marshmallows and nuts over each one and return to the oven. Bake for 2–3 minutes to soften the marshmallows. Remove from the oven and pipe the remaining chocolate over the marshmallows. Leave to cool in the tins for 5 minutes, then remove to cool on a wire rack. Serve warm or cold. Keep for two days in an airtight container.

Difficulty Rating: 2 points

Fudgy Chocolate Bars

Makes 14

Ingredients

25 g/1 oz/²/₃ cup glacé/candied cherries

65 g/2¹/₂ oz/¹/₂ cup shelled hazelnuts

150 g/5 oz dark/semisweet chocolate

150 g/5 oz/²/₃ cup (1¹/₄ sticks) unsalted butter

¹/₄ tsp salt

150 g/5 oz/1 cup chopped digestive biscuits/Graham crackers

1 tbsp icing/confectioners' sugar, sifted (optional)

Preheat the oven to 180°C/350°F/Gas Mark 4, 10 minutes before baking. Lightly oil an 18 cm/7 inch square tin/pan and line the base with nonstick baking parchment. Rinse the glacé/candied cherries thoroughly, dry well on paper towels and reserve.

Place the nuts on a baking sheet and roast in the preheated oven for 10 minutes, or until light golden brown. Leave to cool slightly, then chop roughly and reserve.

Break the chocolate into small pieces, place with the butter and salt into the top of a double boiler, or in a bowl set over a saucepan of simmering water. Heat gently, stirring, until melted and smooth. Alternatively, melt the chocolate in the microwave, according to the manufacturer's instructions. Chop the biscuits/crackers into 5 mm/¹/₄ inch pieces and cut the cherries in half. Add to the chocolate mixture with the nuts and stir well. Spoon the mixture into the prepared tin and level the top.

Chill in the refrigerator for 30 minutes. Remove from the tin, discard the baking parchment and cut into 14 bars. Cover lightly, return to the refrigerator and keep chilled until ready to serve.

To serve, lightly sprinkle the bars with sifted icing/confectioners' sugar, if using. Store covered in the refrigerator.

Difficulty Rating: 2 points

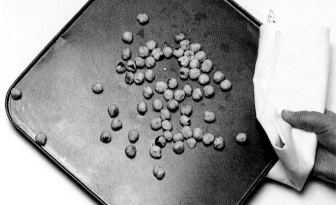

Crystallized Violet Cupcakes

Makes 12

Ingredients

150 g/5 oz/²⁄₃ cup (1¹⁄₄ sticks) butter, softened
150 g/5 oz/²⁄₃ cup caster/superfine sugar
3 medium/large eggs, beaten
150 g/5 oz/1¹⁄₂ cups self-raising flour
¹⁄₂ tsp baking powder
1 lemon

To decorate:

12 fresh violets
1 egg white
caster/superfine sugar
125 g/4 oz/1 cup fondant icing/confectioners' sugar
pale violet food colouring

Preheat the oven to 180°C/350°F/Gas Mark 4 and line a 12–hole muffin tray with deep paper cases.

Place the butter, sugar and eggs in a bowl. Sift in the flour and baking powder. Finely grate in the zest from the lemon.

Beat together for about 2 minutes with an electric hand mixer until pale and fluffy. Spoon into the paper cases and bake for 20–25 minutes until firm and golden. Cool on a wire rack.

To decorate the cupcakes, spread the violets on some nonstick baking parchment. Beat the egg white until frothy, then brush thinly over the violets. Dust with caster/superfine sugar and leave to dry out for 2 hours. Beat the icing/confectioners' sugar with the colouring and enough water to give a thin coating consistency. Drizzle over the top of each cupcake quickly and top with a violet. Leave to set for 30 minutes. Store in an airtight container in a cool place. Keep for two days.

Difficulty Rating: 2 points

Crispy Rice Cakes

Makes 18–20

Ingredients

75 g/3 oz/6 tbsp butter

150 g/5 oz/3 cups mini marshmallows

75 g/3 oz milk chocolate

50 g/2 oz/¹⁄₃ cup finely chopped dried, ready-to-eat apricots

25 g/1 oz/2 tbsp finely chopped glacé/candied cherries

125 g/4 oz/9 cups puffed rice breakfast cereal

Difficulty Rating: 1 point

Place 20 paper fairy-cake/shallow cases in two 12-hole bun trays/shallow muffin pans.

Put the butter and marshmallows in a heavy-based saucepan and add the chocolate broken into pieces. Melt together very gently over a low heat, stirring the mixture, until melted and sticky.

Remove from the heat and add the chopped apricots and cherries. Add the cereal and stir together with a large metal spoon.

While it is still warm, spoon the mixture into the paper cases and leave to set in the refrigerator for 30 minutes. Eat on the day of making.

Chocolate Shortcake

Makes 30–32

Ingredients

225 g/8 oz/1 cup (2 sticks) unsalted butter, softened

150 g/5 oz/1½ cups icing/confectioners' sugar

1 tsp vanilla extract

250 g/9 oz/2 cups plain/all-purpose flour

25 g/1 oz/⅓ cup cocoa powder (unsweetened)

¼ tsp salt

extra icing/confectioners' sugar, to decorate

Preheat the oven to 170°C/325°F/Gas Mark 3, 10 minutes before baking. Lightly oil several baking sheets and line with nonstick baking parchment. Place the butter, icing/confectioners' sugar and vanilla extract together in a food processor and blend briefly until smooth. Alternatively, using a wooden spoon, cream the butter, icing sugar and vanilla extract in a large bowl.

Sift the flour, cocoa powder and salt together, then either add to the food processor bowl and blend quickly to form a dough, or add to the bowl and, using your hands, mix together until a smooth dough is formed.

Turn the dough out onto a clean board lined with plastic wrap. Place another sheet of plastic wrap over the top and roll the dough out until it is 1 cm/½ inch thick. Transfer the whole board to the refrigerator and chill for 1½–2 hours.

Remove the top piece of plastic wrap and use a 5 cm/2 inch cutter to cut the dough into 30–32 rounds. Place the rounds on the prepared baking sheets and bake in the preheated oven for about 15 minutes until firm.

Cool for 1 minute, then, using a spatula, carefully remove the shortcakes from the baking parchment and transfer to a wire rack. Leave to cool completely. Sprinkle the shortcakes with sifted icing sugar before serving. Store in an airtight container for a few days.

Difficulty Rating: 2 points

Chocolate Macaroons

Makes 20

Ingredients

65 g/2½ oz dark/semisweet chocolate
125 g/4 oz/¾ cup ground almonds
125 g/4 oz/⅔ cup caster/superfine sugar
¼ tsp almond extract
1 tbsp cocoa powder (unsweetened)
2 medium/large egg whites
1 tbsp icing/confectioners' sugar

Preheat the oven to 180°C/350°F/Gas Mark 4, 10 minutes before baking. Lightly oil several baking sheets and line with sheets of nonstick baking parchment. Melt the chocolate in a heatproof bowl set over a saucepan of simmering water. Alternatively, melt in the microwave according to the manufacturer's instructions. Stir until smooth, then cool slightly.

Place the ground almonds in a food processor and add the sugar, almond extract, cocoa powder and one of the egg whites. Add the melted chocolate and a little of the other egg white and blend to make a soft, smooth paste. Alternatively, place the ground almonds with the sugar, almond extract and cocoa powder in a bowl and make a well in the centre. Add the melted chocolate with sufficient egg white and gradually blend together to form a smooth but not sticky paste.

Shape the dough into small balls the size of large walnuts and place them on the prepared baking sheets. Flatten them slightly, then brush with a little water. Sprinkle over a little icing/confectioners' sugar and bake in the preheated oven for 10–12 minutes until just firm.

Using a spatula, carefully lift the macaroons off the baking parchment and transfer to a wire rack to cool. These are best served immediately, but can be stored in an airtight container.

Difficulty Rating: 2 points

Florentine-topped Cupcakes

Makes 18

Ingredients

150 g/5 oz/⅔ cup (1¼ sticks) butter, softened
150 g/5 oz/⅔ cup caster/superfine sugar
175 g/6 oz/1½ cup self-raising flour
3 medium/large eggs
1 tsp vanilla extract
75 g/3 oz/⅓ cup chopped glacé/candied cherries
50 g/2 oz/¼ cup chopped angelica
50 g/2 oz/½ cup chopped candied peel
50 g/2 oz/⅓ cup dried cranberries

To decorate:
75 g/3 oz dark/semisweet or milk chocolate, melted
50 g/2 oz/½ cup flaked/slivered almonds

Preheat the oven to 180°C/350°F/Gas Mark 4. Line two 12-hole muffin trays with 18 paper cases.

Place the butter and sugar in a bowl, then sift in the flour. In another bowl, beat the eggs with the vanilla extract, then add to the first mixture and beat until smooth. Fold in half the cherries, angelica, peel and cranberries. Spoon into the cases, filling them three-quarters full.

Bake for about 18 minutes until firm to the touch in the centre. Turn out to cool on a wire rack.

Spoon a little melted chocolate on top of each cupcake, then scatter the remaining cherries, angelica, peel and cranberries and the almonds into the wet chocolate. Drizzle the remaining chocolate over the fruit topping with a teaspoon and leave to set for 30 minutes. Keep for two days in an airtight container.

Difficulty Rating: 2 points

Sticky Toffee Cupcakes

Makes 16–18

Ingredients

50 g/5 oz/¼ cup chopped stoned dates
1 tsp bicarbonate of soda/baking soda
175 g/6 oz/1⅓ cups plain/all-purpose flour
1 tsp baking powder
50 g/2 oz/4 tbsp butter or block margarine, diced
200 g/7 oz/1 cup soft light brown sugar
1 large/extra large egg, beaten
½ tsp vanilla extract

For the icing:
25 g/1 oz/2 tbsp unsalted butter
5 tbsp soft light brown sugar
4 tbsp double/heavy cream

Preheat the oven to 180°C/350°F/Gas Mark 4. Line one or two bun trays/shallow muffin pans with 16–18 fairy-cake cases/shallow cake cases, depending on the depth of the tray holes. Place the chopped dates in a bowl with the bicarbonate of soda/baking soda and pour over 225 ml/8 fl oz/1 cup hot water. Stir, then leave to cool.

Sift the flour and baking powder into a bowl and add the diced butter. Rub in between your fingertips until the mixture resembles fine crumbs. Stir in the sugar and mix well. Add the egg, vanilla extract and the date mixture. Beat with a wooden spoon until smooth.

Spoon into the cases and bake for about 25 minutes until well risen and firm to the touch in the centre. Leave to cool in the tins/pans for 5 minutes, then turn out to cool on a wire rack.

To make the topping, place the butter, sugar and cream in a small pan over a low heat and stir until the sugar dissolves. Bring to the boil and boil for 1–2 minutes until the mixture thickens. Brush quickly over each fairy cake, as the mixture will set as it cools. Keep for two days in an airtight container.

Difficulty Rating: 3 points

Birthday Numbers Cupcakes

Makes 12–14

Ingredients

125 g/4 oz/1 cup self-raising flour
125 g/4 oz/¹/₂ cup caster/superfine sugar
125 g/4 oz/¹/₂ cup soft margarine
2 medium/large eggs, beaten
1 tsp vanilla extract

For the buttercream:
150 g/5 oz/²/₃ cup (1¹/₄ sticks) unsalted butter, softened
225 g/8 oz/2 scant cups sifted icing/confectioners' sugar
2 tbsp hot milk or water
1 tsp vanilla extract

To decorate:
225 g/8 oz ready-to-roll sugarpaste/fondant
paste food colourings
icing/confectioners' sugar, for dusting
small candles

Preheat the oven to 180°C/350°F/Gas Mark 4. Line one or two 12-hole bun trays/shallow muffin pans with 12–14 paper fairy-cake/small paper cases or silicone moulds, depending on the depth of the holes.

Sift the flour into a bowl and stir together with the caster/superfine sugar. Add the margarine, eggs and vanilla extract and beat together for about 2 minutes until smooth.

Spoon the mixture into the cases and bake for 15–20 minutes until golden and firm to the touch. Turn out on a wire rack. When cool, trim the tops flat if they have peaked slightly.

Make the buttercream by beating the butter until light and fluffy, then beat in the sifted icing/confectioners' sugar and hot milk or water in two batches. Add the vanilla extract. Colour batches of sugarpaste/fondant in bright colours. Dust a clean surface lightly with icing sugar. Thinly roll each colour of sugarpaste and cut out numbers freehand, or using a set of

cutters or by tracing round templates. Leave these for 2 hours to dry and harden.

Using a palette knife, spread the buttercream thickly onto the top of each cupcake. Place a small candle into each cupcake and stand the number up against this. Serve within 8 hours as the numbers may start to soften.

Difficulty Rating: 3 points

Fig & Chocolate Bars

Makes 12

Ingredients

125 g/4 oz/¹/₂ cup (1 stick) butter
150 g/5 oz/1 heaping cup plain/all-purpose flour
50 g/2 oz/¹/₄ cup soft light brown sugar
225 g/8 oz/1¹/₂ cups ready-to-eat dried figs, halved
juice of ¹/₂ large lemon
1 tsp ground cinnamon
125 g/4 oz dark/semisweet chocolate

Preheat the oven to 180°C/350°F/Gas Mark 4, 10 minutes before baking. Lightly oil an 18 cm/7 inch square cake tin/pan. Place the butter and the flour in a large bowl and, using your fingertips, rub the butter into the flour until it resembles fine breadcrumbs.

Stir in the sugar, then, using your hands, bring the mixture together to form a dough. Knead until smooth, then press the dough into the prepared tin. Lightly prick the base with a fork and bake in the preheated oven for 20–30 minutes until golden. Remove from the oven and leave the shortbread to cool in the tin until completely cold.

Meanwhile, place the dried figs, lemon juice, 125 ml/4 fl oz/ ¹/₂ cup water and the ground cinnamon in a saucepan and bring to the boil. Cover and simmer for 20 minutes, or until soft, stirring occasionally during cooking. Cool slightly, then purée in a food processor until smooth. Cool, then spread over the cooked shortbread.

Melt the chocolate in a heatproof bowl set over a saucepan of simmering water. Alternatively, melt the chocolate in the microwave, according to the manufacturer's instructions. Stir until smooth, then spread over the top of the fig filling. Leave to become firm, then cut into 12 bars and serve.

Difficulty Rating: 3 points

Chocolate Muffins with Irish Cream Topping

Makes 12–14

Ingredients

125 g/4 oz/¹/₂ cup soft margarine
125 g/4 oz/¹/₂ cup golden caster/superfine sugar
150 g/5 oz/1¹/₂ cups self-raising flour
2 tbsp cocoa powder (unsweetened)
2 medium/large eggs
1 tbsp golden/light corn syrup

To decorate:
150 ml/¹/₄ pint/²/₃ cup double/heavy cream
2 tbsp Irish cream liqueur
chocolate sprinkles

Preheat the oven to 180°C/350°F/Gas Mark 4. Line one or two muffin trays with 12–14 deep paper cases, depending on the depth of the holes.

Place the margarine and the sugar in a large bowl, then sift in the flour and cocoa powder. In another bowl, beat the eggs together with the syrup and then add to the first bowl. Whisk together with an electric beater for 2 minutes, or by hand with a wooden spoon until smooth.

Divide the mixture between the cases, filling them three-quarters full. Bake for about 20 minutes until the centre is springy to the touch. Turn out to cool on a wire rack.

For the decoration, whip the cream until it forms soft peaks. Gently fold in the cream liqueur, then place the mixture in a decorating bag fitted with a plain tip. Pipe the cream in swirls, then top with chocolate sprinkles. Keep refrigerated in a sealed container until needed and eat within two days.

Difficulty Rating: 2 points

Fondant Fancies

Makes 16–18

Ingredients

150 g/5 oz/1¹/₄ cups self-raising flour
150 g/5 oz/²/₃ cup caster/superfine sugar
50 g/2 oz/¹/₂ cup ground almonds
150 g/5 oz/²/₃ cup (1¹/₄ sticks) butter, softened
3 medium/large eggs, beaten
4 tbsp milk

To decorate:
450 g/1 lb/3¹/₄ cups fondant icing/confectioners' sugar
paste food colourings
selection fancy cake decorations

Preheat the oven to 180°C/350°F/Gas Mark 4. Line two 12-hole bun trays/shallow muffin pans with 16–18 paper cases, depending on the depth of the tray holes.

Sift the flour into a bowl and stir in the caster/superfine sugar and almonds. Add the butter, eggs and milk and beat until smooth.

Spoon into the paper cases and bake for 15–20 minutes until golden and firm to the touch. Turn out to cool on a wire rack. When cool, trim the tops flat if they have peaked slightly.

To decorate the cupcakes, make the fondant icing to a thick coating consistency, following the packet instructions. Divide into batches and colour each separately with a little paste food colouring. Keep each bowl covered with a damp cloth until needed. Spoon some icing over each cupcake, being sure to flood it right to the edge. Top each with a fancy decoration and leave to set for 30 minutes. Keep for two days in a cool place.

Difficulty Rating: 2 points

Chequered Biscuits

Makes 20

Ingredients

150 g/5 oz/²/₃ cup (1¼ sticks) butter
75 g/3 oz/¾ cup icing/confectioners' sugar
pinch salt
200 g/7 oz/1½ cups plain/all-purpose flour
25 g/1 oz/¼ cup cocoa powder (unsweetened)
1 small egg white

Preheat the oven to 190°C/375°F/Gas Mark 5, 10 minutes before baking. Lightly oil three or four baking sheets. Place the butter and icing/confectioners' sugar in a bowl and cream together until light and fluffy.

Add the salt, then gradually add the flour, beating well after each addition. Mix well to form a firm dough. Cut the dough in half and knead the cocoa powder into one half. Wrap both portions of dough separately in plastic wrap and then leave to chill in the refrigerator for 2 hours.

Divide each piece of dough into three portions. Roll each portion of dough into a long roll and arrange these rolls on top of each other to form a chequerboard design, sealing them with egg white. Wrap in plastic wrap and refrigerate for 1 hour.

Cut the dough into 5 mm/¼ inch thick slices, place on the prepared baking sheets and bake in the preheated oven for 10–15 minutes. Remove from the oven and leave to cool for a few minutes. Transfer to a wire rack and leave until cold before serving. Store in an airtight container.

Difficulty Rating: 3 points

Streusel-topped Banana Muffins

Makes 6

Ingredients

125 g/4 oz/1 cup self-raising wholemeal flour/whole-wheat flour
    plus 1½ tsp baking powder and ½ tsp salt
25 g/1 oz/3 tbsp plain/all-purpose flour
2 medium ripe bananas, about 175 g/6 oz
1 large egg
50 ml/2 fl oz/¼ cup sunflower/corn oil
50 ml/2 fl oz/¼ cup milk

For the topping:
15 g/½ oz/1 tbsp butter
25 g/1 oz/¼ cup self-raising flour
40 g/1½ oz/scant ¼ cup demerara/turbinado sugar
½ tsp ground cinnamon

Preheat the oven to 200°C/400°F/Gas Mark 6. Line a deep muffin tray with 6 deep paper cases. Make the topping first by rubbing the butter into the flour until it resembles fine crumbs. Stir in the sugar and cinnamon and set aside.

To make the muffins, sift the flours into a bowl, then make a well in the centre. Mash the bananas with a fork and add them to the bowl.

In another bowl, beat the egg, oil and milk together and then add them to the bowl. Mix together until evenly blended, then spoon into the muffin cases, filling them two-thirds full.

Sprinkle the streusel topping over each muffin and bake for about 25 minutes until golden and a skewer inserted into the centre comes out clean. Eat fresh on the day of baking.

Difficulty Rating: 1 point

Coconut & Almond Munchies

Makes 26–30

Ingredients

rice paper
5 medium/large egg whites
250 g/9 oz/2¹⁄₂ cups icing/confectioners' sugar, plus extra for
   sprinkling
225 g/8 oz/2¹⁄₃ cups ground almonds
200 g/7 oz/1 heaping cup desiccated/shredded coconut
grated zest of 1 lemon
125 g/4 oz milk chocolate
125 g/4 oz white chocolate

Preheat the oven to 150°C/300°F/Gas Mark 2, 10 minutes
before baking. Line several baking sheets with rice paper. Place
the egg whites in a clean, grease-free bowl and whisk until stiff
and standing in peaks. Sift the icing/confectioners' sugar, then
carefully fold half of the sugar into the whisked egg whites
together with the ground almonds. Add the coconut, the
remaining icing sugar and the lemon zest and mix together to
form a very sticky dough.

Place the mixture in a decorating bag and pipe the mixture into
walnut-sized mounds onto the rice paper, then sprinkle with a
little extra icing sugar. Bake in the preheated oven for 20–25
minutes until set and golden on the outside. Remove from the
oven and leave to cool slightly. Using a spatula, carefully
transfer to a wire rack and leave until cold.

Break the milk and white chocolate into pieces and place in two
separate bowls. Melt both chocolates set over saucepans of
gently simmering water. Alternatively, melt in the microwave,
according to the manufacturer's instructions. Stir until smooth
and free from lumps. Dip one edge of each munchie in the milk
chocolate and leave to dry on nonstick baking parchment.
When dry, dip the other side into the white chocolate. Leave to
set, then serve as soon as possible.

Difficulty Rating: 3 points

Cherry Garlands

Makes 30

Ingredients

125 g/4 oz/1 cup plain/all-purpose flour
pinch salt
65 g/2½ oz/5 tbsp butter, softened
50 g/2 oz/¼ cup caster/superfine sugar
1 egg yolk
½ tsp almond extract

To decorate:
12 glacé/candied cherries
1 egg white, lightly beaten
extra caster/superfine sugar

Preheat the oven to 190°C/375°F/Gas Mark 5 and grease two
baking sheets. Sift the flour and salt into a bowl or a food
processor, add the butter and rub in with fingertips or process
until the mixture resembles fine crumbs. Stir in the sugar.

In another bowl, beat the egg yolk with the almond extract and
add to the flour mixture. Stir to make a soft dough, then knead
lightly. Roll the dough into pea-size balls and arrange 8 balls in a
ring on a prepared baking sheet, pressing them together lightly.

Continue making rings until all the dough is used up. Cut each
glacé/candied cherry into eight tiny wedges and place three on
each biscuit between the balls.

Bake for 14 minutes until golden, remove the biscuits/cookies
from the oven and brush with beaten egg white. Sprinkle the
tops lightly with caster/superfine sugar and return to the
oven for 2 minutes until a sparkly glaze has formed. Leave to
stand on the baking sheets for 2 minutes, then cool
completely on a wire rack.

Difficulty Rating: 3 points

Peaches & Cream Muffins

Makes 10

Ingredients

225 g/8 oz/1 cup canned peach slices or halves in syrup

125 g/4 oz/1 cup self-raising flour

50 g/2 oz/½ cup wholemeal self-raising flour/whole-wheat flour
    plus ¾ tsp baking powder and ¼ tsp salt

½ tsp ground cinnamon

175 g/6 oz/¾ cup (1½ sticks) butter, softened

175 g/6 oz/¾ cup golden caster/superfine sugar

3 medium/large eggs, beaten

1 tbsp golden/light corn syrup

To decorate:

2 tsp lemon juice

2 tbsp icing/confectioners' sugar

150 ml/¼ pint/⅔ cup whipping cream

Preheat the oven to 190°C/375°F/Gas Mark 5. Line a deep
12–hole muffin tray with 10 paper cases. Drain the peaches and
chop 125 g/4 oz into small chunks.

Sift the flours and cinnamon into a bowl, adding any bran
from the sieve, then add the butter, caster/superfine sugar
and eggs. Beat for about 2 minutes, then fold in the
golden/light corn syrup and chopped peaches.

Spoon the mixture into the paper cases and bake for about
20 minutes until well risen and springy in the centre. Remove
to a wire rack to cool.

Place 50 g/2 oz sliced peaches in a blender or food processor
with the lemon juice and icing/confectioners' sugar to make a
purée (the rest of the can's weight is syrup). Whip the cream until
it forms soft peaks and then fold in half the purée. Place a large
spoonful of cream on top of each muffin, then swirl in a little
extra purée. Refrigerate until needed and eat within 24 hours.

Difficulty Rating: 3 points

Fruity Buttermilk Muffins

Makes 12

Ingredients

175 g/6 oz/1½ cups self-raising flour

50 g/2 oz/½ cup wholemeal self-raising flour/whole-wheat flour
plus ¾ tsp baking powder and ¼ tsp salt

1 tsp mixed ground spice

½ tsp bicarbonate of soda/baking soda

1 medium/large egg

2 tbsp fine-cut orange shred marmalade

125 ml/4 fl oz/½ cup milk

50 ml/2 fl oz/¼ cup buttermilk

5 tbsp sunflower/corn/canola oil

125 g/4 oz eating apple, peeled, cored and diced

125 g/4 oz/¾ cup ready-to-eat pitted prunes, roughly chopped

Preheat the oven to 200°C/400°F/Gas Mark 6. Line a deep 12-hole muffin tray with deep paper cases.

Sift the flours, spice and bicarbonate of soda/baking soda into a bowl. In another bowl, beat the egg with the marmalade, milk, buttermilk and oil and pour into the dry ingredients.

Stir with a fork until just combined, then fold in the apple and chopped prunes. Spoon into the cases and bake for about 20 minutes until golden, risen and firm to the touch.

Leave in the tins for 4 minutes, then turn out onto a wire rack to finish cooling. Serve warm or cold and eat on the day of baking.

Difficulty Rating: 2 points

Chocolate Whirls

Makes 20

Ingredients

125 g/4 oz/¹⁄₂ cup soft margarine
75 g/3 oz/6 tbsp unsalted butter, softened
75 g/3 oz/³⁄₄ cup sifted icing/confectioners' sugar
75 g/3 oz dark/semisweet chocolate, melted and cooled
2 tbsp sifted cornflour/cornstarch
125 g/4 oz/1 cup plain/all-purpose flour
125 g/4 oz/1 cup self-raising flour

For the buttercream:
125 g/4 oz/¹⁄₂ cup (1 stick) unsalted butter, softened
¹⁄₂ tsp vanilla extract
225 g/8 oz/2¹⁄₄ cups sifted icing/confectioners' sugar

Preheat the oven to 180°C/350°F/Gas Mark 4, 10 minutes before baking. Lightly oil two baking sheets. Cream the margarine, butter and icing/confectioners' sugar together until the mixture is light and fluffy.

Stir the chocolate until smooth, then beat into the creamed mixture. Stir in the cornflour/cornstarch. Sift the flours together, then gradually add to the creamed mixture, a little at a time, beating well between each addition. Beat until the consistency is smooth and stiff enough for piping. Put the mixture in a decorating bag fitted with a large star tip and pipe 40 small whirls onto the prepared baking sheets. Bake the whirls in the preheated oven for 12–15 minutes until firm to the touch. Remove from the oven and leave to cool for about 2 minutes. Using a spatula, transfer the whirls to wire racks and leave to cool.

Meanwhile, make the buttercream. Cream the butter with the vanilla extract until soft. Gradually beat in the icing sugar and add a little cooled boiled water, if necessary, to give a smooth consistency. When the whirls are cold, pipe or spread on the prepared buttercream, sandwich together and serve.

Difficulty Rating: 3 points

White Chocolate Christmas Cupcakes

Makes 12–16

Ingredients

150 g/5 oz/²⁄₃ cup (1¹⁄₄ sticks) butter, softened
150 g/5 oz/²⁄₃ cup caster/superfine sugar
150 g/5 oz/1 heaping cup self-raising flour
3 medium/large eggs, beaten
1 tsp vanilla extract
1 tbsp milk
75 g/3 oz/scant ²⁄₃ cup white chocolate, finely grated

To decorate:
250 g/9 oz/²⁄₃ cup white chocolate, chopped
16 holly leaves, cleaned and dried
1 batch buttercream (see page 292)
icing/confectioners' sugar, for dusting

Preheat the oven to 180°C/350°F/Gas Mark 4. Line one or two 12-hole bun trays/shallow muffin pans with 12–16 foil cases. Place the butter and caster/superfine sugar in a bowl, then sift in the flour. Add the eggs to the bowl with the vanilla extract and milk and beat until smooth. Fold in the grated white chocolate, then spoon into the cases, filling them three-quarters full. Bake for 18 minutes until firm to the touch in the centre. Turn out to cool on a wire rack.

To decorate, melt the white chocolate in a heatproof bowl over a pan of barely simmering water. Use one third of the melted chocolate to paint the underside of the holly leaves and leave to set for 30 minutes in the refrigerator. Spread one third of the chocolate onto a clean plastic board. When almost set, make into curls by pulling a sharp knife through the chocolate at an angle until the chocolate curls away from the knife. Stir the remaining cooled chocolate into the buttercream and chill for 15 minutes.

Swirl each cupcake with buttercream, then press on the white chocolate curls. Peel the holly leaves away from the chocolate and carefully place on the cupcakes. Dust with icing/ confectioners' sugar before serving. Keep for two days in the refrigerator.

Difficulty Rating: 4 points

Marbled Toffee Shortbread

Makes 12

Ingredients

175 g/6 oz/³/₄ cup (1¹/₂ sticks) butter
75 g/3 oz/¹/₃ cup caster/superfine sugar
175 g/6 oz/1¹/₂ cups plain/all-purpose flour
25 g/1 oz/¹/₄ cup cocoa powder (unsweetened)
75 g/3 oz/¹/₂ cup fine semolina

For the toffee filling:
50 g/2 oz/4 tbsp butter
50 g/2 oz/¹/₄ cup demerara/light brown sugar
397 g/14 oz can condensed milk

For the chocolate topping:
75 g/3 oz dark/semisweet chocolate
75 g/3 oz milk chocolate
75 g/3 oz white chocolate

Preheat the oven to 180°C/350°F/Gas Mark 4. Oil and line a 20.5 cm/8 inch square cake tin/pan with nonstick baking parchment.

Cream the butter and sugar until light and fluffy. Sift in the flour and cocoa. Add the semolina. Mix together to form a soft dough. Press into the base of the prepared tin. Prick all over with a fork. Bake in the preheated oven for 25 minutes. Leave to cool.

To make the toffee filling, gently heat the butter, sugar and condensed milk together until the sugar has dissolved. Bring to the boil, then simmer for 5 minutes, stirring constantly. Leave for 1 minute, then spread over the shortbread and leave to cool.

For the topping, place the different chocolates in separate heatproof bowls and melt one at a time, set over a saucepan of almost boiling water. Drop spoonfuls of each on top of the toffee and tilt the tin to cover evenly. Swirl with a knife for a marbled effect. Leave the chocolate to cool. When just set, mark into bars using a sharp knife. Leave for 1 hour to harden. Cut into bars.

Difficulty Rating: 3 points

Very Berry Muffins

Makes 10

225 g/8 oz/1¾ cups plain/all-purpose flour

1 tsp baking powder

½ tsp bicarbonate of soda/baking soda

65 g/2½ oz/⅓ cup golden caster/superfine sugar

1 medium/large egg

175 ml/6 fl oz/¾ cup milk

zest and 1 tbsp juice from 1 small orange

50 g/2 oz/4 tbsp butter, melted and cooled

125 g/4 oz/1 cup fresh raspberries

50 g/2 oz/heaping ⅓ cup dried cranberries

Preheat the oven to 200°C/400°F/Gas Mark 6. Line a deep 12–hole muffin tray with 10 deep paper cases.

Sift the flour, baking powder and bicarbonate of soda/baking soda into a large bowl. Add the sugar and make a well in the centre. Beat the egg and milk in a jug/pitcher with the orange juice.

Pour the milk mixture into the bowl together with the cooled butter and the orange zest and beat lightly with a fork until all the flour is combined but the mixture is still slightly lumpy. Gently fold in the raspberries and cranberries and spoon into the paper cases.

Bake for about 20 minutes until firm and risen and a skewer inserted into the centre comes out clean. Cool on a wire rack. Eat warm or cold on the day of baking.

Difficulty Rating: 2 points

Fruit & Nut Refrigerator Fingers

Makes 12

Ingredients

14 pink and white marshmallows
75 g/3 oz/1/2 cup luxury dried mixed fruit
25 g/1 oz/3 tbsp chopped candied orange peel
75 g/3 oz/3 tbsp quartered glacé/candied cherries
75 g/3 oz/3/4 cup walnuts, chopped
1 tbsp brandy
175 g/6 oz/2 1/4 cups crushed digestive biscuits/Graham crackers
225 g/8 oz dark/semisweet chocolate
125 g/4 oz/1/2 cup (1 stick) unsalted butter
1 tbsp icing/confectioners' sugar, for dusting (optional)

Lightly oil and line the base of a 18 cm/7 inch tin with nonstick baking parchment. Using oiled kitchen scissors, snip each marshmallow into 4 or 5 pieces over a bowl. Add the dried mixed fruit, orange peel, cherries and walnuts to the bowl. Sprinkle with the brandy and stir together. Add the crushed biscuits/crackers and stir until mixed.

Break the chocolate into squares and put in a heatproof bowl with the butter set over a saucepan of almost boiling water. Stir occasionally until melted, then remove from the heat. Pour the melted chocolate mixture over the dry ingredients and mix together well. Spoon into the prepared tin, pressing down firmly.

Chill in the refrigerator for 15 minutes, then mark into 12 fingers using a sharp knife. Chill in the refrigerator for a further 1 hour or until set. Turn out of the tin, remove the lining paper and cut into fingers. Dust with icing/confectioners' sugar before serving.

Difficulty Rating: 2 points

Lemon Butter Biscuits

Makes 14–18

Ingredients

175 g/6 oz/3/4 cup (1 1/2 sticks) butter, softened
75 g/3 oz/1/3 cup caster/superfine sugar
175 g/6 oz/1 1/3 cups plain/all-purpose flour
75 g/3 oz/2/3 cup cornflour/cornstarch
finely grated zest of 1 lemon
2 tbsp caster/superfine sugar, to decorate

Preheat the oven to 170°C/325°F/Gas Mark 3. Grease two baking sheets. Place the butter into a bowl and beat together with the sugar until light and fluffy.

Sift in the flour and cornflour/cornstarch, add the lemon zest and mix together with a flat-bladed knife to form a soft dough.

Place the dough on a lightly floured surface, knead lightly and roll out thinly. Use biscuit/cookie cutters to cut out fancy shapes, re-rolling the trimmings to make more biscuits. Carefully lift each biscuit onto a prepared baking sheet with a palette knife, then prick lightly with a fork.

Bake for 12–15 minutes. Cool on the baking sheets for 5 minutes, then place on a wire rack. Once completely cool, dust with caster/superfine sugar.

Difficulty Rating: 1 point

Rhubarb & Custard Muffins

Makes 12

Ingredients

225 g/8 oz/4 stalks pink rhubarb
25 g/1 oz vanilla custard powder/vanilla pudding mix
175 g/6 oz/1⅓ cups plain/all-purpose flour
2 tsp baking powder
125 g/4 oz/¾ cup golden caster/superfine sugar
100 ml/3½ fl oz/½ cup milk
2 medium/large eggs, beaten
½ tsp vanilla extract
125 g/4 oz/½ cup (1 stick) butter, melted and cooled
golden caster/superfine sugar, for dusting

Preheat the oven to 180°C/350°F/Gas Mark 4. Oil or line a 12-hole deep muffin tray with deep muffin cases. Chop the rhubarb into pieces 1 cm/½ inch long.

Sift the custard powder, flour and baking powder into a bowl and stir in the sugar. In another bowl, beat the milk, eggs and vanilla extract together. Make a well in the centre of the dry ingredients and pour in the milk mixture.

Add the melted butter and beat together with a fork until just combined, then fold in the chopped rhubarb. Spoon the mixture into the cases and bake for 15–20 minutes until golden, risen and firm in the centre.

Leave in the tray to firm up for 5 minutes, then turn out onto a wire rack to cool. Serve warm, dusted with golden caster/superfine sugar. Eat on the day of baking.

Difficulty Rating: 2 points

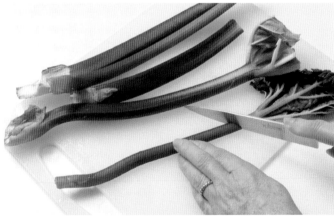

Chocolate Florentines

Makes 20

Ingredients

125 g/4 oz/¹/₂ cup (1 stick) butter or margarine

125 g/4 oz/²/₃ cup soft light brown sugar

1 tbsp double/heavy cream

50 g/2 oz/¹/₃ cup roughly chopped blanched almonds

50 g/2 oz/¹/₃ cup roughly chopped hazelnuts

75 g/3 oz/¹/₂ cup sultanas/golden raisins

50 g/2 oz/¹/₄ cup roughly chopped glacé/candied cherries

50 g/2 oz dark/semisweet chocolate, roughly chopped or broken

50 g/2 oz milk chocolate, roughly chopped or broken

50 g/2 oz white chocolate, roughly chopped or broken

Preheat the oven to 180˚C/350˚F/Gas Mark 4, 10 minutes before baking. Lightly oil a baking sheet.

Melt the butter or margarine with the sugar and double/heavy cream in a small saucepan over a very low heat. Do not boil. Remove from the heat and stir in the almonds, hazelnuts, sultanas/golden raisins and cherries. Drop teaspoonfuls of the mixture onto the baking sheet. Transfer to the preheated oven and bake for 10 minutes, or until golden. Leave the biscuits/cookies to cool on the baking sheet for about 5 minutes, then carefully transfer to a wire rack to cool.

Melt the dark/semisweet, milk and white chocolates in separate bowls, either in the microwave according to the manufacturers' instructions or in a small bowl placed over a saucepan of gently simmering water. Spread one third of the biscuits with the dark chocolate, one third with the milk chocolate and one third with the white chocolate.

Mark out wavy lines on the chocolate when almost set with the tines of a fork, or dip some of the biscuits in chocolate to half coat and serve.

Difficulty Rating: 3 points

Rose Petal Cupcakes

Makes 12

Ingredients

125 g/4 oz/1 cup self-raising flour
125 g/4 oz/½ cup (1 stick) butter, softened
125 g/4 oz/½ cup golden caster/superfine sugar
2 medium/large eggs, beaten
1 tbsp rosewater

To decorate:
1 egg white
about 80 small dry rose petals
caster/superfine sugar, for dusting
175 g/6 oz/1⅓ cups icing/confectioners' sugar
1 tbsp glycerine
2 tbsp rosewater
pink food colouring

Preheat the oven to 180°C/350°F/Gas Mark 4. Line a 12-hole bun tray/shallow muffin pan with foil cases.

Sift the flour into a bowl and add the butter, sugar, eggs and rosewater. Beat for about 2 minutes until smooth, then spoon into the paper cases.

Bake in the centre of the oven for about 14 minutes until well risen and springy in the centre. Transfer to a wire rack to cool. Keep undecorated for up to two days in an airtight container.

To decorate, first place a large piece of nonstick baking parchment on a flat surface. Beat the egg white until frothy, then brush thinly over the rose petals. Set the petals on the paper. Dust with caster/superfine sugar and leave for 3 hours until dry and sparkling.

Beat the icing/confectioners' sugar with the glycerine and rosewater and add enough colouring to give a pale pink colour. Spread over the top of each cupcake and add a circle of rose petals, working quickly as the icing will begin to set. Leave for 30 minutes before serving. Eat on the day of decorating.

Difficulty Rating: 3 points

Madeleine Cupcakes

Makes 10–12

125 g/4 oz/1 cup self-raising flour

125 g/4 oz/¹/₂ cup (1 stick butter), softened

125 g/4 oz/¹/₂ cup golden caster/superfine sugar

2 medium/large eggs, beaten

1 tsp vanilla extract

To decorate:

4 tbsp seedless raspberry jam/jelly

65 g/2¹/₂ oz/³/₄ cup desiccated/shredded coconut

glacé/candied cherries, halved

Difficulty Rating: 2 points

Preheat the oven to 180 C/350 F/Gas Mark 4. Line a 12-hole muffin tray with 10–12 paper cases, depending on the depth of the holes.

Sift the flour into a bowl and add the butter, sugar, eggs and vanilla extract. Beat for about 2 minutes until smooth, then spoon into the paper cases.

Bake in the centre of the oven for about 14–16 minutes until well risen and springy in the centre. Transfer to a wire rack to cool.

To decorate the cupcakes, warm the raspberry jam/jelly in a small pan or in the microwave oven in a heatproof dish on low for a few seconds. Brush the warmed jam over the top of each cupcake. Lightly coat the top of each cupcake with coconut, then finish with a halved cherry. Keep for three days in an airtight container.

Almond Macaroons

Makes 12

Ingredients

rice paper
125 g/4 oz/²⁄₃ cup caster/superfine sugar
50 g/2 oz/¹⁄₂ cup ground almonds
1 tsp ground rice
2–3 drops almond extract
1 medium/large egg white
8 blanched almonds, halved

Preheat the oven to 150°C/300°F/Gas Mark 2, 10 minutes before baking. Line a baking sheet with the rice paper.

Mix the caster/superfine sugar, ground almonds, ground rice and almond extract together and reserve.

Whisk the egg white until stiff, then gently fold in the caster sugar mixture with a metal spoon or rubber spatula. Mix to form a stiff but not sticky paste. (If the mixture is very sticky, add a little extra ground almonds.)

Place small spoonfuls of the mixture, about the size of an apricot, well apart on the rice paper. Place half a blanched almond in the centre of each. Bake in the preheated oven for 25 minutes, or until just pale golden.

Remove the macaroons from the oven and leave to cool for a few minutes on the baking sheet. Cut or tear the rice paper around the macaroons to release them. Once cold, serve or, otherwise, store them in an airtight container.

Difficulty Rating: 2 points

Unbaked Chocolate Cupcakes

Makes 8

Ingredients

For the cases:
450 g/1 lb dark/semisweet chocolate

For the filling:
50 g/2 oz trifle sponges/ladyfingers
2 tbsp sweet sherry or orange liqueur
350 g/12 oz/2¹⁄₃ cups fresh strawberries
450 ml/³⁄₄ pint/2 cups double/heavy cream

Wash eight ridged deep silicone moulds and dry them with paper towels to ensure they are completely free of moisture. Break the chocolate into small pieces and place in a bowl. Set the bowl over a saucepan of warm water and heat the water to barely simmering to melt the chocolate, or place the bowl in the microwave and melt on low in bursts of 30 seconds.

When the chocolate has melted, brush it round the insides of the moulds with a teaspoon or pastry brush, making sure to go into all the ridges. Chill the moulds for 1 hour.

When the chocolate has set, brush on another thicker layer inside the cases and chill again. Once the cases are solid, carefully peel the silicone mould away from the outsides.

Cut a cube of trifle sponge/ladyfinger to fit inside a chocolate case, put inside the case and sprinkle the sponge with sherry or liqueur. Place a small or halved strawberry on top of this. Repeat with the remaining chocolate cases. Whip the cream until it forms soft peaks and place in a decorating bag fitted with a large star tip. Pipe swirls into each case and top with another small or halved strawberry. Refrigerate until needed for up to 24 hours.

Difficulty Rating: 4 points

Pumpkin Cookies with Brown Butter Glaze

Makes 48

Ingredients

125 g/4 oz/¹/₂ cup (1 stick) butter, softened

150 g/5 oz/1 heaping cup plain/all-purpose flour

175 g/6 oz/1 scant cup soft light brown sugar, lightly packed

225 g/8 oz/1 scant cup canned pumpkin or cooked pumpkin

1 medium/large egg, beaten

2 tsp ground cinnamon; 2¹/₂ tsp vanilla extract

¹/₂ tsp baking powder; ¹/₂ tsp bicarbonate of soda/baking soda

¹/₂ tsp freshly grated nutmeg

125 g/4 oz/1 heaping cup wholemeal/whole-wheat flour

75 g/3 oz/³/₄ cup roughly chopped pecans,

100 g/3¹/₂ oz/²/₃ cup raisins

50 g/2 oz/4 tbsp unsalted butter

225 g/8 oz/2¹/₄ cups icing/confectioners' sugar

2 tbsp milk

Preheat the oven to 190°C/375°F/Gas Mark 5, 10 minutes before baking. Lightly oil a baking sheet and reserve. Using an electric mixer, beat the butter until light and fluffy. Add the flour, sugar, pumpkin and beaten egg and beat with the mixer until mixed well. Stir in the ground cinnamon and 1 teaspoon of the vanilla extract and then sift in the baking powder, bicarbonate of soda/baking soda and grated nutmeg. Beat the mixture until combined well, scraping down the sides of the bowl.

Add the wholemeal/whole-wheat flour, chopped nuts and raisins to the mixture and fold in with a metal spoon or rubber spatula until mixed thoroughly together. Place teaspoonfuls about 5 cm/ 2 inches apart onto the prepared baking sheet. Bake in the oven for 10–12 minutes until the cookie edges are firm. Remove the cookies from the oven and leave to cool on a wire rack.

Meanwhile, melt the butter in a small saucepan over a medium heat until pale and just turning golden brown. Remove from the heat. Add the sugar, remaining vanilla extract and milk, stirring. Drizzle over the cooled cookies and serve.

Difficulty Rating: 2 points

Melting Moments

Makes 16

Ingredients

125 g/4 oz/¹/₂ cup (1 stick) butter, softened

75 g/3 oz/¹/₃ cup caster/superfine sugar

¹/₂ tsp vanilla extract

150 g/5 oz/1¹/₄ cups self-raising flour

pinch salt

1 small/medium egg or ¹/₂ medium/large egg, beaten

25 g/1 oz/heaping ¹/₄ cup porridge/rolled oats

4 glacé/candied cherries, quartered

Difficulty Rating: 1 points

Preheat the oven to 180°C/350°F/Gas Mark 4. Grease two baking sheets.

Beat the butter until light and fluffy, then whisk in the caster/superfine sugar and vanilla extract. Sift the flour and salt into the bowl. Add the egg and mix to a soft dough.

Break the dough into 16 pieces and roll each piece into a ball. Spread the oats out on a small flat bowl or plate. Roll each ball in the oats to coat them all over without flattening them.

Place a cherry quarter in the centre of each ball, then place on the prepared baking sheets, spaced well apart. Bake for about 15 minutes until risen and golden. Remove from the baking sheets with a palette knife and cool on a wire rack.

Chocolate & Toffee Cupcakes

Makes 12–14

125 g/4 oz soft fudge

125 g/4 oz/¹/₂ cup soft margarine

125 g/4 oz/¹/₂ cup golden caster/superfine sugar

150 g/5 oz/1¹/₂ cups self-raising flour

2 tbsp cocoa powder (unsweetened)

2 medium/large eggs

1 tbsp golden/light corn syrup

For the cream cheese frosting:

50 g/2 oz/4 tbsp unsalted butter, softened at room temperature

300 g/11 oz/2¹/₂ cups icing/confectioners' sugar, sifted

125 g/4 oz/¹/₂ cup full-fat cream cheese

Preheat the oven to 180°C/350°F/Gas Mark 4. Line one or two bun trays/shallow muffin pans with 12–14 paper cases, depending on the depth of the holes. Cut one quarter of the fudge into slices for decoration. Chop the rest into small cubes. Set all the fudge aside.

Place the margarine and sugar in a large bowl and then sift in the flour and cocoa powder. In another bowl, beat the eggs with the syrup, then add to the flour mixture. Whisk together with an electric beater for 2 minutes, or by hand with a wooden spoon until smooth. Gently fold in the fudge cubes.

Spoon the mixture into the cases, filling them three–quarters full. Bake for about 15 minutes until a skewer inserted into the centre comes out clean. Turn out to cool on a wire rack.

To make the cream cheese frosting, beat the butter and icing/confectioners' sugar together until light and fluffy. Add the cream cheese and whisk until light and fluffy. Do not over-beat, however, as the mixture can become runny. Swirl the cream cheese frosting over each cupcake, then finish by topping with a fudge slice. Keep for 3–4 days chilled in a sealed container.

Difficulty Rating: 2 points

Tropical Mango Muffins

Makes 10

Ingredients

50 g/2 oz soft dried pineapple chunks

50 g/2 oz soft dried papaya pieces

25 g/1 oz soft dried mango pieces

225 g/8 oz/1¾ cups plain/all-purpose flour

1 tsp baking powder

½ tsp bicarbonate of soda/baking soda

75 g/3 oz/heaping ¼ cup golden caster/superfine sugar

1 medium/large egg

275 ml/9 fl oz/1 cup milk

zest and 1 tbsp juice from 1 small orange

50 g/2 oz/4 tbsp butter, melted and cooled

Preheat the oven to 200°C/400°F/Gas Mark 6. Line a deep muffin tray with 10 deep paper muffin cases. Wet a sharp knife and chop the fruits into small chunks. Set them aside.

Sift the flour, baking powder and bicarbonate of soda/baking soda into a large bowl. Add the sugar and make a well in the centre. In another bowl, beat the egg and milk together with the orange juice.

Add the milk to the bowl with the melted butter and the orange zest and beat with a fork until all the flour is combined but the mixture is still slightly lumpy. Fold in three-quarters of the chopped fruit and spoon into the paper cases. Sprinkle the remaining fruit over the top of each muffin.

Bake for about 20 minutes until risen, golden and firm. Cool on a wire rack and eat warm or cold. Keep for 24 hours sealed in an airtight container.

Difficulty Rating: 2 points

Blackcurrant & Lemon Muffins

Makes 12

Ingredients

1 lemon
275 g/10 oz/2¼ cups plain/all-purpose flour
1 tbsp baking powder
125 g/4 oz/½ cup caster/superfine sugar
2 medium/large eggs
275 ml/9 fl oz/1 cup milk
½ tsp vanilla extract
75 g/3 oz/6 tbsp butter, melted and cooled
150 g/5 oz/1½ cups fresh or frozen blackcurrants, trimmed

Difficulty Rating: 1 point

Preheat the oven to 200°C/400°F/Gas Mark 6. Grease or line a deep 12-hole muffin tray with deep paper cases.

Finely grate the zest from the lemon into a bowl, then sift in the flour and baking powder and stir in the sugar. In another bowl, beat the eggs with the milk and vanilla extract.

Make a well in the centre and pour in the egg mixture and the cooled melted butter. Stir together with a fork until just combined and then gently fold in the blackcurrants.

Spoon into the muffin trays and bake for 20 minutes or until firm and golden. Leave in the tray for 4 minutes, then turn out onto a wire rack to finish cooling. Serve warm or cold. Best eaten on the day of baking.

Spiced Palmier Biscuits with Apple Purée

Makes 20

Ingredients

250 g/9 oz prepared puff pastry dough, thawed if frozen

40 g/1½ oz/scant ¼ cup caster/superfine sugar

25 g/1 oz/¼ cup icing/confectioners' sugar

1 tsp ground cinnamon

¼ tsp ground ginger

¼ tsp freshly grated nutmeg

450 g/1 lb/4 cups roughly chopped Bramley/tart cooking apples

50 g/2 oz/¼ cup caster/superfine or granulated sugar

3 tbsp raisins

3 tbsp dried cherries

zest of 1 orange

double/heavy cream, lightly whipped, to serve

Preheat the oven to 200°C/400°F/Gas Mark 6, 15 minutes before baking. Roll out the pastry dough on a lightly floured surface to form a 25.5 x 30.5 cm/10 x 12 inch rectangle. Trim the edges with a small sharp knife.

Sift together the caster/superfine sugar, icing/confectioners' sugar, cinnamon, ginger and nutmeg into a bowl. Generously dust both sides of the pastry sheet with about a quarter of the sugar mixture. With a long edge facing the body, fold each side halfway towards the centre. Dust with a third of the remaining sugar mixture. Fold each side again so that they almost meet in the centre and dust again with about half the remaining sugar mixture. Fold the two sides together down the centre of the pastry to give six layers altogether. Wrap the pastry in plastic wrap and refrigerate for 1–2 hours until firm. Reserve the remaining spiced sugar.

Remove the pastry from the refrigerator, unwrap and roll in the remaining sugar to give a good coating all round. Using a sharp knife, cut the roll into about 20 thin slices and place their cut sides down onto a baking sheet. Bake in the preheated oven for 10 minutes, turn the biscuits/cookies and cook for a further 5–10 minutes, or until golden and crisp. Remove from the oven and transfer to a wire rack. Leave to cool completely.

Meanwhile, combine the remaining ingredients in a saucepan. Cover and cook gently for 15 minutes until the apple is completely soft. Stir well and leave to cool. Serve the palmiers with a spoonful of the apple purée and a little of the whipped double/heavy cream.

Difficulty Rating: 4 points

Peanut Butter Truffle Cookies

Makes 18

Ingredients

125 g/4 oz dark/semisweet chocolate

150 ml/¼ pint/⅔ cup double/heavy cream

125 g/4 oz/½ cup (1 stick) butter or margarine, softened

125 g/4 oz/⅔ cup caster/superfine sugar

125 g/4 oz/½ cup crunchy or smooth peanut butter

4 tbsp golden/light corn syrup

1 tbsp milk

225 g/8 oz/1¾ cups plain/all-purpose flour

½ tsp bicarbonate of soda/baking soda

Preheat the oven to 180°C/350°F/Gas Mark 4, 10 minutes before baking. Make the chocolate filling by breaking the chocolate into small pieces and placing in a heatproof bowl.

Put the double/heavy cream into a saucepan and heat to boiling point. Immediately pour over the chocolate. Leave to stand for 1–2 minutes, then stir until smooth. Set aside to cool until firm enough to scoop. Do not refrigerate.

Lightly oil a baking sheet. Cream together the butter or margarine and the sugar until light and fluffy. Blend in the peanut butter, followed by the golden/light corn syrup and milk.

Sift together the flour and bicarbonate of soda/baking soda. Add to the peanut butter mixture, mix well and knead until smooth. Flatten 1–2 tablespoons of the cookie mixture on a chopping board. Put a spoonful of the chocolate mixture into the centre of the cookie dough, then fold the dough around the chocolate to enclose completely. Repeat with the rest of the dough and filling. Put the balls onto the prepared baking sheet and flatten slightly. Bake in the preheated oven for 10–12 minutes until golden. Remove from the oven and transfer to a wire rack to cool completely before serving.

Difficulty Rating: 2 points

Gingerbread Cupcakes

Makes 14–16

Ingredients

8 tbsp golden/light corn syrup

125 g/4 oz/½ cup (1 stick) block margarine

225 g/8 oz/1¾ cups plain/all purpose flour

2 tsp ground ginger

75 g/3 oz/⅔ cup sultanas/golden raisins

50 g/2 oz/¼ cup soft dark brown sugar

175 ml/6 fl oz/¾ cup milk

1 tsp bicarbonate of soda/baking soda

1 medium/large egg, beaten

125 g/4 oz/1¼ cups golden icing/confectioners' sugar

Preheat the oven to 180°C/350°F/Gas Mark 4. Line one or two muffin trays with 14–16 deep paper cases, depending on the size of the holes.

Place the syrup and margarine in a heavy-based pan and melt together gently. Sift the flour and ginger into a bowl, then stir in the sultanas/golden raisins and sugar.

Warm the milk and stir in the bicarbonate of soda/baking soda. Pour the syrup mixture, the milk and beaten egg into the dry ingredients and beat until smooth.

Spoon the mixture halfway up each case and bake for 25–30 minutes until risen and firm. Cool in the tins for 10 minutes, then turn out to cool on a wire rack.

To decorate the cupcakes, blend the icing/confectioners' sugar with 1 tablespoon warm water to make a thin glacé icing. Place in a paper decorating bag and snip away the tip. Drizzle over the top of each cupcake in a lacy pattern. Keep in an airtight container for up to five days.

Difficulty Rating: 3 points

Chocolate & Vanilla Rings

Makes 26

Ingredients

175 g/6 oz/³/₄ cup (1¹/₂ sticks) butter, softened
125 g/4 oz/²/₃ cups caster/superfine sugar
few drops vanilla extract
250 g/9 oz/2 cups plain/all-purpose flour
15 g/¹/₂ oz/2 tbsp cocoa powder (unsweetened)
25 g/1 oz/¹/₂ cup ground almonds

Preheat the oven to 180˚C/350˚F/Gas Mark 4 and grease two baking sheets.

Put the butter and sugar in a bowl and beat until light and fluffy. Add the vanilla extract, sift in the flour and mix to a soft dough. Divide the dough in two and add the cocoa powder to one half and the almonds to the other.

Knead each piece of dough separately into a smooth ball, wrap and chill for 30 minutes. Divide each piece into 26 pieces. Take one dark and one light ball and roll each separately into ropes about 12.5 cm/5 inches long using your fingers.

Twist the ropes together to form a circlet and pinch the ends together. Repeat with the remaining dough and place on a prepared baking sheet. Bake for 12–14 minutes until risen and firm. Remove to cool on a wire rack.

Difficulty Rating: 3 points

Chocolate Holly Leaf Muffins

Makes 12

Ingredients

125 g/4 oz/¹⁄₂ cup caster/superfine sugar

125 g/4 oz/¹⁄₂ cup soft tub margarine

2 medium/large eggs

125 g/4 oz/1 cup self-raising flour

¹⁄₂ tsp baking powder

50 g/2 oz/¹⁄₄ cup dark/semisweet or milk chocolate chips

To decorate:

12 holly leaves, washed and dried

75 g/3 oz dark/semisweet chocolate, melted

50 g/2 oz/4 tbsp unsalted butter, softened

300 g/11 oz/3 cups sifted icing/confectioners' sugar

125 g/4 oz/¹⁄₂ cup full-fat cream cheese

50 g/2 oz milk chocolate, melted and cooled

1 tsp vanilla extract

Preheat the oven to 190˚C/375˚F/Gas Mark 5. Line a 12–hole muffin tray with deep paper cases.

Place all the cupcake ingredients except the chocolate chips in a large bowl and beat with an electric mixer for about 2 minutes until smooth. Fold in the chocolate chips, then fill the paper cases halfway up with the mixture. Bake for about 15 minutes until firm, risen and golden. Remove to a wire rack to cool.

To decorate the cupcakes, paint the underside of each holly leaf with the melted dark/semisweet chocolate. Leave to dry out on nonstick baking parchment for 1 hour, or in the refrigerator for 30 minutes.

Beat the butter until soft, then gradually beat in the icing/ confectioners' sugar until light. Add the cream cheese and whisk until fluffy. Divide the mixture in half and beat the cooled melted milk chocolate into one half and the vanilla extract into the other half. Fit a decorating bag with a wide star tip and spoon chocolate icing on one side of the bag and the vanilla icing on the other. Pipe swirls on top of the cupcakes.

Peel the holly leaves away from the set chocolate and decorate the top of each cupcake with a chocolate leaf. Keep for three days in an airtight container in a cool place.

Difficulty Rating: 4 points

Chocolate Biscuit Bars

Makes 20

Ingredients

50 g/2 oz/$\frac{1}{3}$ cup sultanas/golden raisins
3–4 tbsp brandy (optional)
100 g/3$\frac{1}{2}$ oz dark/semisweet chocolate
125 g/4$\frac{1}{2}$ oz/$\frac{1}{2}$ cup (1 stick) unsalted butter
2 tbsp golden syrup/light corn syrup
90 ml/3 fl oz/$\frac{2}{3}$ cup double/heavy cream
6 digestive biscuits/Graham crackers, roughly crushed
50 g/2 oz/$\frac{1}{2}$ cup toasted, roughly chopped, shelled
    pistachio nuts,
50 g/2 oz/$\frac{1}{2}$ cup toasted, roughly chopped blanched almonds
50 g/2 oz/$\frac{1}{4}$ cup roughly chopped glacé/candied cherries
grated zest of 1 orange
sifted cocoa powder (unsweetened)

Lightly oil a 20.5 cm/8 inch square tin/pan and line with plastic wrap. Place the sultanas/golden raisins in a small bowl and pour over the brandy, if using. Leave to soak for 20–30 minutes. Meanwhile, break the chocolate into small pieces and put into a heatproof bowl. Place the bowl over a saucepan of simmering water, making sure that the bottom of the bowl does not touch the water. Leave the chocolate until melted, stirring occasionally. Remove from the heat.

Add the butter, golden/light corn syrup and double/heavy cream to a small saucepan. Heat until the butter has melted. Remove the saucepan from the heat. Add the melted chocolate, biscuits/ cookies, nuts, cherries, orange zest, sultanas/golden raisins and the brandy mixture. Mix thoroughly. Pour into the prepared tin/pan. Smooth the top. Chill in the refrigerator for at least 4 hours, or until firm.

Turn out the cake, remove the plastic wrap. Dust liberally with the cocoa, then cut into bars to serve. Store lightly covered in the refrigerator.

Difficulty Rating: 3 points

Pistachio Muffins

Makes 10

Ingredients

125 g/4 oz/1 cup self-raising flour
125 g/4 oz/$\frac{1}{2}$ cup (1 stick) butter, softened
125 g/4 oz/1 cup golden caster/superfine sugar
2 medium/large eggs, beaten
1 tbsp maple syrup or golden/light corn syrup
50 g/2 oz roughly chopped pistachio nuts

To decorate:

225 g/8 oz/2 cups golden icing/confectioners' sugar
125 g/4 oz/$\frac{1}{2}$ cup (1 stick) unsalted butter, softened
2 tsp lemon juice
25 g/1 oz chopped pistachio nuts

Preheat the oven to 200°C/400°F/Gas Mark 6. Line a deep 12-hole muffin tray with 10 deep paper cases.

Sift the flour into a bowl and add the butter, sugar and eggs. Beat for about 2 minutes, then fold in the syrup and chopped nuts.

Spoon the mixture into the paper cases and bake for about 20 minutes until well risen and springy in the centre. Remove to a wire rack to cool.

To decorate the cakes, sift the icing/confectioners' sugar into a bowl, then add the butter, lemon juice and 1 tablespoon hot water. Beat until light and fluffy, then swirl onto each cupcake with a small palette knife. Place the chopped pistachio nuts in a small shallow bowl. Dip the top of each muffin into the nuts to make an attractive topping. Keep for four days in an airtight container in a cool place.

Difficulty Rating: 2 points

Orange Drizzle Cupcakes

Makes 10

Ingredients

75 g/3 oz dark/semisweet chocolate, chopped

125 g/4 oz/$^1/_2$ cup (1 stick) butter

125 g/4 oz/$^1/_2$ cup caster/superfine sugar

2 medium/large eggs, beaten

200 g/7 oz/1$^2/_3$ cups self-raising flour

finely grated zest of $^1/_2$ orange

5 tbsp thick natural/plain yogurt

To decorate:

finely grated zest of 1 small orange

1 tbsp orange juice

1 batch buttercream (*see* page 292)

2 tbsp marmalade

Preheat the oven to 190°C/375°F/Gas Mark 5. Grease 10 deep muffin moulds or line a 12-hole muffin tray with 10 deep paper cases.

Melt the chocolate in a heatproof bowl over a pan of warm water or in the microwave oven on low for 30 seconds and leave to cool.

Put the butter and sugar in a large bowl and whisk until light and fluffy. Gradually beat in the eggs, adding a teaspoon of flour with each addition. Beat in the cooled melted chocolate, then sift in the flour. Add the orange zest and yogurt to the bowl and whisk until smooth.

Spoon the mixture into the paper cases and bake for about 25 minutes until well risen and springy to the touch. Leave for 2 minutes in the moulds or tray, then turn out onto a wire rack.

To decorate, beat the orange zest and juice into the buttercream and fill a decorating bag fitted with a star tip with the frosting. Pipe swirls on top of each cupcake. Warm the marmalade and place drizzles around the sides of the cupcakes with a teaspoon. Keep in an airtight container in a cool place for four days.

Difficulty Rating: 3 points

Coffee & Walnut Muffins

Makes 12

Ingredients

125 g/4 oz/¹/₂ cup (1 stick) butter, softened
125 g/4 oz/²/₃ cup soft light brown sugar
150 g/5 oz/1¹/₂ cups plain/all-purpose flour
1 tsp baking powder
2 medium/large eggs
1 tbsp golden/light corn syrup
1 tsp vanilla extract
4 tbsp sour cream
40 g/1¹/₂ oz/¹/₃ cup chopped walnut pieces

To decorate:
150 ml/¹/₄ pint/²/₃ cup double/heavy cream
1 tbsp golden caster/superfine sugar
1 tsp coffee extract
¹/₂ tsp ground cinnamon
50 g/2 oz/¹/₂ cup walnut pieces

Preheat the oven to 180 C/350 F/Gas Mark 4. Grease or line a 12-hole muffin tray with paper cases.

Beat the butter and sugar together until light and fluffy. Sift in the flour and baking powder, then add the eggs, golden/light corn syrup, vanilla extract and sour cream. Beat together until fluffy, then fold in the nuts.

Spoon the batter into the paper cases, filling them about three-quarters full. Bake for about 25 minutes until a skewer inserted into the centre comes out clean. Turn out to cool on a wire rack.

For the topping, put the cream, sugar, coffee extract and cinnamon in a bowl and whip until soft peaks form. Swirl over the muffins and top each with a walnut piece. Refrigerate until needed, or keep chilled for 24 hours in an airtight container.

Difficulty Rating: 2 points

Golden Honey Fork Biscuits

Makes 20–24

Ingredients

125 g/4 oz/¹⁄₂ cup (1 stick) butter or block margarine, diced

125 g/4 oz/generous ¹⁄₂ cup soft light brown sugar

1 medium/large egg, beaten

¹⁄₂ tsp vanilla extract

2 tbsp clear honey

200 g/7 oz/1¹⁄₂ cups plain/all purpose flour

¹⁄₂ tsp baking powder

¹⁄₂ tsp ground cinnamon

Difficulty Rating: 1 point

Preheat the oven to 180°C/350°F/Gas Mark 4. Grease two baking sheets.

Place the butter and sugar in a bowl and beat together until light and fluffy. Beat in the egg, a little at a time, and then beat in the vanilla extract and honey.

Sift the flour, baking powder and cinnamon into the bowl and fold into the mixture with a large metal spoon.

Put heaping teaspoons of the mixture onto the prepared baking sheets, leaving room for them to spread out during baking. Press the top of each round with the tines of a fork to make a light indentation.

Bake for 10–12 minutes until golden. Cool for 2 minutes on the baking sheets, then transfer to a wire rack to cool completely.

Miracle Bars

Makes 12

Ingredients

100 g/3½ oz/7 tbsp butter, melted

125 g/4 oz/1½ cups digestive biscuit/Graham cracker crumbs
   (about 7 biscuits/cookies)

175 g/6 oz/1 cup chocolate chips

75 g/3 oz/scant ½ cup desiccated/shredded coconut

125 g/4 oz/1 cup chopped mixed nuts

400 g/14 oz can sweetened condensed milk

Preheat the oven to 180°C/350°F/Gas Mark 4, 10 minutes
before baking. Generously butter a 23 cm/9 inch square cake
tin/pan and line with nonstick baking parchment.

Pour the butter into the prepared tin and sprinkle the
biscuit/cracker crumbs over in an even layer. Add the chocolate
chips, coconut and nuts in even layers and drizzle over the
condensed milk.

Transfer the tin to the preheated oven and bake for 30 minutes,
or until golden brown. Leave to cool in the tin, then cut into
12 squares and serve.

Difficulty Rating: 1 point

Nanaimo Bars

Makes 18

Ingredients

125 g/4 oz/¹/₂ cup (1 stick) melted butter
40 g/1¹/₂ oz/3 tbsp granulated sugar
25 g/1 oz/3 tbsp cocoa powder (unsweetened)
1 large/extra large egg, lightly beaten
175 g/6 oz/2 cups digestive biscuit/Graham cracker crumbs
75 g/3 oz/1 cup flaked or desiccated/shredded coconut
75 g/3 oz/³/₄ cup chopped walnuts

For the filling:
50 g/2 oz/4 tbsp butter
2 tbsp custard powder/vanilla pudding mix
1 tsp vanilla extract
3 tbsp milk
225 g/8 oz/2 cups sifted icing/confectioners' sugar

For the topping:
75 g/3 oz dark/semisweet chocolate
15g/¹/₂ oz/1 tbsp butter

Lightly oil a 23 cm/9 inch square tin and line with plastic wrap. Thoroughly combine the butter, sugar, cocoa powder, egg, biscuit/cracker crumbs, coconut and walnuts. Press into the prepared tin very firmly. Chill in the refrigerator for at least 1 hour.

For the filling, cream together the butter, custard powder/vanilla pudding mix and vanilla extract. Add the milk and icing/ confectioners' sugar alternately, about one third at a time, until smooth. Spread this mixture over the chilled base. Return to the refrigerator and chill again for a further hour.

For the topping, melt the dark/semisweet chocolate together with the butter. Stir together until combined well. Pour over the filling and spread quickly to cover the base and filling thinly. Leave for 5–10 minutes until starting to set, then mark the chocolate with a sharp knife into 18 squares. Refrigerate until set. Cut through the marks, dividing the cake into squares. Serve the bars chilled.

Difficulty Rating: 3 points

Ginger & Apricot Mini Muffins

Makes 18

Ingredients

75 g/3 oz/²/₃ cup plain/all-purpose flour
75 g/3 oz/¹/₂ cup wholemeal/whole-wheat flour
2 tsp baking powder
¹/₂ tsp ground cinnamon
50 g/2 oz/¹/₃ cup soft light brown sugar
1 medium/large egg
135 ml/4¹/₂ fl oz/¹/₂ cup milk
75 g/3 oz/6 tbsp butter, melted
125 g/4 oz/¹/₂ cup canned apricots, drained and finely chopped
50 g/2 oz/¹/₂ cup chopped glacé/candied ginger
50 g/2 oz/¹/₂ cup chopped almonds
sparkly sugar pieces, to decorate

Preheat the oven to 200°C/400°F/Gas Mark 6. Line one or two mini-muffin trays with 18 mini paper cases.

Sift the flours, baking powder and cinnamon into a bowl, adding any bran from the sieve, then stir in the sugar. In another bowl, beat the egg and milk together and then pour into the dry ingredients.

Add the melted butter, apricots, ginger and half the almonds and mix quickly with a fork until just combined.

Spoon the mixture into the cases. Scatter the other half of the almonds and the sugar crystals over the top. Bake for 15–20 minutes until risen and golden. Turn out onto a wire rack to cool and eat fresh on the day of baking.

Difficulty Rating: 2 points

Chunky Chocolate Muffins

Makes 12–14

Ingredients

125 g/4 oz/¹/₂ cup soft margarine

125 g/4 oz/¹/₂ cup golden caster/superfine sugar

2 medium/large eggs, beaten

25 g/1 oz/¹/₄ cup cocoa powder (unsweetened)

175 g/6 oz1¹/₂ cups self-raising flour

1 tsp baking powder

2 tbsp milk

50 g/2 oz milk chocolate, chopped

50 g/2 oz dark/semisweet or white chocolate, chopped

To decorate:

75 g/3 oz/heaping ¹/₂ cup granulated sugar

5 tbsp evaporated milk

125 g/4 oz dark/semisweet chocolate, chopped

40 g/1¹/₂ oz/3 tbsp unsalted butter

Make the frosting first in order to allow it to cool. Place the sugar and evaporated milk in a heavy-based pan and stir over a low heat until every grain of sugar has dissolved. Simmer for 5 minutes but do not allow the mixture to boil. Remove from the heat, cool for 5 minutes, and then add the chocolate and butter. Stir until these melt. Pour the mixture into a bowl and chill for 2 hours until thickened.

Preheat the oven to 180°C/350°F/Gas Mark 4. Line one or two deep muffin trays with 12–14 paper cases, depending on the depth of the holes. Place the margarine and sugar in a bowl with the eggs and sift in the cocoa powder, flour and baking powder. Beat with the milk for about 2 minutes until smooth, then fold in the chopped chocolate.

Spoon into the paper cases and bake for 15–20 minutes until firm. Place on a wire rack to cool. Remove the frosting from the refrigerator and beat to soften it slightly. Swirl it over the muffins. Keep in a cool place in a sealed container for 3–4 days.

Difficulty Rating: 2 points

Date, Orange & Walnut Muffins

Makes 12

Ingredients

275 g/10 oz/2¼ cups plain/all-purpose flour

1 tbsp baking powder

125 g/4 oz/½ cup golden caster/superfine sugar

175 g/6 oz/1 cup chopped stoned dates

50 g/2 oz/½ cup chopped walnuts

1 medium/large egg

200 ml/7 fl oz/¾ cup milk

finely grated zest and juice of 1 orange

6 tbsp sunflower/corn/canola oil

Preheat the oven to 200°C/400°F/Gas Mark 6. Line a deep 12–hole muffin tray with deep paper cases.

Sift the flour and baking powder into a bowl and make a well in the centre.

Add all the remaining ingredients and beat together until just combined. Spoon the batter into the paper cases and bake for about 16–18 minutes until well risen and firm to the touch.

Serve warm or cold and eat the muffins on the day of baking.

Difficulty Rating: 1 point

Pineapple, Cream Cheese & Carrot Muffins

Makes 12

Ingredients

175 g/6 oz/1¼ cups self-raising wholemeal flour/whole-wheat
   flour plus 2 tsp baking powder and scant ¾ tsp salt
1 tsp baking powder
½ tsp ground cinnamon
pinch salt
150 ml/¼ pint/⅔ cup sunflower/corn/canola oil
150 g/5 oz/⅔ cup soft light brown sugar
3 medium/large eggs, beaten
50 g/2 oz soft dried pineapple, chopped
225 g/8 oz carrots, peeled and finely grated

To decorate:
75 g/3 oz/⅓ cup cream cheese
175 g/6 oz/1⅓ cups golden icing/confectioners' sugar
2 tsp lemon juice
50 g/2 oz soft dried pineapple pieces, thinly sliced

Preheat the oven to 180°C/350°F/Gas Mark 4. Lightly oil a deep
12-hole muffin tray or line with deep paper cases.

Sift the flour, baking powder, cinnamon and salt into a bowl,
including any bran from the sieve. Add the oil, sugar, eggs,
chopped pineapple and grated carrots.

Beat until smooth, then spoon into the muffin cases. Bake for
20–25 minutes until risen and golden. Cool on a wire rack.

To decorate the muffins, beat the cream cheese and icing/
confectioners' sugar together with the lemon juice to make a
spreading consistency. Swirl the icing over the top of each
cupcake, then top with a piece of dried pineapple. If chilled and
sealed in an airtight container, these will keep for 3–4 days.

Difficulty Rating: 2 points

Pecan Caramel Millionaire's Shortbread

Makes 20

Ingredients

125 g/4 oz/¹/₂ cup (1 stick) butter, softened

2 tbsp smooth peanut butter

75 g/3 oz/¹/₃ cup caster/superfine sugar

75 g/3 oz/²/₃ cup cornflour/cornstarch

175 g/6 oz/1¹/₂ cups plain/all-purpose flour

For the topping:

200 g/7 oz/1 cup caster/superfine sugar

125 g/4 oz/¹/₂ cup (1 stick) butter

2 tbsp golden syrup/light corn syrup

75 g/3 oz/3 tbsp liquid glucose

397 g/14 oz can sweetened condensed milk

175 g/6 oz/1¹/₂ cups roughly chopped pecans

75 g/3 oz milk chocolate

15 g/¹/₂ oz/1 tbsp butter

Preheat the oven to 180˚C/350˚F/Gas Mark 4, 10 minutes before baking. Lightly oil and line an 18 x 28 cm/7 x 11 inch tin/pan with greaseproof/wax paper or baking parchment.

Cream together the butter, peanut butter and sugar until light. Sift in the cornflour/cornstarch and flour together and mix in to make a smooth dough. Press the mixture into the prepared tin. Prick all over with a fork. Bake in the preheated oven for 20 minutes, or until just golden. Remove from the oven.

For the topping, combine the sugar, butter, golden/light corn syrup, glucose, 85 ml/3 fl oz/ 6 tbsp water and condensed milk in a heavy–based saucepan. Stir constantly over a low heat, without boiling, until the sugar has dissolved. Increase the heat and boil steadily. Stir constantly for about 10 minutes until the mixture turns a golden caramel colour. Remove the saucepan from the heat, add the pecans and pour over the shortbread base immediately. Leave to cool. Refrigerate for at least 1 hour.

Break the chocolate into small pieces and put into a heatproof bowl with the butter. Place over a saucepan of barely simmering water, ensuring that the bowl does not come into contact with the water. Leave until melted, then stir together well. Remove the shortbread from the refrigerator and pour the chocolate evenly over the top, spreading thinly to cover. Leave to set, cut into rectangles and serve.

Difficulty Rating: 3 points

Fruit & Nut Flapjacks

Makes 12

Ingredients

75 g/3 oz/6 tbsp butter or margarine

125 g/4 oz/²⁄₃ cup soft light brown sugar

3 tbsp golden/light corn syrup

50 g/2 oz/¹⁄₃ cup raisins

50 g/2 oz/¹⁄₂ cup roughly chopped walnuts

175 g/6 oz/2¹⁄₃ cups rolled oats

50 g/2 oz/¹⁄₂ cup icing/confectioners' sugar

1–1¹⁄₂ tbsp lemon juice

Preheat the oven to 180°C/350°F/Gas Mark 4, 10 minutes before baking. Lightly oil a 23 cm/9 inch square cake tin/pan.

Melt the butter or margarine with the sugar and syrup in a small saucepan over a low heat. Remove from the heat.

Stir the raisins, walnuts and oats into the syrup mixture and mix together well. Spoon evenly into the prepared tin and press down well. Transfer to the preheated oven and bake for 20–25 minutes. Remove from the oven and leave to cool in the tin. Cut into bars while still warm.

Sift the icing/confectioners' sugar into a small bowl, then gradually beat in the lemon juice a little at a time to form a thin icing. Place into a decorating bag fitted with a writing tip, then pipe thin lines over the flapjacks. Leave to cool and serve.

Difficulty Rating: 2 points

Easter Nest Cupcakes

Makes 12

Ingredients

125 g/4 oz/¹⁄₂ cup soft margarine

125 g/4 oz/¹⁄₂ cup golden caster/superfine sugar

150 g/5 oz/1¹⁄₄ cups self-raising flour

2 tbsp cocoa powder (unsweetened)

2 medium/large eggs

1 tbsp golden/light corn syrup

To decorate:

1 batch buttercream (*see page 292*)

50 g/2 oz/1 cup shredded wheat cereal

125 g/4 oz milk chocolate, broken into pieces

25 g/1 oz/2 tbsp unsalted butter

chocolate mini eggs

Preheat the oven to 180°C/350°F/Gas Mark 4. Line a 12–hole bun tray with paper cases.

Place the margarine and the sugar in a large bowl, then sift in the flour and cocoa powder. In another bowl, beat the eggs with the syrup, then add to the first bowl. Whisk together with an electric beater for 2 minutes, or by hand with a wooden spoon until smooth.

Divide the mixture between the cases, filling them three quarters full. Bake for about 15 minutes until they are springy to the touch in the centre. Turn out to cool on a wire rack.

To decorate, swirl the buttercream over the top of each cupcake. Break up the shredded wheat finely. Melt the chocolate with the butter, then stir in the shredded wheat and leave to cool slightly. Line a plate with plastic wrap. Mould the mixture into tiny nest shapes with your fingers, then place them on the lined plate. Freeze for a few minutes to harden. Set a nest on top of each cupcake and fill with mini eggs. Keep for 2 days in a cool place in an airtight container.

Difficulty Rating: 3 points

Viennese Fingers

Makes 28

Ingredients

225 g/8 oz/1 cup (2 sticks) butter, softened
75 g/3 oz/²/₃ cup icing/confectioners' sugar
1 medium/large egg, beaten
1 tsp vanilla extract
275 g/10 oz/2¼ cups plain/all-purpose flour
½ tsp baking powder

To decorate:
4 tbsp sieved apricot jam/jelly
225 g/8 oz dark/semisweet chocolate

Difficulty Rating: 3 points

Preheat the oven to 180°C/350°F/Gas Mark 4. Grease two baking sheets. Put the butter and icing/confectioners' sugar in a bowl and beat together until soft and fluffy.

Whisk in the egg and vanilla extract with 1 tablespoon of the flour. Sift in the remaining flour and the baking powder and beat with a wooden spoon to make a soft dough.

Place the mixture in a decorating bag fitted with a large star tip and pipe into 6.5 cm/2½ inch lengths on the baking sheets. Bake for 15–20 minutes until pale golden and firm, then transfer to a wire rack to cool.

When cold, thinly spread one flat side of a biscuit/cookie with apricot jam/jelly and sandwich together with another biscuit.

To decorate the biscuits, break the chocolate into squares and place in a heatproof bowl and stand this over a pan of simmering water. Stir until the chocolate has melted, then dip the ends of the biscuits into the chocolate to coat. Leave on a wire rack for 1 hour until set.

Chocolate, Banana & Pecan Muffins

Makes 12–14

Ingredients

125 g/4 oz/¹/₂ cup (1 stick) butter, softened

225 g/8 oz1¼ cups soft light brown sugar

250 g/9 oz/heaping cup peeled and mashed ripe bananas

2 medium/large eggs

1 tsp vanilla extract

¹/₂ tsp ground cinnamon

225 g/8 oz/1³/₄ cups plain/all-purpose flour

25 g/1 oz/¹/₄ cup sifted cocoa powder (unsweetened)

1 tsp baking powder

1 tsp bicarbonate of soda/baking soda

85 ml/3 fl oz/scant ¹/₂ cup buttermilk

50 g/2 oz/¹/₂ cup chopped pecan nuts

To decorate:

150 g/5 oz/²/₃ cup granulated sugar

4 tbsp double/heavy cream

50 g/2 oz/¹/₂ cup chopped pecan nuts

225 g/8 oz/1 cup cream cheese

125 g/4 oz/1 cup golden icing/confectioners' sugar

Preheat the oven to 180°C/350°F/Gas Mark 4. Grease or line one or two deep 12-hole muffin trays with 12–14 deep paper cases, depending on the depth of the holes.

Whisk the butter and sugar together. Add the mashed bananas to the bowl with the eggs and vanilla extract. Sift in the cinnamon, flour, cocoa powder, baking powder and bicarbonate of soda/baking soda. Add the buttermilk and fold in with the chopped nuts.

Spoon the mixture into the cases. Bake for 25 minutes until well risen and firm in the centre. Cool on a wire rack.

To decorate the muffins, put the granulated sugar in a small pan with 5 tbsp cold water. Heat gently until every grain of sugar has dissolved, then simmer until the mixture turns golden.

Holding the pan away from you, as the mixture may spit, add the cream and 1 tbsp water and then stir in the nuts. Remove the pan from the heat to cool slightly. In a bowl, beat the cream cheese with the icing/confectioners' sugar and swirl on top of the muffins. Drizzle with the warm caramel nut sauce and leave to set. Keep for 2–3 days chilled in a sealed container.

Difficulty Rating: 3 points

Christmas Pudding Cupcakes

Makes 14–18

Ingredients

125 g/4 oz/$\frac{1}{2}$ cup (1 stick) butter
125 g/4 oz/1$\frac{1}{4}$ cups soft dark muscovado sugar
2 medium/large eggs, beaten
225 g/8 oz/2 cups self-raising flour
1 tsp ground mixed spice/pumpkin pie spice
finely grated zest and 1 tbsp juice from 1 orange
1 tbsp black treacle/molasses
350 g/12 oz/2$\frac{1}{4}$ cups mixed dried fruit

For the apricot glaze:
225 g/8 oz/$\frac{2}{3}$ cup apricot jam/jelly
$\frac{1}{2}$ tsp lemon juice

For the almond paste:
65 g/2$\frac{1}{2}$ oz/$\frac{1}{2}$ cup sifted icing/confectioners' sugar
65 g/2$\frac{1}{2}$ oz/$\frac{1}{3}$ cup caster/superfine sugar
125 g/4 oz ground almonds
1 small/medium egg
$\frac{1}{2}$ tsp lemon juice

To decorate:
450 g/1 lb ready-to-roll sugarpaste/fondant
brown, red, green and yellow paste food colourings

Preheat the oven to 180°C/350°F/Gas Mark 4. Line one or two 12-hole bun trays/shallow muffin pans with 14–18 foil fairy-cake cases/shallow cases, depending on the depth of the holes.

Beat the butter and sugar until fluffy, then beat in the eggs a little at a time, adding 1 teaspoon flour with each addition. Sift in the remaining flour and spice, add the orange zest and juice, treacle/molasses and dried fruit to the bowl and fold together until blended. Spoon into the cases and bake for 30 minutes until firm in the centre and a skewer comes out clean. Leave to cool in the trays for 15 minutes, then turn out to cool on a wire rack. Store undecorated in an airtight container for up to four weeks, or freeze until needed.

To make the apricot glaze, place the jam/jelly, 1$\frac{1}{2}$ tablespoons water and the juice in a saucepan and heat gently until soft and melted. Boil rapidly for 1 minute, then press through a fine sieve with the back of a wooden spoon. Discard the pieces of fruit. To make the almond paste, stir the sugars and ground almonds together in a bowl. Whisk the egg and lemon juice together and mix into the dry ingredients. Knead until the paste is smooth. Wrap tightly in plastic wrap or foil to keep airtight until needed.

To decorate, trim the top of each cake level if they have peaked, then brush with apricot glaze. Roll out the almond paste and cut out circles 6 cm/2$\frac{1}{2}$ inches wide. Place a disc on top of each fairy cake and press level. Leave to dry for 24 hours if possible. Dust a clean flat surface with icing/confectioners' sugar. Colour half the sugarpaste brown, roll out thinly and cut out circles 6 cm/2$\frac{1}{2}$ inches wide. Place on top of the almond paste and press level. Colour the remaining sugarpaste cream or pale yellow, mould into a fluted disc and press on top to represent custard. Colour scraps of sugarpaste green and red and shape into holly leaves and berries. Keep for one week in an airtight container.

Difficulty Rating: 5 points

Lemon & Ginger Buns

Makes 15

Ingredients

175 g/6 oz/³/₄ cup (1¹/₂ sticks) butter or margarine

350 g/12 oz/3 cups plain/all-purpose flour

2 tsp baking powder

¹/₂ tsp ground ginger

pinch salt

finely grated zest of 1 lemon

175 g/6 oz/³/₄ cup demerara/turbinado sugar

125 g/4 oz/²/₃ cup sultanas/golden raisins

75 g/3 oz/¹/₂ cup chopped mixed/candied peel

25 g/1 oz/2 tbsp finely chopped stem/preserved ginger

1 medium/large egg

juice of 1 lemon

Preheat the oven to 220˚C/425˚F/Gas Mark 7, 15 minutes before baking. Lightly oil a baking tray/pan. Cut the butter or margarine into small pieces and place in a large bowl.

Sift the flour, baking powder, ginger and salt together. Add to the butter with the lemon zest. Using your fingertips, rub the butter into the flour and spice mixture until it resembles coarse breadcrumbs. Stir in the sugar, sultanas/golden raisins, chopped mixed/candied peel and stem preserved ginger.

Add the egg and lemon juice to the mixture, then, using a round–bladed knife, stir well to mix. The mixture should be quite stiff and just holding together.

Place heaping tablespoons of the mixture onto a prepared baking tray, making sure that the dollops of mixture are well apart. Using a fork, rough up the edges of the buns and bake in the preheated oven for 12–15 minutes.

Leave the buns to cool for 5 minutes before transferring to a wire rack until cold, then serve. Otherwise, store the buns in an airtight container and eat within 3–5 days.

Difficulty Rating: 2 points

Jammy Buns

Makes 12

Ingredients

175 g/6 oz/1½ cups plain/all-purpose flour
175 g/6 oz/1½ cups wholemeal/whole-wheat flour
2 tsp baking powder
150 g/5 oz/⅔ cup (1¼ sticks) butter or margarine
125 g/4 oz/⅔ cup demerara/turbinado sugar
50 g/2 oz/⅓ cup dried cranberries
1 large/extra-large egg, beaten
1 tbsp milk, plus more for brushing
4–5 tbsp seedless raspberry jam/jelly

Preheat the oven to 190°C/375°F/Gas Mark 5, 10 minutes before baking. Lightly oil a large baking sheet.

Sift the flours and baking powder together into a large bowl, then tip in the grains remaining in the sieve.

Add the butter or margarine to the flours. Cut the butter or margarine into small pieces. (It is easier to do this when the butter is in the flour, as it helps stop the butter from sticking to the knife.) Rub the butter into the flours until it resembles coarse breadcrumbs. Stir in the sugar and cranberries.

Using a round-bladed knife, stir in the beaten egg and the milk. Mix to form a firm dough. Divide the mixture into 12 and roll into balls. Place the dough balls on the prepared baking sheet, leaving enough space for expansion.

Press your thumb into the centre of each ball to make a small hollow. Spoon a little of the jam/jelly into each hollow, and brush the top of the buns lightly with milk. Bake in the preheated oven for 20–25 minutes until golden brown. Cool on a wire rack and serve.

Difficulty Rating: 1 point

Lemon & Cardamom Cupcakes with Mascarpone Topping

Makes 12

Ingredients

1 tsp cardamom seeds
200 g/7 oz/¾ cup plus 2 tbsp (1¾ sticks) butter
50 g/2 oz/½ cup plain/all-purpose flour
200 g/7 oz/1⅔ cups self-raising flour
1 tsp baking powder
200 g/7 oz/heaping ¾ cup caster/superfine sugar
finely grated zest of 1 lemon
3 medium/large eggs
100 ml/3½ fl oz/½ cup natural/plain yogurt
4 tbsp lemon curd

To decorate:

250 g/9 oz tub/1 heaping cup mascarpone
6 tbsp icing/confectioners' sugar
1 tsp lemon juice
lemon zest strips

Preheat the oven to 180°C/350°F/Gas Mark 4. Line a 12–hole muffin tray with deep paper cases. Crush the cardamom seeds and remove the outer cases. Melt the butter and leave to cool.

Sift the flours and baking powder into a bowl and stir in the crushed seeds, sugar and lemon zest. In another bowl, whisk the eggs and yogurt. Pour into the dry ingredients with the cooled melted butter and beat. Divide half the mixture between the paper cases, put a teaspoon of lemon curd into each, then top with the remaining mixture. Bake for about 25 minutes .

To make the topping, beat the mascarpone with the icing/confectioners' sugar and lemon juice. Swirl onto each cupcake and top with lemon strips. Eat fresh on day of baking once decorated or store, undecorated, in an airtight container for up to two days and add the topping just before serving.

Difficulty Rating: 2 points

Mocha Cupcakes

Makes 12

Ingredients

125 g/4 oz/¹⁄₂ cup soft margarine

125 g/4 oz/¹⁄₂ cup golden caster/superfine sugar

150 g/5 oz/1¹⁄₂ cups self-raising flour

2 tbsp cocoa powder (unsweetened)

2 medium/large eggs

1 tbsp golden/light corn syrup

2 tbsp milk

To decorate:

225 g/8 oz/1³⁄₄ cups golden icing/confectioners' sugar

125 g/4 oz/¹⁄₂ cup (1 stick) unsalted butter, softened

2 tsp coffee extract

12 cape gooseberries, papery covering pulled back

Preheat the oven to 180°C/350°F/Gas Mark 4. Line a 12–hole muffin tray with deep paper cases.

Place the margarine and sugar in a large bowl, then sift in the flour and cocoa powder. In another bowl, beat the eggs with the syrup, then add to the cocoa mixture. Whisk everything together with the milk using an electric beater for 2 minutes, or by hand with a wooden spoon.

Divide the mixture between the cases, filling them three quarters full. Bake for about 20 minutes until the centres are springy to the touch. Turn out to cool on a wire rack.

Make the frosting by sifting the icing/confectioners' sugar into a bowl. Add the butter, coffee extract and 1 tbsp hot water. Beat until fluffy, then swirl onto each cupcake with a flat–bladed knife. Top each with a fresh cape gooseberry. Keep for two days in a cool place.

Difficulty Rating: 2 points

Winter Wedding Cupcakes

Makes 12–14

Ingredients

125 g/4 oz/¹/₂ cup (1 stick) butter

125 g/4 oz/²/₃ cup soft dark muscovado sugar

2 medium/large eggs, beaten

225 g/8 oz/2 cups self-raising flour

1 tsp ground mixed spice

finely grated zest and 1 tbsp juice from 1 orange

1 tbsp black treacle/molasses

350 g/12 oz/2¹/₄ cups mixed dried fruit

To decorate:

1 batch sieved apricot glaze (*see* page 340)

2 batches almond paste (*see* page 340)

icing/confectioners' sugar, for dusting

225 g/8 oz ready-to-roll sugarpaste/fondant

fancy paper wrappers (optional)

For the royal icing:

1 medium/large egg white

225 g/8 oz/2 scant cups sifted icing/confectioners' sugar

1 tsp lemon juice

Preheat the oven to 180°C/350°F/Gas Mark 4. Line one or two 12-hole muffin trays with 12–14 deep paper cases, depending on the depth of the holes.

Beat the butter and sugar together until light and fluffy, then beat in the eggs a little at a time, adding 1 teaspoon flour with each addition. Sift in the remaining flour and the spice, add the orange zest and juice, treacle/molasses and dried fruit to the bowl and fold together until the mixture is blended. Spoon into the prepared trays and bake for 30 minutes until firm in the centre and a skewer comes out clean. Leave to cool in the tins for 15 minutes, then turn out onto a wire rack. Store undecorated in an airtight container for up to three weeks, or freeze until needed.

To decorate the cupcakes, trim the top of each cake level, then brush with apricot glaze. Roll out the almond paste and cut out

eight discs 6 cm/2¹/₂ inches wide. Place these over the glaze and press level. Leave to dry for 24 hours if possible.

Dust a clean flat surface with icing/confectioners' sugar. Roll out the sugarpaste/fondant and stamp out holly leaf and ivy shapes. Leave to dry for 2 hours on nonstick baking parchment or plastic wrap.

To make the royal icing, put the egg whites in a large bowl and whisk lightly with a fork to break up the whites until foamy. Sift in half the icing sugar with the lemon juice and beat well with an electric mixer for 4 minutes or by hand with a wooden spoon for about 10 minutes until smooth. Gradually sift in the remaining icing sugar and beat again until thick, smooth and brilliant white and the icing forms soft peaks when flicked up with a spoon. Keep the royal icing covered with a clean damp cloth until you are ready to use it. Swirl the royal icing over the top of each cupcake. Press in the holly and ivy shapes and leave to set for 2 hours. Once decorated, keep in an airtight container for three days.

Difficulty Rating: 5 points

Mint Choc Chip Cupcakes

Makes 12

Ingredients

125 g/4 oz/¹/₂ cup soft margarine
125 g/4 oz/¹/₂ cup golden caster/superfine sugar
2 medium/large eggs
175 g/6 oz/1¹/₂ cups self-raising flour
25 g/1 oz/¹/₄ cup cocoa powder (unsweetened)
1 tsp baking powder
75 g/3 oz/¹/₂ cup dark/semisweet chocolate chips
25 g/1 oz clear hard peppermint sweets, crushed into crumbs

To decorate:
50 g/2 oz/4 tbsp unsalted butter
175 g/6 oz1¹/₃ cups icing/confectioners' sugar
peppermint flavouring or extract
green food colouring
50 g/2 oz chocolate squares

Preheat the oven to 180°C/350°F/Gas Mark 4. Line a 12-hole muffin tray with deep paper cases.

Place the margarine, sugar and eggs in a bowl, then sift in the flour, cocoa powder and baking powder. Beat by hand or with an electric mixer until smooth. Then fold in the chocolate chips and the crushed mints.

Spoon the mixture into the paper cases and bake for 15–20 minutes until firm in the centre. Remove to a wire rack to cool.

Beat the butter and icing/confectioners' sugar together with 1 tablespoon warm water, the peppermint extract and the food colouring. Place in a decorating bag with a star tip and pipe swirls on top of each cupcake. Cut the chocolate into triangles and place one on top of each cake. Keep for 3–4 days in an airtight container in a cool place.

Difficulty Rating: 2 points

Classic Flapjacks

Makes 12

Ingredients

175 g/6 oz/³/₄ cup (1¹/₂ sticks) butter, plus extra for greasing

125 g/4 oz/²/₃ cup demerara/raw sugar

2 tbsp golden/light corn syrup

175 g/6 oz/2 scant cups jumbo porridge/rolled oats

few drops vanilla extract

Preheat the oven to 160°C/325°F/Gas Mark 3. Butter a 20.5 cm/8 inch square baking tin.

Place the butter, sugar and golden/light corn syrup in a saucepan and heat gently until the butter has melted and every grain of sugar has dissolved.

Remove from the heat and stir in the oats and vanilla extract. Stir well and then spoon the mixture into the prepared tin.

Smooth level with the back of a large spoon. Bake in the centre of the oven for 30–40 minutes until golden. Leave to cool in the tin for 10 minutes, then mark into fingers and leave in the tin until completely cold. When cold, cut into fingers with a sharp knife.

Difficulty Rating: 1 point

Coconut & Lime Muffins

Makes 12

Ingredients

125 g/4 oz/^{1}/$_2$ cup soft margarine
125 g/4 oz/^{1}/$_2$ cup golden caster/superfine sugar
2 medium/large eggs
50 g/2 oz/heaping ^{1}/$_2$ cup desiccated/shredded coconut
1 lime
125 g/4 oz/1 cup self-raising flour
1 tsp baking powder
2 tbsp milk

To decorate:
40 g/1^1/$_2$ oz/3 tbsp unsalted butter
125 g/4 oz/1 cup icing/confectioners' sugar
50 g/2 oz coconut chips
grated zest of 1 lime,

Preheat the oven to 180°C/350°F/Gas Mark 4. Line a deep 12-hole muffin tray with deep paper cases.

Place the margarine and caster/superfine sugar in a bowl and add the eggs and coconut. Finely grate the zest from the lime into the bowl, then squeeze in the juice. Sift in the flour and baking powder.

Add the milk and whisk together for about 2 minutes with an electric beater, or by hand until smooth, then spoon into the paper cases. Bake for 15–20 minutes until golden and firm. Cool on a wire rack.

To decorate the muffins, beat the butter and icing/confectioners' sugar together until smooth, then pipe or swirl onto each muffin. Press the coconut chips into the buttercream and then scatter the grated lime zest on top. Keep for three days in an airtight container in a cool place.

Difficulty Rating: 2 points

Shaggy Coconut Cupcakes

Makes 12

^{1}/$_2$ tsp baking powder
200 g/7 oz/1^2/$_3$ cups self-raising flour
175 g/6 oz/^{3}/$_4$ cup caster/superfine sugar
2 tbsp desiccated/shredded coconut
175 g/6 oz/^{3}/$_4$ cup soft margarine
3 medium/large eggs, beaten
2 tbsp milk

To decorate:
1 tbsp coconut liqueur (optional)
1 batch buttercream (*see page 292*)
175 g/6 oz/2 cups large shredded coconut strands

Preheat the oven to 180°C/350°F/Gas Mark 4. Line a 12-hole deep muffin tray with paper cases.

Sift the baking powder and flour into a large bowl. Add all the remaining ingredients and beat for about 2 minutes until smooth and creamy. Divide evenly between the paper cases.

Bake for 18–20 minutes until risen, golden and firm to the touch. Leave in the muffin trays for 2 minutes, then turn out to cool on a wire rack.

To decorate the cupcakes, if you are using the coconut liqueur, beat this into the buttercream, and then swirl over each cupcake. To decorate, press large strands of shredded coconut into the buttercream. Keep for three days in an airtight container in a cool place.

Difficulty Rating: 2 points

Index